THE BUSINESS FACT FINDER

THE BUSINESS FACT FINDER

Edited by Hano Johannsen

Kogan Page

First published in Great Britain in 1987
by Kogan Page Ltd, 120 Pentonville Road,
London N1 9JN

British Library Cataloguing in Publication Data
The Business fact finder.
1. Business
I. Johannsen, Hano
650 HF5351
ISBN 1-85091-211-4

Printed and bound in Great Britain by
Billing & Sons Ltd, Worcester

CONTENTS

CONTRIBUTORS

The Editor, **Hano Johannsen**, currently runs his own research and publishing company Management Update Ltd specialising in business books and readership surveys. Previously he was Head of Information and Library Services and later Head of Research and Publishing at the British Institute of Management. Former editor of *Management Abstracts*, author of several books and surveys on management topics and co-author of the *International Dictionary of Management*, also published by Kogan Page. Has translated a number of books and is a member of the Institute of Linguists.

Michael Armstrong graduated from the London School of Economics, and is a Fellow of the Institute of Personnel Management and a member of the Institute of Management Consultants. For the last nine years he has been a General Manager. His publications include *A Handbook of Management Techniques*, *A Handbook of Personnel Management* and *How to be a Better Manager*, all published by Kogan Page.

C S C Bennett, FCII. Worked in the insurance industry for thirteen years for such companies as General Accident. He lectured at Gloucestershire College of Arts and Technology on professional studies and was later appointed Course Leader in Insurance Studies. Now Head of the School of Short Courses and Languages at the College.

Annabel Beerel, MBA CTA, BCompt (Hons), Dip MM, Head of the Corporate Finance Unit dealing with debt finance for Robson Rhodes. Also lectures on strategic control at Henley Management College. Previously worked with an international firm of management consultants and has written numerous articles on managerial and financial subjects for specialist journals.

Paul Foley, BSc, is a Lecturer in the Department of Town and Regional Planning at Sheffield University. With Howard Green, he is co-author of *How to Choose Business Premises*, published by Kogan Page.

John Gammon, BA, FICSA, FIPS, Managing Director of a company providing a range of commercial, management and personnel advisory services to business organisations and the public sector. He has worked with a wide range of organisations including the City of Manchester Corporation, UK Atomic Energy Authority and South Western Electricity Board. He has particular expertise in the areas of company administration, purchasing and materials control systems.

Howard Green, MA, PhD, DipTP, is a Senior Lecturer in the School of Planning at Leeds Polytechnic. He teaches and researches in the field of property and business.

Joe Horner was formerly one of HM Inspectors of Taxes. He is now a Taxation Adviser with the Manchester branch of Kidsons Chartered Accountants.

Helen Johannsen, BA, studied business law at Lanchester Polytechnic. She is now a Solicitor in a well-known London practice.

Stephen Morse, MA, FIMC, independent Management Consultant. Previously a management consultant with Urwick Orr and Partners, his experience covers the textile, retailing and animal feeding stuffs industries. He was for three years Head of Marketing Training at the Urwick Management Centre and, since 1970, has made regular contributions to MCE courses.

A G Slater is a Principal Manager responsible for physical distribution assignments at Arthur Young Management Consultants. He is the author of *Handbook of Physical Distribution Software* published by Kogan Page, 1986.

James Turner, FCA, FCIArb, FBIM, former Senior Adviser on Financial Management to the British Institute of Management. He is now a Management Consultant and contributes regularly to a number of professional journals including *Accountancy*.

INTRODUCTION

In the highly complex world in which today's businessmen have to operate, personal enthusiasm, knowledge and experience - though important - are rarely enough in themselves to ensure success. While there is a healthy growth in the number of small businesses there is also a growing rate of business failure and liquidations. Research shows that only about a third of all new business ventures survive the first 12 months of trading!

Running a successful business involves the application of a very broad range of managerial skills and techniques as well as ready access to a vast range of information on many diverse subjects ranging from business law, financial control and monitoring, sources of business finance, accounting procedures, employment law, insurance, distribution etc.

Today the individual 'generalist' and even the experienced specialist face a major task in trying to keep up with the changes taking place on all fronts be it new legislation, technology or office equipment etc. Although it is a cliché to talk of the accelerating rate of change and an information explosion there can be few doubts that keeping up with and adapting to ever-changing conditions are an essential ingredient of good management and business survival.

Those running established or new business need ready access to information on such a wide front that needs can no longer be met simply by who or what you know. Business contacts, advisers and colleagues plus personal experience, of course, remain key resources when it comes to tackling new problems, seeking information and testing out new ideas. However, even the most experienced businessman is unlikely to have all the information or contacts to turn to when attempting to find an answer to the hundred and one different issues which arise in the course of a typical week's work.

This handbook is essentially designed as a basic reference book which businessmen, managers, as well as business students, can refer to and keep within arm's reach to check on business information, to consult when coming across some unfamiliar topic or simply to look up some aspect of business law with which they are unfamiliar. It will also be useful for coming to grips with unfamiliar business terms and jargon and establishing the basics of some of the specialised fields which perhaps lie outside their personal experience such as insurance or questions relating to business premises.

Emphasis has been given throughout to signposting further detailed sources of information for no book such as this can hope to be comprehensive. Some may feel that the choice of subjects included has been somewhat arbitrary. To produce a manageable guidebook necessarily implies selectivity in what to put in and what to leave out. However, within the space constraints, we have tried to take an essentially practical and broad view and cover those key topics which justify the title *Business Fact Finder*.

Each section has been prepared by an acknowledged expert with practical experience in their field. Future editions will aim at keeping the material up to date so as to reflect the needs of business operating in an ever-changing environment.

Throughout this work, the use of the personal pronoun 'he' has been adopted solely for the purpose of avoiding the repetitive use of the phrase 'he and or she'. No discourtesy or discrimination is intended towards women who, wherever the context so permits, should always be considered as equally included.

I would like to thank all the contributors for their efforts and June Lines of Kogan Page for patiently gathering all the text together and turning it into what I hope will be a useful handbook!

Hano Johannsen
February 1987

1

BUSINESS ORGANIZATION

Hano Johannsen

Introduction
Basic Management Functions
Types of Business Organization

INTRODUCTION

Management has been variously described by some as an 'art', a 'skill' and a 'science'. In practice effective management is usually a blend of all three. At times it implies the ability to learn and apply specialized techniques and also make rational decisions based on hard facts. At other times it calls for skills in understanding and dealing with people as well as acting on hunch or intuition. Management also calls for less tangible attributes such as 'flair' and the ability to be creative, innovative and challenge existing attitudes, ideas and methods.

BASIC MANAGEMENT FUNCTIONS

Management is all about the effective and profitable use of human and physical resources: people, materials, money and machinery. While there has been a lot of controversy among management theorists over the last hundred years in trying to define the essential elements of the management process, there is general agreement that the key functions involve:

Planning
Organizing
Staffing
Supervising
Directing
Controlling
Coordinating
Innovating

Planning

While one may be able to 'get along' for a short period in a haphazard way, even the smallest business needs to spend time on planning. It involves determining short- and long-term objectives and deciding what methods will be used to achieve them. It implies setting goals and targets for the volume of business to be achieved. It means asking questions about the products or services, the customers, the market conditions, the costs etc, and deciding how and by what methods the business will attain the goals it sets itself.

Planning is not an exact science but it should be seen as an essential prerequisite to any business activity. Planning should be seen as an ongoing process which is never completed, for no sooner have the initial plans been made than the longer term needs to be considered. Many businesses which have got their initial planning right and had a few years of exciting growth, often fail to come up to expectations because of the lack of attention to long-term planning.

Organization

In the one-man business, 'organization' is mainly a matter of making the best use of personal skills and abilities. The emphasis in the 'one-man band' business is on organizing oneself properly and making effective use of time to tackle the variety of tasks.

As the business grows, the volume and variety of tasks make it imperative that some work is delegated to others. It is at this stage that some form of organization structure begins to emerge. At first it may simply be a question of dividing up some of the workload so that certain tasks are delegated. One golden rule in assigning duties to individuals is that responsibility and authority go hand in hand. If an individual is to be responsible for a particular job, he also has to have the appropriate authority to carry it out.

Organization involves two steps. First, the division of the business into key functions and activities which must be performed and then the assignment of each to specific individuals. Where there are a number of related activities these are normally grouped together. The aim should be to assign functions to employees with appropriate skills, interests and experience. Remember that good chemists or salesmen, for example, do not necessarily make good heads of research or sales managers!

As a business grows – to, say, 25 employees or more – the need for rather more formal organization planning and structure becomes apparent.

There are few hard and fast rules about organization charts, but a number of basic guidelines should be observed. The starting point is a clear identification of the organization's real aims and purpose.

First, this should enable the key functions of the business to be established. What are key functions in one firm may be minor ones in another. A detailed analysis should help to reveal the relative importance which the organization attaches to each function.

Second, setting business objectives and key functions helps to highlight the fact that managerial roles cannot operate in isolation but depend on interaction and relationships with others. The typical organization chart unfortunately does not reflect the numerous formal and informal relationships which really make a business work. Often they tend to emphasize reporting levels and status rather than the many lateral links which exist across a hierarchy.

Third, defining objectives and keeping them under review helps to question whether all the activities in which they are engaged really are essential to their business. Must everything be done by the business? What can be subcontracted to others?

Finally, setting objectives will help in organization planning by highlighting attention on the kinds of decision which need to be made. This raises important issues. Among the questions to be raised are:

1. At what levels of responsibility and authority should different kinds of decision be made?
2. What tasks can be delegated?
3. How many levels of management and supervision are necessary for running an effective business?

4. How many activities and individuals can one person effectively look after?

The typical organization chart is really only one way of representing managerial responsibilities and relationships within a business. Whatever their format and purpose such charts usually indicate how work is divided up and who is in charge of what, but all charts have at least one thing in common: they don't reflect how the organization actually works. This is clear from experience and often illustrated by the many charts which are hedged around with caveats to the effect that the position of functions does not indicate degrees of responsibility or authority.

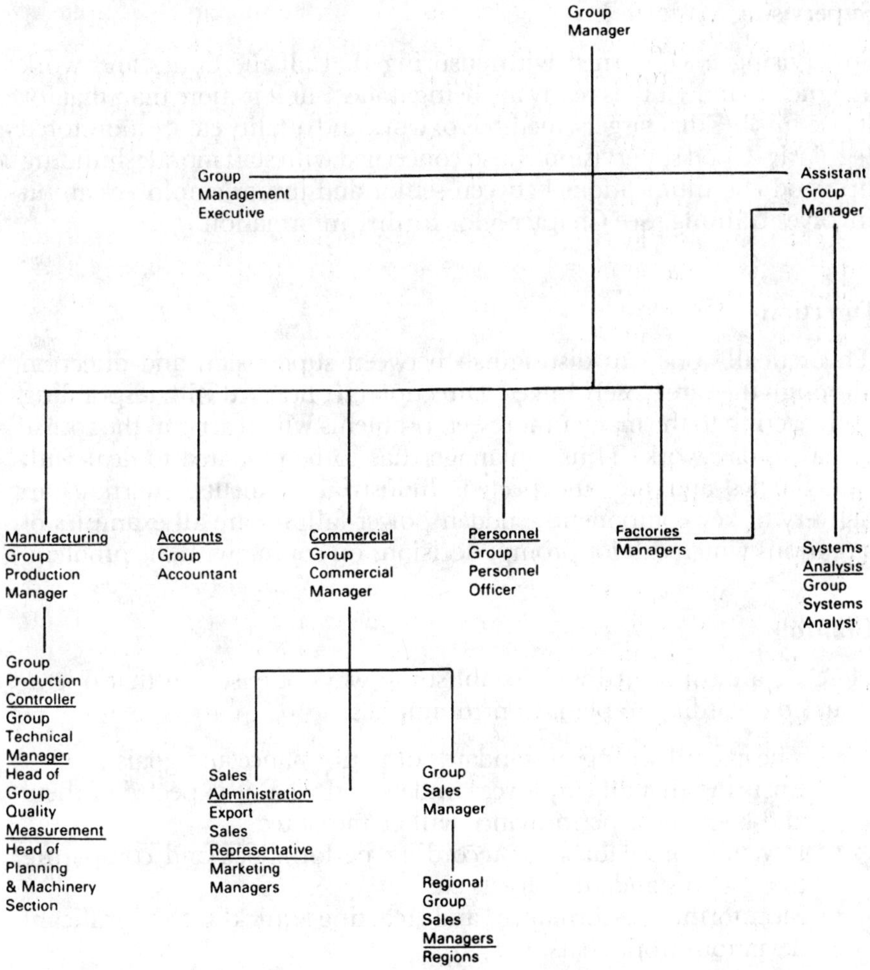

Figure 1.1 *Organization chart*

Staffing

Some would argue that 'staffing' is merely an aspect of organization and especially in the case of an established business. In a new enterprise the right people clearly have to be attracted, selected and appointed to carry out the tasks which the business requires.

In practice it is helpful to see staffing as a separate element in the management process because it focuses attention on the need for sound personnel and training policies and practices: these are discussed in detail in Chapters 4 and 5.

Supervising

Supervising is concerned with ensuring that all the duties and work assigned to individuals really are being done. But it is more than that for it also implies that targets, methods of work and quality etc are monitored regularly. Good supervision is also concerned with staff morale, building up good communications between senior and junior employees and it involves training. See Chapter 5 for further information.

Direction

Theoretically one can distinguish between supervision and direction although they are closely linked. Direction is concerned with responding and reacting to the many unforeseen problems which arise in the course of day-to-day work. Thus a manager has to be prepared to deal with emergencies and the unexpected. Industrial accidents, shortfalls in delivery of key components, sudden power failures are all examples of situations which call for prompt decisions on coping with the problem.

Control

Here we are concerned with establishing ways of ensuring that operations go according to plan. Control implies:

- The careful setting of standards of performance and goals
- Ensuring that all employees understand what is expected of them and know how performance will be measured
- Devising procedures for recording performance and comparing these with standards, targets etc
- Monitoring performance and reacting quickly to significant deviations from goals set.

How control is exercised will depend very much on the type of business concerned and the nature of the activities being controlled, but wherever possible the aim is to quantify performance in terms of units of production, sales or cash terms etc. Normally control systems are developed to deal with activities at both the departmental and company-wide level. See Chapter 12 on accounting for further details of financial control.

Coordination

In the very small business the 'boss' often has to 'wear a number of hats' simultaneously. He may adopt the roles of managing director, head of sales and personnel. His task is to 'coordinate' himself by devoting enough time to each function. As the business grows and he is no longer in complete charge of everything he will want to ensure that his colleagues act as a team and work together. Most business policies and decisions affect one or more areas of the business: coordination is about recognizing the interrelationship between the functions and the importance of all working to a common goal.

Innovation

However well management may perform the basic functions, it also needs to find time to stand back from the day-to-day operations and ask some key questions about longer-term operations. Innovation is not only about technical innovation and new product or service development. It implies keeping pace with the changing world and recognizing trends. It also involves reviewing systems and procedures and exploring ways of improving performance.

In many companies the innovation function is always under threat from the daily demands on management time of just trying to keep the business 'on the road'. While the larger business may have the resources to devote to innovation, the smaller firm often needs to consciously set time aside for this activity: good time management is often the answer. See also Chapter 10 on brainstorming and creative thinking.

TYPES OF BUSINESS ORGANIZATION

Sole trader

This is the simplest type of business structure to run and set up as it involves no legal formalities provided the owners use their own names and there is no intention to register for value added tax. Although sole traders will want to keep proper records for management and tax purposes, there are no rules about the kind of accounts etc to be kept.

A business name needs to be chosen with care and if it is not one's own name, then this must be indicated on stationery etc, as laid down under the provisions of the Companies Act 1981 which came into effect in February 1982. The law demands that the public should be able to establish who the owners of a business really are.

Remember that there is no longer any requirement to register a trade name, as the function of the former Registrar of Business Names - which had to check and record business names - is now abolished. There are, however, still some rules on the choice of name. Permission is required before using any of the so-called 'controlled' names which include names such as 'bank' or 'international'.

Though simple to set up, sole traders have to take upon themselves total responsibility for all the consequences of business decisions. They alone are responsible for all debts, financial risks and obligations. If for some reason the business gets into difficulties or even fails, the creditors have a legal claim to *all* of the sole trader's business *and* personal assets. Similarly, any civil actions also expose sole traders to a variety of potential claims and risks which they have to face personally.

Sole traders are regarded by the tax and National Insurance authorities as being self-employed and therefore subject to Schedule D assessment.

While it is a key advantage for the sole trader's business activities to be private and not open to public scrutiny, this has to be weighed against the fact that there is unlimited personal liability. It is also a fact that a sole trader's business has no continuity but dies with the owner. Raising business finance may present problems especially where little or no securities are offered. Note also that profits have to be distributed annually and cannot be retained within the business to finance further expansion.

Partnerships

Partnerships are legally akin to associations of sole traders. They involve two or more people who jointly and severally are liable for *all* the partners' activities and debts. This means that while all partners share in the profits, they are also individually responsible for all partnership debts and obligations. This liability is not restricted to the size of their own investment in the partnership. In many partnerships some of these risks are deemed to be too high and may therefore in part be alleviated by special forms of insurance.

The essential legal framework providing rules for the operation of a partnership hinges on the partnership agreement. This is a vital document and needs to be drawn up with care and considerable attention to detail. It is all too easy for a number of people to set up in business without realizing that in law they have in fact formed a partnership!

Typically the agreement provides for the ground rules to be spelt out including:

- The duration of the partnership
- The amount of capital to be provided by each partner
- Rules about 'sleeping partners' who put up capital but take no active part in running the business (limited partnership)
- The role and duties of individual partners
- How profits (and losses) are to be apportioned
- The voting rights of partners
- Rules for admitting new partners and removing existing partners
- Rules and procedures for dissolution of the partnership and releasing individual partners.
- The duration of the partnership (normally ongoing unless the partnership is set up for a specific limited period)
- Rules for dealing with the sickness, holidays, death and retirement of individuals
- Rules for accounting and auditing
- Procedures for running a bank account
- Insurance provisions for individuals and the partnership as a whole
- Rules for dealing with disagreements and arrangements for settling them.

As with sole traders the financial arrangements and annual performance of all partnerships are private and do not have to be disclosed to the public.

Private limited companies

These are companies formed under the Companies Acts 1948–1981. An essential feature is that they have to register certain key documents with the official Registrar of Companies at the time of formation and henceforth provide information in the form of annual accounts and returns which reflect significant changes in company ownership etc.

Before incorporation can proceed the Registrar of Companies requires that the following documents be lodged:

Memorandum of Association
Articles of Association
Form PUC 1 showing the nominal value of shares issued or allocated etc.

A declaration by the original subscribers to the Memorandum showing the names of the directors and secretary and the location of the registered office.

After approval of all the documents and payment of fees and stamp duties a Certificate of Incorporation is issued confirming that the company is a 'body corporate'.

A key feature and attraction of the private limited company is that it is an entity which exists quite separately in law from the organization. A limited company can own property, stock and equipment and employ staff, arrange contracts and sue or be sued etc. As a corporate body its existence is not limited to the life span of shareholders and can in theory continue in perpetuity.

Unlike a sole trader or partner, a private company shareholders' liability is limited to the extent of their investment in the company's shares (strictly the paid-up value of their shares). A limited company can raise further capital resources by selling shares.

In reality limited liability is not all that it seems since some (and usually all major) shareholders are often expected to offer personal guarantees and securities to banks etc to cover risks for loans or overdraft facilities made available to the company. Nevertheless, it remains a fact that, apart from such pledges, the shareholders' personal assets and resources are not at risk should the business get into difficulty or fail completely.

There are numerous Acts relating to the legal requirements of company formation, operation and so on. The Companies Act 1986 is the key recent legislation but other acts of 1948, 1967, 1976, 1980, 1981 and 1985 are also relevant.

The minimum number of members of a private company is two: the maximum 50. Exceptions are made to applicants in certain circumstances, such as housing management companies of which the residents are the only shareholders. Shares can be created and sold privately but not by a public offer.

If limited liability is claimed as the key advantage of the private company, then the obligation to make public the activities and financial results of the organization via the Companies Registrar can be seen as a possible drawback. The private limited company's financial activities are deemed to be in the public domain and in addition to the Memorandum and Articles of Association, annual audited accounts which are open to public inspection by bankers, suppliers, credit agencies etc have to be deposited at Companies House.

Companies can be set up by professional advisers or via company registration agents which provide 'off the shelf' companies or can arrange the formation of companies to meet specific needs.

Public companies

These share many of the basic characteristics of limited private companies, but as specified by the Companies Act 1980, they are specifically those who have registered in accordance with section 3. The authorized minimum nominal capital is £50,000 and the name of the company must end with 'Public Limited Company' or the abbreviation 'PLC' (in Wales 'CCC' may additionally be used).

For further information on public companies refer to the appropriate Companies Acts and the detailed rules for Stock Exchange criteria for quoted and so-called 'unlisted' companies whose shares may be traded on the Unlisted Securities Market (USM).

Joint ventures

The rapid development of international trade in recent years has given impetus to the concept of joint ventures especially for exploiting the production and marketing of goods or the setting up of research and development programmes. The parties to the joint venture each contribute their own particular skills and know-how. Whatever kind of legal structure is adopted for a joint venture - perhaps a limited partnership or a limited company - the joint venture calls for detailed agreements and professional advice both in the UK and locally. Often approval of the project by a number of governments and complex financial and taxation considerations are involved.

Workers' cooperatives

In recent years there has been growing interest in setting up businesses which are owned and democratically controlled by their employees. Worker cooperatives have received a new lease of life and created widespread attention. In part this is because of the publicity given to the highly successful cooperatives which have developed in the town of Mondragon in the Basque area of northern Spain. In the UK an additional spur was given in recent years by the realization that worker cooperatives could make a contribution to creating employment and the setting up of the Cooperative Development Agency (CDA) was established by Act of Parliament in 1978. Given all-party support, it was given the specific task of promoting the ideas of setting up cooperatives throughout the United Kingdom and providing information and advisory services nationally.

Worker cooperatives can be set up in a number of ways and detailed guidance is available from CDA and the many other bodies set up to encourage local development. In the London area there are, for example, the Greater London Enterprise Board (GLEB) and the associated London Cooperative Enterprise Board plus separate Cooperative Development Agencies for many of the inner and outer London boroughs.

Additionally, initiatives have been taken in other parts of the country by county councils and organizations such as the Wales Cooperative Development and Training Centre.

Further help and advice can be obtained from the Industrial Common Ownership Movement (ICOM), a membership organization of common ownership firms and individuals providing legal, financial and management advice.

Cooperatives can be incorporated via the Companies Acts (and have the benefits of limited liability) or be registered under the Industrial and Provident Societies Act 1965.

2

FINANCE

Annabel C Beerel

INTRODUCTION

A hackneyed phrase, that finance is the lifeblood of the organization, has often led individuals, entrepreneurs and organizational management to become inhibited by the apparent hazards of raising finance. While this is understandable, the process is never that daunting, provided one can present a sound idea, project or business to the potential financiers. It should not be forgotten that finance is a means to an end and not an end in itself. Unrestricted funding does not guarantee success.

THE FINANCING REQUIREMENT

Both individuals and organizations have ongoing and specific requirements for finance at different stages of their lives. As we are concerned with businesses and not with personal financial planning, we shall confine our discussion to business requirements. These could be:

Ongoing financing	*Specific financing*
Fixed overheads	Start-up capital
Working capital requirements (growth)	Expansion plans
	Special projects
Wear and tear to premises	Fixed asset replacement
Repairs and maintenance of plant	Mergers or acquisitions
Pension fund commitments	Diversification
Research and development*	

*In some cases this could be deemed a special project requiring specific finance.

The purpose for which the finance is required will directly influence:

- The sources of finance to be approached
- The presentation of the financing proposal
- The type of finance which will be most appropriate
- The cost of finance
- The time for repayment
- The security (if any) required by the financier
- The perceived risk of the venture.

It is appropriate at this point to highlight the main differences between lenders and investors.

Lenders lend money for a period of time, usually at a predetermined rate of interest (which is considered their return), secured on assets which have a comparable value. Lenders want their money back in accordance with the agreed repayment terms; in the event of default, they will lay claim to the assets provided as security.

Investors. Investors (termed shareholders) purchase a part of the project or enterprise. This purchase entitles them to a share in the fortunes of the venture, the extent of which is determined by the type of investment. The value of the investment is thus at risk. If the value of the venture increases, so will the constituent stakes invested; and similarly, if the value decreases, so will the value of the constituent stakes. The investor is thus looking to capital gains for his return on his money committed. He usually has no fixed return to compensate him for his investment. (It must be noted that there are hybrid forms of finance, eg preference shares that incorporate the elements of part equity, part debt — often known as loan capital.) As the investor is prepared to take higher risks he demands higher returns.

CRITERIA SET BY LENDERS AND INVESTORS

In putting together your financing proposal it is important to reflect on what the potential financier seeks from the deal, what his perception of the risks and returns is likely to be. Lenders (those that lend money in the form of debt which they intend to recover with interest) have different criteria from investors (who purchase a share of the venture in the hope of making a capital gain later).

Typical lending criteria

The lender will look at the following when making a lending decision.

1. *Management ability and potential.* The lender would want to have some feel for the managerial ability, commercial astuteness and tenacity of either an entrepreneur, or, for an established business, the chief executive and his management team. This would seem to be without fail the main criterion against which a financing application will be assessed. This will be discussed in greater detail under *The business plan,* page 30.
2. *Purpose of the loan.* The purpose for which the finance is raised is very important to the lender as it gives him some indication of the period for which the loan is required and the associated risks.
3. *Amount.* The amount of finance required. Key questions to consider are:

   - Is the amount realistic? Is it sufficient? Most applications are for too little rather than too much.
   - Can the amount be repaid without putting undue stress on the organization, ie how risky will it be from the lender's point of view?

   The size of the loan required will also influence the choice of the source of finance.
4. *Repayment terms.* The lender will look at the repayment terms very carefully as they influence his perception of the risks, as well as the cost to him and to you. The usual term structure of interest rates is that the longer the repayment period, the higher the rate of interest.

5. *General terms.* General terms and conditions form part of most loan agreements. The nature of these terms will be influenced by the lender's overall perception of you and your business. This will be amplified under *The business plan,* page 30.
6. *Security.* All lenders, except very good friends, require some form of security to support their funding and to cover them in the event of default. In the past, retail bankers in particular have been accused of being over-averse to risk and to making unnecessarily stringent security requirements of entrepreneurs and small businesses. This, many say, impedes small business growth and has general negative repercussions throughout industry.

Typical investing criteria

1. *Management.* The same comments apply as for lending criteria. There is possibly even more emphasis on management capabilities as the investors' fortunes are directly linked with those of management. When approaching investors for cash it is a good idea to ascertain their attitude to participation in management. Some wish to be passive and others take an active role in the actual management of the enterprise in which they have invested.
2. *Business prospects.* The investor is very concerned with the potential business prospects of the enterprise or project in which he is investing. Institutional investors are typically looking for an average 35–45 per cent growth rate over the first five years. They like to exit from their investment (at a substantial premium) usually after three to seven years.
3. *Amount.* The larger the amount required for an investment, the higher the return expected.
4. *General terms.* General terms are usually attached to the investment agreement. These will reflect the risk and return perceptions and the stance towards management participation to be adopted by the investor. The investor is also likely to demand access to internal management information.
5. *Exit terms.* Investment agreements include detailed exit terms of how the investor can disinvest, the timing thereof and any constraints placed on the respective parties.

THE INVESTMENT DECISION

How a firm invests its funds is far more important than how it finances the project or business. If the investment does not generate a return greater than the cost of funds, not only is the proposition unviable, but no one will fund you.

All projects and/or businesses that have specific financing requirements, eg a business start-up or the erection of a new plant, should be the subject of vigorous investment appraisal. This entails comparing the amount of cash to be spent now in order to generate a future inflow of cash over a predetermined period of time. The expected cash inflows cannot be predicted with absolute certainty and thus entail a degree of risk, which fact must be taken into consideration when embarking on the venture.

There are many methods of carrying out an investment appraisal of which the Discounted Cash Flow (DCF) is probably one of the most popular. The rigours of investment evaluation will not be pursued in detail here. In essence, all techniques rest on the projection of future cash flows related to the venture.

The apparent returns (or yields) must always be viewed in the light of anticipated risks.

Cash flow evaluations

Projections for the predetermined period of the business should include:

1. Net outlays — original capital investment
2. Annual cash flows — revenue
   — costs

   (a) Sales based on the size of the market, projected market shares and selling prices
   (b) Direct costs excluding depreciation
   (c) Overheads
   (d) Working capital
   (e) Residual values (at the end of the chosen time horizon) of plant and working capital
   (f) Taxation based on taxable profits.

3. Ignore sunk costs, ie investment in resources already made in the past.
4. Interest and financing costs should be excluded from cash flows as evaluation techniques are aimed at evaluating the business before financing costs.
5. Inflation expectations need to be reflected in an appropriate discount or hurdle rate.

RAISING START-UP FINANCE

Raising start-up finance is a fairly stressful experience for most entrepreneurs. Many do not take the time factor into consideration. To raise money for new projects or businesses takes time. It is for this reason that the entrepreneur should talk to potential financiers earlier rather than later. He or she should 'take the financier along' while developing the detailed plans, rather than try to pre-empt a hasty decision after all the thinking and planning is done. Financiers, whether lending or investing, need to be convinced of the soundness of the proposals. They need to feel that they understand *what* you are trying to achieve and *how* you intend going about it. They also want to feel comfortable with the perceived risks and returns associated with the venture.

Presenting yourself

The first and most important criterion for any lender or investor is his view of you as the entrepreneur. He will want to get a feel for your abilities, tenacity and commercial astuteness. Based on his perception of you, the lender/investor is going to make some very subjective judgements about your capabilities.

As the seeker of finance, you have to influence this perception favourably. There are no hard and fast rules on how to do this; however, the following are always taken into consideration:

1. How you present yourself
2. Your business track record
3. The amount of research you have carried out
4. Your familiarity with the detail of your project or venture
5. How you present your business plan.

The lender/investor has certain lending criteria: in trying to evaluate your management experience and potential he will be very interested in your track record. This usually means qualifications, experience, demonstrable successes and above all a good relationship with your present or past bank manager. If this last point proves a stumbling block you are advised to come clean at the outset.

Presenting your case

Ideas alone do not make money. A sound business idea needs to be encapsulated in a detailed commercial proposition in which risks and returns should attract financiers. There is no shortage of funds to back sound management with good propositions — sadly, it is the latter rather than the former that is lacking.

The high failure rate of start-up businesses is due essentially to five key issues:

1. Incompetent management
2. A badly researched proposal (especially with regard to marketing and the competition)
3. Wrong or inadequate financing
4. A basic lack of understanding of the economics of the business
5. Poor management information systems.

In presenting your case, your well thought out proposal needs to attract the financiers' attention. It needs to elicit their confidence.

The key to presenting your case well is not only to try to cover all aspects of the business but to demonstrate realism, eg discuss the weaknesses and the risks.

The business plan

The business plan is a statement of intent. It is the documentary evidence of your business idea supported by research information and plans of action which you intend pursuing. It is the selling document that you will use in order to raise the appropriate finance for your venture. Having set out your plans in both qualitative and quantitative form you need to include a write-up on the type and purpose of financing required. In developing your business plan take cognizance of the typical lending and investing criteria set out earlier.

The financing requirement should be discussed in detail and should include:

1. The finance required and the potential financier, eg bank, venture capital institution
2. The form in which the finance is needed, eg lump sum or instalments
3. When it is needed
4. Proposed repayment details
5. Proposed security in order to back the amount of funds required.

It is better to discuss a range rather than an exact figure when it comes to the financing requirement. Remember also to budget for contingencies and worst case scenarios and to address sensitivities and risks.

An example of how detailed trading projections should be set out is shown on pages 31–35.

Section	Item	Detail
Overview	• General business profile • Product/services • Management • Key financial data • Financing required	Give a brief and 'punchy' description sufficient to convey the essence of the business. The finance required should cover the purpose and amount.
History	• Business evolution • Historical financial results • Structural details	Discuss major changes. Highlight good and bad points and discuss trends. Discuss shareholders and directors and note changes.
Management and organisation	• Reporting structure and responsibilities • Management team • Employee details • Premises and facilities	Discuss. Provide CVs and salient details. Set out size, relevant contracts, trade union details etc. Discuss developments and planned major changes.
Product or service	• Detailed description of mix • Research and development commitments • Production methods • Patents and licensing • Resource requirements	Discuss volumes, profitability and pricing. Note technology involved and capital expenditure plans. Discuss strengths, weaknesses and opportunities. Note these if relevant and explain implications. Discuss salient points.
Marketing and markets	• Market research • Size of the markets • Competition • Customers • Pricing, sales and distribution • Promotion	Discuss market research carried out and future plans. Note relevant points. Discuss marketing strategy, who the competitors are etc. Explain present and potential customer bases. Discuss policies and the competitive edge. Highlight strategy and programmes.
Financial aspects	• Historic results • Future projections (three to five years) Profit and loss accounts Balance sheets Cash flows • Timing of cash injections • Repayment capability	Discuss important points. Describe assumptions in detail. Carry out a sensitivity analysis and explain the implications. Highlight potential timing of cash peaks and troughs. Explain. Propose repayment terms in line with projections.

Detailed trading projections

Projected balance sheets						
Assets employed		**Year 1**		**Year 2**		**Year 3**
Fixed assets (see below)		(a)		(a)		(a)
Stock value						
Debtors						
Cash						
Current assets	(b)____		(b)____		(b)____	
Bank overdraft						
Creditors						
Tax payable	____		____		____	
Current liabilities	(c)____		(c)____		(c)____	
Net current assets		(b-c)____		(b-c)____		(b-c)____
Net assets		____		____		____
Sources of finance						
Share capital						
Reserves		____		____		____
Shareholders' funds						
Loans						
Total sources of finance		____		____		____
		====		====		====
(a) Fixed assets						
Previous fixed assets						
+ Capital expenditure						
– Depreciation		____		____		____
Fixed assets		====		====		====

Projected monthly profit and loss account (£000)

	Projections 1	2	3	4	5	6	7	8	9	10	11	12	Total
1. Sales													
(per major product group)													
(a)													
(b)													
(c)													
2. Total Sales													
3. Materials, labour and overheads													
Opening stock													
Purchases													
Labour													
Production overheads													
Closing stock													
4. Selling costs													
Sales commission													
Freight and duty													
5. Cost of sales													
6. Gross profit													
Marketing and promotion													
Other selling + distribution overheads													
Administrative costs													
Premise costs													
Travel and entertainment costs													
Interest - bank loans													
- other													
Sub-Total													
7. Pretax profit (loss)													
8. Gross profit percentage (6) × 100 - (2)													
9. Net profit percentage (7) × 100 - (2)													

10. Breakeven point = $\frac{\text{Fixed expenses}}{\text{Sales less variable expenses}} \times 100$

Note: Years 2 + 3 should be projected on a quarterly basis
Years 4 + 5 should be projected on an annual basis

Schedule of changes in working capital (cash flows)

	Actual	**Projections Net current assets per balance sheet**												
	Opening balances	**1**	**2**	**3**	**4**	**5**	**6**	**7**	**8**	**9**	**10**	**11**	**12**	**Total**
Debtors														
Trade														
Other														
Stock														
Raw material														
Work in progress														
Finished goods														
(Progress payments)														
Sub-Total														
Creditors Trade														
Other														
Sub-Total														
Net current assets														
(Increase) Decrease in working capital +/–														
			Cash flow statement											
Cash out														
Increase (Decrease) in Working Capital														
Capital Expenditure														
Repayment of existing loans														
Sub-Total														
Cash in														
Profits (Losses)														
Depreciation and other write-offs														
Sub-Total														
Net cash requirements (surplus)														

Monthly cash flow

Funding statement

	Actual	Projections												
	Opening balances	**1**	**2**	**3**	**4**	**5**	**6**	**7**	**8**	**9**	**10**	**11**	**12**	**Total**
Equity														
Preference shares														
Other														
Borrowings														

Potential financiers

Financiers of start-up ventures are usually people or institutions looking for high capital gains rather than high debt yields. Some sources to be considered are:

- *Specific venture capital institutions.* They typically prefer a significant shareholding and prefer an active management approach.
- Private investors (most often exploiting Business Expansion Scheme opportunities). Those investors who usually have a high tax profile are looking to capital gains and tax benefits. Most are inclined to be passive investors.
- *Venture capital arms of pension funds or banks.* They have a similar outlook to specific venture capital institutions. They are often the most passive but risk-averse in their approach.
- *Banks* (general financial institutions). Banks typically do not want to play the role of investor or shareholder in a start-up venture. They wish to be assured that the business is adequately capitalized and that their finance will be in the form of secured debt with a fairly predetermined return.
- *Local authority and government organizations.* These institutions participate in business largely to the extent that they advance grant money in order to stimulate local businesses.

METHODS OF RAISING EQUITY CAPITAL

The methods for raising equity capital vary depending on:

1. Whether a company is public or private
2. The number of shares available for issue
3. The size of the company in profit terms
4. The company's track record
5. The general market conditions at the time of wishing to go to the market.

Private companies

A private company is prohibited from offering its shares or debentures to the public. In return private companies enjoy certain privileges that afford them a degree of privacy denied to public companies.

If a private company wishes to issue new shares to raise finance, either existing shareholders have to subscribe or the new shares have to be carefully placed through an issuing house. Shares in private companies are not marketable, cannot be easily transferred, and are thus not very attractive to investors.

Public companies

Public companies have no restrictions on the transfer of their shares and if they have a Stock Exchange quotation they can raise new equity funds through the market. Unquoted companies often find that their growth is limited by a shortage of funds and so seek a quotation in order to gain access to additional sources of finance.

Any offer to the public to subscribe for shares or debentures in a company must be accompanied by a prospectus. This is a document which sets out the advantages that accrue from investing in the company.

There are several methods of issuing new shares via the stock market:

Offer for sale. The company's shares are offered to an issuing house, which in turn offers these to the general public by advertising a prospectus. This is often used by a private company wishing to change its status to public.

Public issue. Here the offer is made direct by the company to the public. The vendors of the shares may either be shareholders or the company. The issuing house acts purely as agent in this instance.

Placing. A placing occurs when shares, debentures or other securities are sold privately to the clients of the issuing house or broker handling the issue, rather than being offered to the general public.

Tender issue. By this method shares are offered to the public and potential investors are invited to tender a price they would be prepared to pay. The company usually puts a reserve on the shares, being the minimum price below which they shall not be sold.

The Stock Exchange

The Stock Exchange is a self-regulating body, governed by a council which has drawn up a series of regulations governing its internal affairs and its supervision of companies whose securities are listed. The 'Admission of Securities to Listing' or 'Yellow Book' sets out the requirements of companies before their securities are listed as well as the rules for the conduct of their affairs with respect to the stock market once listed. The Stock Exchange is known as the 'main market' and is not only the most regulated but is the most costly to join.

The Unlisted Securities Market (USM)

This is the second market to the main market. It has less onerous obligations and is less costly on listing. The smaller company or company that wishes the general public to hold only a minority holding often favours this market.

The Over-the-Counter Market

This is a small market that has developed for dealings in unlisted securities. It is typically used by small and medium-sized companies which do not qualify for a main or USM listing. This type of unofficial market is very active in the USA and also exists in some European countries, notably West Germany and France.

During the 1970s a requirement for a London market dealing in unlisted securities was recognized by an investment banker, M J H Nightingale. He began to operate in unlisted securities on this unofficial market and his organization, now known as Granvilles, has spurred on the development and growth of this market. Initially only some dozen stocks were traded; however, the OTC has gained in public recognition and popularity and some 100 stocks are now active.

SHORT- AND MEDIUM-TERM FINANCE

Short- and medium-term finance is normally raised in the form of debt finance by most businesses. Although there is no strict definition of the terms, it is commonly accepted that:

Short term is up to two years.
Medium term is two to seven years.
Long term is longer than seven years.

Short-term financial needs should be financed with short-term borrowing and long-term needs by long-term funds. It is dangerous to finance long-term needs with short-term funds as they take longer to generate a positive cash flow and thus it might be difficult to raise the cash to repay any short-term loans.

Bank borrowing

Bank borrowing in the form of overdrafts is the most popular form of finance especially for small and medium-sized businesses. It is comparatively cheap as the risks to the lender are not as great as for long-term loans, and the interest is tax deductible. Bank advances are, however, legally repayable on demand which could be awkward if the funds have been used to finance anything other than short-term assets.

The high degree of competition among financial institutions has resulted in the banks being more approachable with respect to medium-term, and in some cases long-term, finance.

Banks are very keen to obtain adequate security to support any advances that they might make. The greater the security required the higher the perceived risk of the loan. It is common for them to obtain fixed or floating charges on assets as security for overdrafts and other advances. In some instances they even insist on a personal guarantee from owners.

The cost of bank borrowing depends on the creditworthiness of the borrower and upon the level of interest rates in the market. Bank borrowing is usually offered at a margin above the base rate.

Trade credit

A vital source of funding to almost all organizations is trade credit extended by one company to another on the purchase and sale of goods, services and equipment. This is often considered to be a no cost form of financing. If a discount is offered for prompt payment and is not taken advantage of, then this can prove to be a fairly costly form of finance. For example, a 1 per cent cash discount for payment within 30 days which is not availed of amounts to a cost of capital of 12.7 per cent per annum.

Trade credit is a normal part of business in most industries. Part of the terms of sale of goods and services includes an offer for trade credit. As a buyer, obviously one would wish the terms to be as lenient as possible. As a seller one would strive to make the credit terms tight and collect the cash as quickly as possible without negatively affecting sales. The varying terms of credit in different industries must be taken into account when establishing terms of trade and calculating the working capital requirement.

Factoring

This has become a very popular source of financing for small businesses. Factoring involves raising funds on the security of the company's trade debtors without having to wait for the normal period that debtors take to pay. Factoring houses usually allow a draw down rising to 85 per cent of the outstanding debtors' balance in cash. The company thus has an apparent 'cash' generating business at a cost of X per cent of the outstanding debtors' balance. Factoring can be a fairly expensive form of financing as the X per cent can be anything between 2 and 4 per cent.

Most factors offer several services of which the client may choose only those that it requires. These are usually:

1. A sales ledger accounting, sending out of invoices and a collection service
2. A credit insurance which acts as a guarantee against bad debts
3. Cash advances against the outstanding debtors' balance.

Factors also offer recourse and non-recourse factoring. In the former case the client is responsible for and carries any bad debts and in the latter the factor assumes those risks. Obviously, the fee for non-recourse factoring is higher.

Factoring improves the company's liquidity position. There is a danger, however, that this can give management a misleading impression of the true economics of the business. Experience has also shown that when the company wants to cease the use of factoring it often has to face a daunting liquidity crunch.

Invoice discounting and credit insurance

This is another method of factoring aimed at assisting the liquidity of a business by not tying up working capital in the book debts. Specific invoices can be converted into cash by discounting the invoice through specialized finance companies. The cost of this service depends on the size of the invoice or block of invoices, the administrative costs and the risks involved. Costs include interest and service charges.

Credit insurance is available from insurance companies and credit insurance agencies. A premium is paid in return for the amount of the invoice if the debt goes bad. A company wishing to discount invoices will find institutions more receptive if they have some form of credit insurance.

Bills of exchange

These are mainly used for overseas payments. A supplier prepares a bill which requires the person to whom it is addressed (the buyer) to pay on demand or at a fixed future time a certain sum of money, to the order of a specified person or bearer. In other words, a bill of exchange is akin to a post-dated cheque. This bill can be discounted at a bank or discount house at a discount rate set by the financial institution, based on the creditworthiness of the payer, the amount and general market conditions.

Acceptance credits

These are similar to bills of exchange only in this instance one of the parties is a bank. An acceptance credit is an arrangement whereby a company draws a bill of exchange on a bank. The bank, by accepting the bill, agrees to pay out the amount of the bill at some determined future rate. This bill now has some value as it entitles the holder to receive some money at some time in the future and it can be discounted with, for example, a discount house. A bill bearing a reputable bank's name can be sold at a lower discount than a bill bearing the name of a small or medium-sized company.

A company does not have to discount the bill when it is issued but can use this credit as and when required. The length of credit available can be up to five years and can represent a cheaper and even more flexible method of financing than the normal bank overdraft.

Export finance

Export business is always that much more risky than domestic business due not only to the distance of markets, but the potential insolvency of the customer as well as foreign exchange risks. The Export Credits Guarantee Department (ECGD) insures exporters against default resulting from buyer insolvency or currency problems.

Credit insurance is achieved by the company paying a premium to the ECGD which effectively guarantees reimbursement for the invoice amount of goods sold to overseas buyers.

The ECGD will also guarantee a bank, that any loan that it (the bank) has advanced to an exporter in order to provide enticing credit terms to its overseas customers, will be made good should the overseas buyer default. In this way the ECGD assists an exporting company in the raising of funds and in return receives a premium from the exporter for this service.

The ECGD also provides a buyer credit scheme whereby, for large contracts especially of capital goods, the exporter is paid in cash on acceptable delivery to the buyer of the goods or installation. The buyer typically pays up to 20 per cent out of his own resources and the balance is financed by a UK institution guaranteed by the ECGD. The ECGD assists in providing lines of credit to overseas buyers if they are buying goods manufactured in the UK.

The ECGD provides exchange rate cover as the exporting company can run the risk of exchange exposure on every sale. A special scheme is available in order to protect exporters against the risks of financing exports through the currency markets.

Performance bonds

Performance bonds most often relate to the financing of large construction and capital expenditure projects. Many such projects which are offered on a contract basis dwarf the size of the organizations contracted to undertake the work. Usually the customer or buyer is asked to advance a portion of the value of the contract to the contractor in advance of the commencement of the project. Naturally, a concern then exists that the work will be completed and/or any losses will be recovered. In order to provide comfort to the buyer the supplier organizes a guarantee from the bank in favour of the foreign buyer which he can exercise in the event of bad or non-performance by the supplier. The performance bond has a cost to the supplier which he naturally tries to recover in the pricing of the contract.

The ECGD issues performance bonds as yet another method of facilitating the financing of overseas trade.

Project finance

Project finance is essentially medium-term borrowing arranged to support a particular project and secured against the assets and/or positive cash flow of that project rather than against the standing or potential of the borrower. In establishing the amount and the cost of the finance the key consideration is thus the financial viability and the risks of the project.

The biggest single source of project finance is held to be the World Bank. This organization lends not only to larger multinationals but mainly to sovereign borrowers in the less developed or newly industrialized countries where the capital markets are relatively under-developed.

Hire purchase

This is a very popular source of medium-term credit most often used to finance the purchase of plant, equipment and motor vehicles. The hire purchase company hires the equipment to the intended purchaser at a fixed monthly hire purchase instalment over a predetermined HP period. At the end of the period the hirer has the option of acquiring legal title to the equipment by paying a nominal amount.

Throughout the HP period the asset serves as security against the loan amount which makes this a very convenient way of financing. Hire purchase is an expensive way of obtaining credit as the effective interest rate is usually between 20 and 30 per cent.

Leasing

This is a similar form of finance to hire purchase except that ownership remains with the lessor. The lessee acquires the right to use an asset for a fixed rental. The growth of leasing was largely stimulated by highly geared companies using this method of off-balance sheet financing whereby they attained use of assets, the financial implications of which are not reflected on the balance sheet. In recent years reporting accountants have been concerned with fair disclosure in the annual financial statements. These statements should reflect substance over form which is particularly relevant with respect to off-balance sheet finance and especially leasing. Leases are now classified between finance and operating leases.

Finance leases are those where in reality the lease is entered into as a basic financing agreement rather than a rental agreement. The lessee has the use of the asset for 75 per cent or more of its estimated economic life and has substantially all the risks and rewards associated with the ownership of the asset other than legal title. A finance lease usually also involves payment by a lessee to a lessor the full cost of the asset plus a return on the finance provided by the lessor.

Finance leases require to be capitalized in the books of the lessee and the liability for the cost of the asset (excluding the financing cost) to be raised as a liability in the accounts.

With an *operating lease,* ownership, risks and the responsibility for repairs, maintenance and insurance remain with the lessor. The rental paid for the hire of the asset is for a period shorter than 75 per cent of the estimated economic life, and the net cost of the equipment is not usually recovered by the lessor.

Sale and lease-back

Companies can often generate cash by selling assets that they own and leasing them back from the purchaser. This is a fairly popular method with land and buildings which can be sold to institutions such as insurance companies and pension funds which like holding long-term assets likely to appreciate in value.

Selling the asset might result in a capital gains tax liability which will arise if the sale price is greater than the book value of the asset. The rental payable for use of the asset will, however, be tax deductible.

MANAGING WORKING CAPITAL

Working capital is defined as the net current assets of a business, its three main items being stock, debtors and creditors. It is essentially these items that reflect the trading cycle of the business. A company must strive to achieve an optimal balance between not having too much capital tied up in its working capital and being sufficiently liquid, ie having sufficient resources tied up in current assets that can be quickly converted to cash to meet short-term requirements. The optimal mix varies from business to business as the working capital requirement will reflect the terms of trade in the respective industry.

In order to determine future working capital requirements it is necessary to project the future profit and loss account, balance sheets and to generate a cash flow statement (see page 28). Generally, it is considered expedient to budget for spare cash to cope with short-term requirements and to borrow for longer-term needs. Cash balances are usually considered to be idle assets as the return on cash is usually far less than the return on investment in another form of asset.

The current assets of a business usually need to be 1.7 to 2 times the current liabilities for the company to be considered as safe by anyone considering advancing it short-term funds. This is because the largest current asset is usually inventory which can rarely be quickly converted into cash. A forced sale is also likely to result in not recovering the full value.

EXPANSION

It is inherent in the nature of the management of enterprises that they see business expansion as virtuous, something to be pursued. The motivations underlying expansion plans are many, and again a business plan would be the appropriate document to attract outside finance if this is required. It is rare that a small company can fund its own expansion plans. Financial institutions are amenable to financing expansion provided the motivation is plausible and the figures stackup. Some examples of specialist financial institutions are:

- Finance for the development of new inventions — The National Research Development Corporation
- Finance for the development of small and medium companies — Investors in Industry (3is)
Charterhouse Development Ltd
Venture capital arms of the clearing banks
Local enterprise boards

• Finance for regional development	Government and regional development grants

CONCLUSION

The subject of finance is large and dynamic. New financing methods are continuously being introduced, while traditional sources of funding are changing. Tomes continue to be written about the subject and thus only a window on to this intriguing vista can be revealed here. Raising and managing financial resources is not an exact science. Each organization must continue to strive to obtain its optimal financing mix, at least cost, with least risk, and maximum flexibility. A challenging task to say the least.

Sources of finance

1. *Equity*
   Private individuals
   Listing on the OTC, USM or London Stock Exchange
   Venture capital institutions
2. *Debt*
   Private individuals
   Banks
   Discount and finance houses
   Other large corporations

3

PROPERTY AND PREMISES

D Howard Green and Paul D Foley

INTRODUCTION

Premises are a vital element of all businesses; for the would-be entrepreneur the problem may be finding premises at all; further established business issues such as space management, service provision, tenancy arrangements, property maintenance or even location will arise from time to time. For the larger company with a range of premises, property will be the responsibility of an individual or even department. Property issues can be complex and involve dealing with a bewildering array of expert professionals, such as solicitors, town planners, estate agents, accountants, bank managers, architects, builders, building inspectors, fire officers, health and safety officials, insurance agents, interior designers and estate managers. The aim of this section is to identify and discuss the key issues of property selection and management to provide thought, planning and informed decision making. The section begins by identifying nine key items which make up the property balance sheet:

1. *Geographical location.* Location can have a major impact on business prospects and profitability.
2. *Size and layout.* The physical characteristics of a building can condition patterns of work and productivity.
3. *The environment.* The environment in which employees work can have a major impact on individual and group performances, energy and enthusiasm.
4. *Image.* Property creates an image for a business.
5. *Purchase costs.* For those who own property it constitutes a major financial commitment and resource.
6. *Rentals.* Rentals and the buying and selling of leases can represent major financial burdens.
7. *Overheads.* Rates, heating, lighting and maintenance costs can be substantial.
8. *Technical problems.* Mistakes on a range of technical issues such as planning permission, building regulations or the small print in leases can cost a lot of time and money.
9. *Moving.* Moving premises is a major undertaking which can influence company performance. Moving to the wrong premises will bring many more problems than opportunities.

THE CHOICE OF PREMISES AVAILABLE

In all sectors of the industrial and commercial property market there is a wide range of premises available. Markets for retail, commercial and manufacturing property are characterized by premises ranging from the cheap but scruffy end of the market to high quality premises in prestigious locations. It is up to the individual business person to decide the appropriate place in the market for his or her business. Within any local market it is probable that the full range of premises listed below will not be available. It is therefore important for individual businesses to familiarize themselves with the different kinds of property available within their local market. This review cannot cover all the different elements of the market but rather gives an indication of what is available. It begins with a discussion of the possibilities of working from home, for while it will be appropriate only to a small minority it is an option which current government policy is encouraging. It then examines separately manufacturing, retail and office accommodation.

Working from home

A large proportion of businesses in the United Kingdom start by trading from home. Working from home can have a lot of advantages for new businesses: by removing the costs of providing and running premises it minimizes overhead costs. Since even the smallest workshop or office is likely to cost well over £1000 a year considerable savings can be made by the entrepreneur working from home.

Working from home can save the time that would otherwise be spent commuting to and from work. It also allows some small-business people the opportunity to involve their family in the day-to-day running of the business. A spouse prepared to deal with telephone enquiries, help with correspondence, typing and other secretarial tasks can provide valuable (and possibly unpaid) assistance.

However, there are disadvantages in working from home. Domestic tensions can accumulate as the business expands and takes over ever-increasing areas of the house. Other problems of working from home are that businesses might contravene local regulations regarding the use of domestic premises. The deeds of many houses forbid this use. Leaseholders should check the terms of their leases and tenants should notify their landlords before using their home for business. Working from home may also infringe town planning regulations. Planners have designated many areas of towns and cities for residential use only. Setting up business and working from home can actually contravene these regulations by making what is called 'a material change in the use of land'.

Businesses which do not generate much traffic or noise and do not annoy neighbours will not normally be required to obtain planning permission, but more troublesome kinds of firm will be expected to apply for permission. This might, in many cases, be refused.

Working from home can have a number of implications for other aspects of normal household life. House insurance policies may be invalidated by businesses trading from home; if a business increases the risk of fire or theft by increasing the number of visitors, both house and home contents policies may need to be changed. Rates and tax allowances may also be affected by trading from home. Rates bills should increase slightly because a higher level of rates will be payable on the parts of a home which are used for business purposes. Although there is no legal obligation to inform the local authority rates officer of business activities he may find out about these if an application for planning or building permission is made to the local authority.

Tax relief is available to those trading from home on the part of their rates bill which is paid for business use. Tax allowances can be claimed from the Inland Revenue for heating, lighting, repairing and maintaining the room(s) which are used by the business. Regulations state that allowances are only granted if rooms are used exclusively for business but in practice many Inland Revenue officials are reasonably lenient on this issue and too busy to make exhaustive checks.

Manufacturing accommodation

Old cheap premises

In many of the more run-down inner areas of Britain's towns and cities there is a stock of older pre-First World War properties which are generally inexpensive but often shabby and in need of repair or redecoration. Although relatively poor aesthetically, these premises are usually very cheap and therefore provide ideal quarters for new companies or companies moving from home which want to keep their property costs down. Although these older buildings were not designed or laid out for modern industry, a little bit of work and a coat of paint can transform them into premises which provide tolerable working conditions. Many of these buildings were designed and constructed before the car was invented and as a result parking and vehicle access problems are often prevalent.

Rents for these cheaper types of premises vary throughout the country, but they can be as low as 25 pence per square foot in some of the more run-down areas. Variations in rent are generally caused by local market demand and the condition of the individual property; average rents (excluding rates and other charges) are about £3 per square foot in London and between £1 and £1.50 in the provinces.

Refurbished premises

The growth in recent years in the amount of redundant floor space has led both public and private developers to fund refurbishment schemes. These schemes bring property up to standards appropriate to today's needs and may also include subdivision to create units for small business.

Levels of refurbishment vary greatly from scheme to scheme and rental charges are generally dependent upon the degree of modernization which is undertaken and the site's geographical location.

Rental charges (exclusive of rates and other charges) vary considerably from under £1 per square foot in parts of Yorkshire and northern England to over £5–£6 per square foot in parts of London. Average rents lie in the range between £1.50 and £2.50 per square foot.

Modern factory units

The traditional form of modern factory unit consists of a steel framed and clad structure with roller shutter doors, and eaves heights of 18ft or more. These have traditionally been built in sizes upwards of 10,000 sq ft on industrial estates in the suburbs of towns and cities. Levels of finish and detailed design vary, but in general they provide the bread and butter of modern factory building. In many parts of the country they are built speculatively and are readily available for occupation.

More recently there has been an increase in the number of new small units built to standardized designs aimed to appeal to a wide range of small business tenants. These small units generally take one of three forms: terraced, semi-detached or detached. Terraces are the most common because this design lowers building costs by reducing the amount of exterior walls. This in turn can help to reduce heating and maintenance costs. Detached and semi-detached units are generally confined to the larger end of the small factory market. Nearly all newly built units have very large roller doors enabling them to be used not only for manufacturing but also as small warehouse units.

Rental charges for modern units are variable, depending not only upon the type of unit but also the physical layout, location, site services and the quality of the local environment. Rents for modern units at prime sites can reach up to about £6 per square foot, but charges between £1.50 and £3 are more typical.

Science parks

Science parks are a new development in the property market. They are usually in green field locations and consist of 'high tech' buildings built at very low densities. The appeal is to high tech research and development companies seeking a pleasant working environment. Perhaps the best known in Britain are at Cambridge and Warrington. Innovative variations on this theme are found at Listerhills in Bradford and at Aston in Birmingham. Here the development is located close to the universities and emphasizes the needs of technology transfer. Rents vary from £4.50 to £6 per square foot in the provinces to £9–£12 in the south.

Serviced workshops

Serviced workshops are a fairly recent innovation primarily designed to help new small businesses become established. As well as working accommodation, at these sites a wide range of business services is available. The underlying rationale for this type of development is that individually small businesses could not afford these services but collectively they can create enough demand to make them economic. Services generally fall into three main groups. First, office services such as typing, photocopying and telephone answering. Second, property-related services including heating, lighting, insurance and maintenance. Finally, business services such as business advisers, accountants and marketing services.

The type of premises used for serviced workshop accommodation can vary widely from purpose-built workshop schemes to refurbishment schemes. The main advantage of this type of scheme is that most tenants are in a similar situation suffering similar problems; the sharing of experience, and mutual assistance and co-operation which a workshop environment can therefore engender, can be particularly useful. The main disadvantages lie in the general level of noise and distraction which is often prevalent in workshop schemes.

Rentals for serviced workshops can vary greatly depending how services are charged for. Most adopt a fully inclusive method in which all costs except individual tenants' electricity and telephone bills are included. Typical rents at serviced workshop schemes range between about £4.50 and £7.50 per square foot.

Retail premises

Although the premises so far reviewed might suit some types of retail company such as wholesalers or retailers handling bulky goods (timber merchants, for example) retailers generally require different types of property. When purchasing retail premises, it is more common to buy an existing business together with the freehold or lease of the actual premises. In such cases it is important to explore the track record and future prospects of the business as well as the merits of the property.

Further details of these considerations can be found in *Buying a Shop* by A St J Price and *How to Buy a Business* by P Farrell.

The age and condition of retail premises can vary greatly but retail outlets can be classified into three main groups in terms of location:

Town centres
In town centres the number of prospective tenants passing a particular property reaches a maximum and the turnover per unit area of the property should be at a peak. The majority of shops in town centres are selling comparison goods (eg clothes and shoes) where customers check on alternative products for style, quality and price before making a purchase. These buildings tend to be of a fairly good quality, with good interior design and high levels of finish.

The quality of shops and the number of prospective tenants passing by a property tends to decrease with distance from the town centre. On the margins of most town centres and the roads leading away from them there is often a stock of older, less glamorous shops.

District high streets
District high streets operate as 'mini town centres' and generally serve a large local neighbourhood rather than a whole town. These centres also contain shops selling comparison goods, but there is an increased number of shops dealing in convenience goods (everyday grocery and household items) too. The quality of the buildings in these areas, their interior finish and the products sold usually reflect the social class and income level of the population in the surrounding area.

Local stores
Local stores can vary from an isolated corner shop to a group of a few shops serving a particular town or small neighbourhood of a city. Their general function is to provide convenience goods for the immediate locality. These shops, once again, reflect the social characteristics of the area they serve. Since their turnover is lower than both of the previous groups the shops are generally of a lower quality.

Variation in rents for retail premises is far greater than for the industrial and workshop premises considered earlier. The most important determinant of rent is probably the shop's location. Prime retail locations can attract exceedingly high rents; in central London prime retailing space currently costs about £70–£100 per square foot (excluding rates). By contrast a local corner store in a provincial city might cost about £4–£6 per square foot. Contrasts between rental levels can be considerable and it is important to become familiar with local rents before making a firm commitment to any property.

Offices
Easy access to customers is usually a key locational consideration for most office users, as well as retailers. The supply of office premises therefore shares some common features with the geography of retailing. In terms of location, offices can be classified into four main groups:

Town centres
The prime location for offices is a town centre site. The recent service sector boom has seen a concentration of office accommodation in central locations. Town centres provide advantages not only in attracting qualified staff but also in access to customers and to other offices offering related services. Much of this central office space takes the form of high-rise blocks, often built during the 1960s and 1970s.

Prestigious historical premises
Some professional services, such as solicitors, like to advertise the antiquity and respectability of their businesses by obtaining a prestigious address in an historic part of town. Most of these premises are located in the historical core of many older towns and cities, in an area usually within or adjacent to the existing town centre. A limited supply of this type of office space can therefore often be found close to cathedrals, abbeys, town halls and in areas of elegant architecture.

District high streets

In some areas of the south east and around larger cities purpose-built office blocks have been developed at district high street centres. However, the main stock of office premises in district high streets is upper floor accommodation above existing shops. The geographical catchment area for attracting customers is more localized at high street centres and this is consequently reflected in the lower rents required for such premises.

The suburbs
As a result of changing patterns of communication, new developments in the transmission of data, and lower land prices in the suburbs, many new office developments have been built in suburban locations. Large suburban office developments are now common around many major cities. Favoured sites are usually areas with high accessibility along main roads or at transport interchanges.

Office rents are highly sensitive to location and there are striking geographical variations. Prime office space in the city of London can cost about £45 per square foot (excluding rates and other charges). Similar modern premises in the provinces may cost about £10 per square foot.

Rents for other types of office accommodation can be as little as £2 per square foot in some northern towns and district high street centres. Once again, these steep variations underline the need to get to know the local property market.

RENTS AND COSTS

It is important to emphasize a few key points about the way rents and costs are frequently quoted. At all premises you should enquire fully into exactly what rental cost covers. Be sure to enquire whether the figure quoted includes rates or any other form of supplementary or 'service' charge. Service charges can vary considerably from a small maintenance charge at a manufacturing unit to the full cost of a wide range of business and other services at a shared service workshop. All the extras which are sometimes attached to rent can more than double the cost of premises.

When considering moving to premises where a lease already exists it is important to remember that some cost may be involved in purchasing the lease. The purchase price for a lease will depend upon the rental value of the property and the period (in years) before the next rent review is due. The payment for the lease is therefore essentially 'key money' which secures the tenant the right to use the premises.

Rents for larger premises tend to be cheaper, on a square foot basis, than those for smaller properties. This is because scale economies exist at larger premises. Many public sector bodies, such as local authorities, see their main goal as encouraging businesses and employment rather than making money from property. For this reason their rents often tend to be lower than the private sector; some local authorities even offer reduced rents or rates for the first few months as a method of helping new businesses in their area.

This section has tended to concentrate on the cost of rentals for premises rather than freehold costs. For companies contemplating ownership it is worth pointing out that the same factors which shape rentals also shape purchase costs and there are equally steep variations, especially for shops and offices, between premises. In general, freehold costs in all sectors are about ten times the annual rental charge.

SOURCES OF PROPERTY INFORMATION

Searching for industrial property, like searching for houses, can be a difficult and dispiriting process. The difference between an agent's glowing description and the reality encountered on inspection can be considerable. The search process therefore usually results in a downward adjustment of requirements and an increased willingness to make compromises.

There are six main sources of information about industrial and commercial property; these are listed below. Those likely to be most useful are given first but much depends on the particular kind of property required.

Local authorities

Many local authority planning, employment or estates departments now keep a register of available premises. These are usually compiled in consultation with local estate agents. They tend to concentrate on industrial property but some also have lists of shop and office accommodation. The lists are usually updated regularly and, although they inevitably fall short of being absolutely comprehensive, they are often the single best source of information.

Estate agents

Not all agents deal with industrial and commercial property. Industrial property is usually dealt with by larger agents only. Some companies specialize in commercial and industrial property. Estate agents have a tendency to promote their most expensive premises, cheaper premises being revealed only after specific questioning about this area of the market. It is usually best to call in at an agent's office and make regular repeated visits. In this way they know that an enquiry is serious, and as a result clients usually receive a better service.

Local newspapers

The local press usually have industrial and commercial property sections in which businesses can either advertise their requirements or review properties advertised for lease or sale. Most newspapers have a particular issue during the week which is generally accepted as the 'industrial/commercial property day'.

Walking or driving around the local area

At some properties, the only advertising undertaken is by billboards outside the premises. A drive around the local area can sometimes bring to light vacant properties which are not advertised elsewhere.

Personal contacts

It is always worthwhile for any company to tell its business colleagues, suppliers and customers that it is looking for new premises; they may well know of suitable premises in their locality. Members of local business organizations can be particularly helpful in this respect. It is also useful to discuss your property requirements with your contacts. Their experience may help to highlight items or locations which had not been considered.

Other sources of advice

Other groups which can also be useful include local enterprise agencies, the Department of Employment's Small Firms Service, CoSIRA and English Estates.

SEARCHING FOR PREMISES

The previous section gave a broad indication of the types of premises available within any local area. Precise details of what is available within a particular area can only be found after a thorough search of locally available properties. If you do not have your own estates department you may consider employing a consultant to undertake the search and selection on your behalf.

Before undertaking any search it is essential to have a clear set of objectives to help the search proceed more efficiently. If a company knows what it is looking for, it will not waste time visiting premises which do not meet requirements. A written checklist of requirements makes it far easier to evaluate the sites that are inspected. It is unlikely that during the search any business will ever find the exact type of premises it wants. The search inevitably develops into a series of compromises and trade-offs between particular premises, but by preparing a checklist this process of compromise can be undertaken in a more structured way.

The preparation of a checklist is a valuable exercise in itself. It ensures that the company has fully considered the type of premises that it wants. It should also ensure that premises requirements fit in with the company's future business and investment plans. While preparing a checklist of priorities it is worth talking to people in your search area who have a knowledge of property matters and the state of the local property market. Although you will accumulate knowledge about the market over time, this process can be accelerated by discussions with estate agents, local businessmen and local authority industrial development officers. Through their network of contacts they might have some useful ideas about your checklist and the prospects of finding what you want locally. Outside advice can be particularly helpful for businesses looking for premises for the first time.

Every business will obviously have its own individual requirements (no two checklists will have exactly the same detailed contents) but at a broad level there are certain items which virtually all checklists will need to consider. These are discussed below.

Location

The importance of location varies enormously between different businesses. Location matters most if customers come to collect goods or services. Retailers are therefore especially sensitive to location. The two key ingredients of a good retail location are high pedestrian flow and a large local resident population.

The importance of location for office activities depends upon the precise nature of the business. For activities such as solicitors and accountancy, where customers visit the premises, the locational needs are broadly similar to those of specialist shops. If the office function is simply processing forms or invoicing, with little direct customer contact, a more decentralized location can be considered. Many companies are now splitting up their office activities to take advantage of lower rentals in more peripheral locations, while retaining a small centrally located headquarters.

Even among manufacturing companies location can be important; it will depend upon the frequency and urgency of contacts with customers and suppliers. Many firms are now seeking highly accessible locations at motorway intersections or with easy access to the motorway network.

A further locational consideration may be the variety of local authority and central government assistance which is available to companies locating in certain parts of the country.

Size

Deciding on the correct area or size for any business can be difficult. Some reserve space is always required for expansion, but businesses have to be careful not to overburden themselves with large areas of space which they may not use. Unused space costs money. Overheads such as rents, rates, heating, lighting and insurance are all incurred on unused space. Obtaining the correct balance of sufficient space for existing operations and enough space for future expansion requires a careful and realistic review of the company's development plans.

Recent business surveys suggest that the average floor space per employee in manufacturing is about 300–400 sq ft. Office orientated businesses tend to need rather less space, averaging about 200 sq ft per employee. By contrast, wholesale and warehousing businesses are more space extensive and figures of 600–700 sq ft are common. These figures are only a very rough guide to floor space requirements: different firms will have very different needs.

Costs

A major item on any checklist will be cost. A company's ability to pay for premises will play a key role in determining the kind of premises which should be considered. By expressing property costs as a proportion of expected turnover it is possible to clarify how sensitive a business is to differences in accommodation costs. This can help to indicate whether a business can afford to pay a little extra for superior premises. It is always worth consulting an accountant about immediate and projected costs associated with a fixed overhead such as property.

Because of the higher costs associated with buying property most companies rent premises. Rent charges can vary considerably for premises of broadly similar size and quality. This is particularly the case with smaller premises. A broad indication of price variation can be obtained from the major national estate agents, such as Jones Lang Wootton, who produce regular reviews and analyses of industrial and commercial property prices. The way in which prices are quoted can vary considerably. Normally only rents are quoted; occasionally the rateable value is given, sometimes associated service charges are also included. Rents are usually expressed as the price for premises per square foot per annum; some agents quote prices per square metre.

Tenure

Most businesses rent rather than buy property so as to minimize the capital locked up. A detailed discussion of the different forms of tenure will be found on page 69.

Condition

The condition of premises occupied by a company can greatly influence its customers' image of the business. It can also affect the productivity of employees: a shabby working environment can lower their productivity and morale. Take care not to be tempted into over-glamorous property at costs far beyond what the company can afford.

Layout

Before visiting any premises it is useful to consider the day-to-day operations of the business to develop an idea of the property layout and shape that would be most suited to the company's needs. For example, what is the best shape and layout of premises for particular companies' production, storage, office and sales functions? What are the requirements of each element of the business and how do they interrelate? A company using heavy machinery will have to consider floor loadings. In many properties the only areas capable of withstanding the load and vibration caused by heavy machinery are on the ground floor.

Parking and access

It is important to consider car parking and access requirements carefully. Estimates should be made of how many visitors call by car and thus how many car parking spaces will be required to allow all customers to park easily. If sufficient car parking space is not available, on-street parking will have to be considered. Ensure that the property is visited during midweek working hours and at peak times to obtain a representative view of normal parking conditions. It is also important to consider access for large lorries and vans entering or leaving the premises.

FINANCING PROPERTY

The two processes of finding a property and obtaining the money to pay for it are closely interwoven and tend to proceed in tandem. For those businesses intending to finance the purchase of premises or the move by means of a loan, obtaining the necessary capital is an essential task. Once businesses have drawn up a preliminary checklist of property requirements it is important to investigate the availability of funds. Exploratory discussions with accountants and funding agencies at this early stage will help to test the feasibility of plans, and may suggest some changes to ideas or adjustments to the checklist. Most firms requiring finance will have to borrow from a commercial lender.

Sources of finance

High street banks

Under the right circumstances most high street banks are prepared to lend money for up to 20 years for the purchase of industrial property. They will also consider lending money to finance longer-term leases or company moves provided that suitable security is available.

Merchant banks
Because merchant banks tend to lend larger amounts of money (over £50,000) they normally lend only to companies or individuals with a proven track record. They usually lend up to about 75–80 per cent of any property's value.

Building societies
Some building societies, predominantly the smaller ones, give mortgages to purchase industrial and commercial property. Indeed, many societies are keen to expand their lending in this area.

Local authority finance
Many local authorities, anxious to encourage local economic regeneration and employment growth, offer loans and in some cases grants to help businesses purchase premises.

Approaching the financial institutions

Although each financial institution has its own methods of dealing with applications the procedures set out below are those which commonly apply when borrowing sums between £5000 and £50,000.

A brief exploratory visit should be made to a number of financial organizations before the process of selecting a property begins. The aim of this visit is simply to make them aware that the business is considering new or additional premises and, unless the probability of lending is rejected at the outset, the company will return in the future when a suitable property has been found. Once a property has been identified a second visit should be arranged. Prior to this second meeting a brief document (three or four pages) should be prepared which gives basic information about the property (use details from the estate agent's handout), the company, the amount of finance required and the preferred method of repayment. If the lenders are satisfied with the initial ideas presented at this meeting and are interested in the proposition, they will invite the company back for another interview and a more thorough assessment.

For this final interview the lenders will require a much more detailed document which should include the following information:

1. Details of the business (products, markets etc) together with any sales or publicity material.
2. Details of the property (use the estate agent's brief).
3. The amount of finance required and the preferred method of borrowing.

4. An historical analysis of the company's finances (generally three years minimum).
5. The most recent trading figures and audited accounts for the company.
6. A forecast of cash flow and the company's future trading position.
7. Details (if appropriate) of the company's management structure.
8. A list of the company's major shareholders.
9. Details of current banking arrangements.
10. Details of any assets which are available as security.

Because of its essentially financial nature this document is best prepared with the help of an accountant. During the final meeting companies are asked in detail about the accuracy of the facts and forecasts which they make in the document. Business people who do not have a good knowledge of accounts are generally advised to take an accountant with them. Although accountants can deal with more detailed financial information, business people are also required to have a thorough understanding of the general principles of the document and forecasts which they are presenting. The lenders' personal impressions of business people are very important. It is often a gut feeling about the applicant which will sway their final decision.

The appointment of a surveyor to examine a property and ensure its value and future well-being is usually undertaken near the end of the financial negotiations. In this way surveyors are not employed until the lending organization is fairly confident that it will lend money for the purchase of the premises or to assist with the company's move.

Major sources of grants and preferential loans for the purchase of property

Numerous sources of financial assistance are available from central government, local government and other organizations to help companies move or relocate their premises. The following list outlines some of the most commonly used sources. It focuses on the assistance which may be given if a property is located in a certain geographical area or the business is eligible for certain other types of assistance. Full details of this complex subject are to be found in *Industrial Aids in the UK: a Businessman's Guide* by Mishka Biewkowski and Kevin Allen.

Assisted areas eligible for regional policy

Some areas of the country with particular economic problems or high levels of unemployment have been designated by central government as 'assisted areas'. There are two types of regional aid available in assisted areas:

- *Regional Development Grants.* These offer tax-tree contributions towards expenditure on premises. The rate of the grant is set at about 15 per cent subject to a limit of £10,000 for each new job created.
- *Regional Selective Assistance.* This form of aid is discretionary. Relocation schemes are eligible but only if there is an increase in jobs. The amount of assistance is negotiated on an individual basis and is fixed at the minimum sum needed to bring about the project.

Inner city areas
Certain inner city areas, designated under the Inner Urban Areas Act 1978, are eligible for loans and grants to assist with property improvement and purchase. Grants and loans are available for the conversion, improvement, modification or extension of industrial or commercial buildings located in industrial or commercial improvement areas.

Enterprise zones
Financial and tax incentives are available to companies purchasing or leasing properties in any of the 25 enterprise zones located throughout the United Kingdom. All companies located in premises in these areas are exempt from rates on property.

British Technology Groups
The British Technology Groups were established to promote innovation and investment in British industry. They can provide money to finance the purchase or relocation to premises if this is part of an overall improvement programme within a company.

Council for Small Industries in Rural Areas (CoSIRA)
CoSIRA provides loans for small businesses in certain rural areas of England. Loans for building capital are available at up to 50 per cent of the project costs up to a maximum of £75,000.

English Estates
English Estates are primarily concerned with providing industrial and commercial property, but they can also arrange mortgages with financial institutions at favourable interest rates.

British Coal Enterprise Ltd
British Coal Enterprise Ltd, set up by British Coal in 1985, can provide

preferential loans to small businesses which may be used for the purchase of premises in coalfield areas.

THE PROPERTY DECISION

After the first meeting with lenders, when outline confirmation has been given that funding to purchase or move into new premises will be considered, the detailed search for property can begin. The process of looking for suitable industrial or commercial property is not unlike looking for a new house. There are certain obvious things to look out for and check; these include the state of the walls, roof, window frames and doors, the condition of the electrical wiring system and the overall state of decoration of the property. It is virtually essential to consult a chartered surveyor about the property which is finally chosen (if borrowing money to purchase a property, bankers will almost certainly insist on this). However, most obvious problems and difficulties can usually be spotted during the course of a visit by any business person. If there is any doubt about aspects of the premises, talk to the current tenants or try to find out why the previous occupier left. If the landlord or existing tenant is not helpful ask nearby businesses about the premises.

Before visiting any premises it is a good idea to make a list of all the items which should be examined. It is easy to become engaged in conversation with an eager vendor or his agent and miss many important points. Such a list should include the following features:

Structure

Examine structural stability (cracks or bulges in walls and surfaces out of plumb indicate weaknesses). Examine roof timbers and the general state of the roof. Check that floors are in a good condition (wooden flooring at multi-storey premises may indicate that they will be unsuitable for taking heavier loads). Look for signs of dampness and condensation.

Layout

Make a drawing or sketch of the layout of the property noting doors, windows and all dividing walls; the use of graph paper can help in maintaining the scale of the drawing. After the visit the drawing should be consulted to ensure that the layout of the premises is suitable for the company's activities.

Services

Make a note of all the services installed. Look carefully at the electricity supply and wiring (is three-phase electricity supplied? Is the wiring in good condition?). Check the heating system. Ask about electricity and fuel costs (if in doubt ask to see previous year's bill). Are there sufficient car parking spaces for visitors? Is there adequate access for customers and suppliers? Are nearby businesses likely to conflict or cause a nuisance?

Many people's final judgement is based largely on intuition. However, a detailed checklist of property requirements and the above list of items to review when visiting premises can ensure that even the most intuitive decisions are based on factual information. When a property has finally been chosen chartered surveyors should be engaged to undertake a survey. This is most important for companies buying or taking a long lease on property, since the survey will indicate the state of repair of the property, for which the new occupant may well be responsible. A full structural survey rather than a valuation survey should be specified since this will give far greater detail about the property. If certain aspects of the property give cause for concern inform the surveyor; they do not always undertake a full investigation - for example roofs are not always fully examined, and floor loadings calculated. The cost of a structural survey varies considerably and it is wise to obtain two or three quotations before commissioning one.

Information contained in the surveyor's report can be particularly valuable when negotiating terms for the purchase or lease of a property. Defects in the fabric of the building can be a good reason to negotiate the asking price downwards. Such defects may also necessitate exclusion clauses within a lease so that the occupant does not become liable for their repair at a future date.

Commissioning a solicitor

When a property has been found and the surveyor's report confirms its suitability a solicitor should be appointed to finalize the transaction. Do not sign anything straight away! Every year a number of businesses lease, and in some cases, buy, property which they are later unable to use. This is because the regulations described in the next section place restrictions on the use of the property. Solicitors will ensure that the property can legally be used by the prospective purchaser or tenant. The solicitor's searches with the local authority will also reveal whether the property will be affected by future town planning proposals such as urban redevelopment or road building. The solicitor's other main duties are to investigate the title (to ensure that the person selling actually owns the property or lease) and to make arrangements for the preparation and exchange of contracts. In all these legal matters the solicitor will be protecting the legal interests of the prospective purchaser. Many business people prefer to use a solicitor who is willing to visit the premises and look for hidden snags or problems such as easements (drains underneath a property which could be accessed by other tenants).

Solicitors can also be useful in performing a variety of other tasks. They can, for example, appoint a surveyor and interpret the report; advise on finance and negotiations over the price; examine leases and licences to ensure their suitability.

The average charge by a solicitor for conveyancing a 1000 sq ft unit is between £300 and £500 plus disbursements. It is also important to note that during these legal transactions the prospective tenant is usually expected to pay the landlord's legal costs for administering the tenancy. It is worth including a clause in the lease or in negotiations prior to the move that these costs should be 'fair and reasonable'. In most cases landlords' costs are similar to those of the prospective tenant.

MOVING

At some stage in the development of most companies moving premises, or reorganizing into fewer buildings, will arise. Some firms are compelled to move because of push factors such as the expiry of a lease or a sharp increase in rent. Some move in response to pull factors, such as cheaper labour or better communications. An increasing number of companies in recent years have moved because of internal restructuring and an increasing awareness of property costs within the company balance sheet. Research on the movement of industry and commerce has shown the following factors to be the most common reasons for movement.

1. *Shortage of space.*
   - new product requires new machines
   - inadequate storage to cope with increased sales.

   Frequently, space shortage becomes a problem slowly and is brought to a head by a crisis.
2. *Too much space.* The recession and technological change with associated labour shredding has meant that many businesses no longer require all available space.
3. *Poorly laid out premises.* Many companies add to premises piecemeal, eventually leading to inefficiency.
4. *Status.* Many companies regard premises as important to their status and move up the premises ladder to increase that status.

5. *Compulsory purchase.* Compulsory purchase, frequently associated with road development schemes, is less common a factor than in the 1950s and 1960s. It is still important for the smaller firm, though, which tends to be located in older, main road locations.
6. *Labour issues.* Labour issues are particularly important reasons for larger companies. Union activity, labour shortage, skill shortage, and high labour turnover are typical reasons.
7. *Developing new markets.* Many businesses, particularly in the service and retail trades, set up branch units to develop new markets.
8. *Personal reasons.* Many companies are now realizing the importance of a pleasant working environment to maximize efficiency and maintain morale. The growth of smaller businesses in rural areas such as north Yorkshire, East Anglia, Devon and Cornwall are attributed to these environmental and personal reasons.
9. *Government aid.* Various aspects of government aid have been discussed earlier. It is possible to make financial gain by moving from one area to another. Several large companies have received considerable bad press coverage from such activity. It is best to see government inducements as a bonus from relocation, not a reason for it.
10. *Property values.* Many companies are recognizing the development value potential of their sites. Movement, involving sale for redevelopment, can release considerable funds for use elsewhere in the business.

Relocation is a major upheaval for any company and the decision to move should be taken only when all other avenues have been explored and analysed. Location decisions should not be taken in isolation but as part of a wider business strategy and should be carefully costed and placed within the framework of company investment plans.

Much of the uncertainty of relocation can be avoided by employing relocation consultants to advise and organize the entire project. Most of the major property agents such as Knight Frank and Rutley or Healey and Baker undertake such work.

The removal process

Many smaller companies are tempted to undertake the actual removal themselves. Larger companies employ specialist firms. There is little to be gained from using your own specialist employees as packers and porters when they could be doing their own jobs. Relocation can also be disruptive to business. Professional help can minimize this.

The major removal companies, such as Pickfords, have sections dealing solely with industrial and commercial moves. Special packages are available which also include movement of personnel.

Preplanning is crucial to a successful move. Appoint one member of staff to coordinate the operation and draw up an actual path diagram of the move. Mark on it the key dates when certain actions need to be undertaken. These will include:

1. Informing gas, water and electricity boards of the move.
2. Arranging with British Telecom for the transfer of your telephone number if the move is local or for the redirection of calls if a longer distance move necessitates a new number.
3. Inform the Post Office of your change of address and arrange for the redirection of mail.
4. Obtain quotations from removal companies.
5. Inform suppliers and customers of the impending move and your new address and telephone number.
6. Arrange for headed paper and business cards to be produced with the new address and telephone number.

Moving employees

One of the major concerns for companies moving longer distances is the loss of key personnel. While management may take for granted the need to move with the company, other employees may not.

Experience shows that there are several ways by which you may encourage the workforce to move with you. These will include:

1. Involvement in the search for a new site.
2. The offer of a package of incentives.
3. 'Selling' the new location as an attractive place to live.
4. Taking advantage of any assistance for worker transfer offered in the new area.

Publicizing your move

Relocation can be disruptive to business, particularly in the short term. It is vital that it is properly advertised. This publicity campaign should begin many months before your move and continue long afterwards. It is important to publicize the move at both the old site and the new one. Inform all your suppliers and customers of your change of address. Produce a leaflet which includes a map of your new location. Ensure that the agent dealing with your former property indicates on the sale board that you have moved and not gone out of business. Because of the recession a 'to let' sign frequently indicates a company which has ceased trading.

One potential source of disruption is the loss of customers and suppliers. There is considerable evidence to suggest that these concerns can be exaggerated. If you look at the pattern of your business links you will probably find they already cover a wide area. Although it is often suggested that small businesses trade over a small area this is in fact rarely the case. If you then analyse the amount of face-to-face contact involved in running your business (compared with telephone, telex and other forms of communication) you will have an assessment of the danger of dislocation. As many of your contacts will already be outside the 'local' band of telephone charges, even these costs will probably be little affected. Companies who have moved longer distances usually suggest that they have few, if any, problems in keeping their business links. Indeed, many continue to trade with their former suppliers and customers as if no move had taken place.

TENURE

For many companies the choice between freehold and leasehold as forms of tenure does not arise. For simple financial reasons, purchase of property is out of the question. The purchase of property, however, can be extremely tax efficient and is worth considering if it does not direct resources away from the business itself. Normally the freehold of property is useful as security for loans and looks good on the balance sheet. The recession has undermined the market value of much industrial and commercial property, though.

Many companies who decide to buy the freehold of their premises do so either through a holding company or through a subsidiary company set up for the sole purpose of financing and managing property. The premises are then leased in the normal way by one company to the other. This can have major tax advantages. It also ensures that if the operating company fails at some time in the future, liquidators cannot possess the premises. The holding company and its directors still retain a valuable asset. In some instances more complex arrangements involving company pension funds can be made. Your accountant and lawyer will be able to advise on the precise advantages to your particular company.

Purchase prices vary considerably throughout the country, and can vary from as little as five to as much as 12 times the annual rental.

Leasehold is the more common tenure with several minor variations including lease and lease back and a head lease with subsidiary leases. The licence, a more flexible arrangement, is becoming increasingly common for small business premises as it offers an 'easy in, easy out' approach to tenure. It may have some of the same conditions attached as a longer-term lease, but without the longer-term commitment. Licences save money because they do not require the services of a solicitor to negotiate them. A licence is not a 'valuable' interest and cannot be sold in the way that a tenant can sell a lease - at a premium.

Detailed aspects of a tenancy agreement are normally negotiable. In many parts of the country a buyer's market exists and prospective tenants have the upper hand in negotiations.

The traditional business tenancy is on a fixed-term lease of anything from three to 21 years' duration. It may be even longer. The lease will specify the conditions under which you occupy the property. Included will be details of:

Rent review

Rent reviews provide for rent increases, usually on a three-, five- or seven-year basis. Review periods are negotiable and it is in the tenant's interest to keep the period as long as possible. Six months' notice should always be given before the changes come into operation.

Property use

It is normal for a lease to specify the use to which a building may be put. Restrictions may be included which relate to specific businesses or types of nuisance. While changes of use can be negotiated, the landlord may levy a charge for the addition of new clauses.

Subletting

A clause is frequently included in leases to control the practice of subletting. These restrictions are usually in one of two forms: an absolute covenant preventing subletting or a qualified covenant in which subletting may take place, only with the landlord's consent. Normally leases will prohibit the subletting of only part of the premises but will often permit the subletting of the whole, subject to landlord's consent.

Usual covenants

This term is used to cover a wide range of circumstances which come within a commonly held convention. These may include:

- payment of rent, rates and other taxes

- maintenance and repair of property
- landlord access to examine the condition of the property
- repossession in the event of non-payment of rent.

Maintenance and repair are of particular importance because of the possible expenditure involved. Many landlord-tenant disputes have revolved round levels of maintenance and liabilities associated with repair. It is important to minimize liabilities associated with joint wear and tear clauses and insure against as many risks as possible.

Alterations and improvements

The lease will specify any restrictions on modification to the buildings. It may insist that the property is put back to its original state. Ensure that value you have added to the property is not included at a rent review. While the Landlord and Tenant Act offers protection against double payment, it is not uncommon for tenants to find themselves paying twice for improvements: once for building work and once for the rent increase.

Termination of leases

Normally a lease will be terminated either because the occupier gives the landlord an agreed period of notice or because the terms of the lease have been broken. The agreed period will be one month for a monthly tenancy, three months for a quarterly and so on. In a fixed-term lease, it will be at the end of the term. The early termination of a fixed-term lease may involve the sale of the lease, sometimes at a premium. However, as the property market has become considerably depressed in many parts of the country, even the sale of a lease can prove a major problem. To avoid the costs of an unwanted property where a lease cannot be sold, it is obviously preferable to negotiate a more flexible, shorter-term contract.

Insurance

Property insurance is an important issue for all companies (see Chapter 13). There are four broad areas of insurance which you should consider:

- Property
- Contents and work in hand
- Public liability (business risks)
- Employer's liability.

Property
The most important consideration is fire cover. The precise nature of

cover varies with different companies; some, for example, will include a 'loss of profits' component. Such policies cover charges such as rent, rates, salaries and interest payments incurred as a result of fire.

Precise premiums depend on the size and structure of the building. An installed sprinkler system can reduce a premium by as much as 50 per cent. Trades are frequently grouped according to fire risk. Companies group trades in different ways so it is always worth shopping around.

Normally, insurance of 'other perils' has to be taken out in association with fire cover, although occasionally separate cover is possible. Such cover would include storm, burst pipes, riot and explosion. Other special areas of cover are available such as that for glass in businesses which have large areas of display windows.

Contents and work in hand

Contents cover is very similar to normal domestic contents cover. Loss from theft, fire or accidental damage to equipment can cause serious financial embarrassment.

Public liability

Public liability policies cover your legal liability in the event of injury to persons or loss of or damage to property caused by accidents associated with your business. Cover is for third parties (visiting customers, for example) and not you or your employees.

Employer's liability

The Employers Liability (Compulsory Insurance) Act 1969 requires employers to take out and maintain approved insurance policies with appropriate insurers against liability for bodily injury or disease sustained by employees in the course of employment. The certificate of insurance or an appropriate copy must be displayed at the place of work.

Insurance premiums vary considerably throughout the country, for different trades and between different companies. Consequently, it is always wise to shop around or take professional advice from a broker.

MAJOR REGULATIONS CONCERNING BUSINESS PREMISES

Various pieces of legislation apply to business premises and several agencies may need to be consulted from time to time. Many larger companies will have specialist staff or even separate departments dealing with these issues; for the medium-size and smaller company a general understanding will guide the business person through the maze and will assist in the decision to engage experts or not. The main regulations and authorities concerned are discussed below.

Town planning regulations

Planning controls over industry and commerce have been the subject of considerable debate and change in the last two or three years. Three very useful booklets produced by the Department of the Environment are available free of charge from your local authority planning department:

'Planning Permission: A Guide to Industry'
'A Step by Step Guide to Planning Permission for Small Business'
'Planning Appeals: A guide'.

Planning permission is required for most construction and building works. There are some exceptions including temporary buildings, small extensions, internal alterations and property demolition (except listed buildings or property in conservation areas). Permission is also required if you wish to change the use of a building. You will be required to submit scale drawings and plans and it will be worth engaging an architect or surveyor. In cases where the process is not straightforward it may be worth hiring a planning consultant. Names and addresses can be obtained from Yellow Pages or from the Royal Town Planning Institute, 26 Portland Place, London W1N 4BE. In all cases shop around as the fees charged vary considerably.

Advice on planning matters is normally obtained from the local authority planning department, to which all applications should be made. There are some exceptions:

- *Enterprise zones.* Currently 25 designated areas in which planning controls are more limited.
- *New towns.* Contact the New Town Development Corporation planners.
- *Urban development areas.* Contact either the London Dockland Development Corporation or Merseyside Development Corporation.

Scotland and Northern Ireland have a slightly different system. In Northern Ireland contact one of the eight divisional offices. In Scotland contact the district authority in Central Region, Fife, Grampian, Lothian, Tayside and Strathclyde. In Borders, Dumfries and Galloway, and Highland regions contact the regional authority.

Elected members of the local authority make the final decision to grant permission on the advice of the planning officers. If permission is refused, it is worth considering appealing to the Secretary of State for the

Environment. The appeals procedure is not (in most cases) very complex.

A charge is made for a planning approval; the charge is on a sliding scale depending on the size of the development. Planning approval lapses after five years if not acted upon.

Building regulations

Building regulations, administered by the local authority, are to ensure that buildings are safe and structurally capable of fulfilling their intended use. In general, applications are required for all building works, including internal and external alteration and changes of use, even if no building work is involved. While there are many exceptions where permission is not required, it is always wise to consult. It will be necessary to prepare detailed plans and drawings if permission is required. In 1985 the system of building control was simplified and the process of approval modified to allow 'self-certification' as well as local authority approval. However, it will be several years before the new system becomes established so the local authority is still the first point of contact.

As well as structural stability, the building control officers are concerned with the fire resistance of buildings and means of escape. Building regulations approval is given by technical officers of the local authority. Officers will visit the site during the course of construction to check that work is being undertaken correctly. A charge is made for both the approval and site visits. Building control approval lapses after three years from the date of approval if it is not acted upon.

Environmental health

The environmental health officers of the local authority will have an interest in your premises in so far as they affect the surrounding area. Their major concerns are in the activities within the building and the degree of dust, odours, fumes and noise which they create. They will be concerned to ensure that grit, dust and smoke from boilers are kept within reasonable limits. Food and food hygiene are of particular importance as premises must conform to the Food Hygiene (General) Regulations 1970. These lay down standards of construction, lighting, ventilation and sanitary provision which must be met. Leaflets are available on a variety of topics from the environmental health department of the local authority. One such, 'Your Guide to the Food Hygiene (General) Regulations 1970', produced by the Health Education Council is available free from the Council or from the local authority.

Fire certificates

In addition to the fire related requirements of the building regulations it is important to ensure that your property has an appropriate fire certificate. Certain small buildings do not require a certificate, but never leave the possibility in doubt. Even if the building has an existing certificate, it may need revalidation if certain changes take place. These include:

- any change of use
- any change in processes to be used or the materials stored
- subdivision of the building into smaller units.

Buildings which require a fire certificate will normally require a fire alarm system, fire fighting equipment and possibily emergency lighting. The fire prevention officer in your area will be pleased to discuss the fire safety of your property. Several leaflets covering aspects of fire safety are available free from The Fire Protection Association.

Other legislation

Two other major pieces of legislation affect the way in which you use your premises. These are the Health and Safety at Work Act 1974 and the Offices, Shops and Railway Premises Act 1963 and their various amendments.

In general, both Acts require employers to ensure that premises are safe and reasonably comfortable - not too hot, cold, damp or noisy. Welfare, catering and toilet facilities must be kept clean and safe, equipment must be correctly guarded and maintained, floors, steps, stairs and passages must be kept safe and free from obstruction. The legislation is enforced by the Health and Safety Executive and its various inspectorates.

Periodic visits are made by the inspectorate to assess whether your property is up to the appropriate standard. If any improvements are required one of two courses of action is usually taken:

1. Informal advice may be given, either verbally or in writing, usually backed up by one of the many leaflets produced by the Executive.
2. Formal action including improvement notices, prohibition notices and prosecution.

Both the Health and Safety Commission and Health and Safety Executive produce a series of excellent leaflets which address both general and specific health and safety issues. Copies are available from the area offices of the Executive.

More detailed comment on the health and safety issues can be found in *An Employer's Guide to Health and Safety Management: A Handbook for Industry* by Peter Arscott.

MANAGING PROPERTY

It is important to lay out and maintain your property carefully to maximize its role within the company. It is very easy to regard questions of space use, interior design and day-to-day caretaking as frills not to be taken seriously. However, property management is a vitally important management function.

Services

Electricity
The electricity supply in Great Britain is 240 volts at 60 Hz. Some equipment uses a three-phase supply. Periodic reviews of the electrical system should be made to ensure its safety and adequacy for the loads being placed on it. Take great care to avoid overloading the system. Do not be tempted to use multiple extension sockets to overcome a basically inadequate system. If in any doubt contact your local electricity board.

Heating
Heating needs will be greatly affected by the orientation and design of the buildings as well as the activity carried on within them. Certain maximum and minimum temperatures are laid down by law:

1. Minimum of 60°F (15.5°C) for work rooms where a substantial proportion of the work is done sitting and does not involve 'serious' physical effort.
2. In shops and offices a temperature of 60.8°F (16°C). (See *Health and Safety at Work Handbook* edited by Malcolm Dewis.)

Humidity should also be carefully controlled. Adequate ventilation will assist in this and create a healthy working environment with sufficient oxygen, and minimize smells and fumes.

Lighting
Lighting requirements will vary depending on the type of activity being undertaken. Ensure that your lighting provision is adequate and appropriate. Make maximum use of natural daylight. It is important to maintain lighting facilities regularly and in the case of fluorescent tubes,

ensure that the diffusers are cleaned regularly. Keep a ready supply of spare tubes and spotlight bulbs.

Waste disposal
While an untidy work space may reflect a busy order book, it frequently indicates inefficient management. Waste product can be a danger in office, shop or factory, potentially causing both personal injury and fire. It is vital to develop a waste disposal system, which may range from day-to-day caretaking activities to a regular contract with a waste management company.

Cleaning activities, other than normal caretaking duties, such as windows and carpets, should be dealt with regularly.

Security
How much to spend on security at your premises will greatly depend on the value of the goods held in stock and the degree of disruption which burglary or vandalism would cause. It is wise to take precautions. For larger firms it is appropriate to designate a member of staff with responsibility for security. Advice may be sought from the police crime prevention officer. Security can be achieved in four main ways:

1. *Physical barriers.* Barriers may include security fences, then thick security glazing and security locks, and alarms.
2. *Careful layout.* A reception desk or customer service point placed carefully to monitor the movement of people into and out of premises.
4. *Employment of a security firm.*

None of these approaches is mutually exclusive. The combination will depend on individual needs.

Layout and decor

Organizing space
The efficient use of space is vital for all companies. A regular review of the use of space is vital to efficient working. Obviously, the larger the premises, the greater the scope for alternative layout. However, the smaller the space the greater the need for its effective use. It is useful to identify the various stages or sections within the company's operations and ask:

- How much space does each activity require?
- Does the activity have particular locational needs?
- Does it have special access needs?

- Does it relate closely to other activities within the company?

It is useful to discuss layout with your employees. The planning process may benefit from physical models or at least scale diagrams showing spaces, machinery, fittings, furnishings and lines of communication.

Clearly, what is possible will be constrained by the building and the degree of flexibility offered by its structure. Your review may confirm the need for a move.

Reception areas are particularly significant. First impressions count. A client must be made to feel welcome and comfortable. The reception area also provides an opportunity to display your products and services.

Display signs will be necessary to identify your premises for clients or visitors. Signs and advertisements attached to buildings are subject to town planning controls and the regulations are complex. At present the position in outline is that planning consent is needed for signs and advertisements if any of the following conditions apply: if they are illuminated, include letters more than 0.75 m high, are above 4.6 m from the ground, are above the bottom level of the first floor windows, or are on a shop wall without a display window. Still tighter controls are enforced in 'areas of special control' (mainly sensitive rural locations). In addition, all directional signs on or near a public highway require the approval of the local highway authority (normally the county council) or the Department of Transport.

Both decoration and furnishings can be important to company image. Careful choice of colours can create an atmosphere appropriate to the activity being undertaken. It is frequently worth engaging an interior designer for this work. Names of suitable designers can be obtained from The Designer Selection Service, The Design Council, 28 Haymarket, London SW1Y 4SU, or Clients Advisory Service, Royal Institute of British Architects, 66 Portland Square, London W1N 4AD.

Provision for disabled employees

If you are to benefit from the skills which disabled people have to offer, it is vital to consider their special needs. 'Disabled' covers a wide range of individual conditions; here we include blind, deaf and chairbound disabled people. The key to their successful integration within the firm is to take account of the range of property-related difficulties which may be encountered. The following will give you an indication of what to consider.

1. *Site layout*
   Parking: wide marked-out spaces to allow full opening of doors.
   Walkways: unobstructed, no furniture.
   Ramps (not steps): not steep and with level 'rest areas'.

Surfaces: non-skid, covered if possible.
Doors and doorways: wide enough for wheel chairs (34 ins) with ample room for opening. Handles at wheelchair height.

2. *Internal layout*
Restroom/toilets: at least one specially set out for disabled people. Appropriate washbasins and grab handles. Locate on a level which minimizes difficult travel.
Shelves and counters: at appropriate height.
Public telephones: at least one at wheelchair height

All these and many other detailed points can be followed up in: *Building without Barriers* by Sarah P Harkness and J N Groom.

Do remember that a disabled employee does not want to feel different from others. If you need to be convinced of the difficulties which the workplace can pose for the disabled, borrow a wheelchair for the morning and use it to undertake your normal tasks.

Specific layouts

Shops

The retailer needs to encourage the purchase of goods; hence it is important both to maximize sales space and make it convenient and attractive to customers. Some general guidelines are appropriate here:

1. Perimeter walls are normally used for display fittings on counters, with the main floor area subdivided into display islands known as gondolas which run lengthwise from front to rear, forming a series of circulation corridors. Cul-de-sacs (or dead-ends) should be avoided.
2. Commodities should be arranged so that similar or related products are grouped together.
3. High demand goods should be placed at the back of the shop so that impulse purchases of other goods are stimulated.
4. The layout should allow easy supervision to minimize the problems of shop-lifting. Black spots can easily be covered by anti-theft mirrors or closed circuit television.
5. Special attention should be given to the shop entrance and display windows.

For further information and ideas about shop layouts, *Shops — a manual of Planning and Design* by David Man, published by the Architectural Press in 1981, is a useful source.

Offices
The main decision in laying out an office is whether to adopt an open plan format. When considering open plan for your office the following factors will guide your decision.

Advantages of open plan:

1. It mimizes building and fitting-out costs.
2. It promotes communication and team work.
3. It encourages a spread of workload.
4. It facilitates supervision.
5. It maximizes the flexibility of use of space.

Disadvantages of open plan:

1. It removes the privacy and feeling of territoriality which many people need at work.
2. Levels of performance can be lowered as the general hubbub can easily distract.
3. Some staff may feel that their status demands separate accommodation.

One way around this dilemma is to use a system of movable partitions which give both privacy and flexibility.

Property maintenance

It is important to undertake property maintenance in a regular, systematic way. Neglected maintenance can be very costly. Devise a schedule of maintenance activities. The following list will give you an idea of how such a schedule can be built up:

1. General cleaning, replenishing soap and servicing toilet facilities — daily
2. Cleaning of windows, floor maintenance — three-monthly intervals
3. Checking and replacement of lights — three-monthly intervals
4. Maintenance of lifts — annually
5. Servicing of heating system — annually
6. Checking roof, gutters etc and cleaning as appropriate - annually
7. Painting (interior and exterior) — three-yearly intervals.

Enter each of these activities into a maintenance programme to ensure they are undertaken. It is all too easy to forget. Activities can then be undertaken in a controlled way, rather than as an emergency.

4

PERSONNEL MANAGEMENT

Michael Armstrong

Statutory sick pay and maternity pay
Health and safety

INTRODUCTION

Personnel management is concerned with what the organization needs to do about one of its two key resources — people (the other is, of course, money). It is the responsibility of all those who manage people. All managers are personnel managers. They cannot leave it to the specialists in the personnel department.

Personnel management is about obtaining, developing and motivating the human resources required by the organization to achieve its objectives. It is also concerned with developing and maintaining a cooperative climate of relationships between management, employees and trade unions or staff associations representing employees. These functions have to be carried out within the legal framework which has been built up in recent years to protect employees and to regulate industrial relations.

This chapter covers the main techniques used in personnel management and provides background information on relevant legislation and government provisions affecting people at work.

MANPOWER PLANNING

Manpower planning helps you to decide how many and what sort of people you need in your organization so that you can take steps to obtain them.

Manpower planning techniques ensure that you can fully take into account the factors in assessing future requirements. They provide the basis for action plans dealing with recruitment, management development, training, retraining, career progression, redundancy (if necessary) and the improvement of productivity.

Manpower planning uses demand and supply forecasting techniques.

Demand forecasting

Demand forecasting is the process of estimating the future quantity and quality of manpower required. The basis of the manpower forecast is the annual budget and longer-term corporate plan, translated into activity levels for each function and department. The three techniques used in demand forecasting are:

1. Ratio-trend analysis
2. Work study
3. Econometric models

Ratio-trend analysis

Ratio-trend analysis is carried out by studying past ratios between, say, the number of direct and indirect workers in a manufacturing plant, and forecasting future ratios, having made some allowance for changes in organization or methods. Activity level forecasts are then used to determine direct labour requirements and the forecast ratio of indirects to directs is used to calculate the number of indirect workers needed.

Work study

Work study techniques can be used when it is possible to apply work measurement to calculate how long operations should take and the amount of labour required.

Econometric models

To build an econometric model for manpower planning purposes it is necessary to analyse past statistical data and to describe the relationship between a number of variables in a mathematical formula. The variables affecting manpower requirements may be identified under headings such as investment, sales or the complexity of the product line. The formula could then be applied to forecasts of movements in these variables to produce a manpower forecast.

Supply forecasting

Manpower resources comprise the total effective effort that can be put to work as shown by the number of people and hours of work available, the capacity of employees to do the work, and their productivity. Supply forecasting measures the quantity of manpower that is likely to be available from within and outside your organization, having allowed for absenteeism, internal movements and promotions, wastage, and changes in hours and other conditions of work. The supply analysis covers:

1. Existing manpower resources;
2. Potential losses to existing resources through labour wastage;
3. Potential changes to existing resources through internal promotions;
4. Effect of changing conditions of work and absenteeism;
5. Sources of supply from within the firm.

RECRUITING

Your aim is to recruit the sort and number of people you need without wasting money or time. To achieve this objective there are three things you need to do:

1. Define what you need.
2. Attract a wide field of candidates.
3. Select people who will meet your requirements.

Defining needs

Defining needs is a matter of:

- job analysis, leading to the preparation of a
- job description, from which are derived the
- job requirements, which lead to the final decisions on
- terms and conditions of employment.

Job analysis
Your starting point is job analysis. This should provide the data required to prepare job descriptions and specifications and to fix terms and conditions of employment.

Job analysis is the key stage in recruitment. It gives the base for deciding where to look for people, for drafting advertisements, for interviewing and for making the final selection.

Job descriptions

Job descriptions record the facts shown about the job derived from job analysis. These consist of:

1. Job title of job holder.
2. Job title of person to whom job holder reports.
3. Job titles of subordinates.
4. A brief summary of the overall purpose of the job.
5. A short description of each of the main activities or tasks carried out by the job holder.
6. Any further information required to convey the size or 'flavour' of the job: resources controlled, level of responsibility, extent of guidance or supervision received etc.

Job descriptions should be brief and to the point. One side of one sheet of paper is the ideal. Never produce job descriptions more than two pages long. They will be ignored. In any case, there is a limit to how much you can convey about a job on paper.

Job requirements

The experience, qualifications, training and personal qualities required to do the job constitute the job specification. This will also state age and trade union membership requirements, where relevant.

The starting point for writing a job specification is the description of what the job holder actually has to do. Ideally, you should look at each of the main tasks and ask yourself what sort of experience, personal qualities etc are required to do them. Identify the key tasks first and then define your minimum requirements. Without these no one can do the job.

Take care not to over- or understate requirements. People often ask for too much, only to fail to attract a sufficient number of candidates or to be disappointed when they feel their final selection is a compromise. It is best to distinguish between essential and desirable requirements.

Terms and conditions of employment

The terms and conditions of employment should then be defined or reviewed. They will include:

- Pay
- Bonuses
- Fringe benefits (car, medical insurance etc)

- Pension arrangements
- Holidays
- Sick pay
- Notice and redundancy entitlement
- Removal and settling in allowances.

Attracting candidates

Before going outside by advertising or using agencies or consultants you should first make sure that there is no one suitable for the job within your company. If there is no one available in your company consider using one or other of these external sources:

- Jobcentres
- Advertising
- Agencies
- Selection consultants
- Executive search consultants (head hunters).

Selecting people

When you have defined the job and attracted a field of candidates you can set up the recruitment procedure consisting of these steps:

1. Obtain information on candidates.
2. Sift candidates.
3. Make interview arrangements.
4. Interview (dealt with in section on page 87).
5. Obtain references.
6. Make final decision.

Obtaining information on candidates
Information on candidates can be obtained by asking them to do any one of the following:

- Call in person
- Telephone
- Write a letter of application with or without a curriculum vitae (CV)
- Complete an application form.

Obtaining references
Only take up references with the prior permission of the candidate. They can usefully confirm the nature of the previous job, the reason for leaving

(if relevant) and the pay. Opinions about characters and suitability are unreliable. Personal referees are, of course, entirely useless. All they prove is that the applicant has at least one or two friends.

Although references may be useful if they are given without malice and are factually correct, most people avoid conveying unpleasant truths in writing. If you want an honest opinion it is therefore advisable to telephone.

Whether you ask for the reference in writing or obtain it over the telephone it is best always to ask the following questions:

1. What was the period of employment?
2. What was the job title?
3. What work was carried out?
4. What was the rate of pay or salary?
5. How many days' absence has the employee had in the last 12 months?
6. Would you re-employ (if not, why not)?

Question 6 is the key one.

Making the final decision

Your final decision should be based on an analysis of the data provided by the application form, the interview and the reference. You may, in practice, have to narrow your choice to one before taking up references, but if there is a choice of suitable candidates you should keep one or two in reserve in case the reference is unsuitable or the final offer is turned down. You can then confirm the offer, subject to any medical examination that the candidate may have to undergo for pension purposes or because a certain standard of physical fitness is required for the work.

Your final step in a selection procedure should be to write letters of rejection to unsuccessful candidates.

INTERVIEWING

Function of the interview

An interview has been described as a conversation with a purpose. It is a conversation because the candidate should be drawn out to talk freely about himself and his career. Except for the time he spends describing the job and the company, the interviewer should restrict himself to asking open-ended questions and making encouraging noises. Open-ended questions invite the applicant to expand about himself. If you simply say, 'Tell me about your present job' you will get most of what you want. Gaps can be filled by asking follow-up questions. Avoid leading questions which indicate the answer you are expecting. Minimize questions demanding only a 'yes' or 'no' response.

The interview has a specific purpose, which is to provide the evidence upon which a prediction can be made of the candidate's future performance in the job for which he is being considered. The interview, however, has two other aims: first, to provide the candidate with information about the job and the company, and, second, to give the candidate a favourable impression of the company. This should encourage the good candidate to join and should leave the rejected candidate without any ill-feelings.

Planning and the interview

The interview must be planned to elicit information from the candidate which will enable his experience, qualifications and personal qualities to be compared with the requirements of the job as set out in the job specification. Having done this, there is no one best way of sequencing the interview. A fairly typical approach is to:

1. Put the candidate at his ease; he will be nervous and you want him to relax so that he will express himself freely.
2. Explain how you are going to handle the interview.
3. Start with a brief description of the job and the company. Do not spend too long on this, especially if the candidate is a marginal one. You can elaborate at the end of the interview.
4. Use a biographical approach, inviting the candidate to describe in his own words his education and career to date. Do not delve too deeply into the distant past; spend most time on the current job. Probe if necessary to ensure that the candidate is giving you the full picture. He will naturally try to gloss over any less successful periods in his career. Get him to tell you not only what he did but why he did it. This is particularly relevant when discussing choice of career and reasons for leaving jobs. It will give you a chance to assess how well he is motivated.
5. Give him the opportunity to talk about his achievements as well as to explain any setbacks.
6. Allow time at the end of the interview for him to ask questions.

The information gathering part of the interview should last between 20 and 40 minutes, depending on the level of the job. For key jobs, second interviews by someone in a higher position are desirable.

Evaluating the interview

The only questions you need to answer at the end of the interview are:

1. Does this candidate measure up to the job?
2. How does this candidate compare with other candidates?

Qualifications are relatively easy unless they have been obtained from some obscure institution. Experience should not be too difficult to evaluate as long as you systematically probe to ensure that the candidate has really been doing what he claims to have done. Job titles are misleading; you must have information on the actual level of responsibility and how this compares with what he will be expected to do in each of the key areas of the job for which he is being considered. Information on specific tasks and achievements is helpful.

His progress to date will give you some indication of how he will perform in the future. A steady progression in line with his ambitions is obviously what you are looking for. Anyone can fail once for reasons which are not particularly blameworthy. A pattern of failure characterized by short stays in jobs is highly suspect. Ensure that there are no gaps in his career. If any emerge, find out where he was and what he was doing.

The most difficult aspects of a candidate to evaluate are his personal qualities. You can quickly assess his speech and decide whether you like his manner or not, but it is much harder to assess qualities such as drive, ability to work with others and leadership.

Interviewers are always advised against the 'halo effect' which means taking one characteristic (usually appearance or manner) and allowing a favourable impression to override judgement on other factors. Unfavourable judgements based on one undesirable characteristic (the horns effect) can be equally misleading. A balanced view must be achieved, which means looking at all aspects of the candidate's career as well as the initial impression he makes, however important that may be in many jobs which involve relating to people.

The final assessment

The evidence required to make an assessment of the candidate comes from various aspects of the interview backed by the prior information obtained from the letter of application or application form. It needs to be compared with the specification and summarized on an assessment form, especially if there are a number of candidates whose relative merits need to be assessed.

CONTRACTS OF EMPLOYMENT

The basis of the contract

Contracts contain:

- *Express terms.* Those defined in writing or orally (eg pay, hours, holidays, pensions);
- *Implied terms.* Those that can be implied into the contract of employment (eg duty to pay wages).

Contracts may consist of one or a number of documents. These include:

- The letter of appointment;
- A written statement of express terms;
- Other documents, such as staff handbooks, works rules and collective agreements, which are incorporated into the contract by being expressly referred to in the letter of appointment or written statement.

Contracts are accepted by the employee signing a document or simply by starting work.

Written particulars

Written particulars of the terms of employment must, under the Employment Protection (Consolidation) Act 1978, be given to all employees not later than 13 weeks after they start work (employees working less than 16 hours a week are excluded).

The written statement must contain or refer to particulars of the following terms:

1. The names of the parties;
2. The date when employment began;
3. A statement as to whether any employment with a previous employer counts as part of the employee's continuous period of employment and, if so, the date when the continuous period of employment began;
4. Rate of pay;
5. Interval at which payment is made;
6. Hours of work;
7. Holiday pay, including entitlement to accrued holiday pay on terminating employment;
8. Sick pay (if any);
9. Pension arrangements;

10. The length of notice from the employer or employee to terminate employment;
11. Job title.

The statement should also contain or refer to details of:

- Disciplinary rules and procedures;
- Grievance procedures.

Note that the written statement is not the contract itself, although it can be taken as an accurate record of it unless the contrary is proved.

To minimize problems arising from changes, it may be advisable to:

- include a clause indicating that employees might be required to move to other places of work;
- avoid too precise a description of the job in case the work changes; if a job description is issued, a 'catch-all' phrase such as 'and such other duties as may have to be carried out' may be helpful.

Changing the contract

The Employment Protection (Consolidation) Act states that not more than one month after a change in the terms of employment specified in the statement the change must be announced by:

- individual notification to each employee; or
- telling employees where details of the changes can be seen on a notice board or in some reasonably accessible place; or
- entering the change in a specified document, provided that employees were told that this would be done in their original statement or in a subsequent change.

INDUCTION

Induction is the process of receiving and welcoming an employee when he first joins a company and giving him the basic information he needs to settle down quickly and happily and start work. Induction has three aims:

1. To smooth the preliminary stages when everything is likely to be strange and unfamiliar to the new starter;
2. To establish quickly a favourable attitude to the company in the mind of the new employee so that he or she is more likely to stay;
3. To obtain effective output from the new employee in the shortest possible time.

Company induction

The first stage in induction is when the employee arrives at the company. He or she should be welcomed by a responsible person (not simply a commissionaire or a junior wage clerk) who can provide basic information about the company and terms and conditions of employment. Some of the information will confirm what the employee has already been told, some will be new, but there is a limit to how much can be conveyed at this stage.

The information should cover:

- A brief description of the company — its history, products, organization and management;
- Basic conditions of employment — hours of work, holidays, pension scheme, insurance;
- Pay — pay scales, when paid and how, deductions, queries;
- Sickness — notification of absence, certificates, pay;
- Leave of absence;
- Works rules;
- Disciplinary procedure;
- Grievance procedure;
- Promotion procedure;
- Union and joint consultation arrangements;
- Education and training facilities;
- Health and safety arrangements;
- Medical and first-aid facilities;
- Restaurant and canteen facilities;
- Social and welfare arrangements;
- Telephone calls and correspondence;
- Travelling and subsistence expenses.

Ideally, this information should be conveyed in an employee handbook.

Departmental induction

The departmental induction programme should, wherever possible, start with the departmental manager, not the immediate supervisor. The manager may limit his remarks to a general welcome and a brief description of the work of the department before handing the new employee over to his supervisor for the more detailed induction, but it is important for the manager to be involved at this stage so that he is not seen as a remote figure by the new employee. And at least this means that the new starter will not be simply a name or a number to him.

The detailed induction is probably best carried out by the immediate supervisor. He should have five main aims:

1. To put the new employee at his ease;
2. To interest him in his job and the company;
3. To provide basic information about working arrangements;
4. To indicate the standards of performance and behaviour expected of him;
5. To tell him about training arrangements and how he can get on in the company.

JOB ENRICHMENT

Job enrichment maximizes the interest and challenge of work by providing employees with a job that has these characteristics:

1. It is a complete piece of work in the sense that the worker can identify a series of tasks or activities that end in a recognizable and definable product.
2. It affords the employee as much variety, decision-making, responsibility and control as possible in carrying out the work.
3. It provides direct feedback through the work itself on how well the employee is doing his job.

Job enrichment is not just increasing the number or variety or tasks, neither is it the provision of opportunities for job rotation. These approaches may relieve boredom, but they do not result in positive increases in motivation.

Techniques

There is no one way in which you can enrich a job. The technology and the circumstances will dictate which of the following techniques or combination of them is appropriate:

- Increasing the responsibility of individuals for their own work;
- Giving employees more scope to vary the methods, sequence and pace of their work;
- Giving a person or a work group a complete natural unit of work, ie reducing task specialization;
- Removing some controls from above while ensuring that individuals or groups are clearly accountable for achieving defined targets or standards;
- Allowing employees more influence in setting targets and standards of performance;

- Giving employees the control information they need to monitor their own performance;
- Encouraging the participation of employees in planning work, innovating new techniques and reviewing results;
- Introducing new and more difficult tasks not previously handled;
- Assigning individuals or groups specific projects which give them more responsibility and help them to increase their expertise.

Steps to job enrichment

The following steps should be taken if you wish to introduce job enrichment:

1. Select those jobs where better motivation is more likely to improve performance.
2. Set up a controlled scheme before launching the full programme of job enrichment.
3. Brainstorm a list of changes that may enrich the jobs, without concern at this stage for their practicability.
4. Screen the list and concentrate on motivation factors such as achievement, responsibility and self-control.
5. Ensure that the changes are not just generalities like 'increase responsibility' but list specific differences in the way in which the jobs are designed and carried out.
6. Set precise objectives and criteria for measuring success and a timetable for each project, and ensure that control information is available to monitor progress and the results achieved.

Benefits

The benefits provided by job enrichment arise because it helps to make the job intrinsically motivating, ie people are motivated to achieve high productivity and high quality by the work itself, not simply by the extrinsic motivation provided by money. This happens as a result of:

1. *Feedback.* The individual receives meaningful feedback about his performance, preferably by himself evaluating his own performance and defining the feedback he needs. This implies that he should ideally work on a complete product, or a significant part of it which can be seen as a whole.
2. *Use of abilities.* The job is perceived by the individual as requiring him to use abilities that he values in order to perform the job effectively.

3. *Self-control.* The individual feels that he has a high degree of self-control over setting his own goals and defining the paths to these goals.

APPRAISAL SCHEMES

Appraisal schemes are used to review an individual's performance and progress in a job and to assess his potential for future promotion. They provide you with a systematic method of obtaining, analysing and recording information about a person that is needed:

- for the better running of the business;
- to help you improve the job holder's performance and plan his career;
- to help the job holder to assist in his own performance and develop himself.

Schemes

Each of the schemes described below aims in its different way to help you to analyse what a person has done and is doing in his job so he can be helped to do better by developing his strengths or overcoming his weaknesses.

1. *Overall assessment,* which simply asks assessors to write down in narrative form their comments about the employee. They may be helped with a checklist of personality characteristics to consider, such as reliability, enthusiasm, appearance and acceptability.
2. *Guideline assessment,* which attempts to obtain specific judgements from assessors who are asked to comment separately on a number of defined characteristics; for example, industry and application, loyalty and integrity, cooperation, accuracy and reliability, adaptability, knowledge of work and use of initiative.
3. *Grading,* a further development of the guideline approach, which attempts to provide a framework of reference by defining a number of levels at which the characteristics are displayed and asking managers to select the definition which most closely describes the individual they are assessing. For example, in rating effective output, the manager in a typical grading scheme is asked to choose between:
   - Outstanding — outstanding output of high quality work
   - Satisfactory — satisfactory level of output and effort

- Fair — completes less than the average amount of effective work
- Poor — low output and poor worker.

4. *Merit rating*, which is similar to grading except that numerical values are attached to the judgements so that each characteristic is rated on a scale of, say, 1 to 20. The ratings are then added up to produce a total score.
5. *Results-orientated schemes*, which embody the philosophy of management by objectives and relate assessments to a review of performance against specific targets and standards of performance agreed jointly by superior and subordinate. This procedure has marked advantages in general over the other four because it is related to actual performances and can therefore be more objective. The other schemes inevitably bring qualitative and subjective judgements of personality characteristics into play. The results-orientated approach has three specific advantages:
   (a) The subordinate is given the opportunity to make his own evaluation of the results he obtains. When he is discussing results and the actions that produced them, he is actually appraising himself and gaining insight on how he can improve his own methods and behaviour.
   (b) The job of the manager shifts from criticizing the subordinate to helping him to improve his own performance.
   (c) It is consistent with the belief that people work better when they have definite goals which they must meet in specified periods.

SALARY ADMINISTRATION

Salary administration is concerned with the design, development and maintenance of salary systems which determine what and how staff should be paid. These systems consist of the policies, techniques and procedures used for:

1. Fixing salary levels
2. Designing and maintaining salary structures
3. Progressing individual salaries
4. Exercising control over gradings, individual salaries and general salary reviews
5. Planning and administering total benefit packages for staff.

The aim of salary administration is to help you to develop and maintain salary systems, policies and procedures which enable the organization to attract, retain and motivate staff of the required calibre and to control payroll costs.

Techniques

The basic techniques used in salary administration are:

1. *Job analysis* — establishing job content and levels of responsibility.
2. *Job evaluation* — developing job hierarchies according to the relative values of jobs.
3. *Salary surveys* — finding out the market rates of jobs.
4. *Salary structure design* — designing and maintaining salary structures which are internally equitable and externally competitive.
5. *Salary control* — monitoring the salary system, conducting reviews and grading jobs.

Benefits

Salary administration can:

- Ensure that the organization can recruit the quantity and quality of staff it requires.
- Encourage suitable staff to remain with the organization.
- Provide rewards for good performance and incentives for further improvements in performance.
- Achieve equity in the pay for similar jobs.
- Create appropriate differentials between different levels of jobs in accordance with their relative value.
- Maintain control over salary costs.

WAGE PAYMENT SYSTEMS

Pay structure

Your basic pay structure for hourly paid or manual jobs will have some similar features to a typical salary structure. There will be a hierarchy of jobs related to the levels of responsibility that exist in your organization. Between these jobs pay differentials which attempt to reflect levels of responsibility will have to be established.

Your choice of payment systems is between:

1. Time rates
2. Individual piece-work or payment-by-results systems

3. Group or factory-wide incentive schemes.

Time rates

Time rates, also known as day-work, day rate, flat rate or hourly rate, simply involve paying operators a predetermined rate for the actual time worked. You should use them when you believe that it is impossible or undesirable to apply a payment-by-results system.

Some people like time rates because earnings are predictable and steady. Others, especially managers, dislike them because they do not provide the motivation of a direct incentive relating the reward to the effort, hence the various forms of incentive schemes discussed below.

Individual piece-work or payment-by-results systems

Straight piece-work means paying a flat money price for each piece of work completed. The alternative time-allowed payment-by-results system pays the worker his basic rate for the time allowed, preferably established by work measurement, and, if he completes the job in less time, he gains the advantage of the time saved, as he is still paid for the original time allowed.

To achieve success in introducing and maintaining an individual piece-work or payment-by-results scheme you need to:

1. Ensure that individuals carrying out the work will by their own efforts directly determine their level of output and therefore their bonus payments without interference from outside sources.
2. Use work measurement to determine output levels and times.
3. Provide good quality work measurement staff to set up and maintain the system.
4. Train managers and supervisors to use the system.
5. Build in provisions which control the amendment of rates and prevent the scheme getting out of hand.
6. Conclude a formal agreement with the trade union consisting of these provisions and all the other procedures included in the scheme.
7. Ensure through firm but fair management that the agreement is honoured by all parties.

Group or factory-wide incentive schemes

Group incentive schemes are individual schemes written large. The bonus is earned by a group of workers together and is related to the output achieved over an agreed standard or to the time saved on a job: the difference between allowed time and actual time. They have the same basic advantages and disadvantages as individual schemes, except that it is the group as a whole and not each individual in it which must feel it can directly affect output. Group schemes are particularly useful where groups of workers are carrying out interdependent tasks.

Factory-wide incentive schemes provide a bonus for all workers which is related to an overall measure of performance such as output or added value. These schemes can create interest in increasing productivity, especially when they are linked to arrangements for participation in the planning of changes to methods or in overcoming production problems. The difficulty these schemes often face is that of establishing a formula for relating the bonus to performance which is reliable and can be understood by all those concerned.

JOB EVALUATION

Definition

Job evaluation schemes:

1. Establish the rank order of jobs within an organization, measure the difference in value between them, and group them into an appropriate grade in a job grade structure;
2. Ensure that, as far as possible, judgements about job values are made on objective rather than subjective grounds;
3. Provide a continuing basis for assessing the value of jobs which is easy to understand, administer and control, and is acceptable by the staff as fair.

Types of job evaluation

Job evaluation schemes are usually grouped into two basic types:

1. *Non-analytical* which is based on whole job comparison. The main non-analytical schemes are job ranking and job classification.
2. *Analytical* which is based on comparing separately defined characteristics or factors which are assumed to be common to all jobs. The basic scheme is points rating, although there are a number of proprietary brands, of which the best known is the Hay/MSL scheme.

Job ranking
The simplest form of job evaluation is job ranking. This is a non-analytical approach which aims to judge each job as a whole and determine its relative value in a hierarchy by ranking one job against another. The rank order is established by considering the worth of each job to the organization: a grading structure has then to be developed and the jobs are slotted into the grades.

Job classification
Job classification is based on an initial definition of the number and characteristics of the grades into which the jobs will be placed. The grade definitions attempt to take into account discernible differences in skill and responsibility and may refer to specific criteria, such as level of decision, knowledge, equipment used and education or training required to do the work. Jobs are allotted to grades by comparing the whole job description with the grade definition.

Points rating
Points rating schemes use what are called factor comparison techniques. The factors selected are those considered to be most relevant is assessing the comparative value of jobs. Typical factors include resources controlled, decisions, complexity, and knowledge and skills.

Each factor is given a range of points so that a maximum number of points is available. The relative importance or 'weighting' of a factor is determined by the maximum number of points allotted to it. In each factor, the total range of points is divided into degrees according to the level at which the factor is present in the jobs. The characteristics of each degree in terms of, say, level of complexity, are defined as yardsticks for comparison purposes.

Jobs are evaluated by studying job descriptions containing analyses of the degree to which the factor is present in the job and comparing them with the factor level definition. The jobs are graded for each factor and the points for each grading are added to produce a total score. This score can then be related to the scores of other jobs to indicate the rank order.

EQUAL PAY

The basic law

The Equal Pay Act 1970, as amended by the Equal Pay (Amendment) Regulations 1983, is concerned with:

- Individual rights

- Collective agreements and published pay structures.

Individual rights

Equal treatment with regard to terms and conditions of employment is required when:

1. Women are employed on 'like work' to men, ie work of the same or broadly similar nature. The two guidelines on the existence of 'like work' are that:
   - like work exists when 'the difference (if any) between the things she does and the things she does not do are of practical importance in relation to terms and conditions of employment';
   - when making comparisons between men's and women's work account should be taken of the 'frequency or otherwise with which any such differences occur in practice as well as the nature and extent of the differences';
2. Women are in a job which, although different from those of men, has been given an equal value to men's jobs under a job evaluation exercise. Job evaluation is defined as being a study undertaken with a view to evaluating, in terms of the demand made on a worker under various headings (eg effort, skill, decisions), the jobs to be done by all or any of the employees in an undertaking or group of undertakings. The same terms and conditions of employment must therefore be given to men and women where:
   - Job evaluation has been carried out;
   - Terms and conditions of employment are based on the job evaluation;
   - A job carried out by women has been given an equal value to a job carried out by men;
3. When neither 1 nor 2 applies, equal pay is due where a woman is employed on work which is, in terms of the demands made on her (for instance, under such headings as effort, skill and decision), of equal value to that of a man in the same employment. Whether or not the work is of equal value should be determined by a job evaluation study which in itself is not discriminatory.

Area of comparison

Comparisons may be made between different establishments if:

1. Both establishments are owned by the same employer or an associated employer;

2. Terms and conditions of employment are common to the two establishments.

Reference to an industrial tribunal

The individual affected, her union representative, or, in special cases, the Secretary of State for Employment, can take up a case alleging discrimination with an industrial tribunal for a decision.

The individual or her representative must show that she has the right to equal treatment with a man.

In relation to a variation between the woman's and the man's contract, discrimination will not be held to have taken place if the employer proves that the variation is genuinely due to a material factor which is not a difference of sex, and that factor must be a material difference between the woman's case and the man's.

Collective agreements

The Act also applies to:

1. Negotiated collective agreements
2. Employers' pay structures where 'the provisions are generally known or open to be known to the employees concerned'.

The Act requires that in respect of such agreements or pay structures:

- where a category of work exists with separate men's and women's rates attached to it, the women's rate will be raised to the level of the men's rate;
- where a category of work is defined with a women's rate only attached to it (ie where no provision is made for a specific men's rate for that type of work) the women's rate must be raised to the level of the lowest men's rate in the agreement.

In short, agreements should first equalize men's and women's rates for any class of work which both sexes carry out, and, second, ensure that the rates for work carried out by women only should not be less than the minimum male rate.

Issues raised on collective agreements are heard by the Central Arbitration Committee (CAC).

Equal value cases

If a claim under the equal value rules is submitted to a tribunal and is not rejected by the tribunal, for example because the employer successfully invoked the genuine material factor provisions, the tribunal may refer the case to an expert. The expert will report back to the tribunal on his or her findings and the tribunal will take account of those findings in making its judgement. The tribunal can exclude the report but in this case must obtain another one. It cannot decide whether or not the jobs are equal value without an expert's report.

Equivalent work

An employee can use the equivalent work section of the Act to show that a job evaluation study rates her work equivalent to a man's or would do so if some discriminatory element was removed.

An employer can also use job evaluation to justify a higher grading for a man's job. The job evaluation study, however, must be valid in accordance with the following criteria:

- It should be thorough in analysis and capable of impartial application;
- It should not be dependent upon subjective managerial judgements concerning the nature of the work before the employee can be fitted into the appropriate place in the appropriate salary scale.

EXPATRIATES' REMUNERATION

When staff are sent overseas on short- or long-term assignments the complex question of what and how they should be paid arises. The aims of an expatriate remuneration policy are quite simply:

1. To pay the appropriate salary, taking into account the content of the job and the salary levels for similar jobs held by nationals employed by the company in the same overseas locations.
2. To protect the employee from the increased costs of living abroad.
3. To provide an incentive to work abroad.

Achieving these aims, however, is more difficult. The factors to be considered are:

- Salary and overseas allowance
- Special benefits, including education.

Salary and allowances

There are a number of methods of tackling the question of how much to pay. The choice depends partly on whether staff are being moved from a high cost to a low cost country or vice versa, and partly on the extent to which the pay of nationals employed by the company has to be taken into account. When staff move from high cost to low cost countries it is normal to maintain the home country salary and pay some form of additional overseas allowance, although this may result in problems when comparing the salaries of expatriates and nationals in similar posts. When staff are moved from low to high cost countries, it is necessary either to ensure through allowances that the expatriate's standard of living does not suffer, or to pay the going rate for a similar job locally, which may also have to be topped up by special allowances. The choice is between using:

1. A home base
2. A local base
3. A home base in low paid countries and a local base in high paid countries.

Using a home base

The home based approach starts from the UK salary for the post to which is added an overseas allowance to cover increased living costs and, if it is thought to be appropriate, to provide an incentive payment to compensate for the alleged hardship of an overseas assignment.

The aim of the cost of living allowance is to allow the expatriate to maintain living standards similar to those at home without spending a greater proportion of his income than he would at home. Its calculation should be related to the employee's net disposable income, which is his home salary less tax, social security payments and pension contributions. This disposable income is the amount that will be affected by changes in the cost of living.

The overseas premium to provide an incentive for staff to live overseas is an optional and variable item. Some firms rely entirely on fixing the right salary level for the job and compensating for increased living costs when they send staff to reasonably attractive assignments in Europe and North America. Others feel that some additional incentive is required for staff moved to the Middle East or other less attractive African or Asian locations. The size of premiums varies, but it is generally between 10 and 20 per cent of salary, with higher rates for particularly unpleasant postings.

Using a local base

The local based method is quite simple, consisting of:

- The basic salary for the post which would be payable to a local national with the same responsibilities; plus
- An allowance to cover those expenses which are unavoidably incurred

by an expatriate, not by a local national; plus (optionally)
- An overseas premium to compensate for the inconvenience of working in an unfamiliar environment.

This approach caters for employees transferred from a low pay country to a higher pay country, where the home base method produces a lower salary than that payable to a local employee with similar, or even less, responsibility. It also means that the salaries of expatriates and nationals can be calculated on the same basis thus reducing the scope for invidious comparisons and facilitating the replacement of expatriates with local nationals. If a local base is used in a number of countries it is advisable to establish job grades throughout each area so that the local salary can be related to an international grade structure.

Home or local base
Some companies use both a home and a local base depending on the country. In highly paid countries the local rate is used plus any special accommodation allowances. In low paid countries the home rate is used although, to avoid invidious comparisons, this is expressed as the local rate plus a special overseas allowance.

Special benefits

The most important special benefit provided for expatriates is help with the costs of education. Assistance towards local education is given where travel or high fees are involved, but the main benefit is to cover all or most of the costs of day or boarding school education at home. If a foreign assignment terminates while children are still being educated at home, companies usually continue their help for an adjustment period, or more generously, until education is completed.

The other benefits provided by companies to expatriates include separation allowances, entertainment allowances and club subscriptions.

EMPLOYEE BENEFITS

Employee benefits are items in the total package offered to employees over and above salary, which increase their wealth or well-being at some cost to the employer.

Apart from pension schemes (dealt with in a separate section), employee benefits fall into the three categories described below.

Personal security and help

Personal security benefits include:

1. Medical insurance with organizations such as BUPA or PPP, which provide either company financed cover or group discount schemes.
2. Personal accident and travel insurances.
3. Permanent disability cover to provide for the tragedies of long-term or terminal illness.
4. Sick pay. This is an almost universal benefit. Entitlements still vary by employee category but most organizations accept that financial security through periods of unavoidable illness is a basic employee need. Schemes are usually on a sliding scale relating to service, often starting with four weeks' full and four weeks' half pay after six to 12 months of service, building up to 13 weeks' full and 13 weeks' half-pay after five years of service.
5. Additional redundancy provisions. These constitute extra payment according to service, often two weeks' pay for every year, although one month's pay per year is becoming quite common.
6. Service contracts are sometimes made available to directors and senior management to give them extra security. As a means of locking people into the company their value is, however, doubtful.

Leave and retirement policy

Holidays
Many staff in the UK now receive at least four weeks' paid annual holiday and, for management, five weeks is increasingly becoming the rule. There has traditionally been a differential between staff holidays and those given to manual workers and this has been maintained in a certain degree as manual worker holidays have increased. In the EEC countries, holidays tend to be longer than in the UK but in North America, executives' holidays lag behind - many still have only two weeks a year.

Retirement
Early retirement options are becoming more common. It is recognized that many people do not want to grind until they are 60 or 65, and if they leave earlier, they provide opportunities for promotion or new vacancies to be filled from outside.

Many companies recognize the need to help their employees to bridge the gap between work and retirement. Schemes preparing people for retirement are available through the Pre-Retirement Association which also gives advice on locally based courses.

Additional financial assistance

Additional financial assistance can be provided in the form of:

1. Loans, usually in short-term emergencies, although companies in the financial sector often provide facilities for generous long-term loans.
2. Season ticket loans to purchase an annual season ticket.
3. House purchase assistance in the form of a bridging loan, a guarantee to a building society, or a loan to supplement an advance from another source.
4. Removal and relocation expenses to attract employees who are being recruited from other parts of the country and to help employees who are transferred to other locations of the company.
5. Credit cards for the purchase of petrol (taxable) or for use on company business.
6. Payment of the fees of job-related professional associations.
7. Personal financial counselling for the more highly paid executive.
8. Discounts in company products.

Other benefits

1. Company cars. After pensions and holidays, which are usually taken for granted, cars have been the most highly regarded fringe benefit in the UK. The provision of a company car saves the executives both the capital costs of acquisition and, usually, the heavy running costs, but this advantage has been eroded by recent UK legislation. From the company's point of view, the provision of a car can still be less costly than paying the extra salary needed to compensate the executives for not having a car when allowance is made for tax. And in the UK at least, where over 90 per cent of top management have company cars, it has been almost impossible to be competitive without giving a car or the equivalent net salary.

   But there are some disadvantages. A car is a very visible sort of benefit and great care has to be taken to ensure that the size or cost of cars accurately reflects differentials. It is also costly to administer a car fleet. A further point to consider is that not all people like to have a company car imposed upon them. Many would prefer to spend the equivalent money as they wish.
2. Subsidized meals. It is normal practice in large organizations to provide in-house eating facilities. Smaller companies in urban areas frequently provide luncheon vouchers.
3. Sports and social facilities. These are one of the oldest forms of

employee benefit and are common among old established larger employers. Although welcomed by those who patronize them, they are often under-used and under-appreciated.

4. Day nurseries. These are relatively rare but companies that wish to attract or retain female staff have found them useful.

PENSION SCHEMES

Pension schemes are designed to provide employees with security by currently building up rights which will give a guaranteed income to the employee or his dependants on retirement or death. Pensions are essentially deferred pay and they are financed by contributions from the company and in most, but not all, cases, the employee.

Pensions are generally regarded as the most important employee benefit after basic pay, although many employees, especially younger ones, express little interest in their pension arrangements until in many cases it is too late.

The need to ensure that the pension arrangements are the best the company can afford arises from three reasons:

1. A company has a moral obligation to do the best it can to provide a reasonable degree of security for its employees, especially its longer-service employees.
2. A good pension scheme demonstrates that the company has the long-term interests of its employees at heart.
3. A good scheme will help to attract and retain high quality staff, especially older staff employed at senior levels who are likely to be most interested in pension rights.

Main features of pension schemes

Pension schemes are usually complex affairs and their provisions can vary considerably. Professional advice from pensions specialists is always required when reviewing pension arrangements to assess what the company needs, what it can afford and all the legal and tax considerations surrounding pension schemes. The following is a list of the main features that have to be dealt with when reviewing pension schemes.

Pension formulae

There are four main types of formula for determining pensions on retirement:

1. Final salary (salary service), where the pension is calculated as a fraction of the salary at retirement or as an average over the closing

years or months of service. If the arrangement is to pay one-sixtieth of final salary for every year's service the formula would be described as n/60ths. In this case, someone on retirement with 40 years' service would obtain 40/60ths of his final salary as a pension, the maximum allowed in the UK under the Inland Revenue code of approval for pension schemes.
2. Average salary (salary graded), where fixed amounts of pension are given for each year spent in a salary bracket.
3. Flat rate, where a flat rate payment is made which is quoted as a given rate for each year of service.
4. Money purchase, where contributions are fixed and accumulate in a 'pool' for each employee.

A final salary scheme is clearly preferable for the employee because the pension will be based on earnings just before retirement, which should keep pace with increases in the cost of living.

Contributions

Schemes can be either contributory — requiring contributions from both the employer and the employee — or non-contributory, in which case only the employer makes the contribution. The contributions of employees tend to average about 5 to 6 per cent of basic salary.

The arguments advanced in favour of contributory schemes are that sharing the cost means that more money is available to buy better benefits, and that employees appreciate benefits more when they have to pay for them. The arguments in favour of non-contributory schemes are that they are an attraction to employees, are more flexible in response to change and cost less to run.

Entry age

The entry age can be fixed at 25 or, preferably, 21. There is usually a qualifying period of six months to a year.

Contracting out

Occupational pension schemes can be 'contracted out' of the state earnings related pension scheme, known as SERPS, as long as the company pension scheme provides at least the equivalent of SERPS. This means that no contributions have to be made to SERPS. If the scheme is contracted in, contributions to SERPS continue to be made, and on retirement the employee will receive the state old age pension and the SERPS benefit in addition to the company pension.

Transferability
Pension schemes can offer some degree of transferability if an employee moves to another firm with a scheme that will accept the transfer. The pension in the new scheme bought by the transfer is almost always lower than the amount of pension rights accrued in the previous scheme. The government's proposals on personal pension schemes referred to later in this chapter are designed to encourage mobility by eliminating the risk of losing pension rights.

Post-retirement pension increases
Pension schemes can be more or less inflation-proofed by the process of escalation - allowing for increases in pensions in response to changes in the cost of living. This is a highly desirable but potentially expensive feature.

Lump sum on retirement
Pension schemes can offer the right of commutation of pension on retirement which allows the exchange of part of the pension for a tax-free lump sum. This provides a useful aid to those wanting to buy a retirement home, or it can be used for special purchases or investment.

Widows' benefits
Pension schemes support a widow whose husband has died in service either by providing a lump sum, a reduced widows' pension or a combination of the two. If wisely invested, a lump sum can often provide a better income than a pension. During his working life a man should know that there will be adequate provision for his dependants.

Arrangements for paying a widow's pension after the husband's death in retirement vary widely. The best method is to provide a pension of up to two-thirds of the husband's pension.

Early and late retirement
Early retirement pensions are usually calculated at a reduced rate and schemes may define the reduction that will apply for each year between the year of early retirement and the normal retiring age. If an employee retires early through ill-health he or she should at least be entitled to the pension earned up to retirement age. A more favourable arrangement would be to pay an improved pension which would take account of potential service up to normal retirement age.

There may be situations in which the company wants employees to stay on after normal retiring age, but their continued service should be reviewed regularly from the point of view of their health. Pension schemes should always provide for a 'late retirement increment' under which an employee who continues to work after his normal retirement date can receive an enhanced pension without any further contributions from himself or his employer.

'Top hat' arrangement

A 'top hat' arrangement is one in which a pension scheme for directors or senior staff is topped up by means of an additional non-contributory scheme. A 'top hat' scheme is offered when a company wishes to provide a greater benefit to individuals over and above that supplied under its main fund. Such benefits could usually be provided by augmentation within the fund but there are sometimes internal company reasons for requiring a separate policy.

Funding

All schemes have to be funded so that the money is available to pay the promised benefits. The usual arrangement is to build up funds by contributions which are invested in securities or in an insurance policy or both. The basic choice is between running a private self-administered fund through trustees or operating a scheme through an insurance company. Private schemes require considerable investment expertise and administrative effort to organize, although some large companies feel they can run a better and less costly scheme if they go it alone with specialist actuarial advice. The majority of schemes are designed and administered for their clients by insurance companies who have the actuarial, investment and administrative skills required.

Choice of scheme

Pension schemes are complicated affairs, subject to a number of legal and fiscal considerations. The choice of what goes into the scheme in the shape of alternative types and levels of benefit will depend largely on what the company can afford to pay. It may be necessary to trade off one benefit against another by, for example, reducing the pensions formula from n/60ths to n/80ths in order to introduce a 50 per cent widows' pension. If there is any choice within a budget, employees should be consulted about their preferences.

The cost of pension schemes can be anything up to 25 per cent of payroll, so it is worth taking care in setting them up and maintaining them. They should be reviewed regularly with the help of expert advice to ensure that they are properly funded (although in periods of high inflation this is difficult) and that a reasonable mix of benefits is being provided for the money subscribed by the company and its employees.

Additional voluntary contributions

A facility which many employers provide is for additional voluntary contributions (AVCs) which are usually organized through a finance institution. The beauty of these schemes is that the employee gets the maximum tax relief on the contributions he makes to the scheme. This fact, plus the bonuses that can be earned over the years, make AVCs one of the best, if not the best form of saving available. Employees are limited to contributing a maximum of 15 per cent of their salary, and their final pension, including the effect of their voluntary contributions, cannot exceed the statutory two-thirds of final salaries.

Recent and forthcoming legislation

The government has introduced a number of important changes to pension arrangements in recent years, or made proposals to do so.

Changes introduced
The most significant of the changes incorporated in the Social Security Act 1985 are:

- Better benefits for pension scheme members who leave service on or after 1 January 1986. These take the form of an increase to that part of the pension relating to service after January 1985 at the rate of 5 per cent per annum subject to a maximum of the cumulative increase in prices over the period of service concerned.
- More disclosure of information to members in the reports of trustees, including statements on pension increases made during the year, transfer values paid and a fair review of the financial development of the scheme.
- Schemes are compelled to provide transfer values for members who leave service.

Proposed change
The major change proposed by the government for introduction in April 1988 is the abolition of compulsory membership in a company's pension scheme and the establishment of the right of every employee to choose a personal pension.

The main features of this proposal are as follows:

- All new employees will be able to choose freely whether or not they join the company's pension scheme.
- Existing employees will be given the choice of staying with the employer's scheme or opting out.

- Personal pensions will be contracted out of the state earnings related pension scheme (SERPS), which means that at retirement age anyone who has taken out a personal pension will only receive the basic state old-age pension plus whatever personal pension they have been able to provide.
- At present, for those with SERPS benefit, employees pay 2.15 per cent of certain earnings and employers pay 4.1 per cent. Instead of that money being deducted from their income and passed to the state, it will be deducted and passed to a personal pension scheme if that is what the employee wants.
- As an incentive, the state will pay an additional 2 per cent of salary into a personal pension scheme for a five-year period from 1988 to 1991 to all those who start a personal pension during that time, provided they have not been in an employer's contracted-out scheme.

INDUSTRIAL RELATIONS

Industrial relations is about how you, as an employer, deal with your employees collectively, and how your employees deal collectively with you. It is primarily concerned with relationships between management and trade unions or staff associations.

The role of management

Management typically sees its function as that of directing and controlling the workforce to achieve objectives — usually involving economic growth — which it sets itself. But management and workers are equally interested in the prosperity of the business and its future security, as long as both parties feel that they are sharing the benefits equitably. However, in many other ways their interests do not coincide, and the basis of all industrial relations is that both sides will be using their bargaining power to advance and protect their own interests.

The role of the trade unions

Trade unions have four major objectives:

1. To redress the bargaining power of the employer by providing collective support to the individual worker.
2. To secure improved terms and conditions of employment for their members and the maximum degree of security to enjoy these terms and conditions.
3. To obtain improved status for the employee.

4. To increase the extent to which the unions can exercise democratic power over decisions that affect their members by power-sharing at the national, corporate or plant level.

Shop stewards can be militant and aggressive. They sometimes seem to act in ways which not even their own union can control, but they can help management and supervision by overruling unreasonable complaints.

Industrial relations policies

You need to take a carefully considered view of your attitude to trade unions, whether or not you have them in your company. If there is no union, you should decide whether or not you would want to recognize one and the circumstances in which you would do so. If you have a union or unions you need to decide how you are going to deal with them. Your aim should be to achieve a reasonable degree of harmony without either exaggerating militancy or underestimating it.

It is sometimes said that management has the unions and shop stewards it deserves. If you treat them autocratically or refuse to recognize that they have any right to represent the interests of their members, you can expect a negative reaction. Aggression breeds aggression. If, on the other hand, you treat them as responsible people, they are more likely to act responsibly. It would be naive to suggest that this approach will eliminate trouble-makers. They will continue to exist. But it will at least reduce the danger of pushing reasonable people (by far the majority of shop stewards) into unreasonable behaviour.

PARTICIPATION AND INDUSTRIAL DEMOCRACY

Participation is the joint involvement of management and employees in making decisions on matters of mutual interest. These decisions can be restricted to amenities such as social affairs, canteens and working conditions; or they can deal more positively with health and safety matters; or they can go more deeply into management affairs: the organization of work and policies affecting the future of the company.

Participation is sometimes regarded as being synonymous with industrial democracy, which it is not. Participation can be fairly well circumscribed, whereas industrial democracy implies a much greater degree of involvement and produces the joint regulation and control by unions and management of decisions which affect the present and future conduct of the business.

The attitude of your staff may not be as predictable as you imagine. It is not necessarily the case that trade unionists at office or factory level welcome participation. They may feel that it cuts across their traditional role as negotiators and is a device introduced by management to emasculate them.

Aims of participation

The Industrial Participation Association has summed up the aims of participation as follows:

1. It is both reasonable and just that the employees of a company should have the means to influence the major decisions that may determine the conditions of their own working lives.
2. Its essential purpose must be to improve the efficiency and productivity of the enterprise, by enabling employees at all levels to make a more effective contribution.

Methods of participation

At the job level participation should be as informal as possible, although one of the latest imports from Japan — quality circles — introduces a degree of formality among groups, voluntarily meeting to discuss productivity issues, which is said to be highly successful.

At a higher level more formality may be required. But joint consultation committees often fail because both management and trade unions keep the real issues off the agenda, with the result that they degenerate into trivial discussions about the quality of the sausages in the canteen.

Requirements for successful participation

If you decide to introduce participation there are four requirements for success:

1. Define the objectives and scope of participation. These should be related to tangible and significant aspects of the job in addition to welfare.
2. You must believe and be seen to believe in it. Actions speak louder than words and you should quickly put into effect what was agreed in joint consultation.
3. Don't try to use joint consultation as a means of reducing the effectiveness of an existing union. It won't work.
4. Keep managers and supervisors in the picture. There is a danger of them being bypassed.

TEAM BRIEFING

Team briefing, also known as briefing groups, is a communications technique developed by the Industrial Society. As described by the Society, team briefing is a system of communication operated by line management. Its objective is to make sure that all employees know and understand what they and others in the company are doing and why. It is a management information system. It is based on the leader and his/her team getting together in a group for half an hour on a regular basis to talk about things that are relevant to their work.

Team briefing enables face-to-face communications to be planned and conducted systematically, although the actual briefing sessions are conducted informally. It enables people to discuss with their line manager or supervisor company matters which affect them personally. Through team briefing, the company can ensure that the reasons for change are brought out into the open so that understanding and acceptance can be increased.

Team briefing operates as follows:

1. Organization

- Cover all levels in an organization;
- Fewest possible steps between the top and bottom;
- Between four and 18 in each group;
- Run by the immediate leader of each group at each level (who must be properly trained and briefed in his task).

2. Subject

- *Policies.* Explanations of new or changed policies;
- *Plans.* As they affect the organization as a whole and the immediate group;
- *Progress.* How the organization and the group are getting on: what the latter needs to do to improve;
- *People.* New appointments, points about personnel matters (pay, security, procedures).

3. Timing and duration

- A minimum of once a month for those in charge of others and once every two months for every individual in the organization — but only meet if there is something to say;
- Duration not longer than 20–30 minutes.

QUALITY CIRCLES

Quality circles are groups of workers, usually led by their supervisor, who meet voluntarily and often in their own time to discuss the problems they face in achieving quality, or some other important target. The circle is given training in problem-solving techniques and the resources to solve the problem it identifies.

Quality circles can help you to improve quality and productivity by obtaining employee involvement and commitment in solving problems jointly, and getting the solutions implemented. Chapter 9 mentions quality circles in the context of purchasing and supply.

Method

The idea of quality circles was developed in Japan. In the UK and other western countries there are a number of different methods in operation but the essential ingredients are the same. The group consists of five to ten members, and attendance is voluntary. They may meet in company time. They are usually led by their immediate supervisor, although the leader is often chosen by the group. The leader has to be thoroughly trained in how to run the circle. He cannot be too directive, but he must ensure that the problem is identified and defined clearly and that analytical problem-solving techniques are used to solve it. He must help the group to keep its feet on the ground and come up with practical solutions, and he has to guide the circle when the agreed answer is being implemented. His role is a key one. Quality circle members are usually employees doing similar work.

The sequence of events in a typical quality circle is as follows:

1. The members identify problems in their work area, although on occasions supervisors or managers can indicate problems that need to be solved.
2. When the problem has been indentified the circle agrees a realistic goal for its activities, such as to reduce defects from 6 to 3 per cent over a period of three months.
3. The circle draws up a plan for solving the problem using appropriate analytical techniques.
4. The base data are collected by members of the circle and possible solutions to the problem are reviewed. Expertise from supervision or technical personnel can be called on.
5. When a solution has been agreed the circle presents to management its analysis of the problem and its proposals for solving it.
6. The circle is responsible for implementing solutions agreed by

management. It monitors results, carries out tests as necessary, and reports on progress.

Requirements for success

Quality circles are only effective if you can meet the following conditions:

1. You must introduce them carefully. Pilot tests are essential.
2. You must appoint a trained and experienced individual (probably an outside consultant) to initiate the scheme.
3. Top management must fully support the scheme.
4. The environment and technology in your company should be such that the quality circle groups will have plenty of scope for developing improvements.
5. The management style of your company should be sympathetic to this form of participation.
6. The members of quality circles should be trained in problem-solving and analytical techniques.
7. You should appoint an organizer to coordinate and monitor the programme.

PERSONNEL RECORDS AND THE DATA PROTECTION ACT

The basic law

The aim of the Data Protection Act 1984 is 'to regulate the use of automatically processed information relating to individuals and the provision of services in respect of such information'.

The Act regulates the use by data users or computer bureaux of personal data by a system of registration.

'Personal data' is defined by the Act as 'data consisting of information relating to a living individual who can be identified from it or from the data and other information'.

A 'data user' is a person who 'holds data' which forms part of a collection intended to be processed by him or on his behalf and controls the contents and use of the data.

Data protection principles

The eight principles set out in the Act are as follows:

1. The information to be contained in personal data shall be processed fairly and lawfully.
2. Personal data shall be held only for one or more specified purposes.
3. Personal data held for any purpose or purposes shall not be used or disclosed 'in any manner' incompatible with that purpose or those purposes.
4. Personal data held for any purpose or purposes shall be adequate, relevant and not excessive in relation to that purpose or those purposes.
5. Personal data shall be accurate and, where necessary, kept up to date.
6. Personal data held for any purpose shall not be kept for longer than is necessary for those purposes.
7. An individual shall be entitled:
   (a) at reasonable intervals and without undue delay or expense:
      (i) to be informed by any data user whether he holds personal data of which that individual is the subject; and
      (ii) to access any such data held by the data user; and
   (b) where appropriate to have such data corrected or erased. Note, however, that the Act provides a safeguard against reasonable or 'vexatious' requests for access.
8. Appropriate security measures shall be taken against unauthorized access to, or alteration, disclosure or destruction of, personal data and against accidental loss or destruction of personal data.

Modification of the principles

These principles may be modified in the following circumstances:

- Where data is held for historical, statistical or research purposes and is not used in such a way that damage or distress is (or is likely to be) caused to any data subject, this information:
  (a) shall not be regarded as obtained unfairly only because its use for historical, statistical or research purposes was not disclosed when it was obtained;
  (b) may be held indefinitely;
- The government has the power to amend the principles to provide additional safeguards for sensitive data, ie data relating to racial origin, political opinions, religious or other beliefs, health or sexual life, or criminal convictions.

Registration

Data users who hold personal data must register with the Data Protection Registrar giving details of:

- The data to be held;
- The purposes for which the data will be used;
- The sources of the data;
- The name(s) of any person(s) who may disclose the data;
- One or more addresses for the receipt of requests from data subjects for access to the data;
- The names of any territories outside the UK to which the data may be transferred.

The only data excluded is that which is used for payment purposes *only*. But if the data is used in any other way, registration has to take place.

When a data user has registered an entry he must not:

- hold any personal data other than that specified;
- hold any data for purposes other than those described;
- obtain such data from any sources not specified;
- disclose such data to any person not described in the entry;
- transfer such data to a territory not specified.

Contravention of any of these prohibitions is a criminal offence. The Registrar can refuse to accept applications but an appeal can be made to the Data Protection Tribunal against such a decision.

Enforcement

The Registrar has the power to issue three types of notice:

1. Enforcement notices requiring the user to take specified action within a specified time to comply with the principles;
2. Deregistration notices which may totally prohibit the holding of any personal data or may prohibit the holding of certain types of personal data;
3. Transfer prohibition notices prohibiting the transfer of personal data to countries which do not provide comparable safeguards.

Appeals against a decision of the Registrar can be made to the Data Protection Tribunal.

The Registrar may start criminal proceedings for an offence under the Act, eg:

- The holding of personal data by an unregistered user;

- Knowing or reckless contravention of any of the particulars contained in a register entry, eg holding data other than registered, or using it for an unspecified purpose;
- Knowing or reckless contravention of particulars in the register by a servant or agent of a data user other than particulars about what data may be held.

The penalty for committing an offence is a fine (unlimited in a crown court) and a court order to forfeit, destroy or erase the data.

Implications for personnel records

The implications are quite clear. It is necessary to register if any personal data is held on a computer and ensure that anyone who has access to the computer conforms to all the eight principles.

A review will have to be made of what data is held on the computer if it may have to be revealed. For example, should the results of appraisals be held if such results have not previously been communicated to the employees concerned?

It will also be necessary to check where personal data is held. Departmental managers who maintain records of their own staff on their own personal computer will be contravening the Act if they do not register. It may be advisable to prohibit any records being kept on a computer unless they are under the direct control of an authorized and registered department, eg the personnel or payroll departments.

The security of personal records on the computer should be checked.

Consideration should be given to issuing all employees with a print-out of the data held about them on the computer on a regular basis, then giving them an opportunity to update the information and, incidentally but still important, ensuring that they know what is held.

HANDLING DISCIPLINE AND DISMISSAL CASES

In the UK the way in which disciplinary problems are handled is very much influenced by the statute law on unfair dismissal as interpreted by case law and backed up by the code of disciplinary practice and procedures in employment. Although only applicable in the UK, the regulations are based on principles of natural justice which are, or should be, universal.

Natural justice

Three basic principles should govern the way in which you handle potential discipline problems:

1. The individual should know the standards of performance he is expected to achieve and the rules to which he is expected to conform.
2. He should be given a clear indication of where he is failing or the rules he has broken.
3. Except in cases of gross misconduct, he should be given an opportunity to improve before disciplinary action is taken.

Four further principles governing how disciplinary cases should be dealt with have been defined in case law:

1. The person should know the nature of the accusation against him.
2. He should be given the opportunity to state his case.
3. The disciplinary tribunal should act in good faith.
4. The employee should be allowed to appeal.

The law of unfair dismissal

The law of unfair dismissal applies generally to employees with more than two years' service. Under this law, dismissals are fair if the principal reason was one of the following:

1. Incapability, which covers the employee's skill, aptitude, health and physical or mental condition.
2. Misconduct.
3. Failure to have qualifications relevant to the job.
4. A legal factor which prevents the employee continuing work.
5. Refusal to join a trade union where a closed shop exists and it cannot be shown that the employee objects on grounds of deeply held personal conviction to joining the union.
6. Redundancy, where this had taken place in accordance with a customary or agreed redundancy procedure.
7. The employee broke or repudiated his contract by going on strike (as long as he was not singled out for this treatment).

Dismissals are unfair if:

1. The employer fails to show that he has good reasons to dismiss the employee (one of the admissible reasons listed above).
2. The employer has not acted reasonably in the circumstances, which can arise when he has not followed the principles of natural

justice set out earlier, especially those concerning proper warnings, the opportunity for the employee to state his case and the right to appeal. But this requirement to follow a fair procedure is modified under case law if it can be shown that adherence to the agreed procedure would have made no difference to the employer's decision.

3. 'Constructive' dismissal takes place, ie where the employer's conduct is such that the employee would be entitled to regard his contract of employment as having been repudiated by his employer. But the employee is only entitled to leave and claim constructive dismissal if his employer is in breach of some express or implied term of the contract and the breach is so serious that it goes to the root of the contract.

Examples of constructive dismissal are:

1. Giving unjustified warnings.
2. Using extremely provocative or denigratory language.
3. Forcing the employee to resign.
4. Failing to provide a safe system and place of work.
5. Forcing an employee to do work clearly outside his contract.

When assessing whether or not a dismissal is fair, an industrial tribunal asks itself the following questions:

1. Was the manner of the dismissal correct, ie did the employer follow a proper procedure, giving fair warning of the consequences of continued misconduct or incapability?
2. Was the employer's decision to dismiss based on sufficient evidence?
3. Did the employee's offence or misbehaviour merit the penalty of dismissal or would a lesser penalty have been appropriate in the circumstances?
4. Were there any mitigating circumstances which the employer should have taken into account?

Approach to handling disciplinary cases

Your approach should be clearly governed by the principle of natural justice and the legal considerations set out above. You should have a disciplinary procedure (you are, in fact, required to have one by law) and you should ensure that it is understood and applied by all your managers and supervisors.

A disciplinary procedure should provide for a three-stage approach before action is taken.

1. Informal oral warnings.
2. Formal oral warnings which, in serious cases, may also be made in writing. These warnings should set out the nature of the offence and the likely consequences of further offences.
3. Final written warnings which should contain a statement that any recurrence would lead to suspension, dismissal or some other penalty.

The procedure should provide for employees to be accompanied by a colleague or shop steward at any hearing. There should also be an appeal system and a list of offences which constitute gross misconduct and may therefore lead to instant dismissal.

Your managers and supervisors should be told what authority they have to take disciplinary action. It is advisable to have all final warnings and actions approved by a higher authority.

ABSENTEEISM AND LATENESS

Absenteeism and lateness are not usually regarded as gross misconduct and, if persistent, should be dealt with through the normal disciplinary procedure.

It is up to you to decide what level of absenteeism without proper explanation or lateness is unacceptable. Employees should be made aware of this level and warned of the consequences if they do not meet the standards expected of them.

Warnings require a continuous commitment from the employee not to take days off without leave or satisfactory explanation, or to be late. They do not lapse simply because you retain the employee. But if the employer has agreed to ignore previous offences they cannot be taken into account if persistent absenteeism or lateness recurs.

This raises the difficult question of time limits. You may give a final warning that timekeeping must improve by a certain date or else. If it does improve by that date, and the slate is wiped clean, it could be assumed that the disciplinary procedure starts again from scratch if timekeeping deteriorates again. Some people cannot sustain efforts to get to work on time for long and deterioration often occurs. In these circumstances, do you have to keep on going through the warning cycle time after time? The answer ought to be no, and, although there are no conclusive rulings in case law on this point, the best approach seems to be avoid stating a date when a final warning period ends. Instead, the final warning letter should simply say that timekeeping performance will be reviewed on a stated date. If it has not improved, disciplinary action can be taken. If it has, no action is taken, but the employee is warned that further deterioration will make him liable to disciplining which may well circumvent the normal procedure, perhaps by only using the final warning stage and by reducing the time between the warning and the review date.

REDUNDANCY

Redundancy is the saddest and often the most difficult problem concerning people you will ever have to deal with. There are four things you can do to make it less painful:

1. Plan ahead to avoid redundancy.
2. Use other methods of reducing numbers or man-hours to avoid or minimize the effects of redundancy.
3. Call for voluntary redundancy.
4. Develop and apply a proper redundancy procedure.

Plan ahead

Planning ahead means anticipating future reductions in manpower needs and allowing natural wastage to take effect. You need to forecast the amount by which the labour force has to be reduced and the likely losses through labour turnover. You can then freeze recruitment at the right moment to allow the surplus to be absorbed by wastage.

The problem is that forecasts are often difficult to make, and in periods of high unemployment natural wastage rates are likely to be reduced. You may therefore overestimate the extent to which they will take up the slack. It is best to be pessimistic about the time it will take to absorb future losses and apply the freeze earlier rather than later.

Ideally, you should take whatever steps you can to transfer people to other, safer jobs and retrain them where possible.

Use other methods

The other methods you can use to avoid or at least minimize redundancy include, in ascending order of severity:

1. Calling in outside work.
2. Withdrawing all subcontracted labour.
3. Reducing or preferably eliminating overtime.
4. Developing work-sharing: two people doing one job on alternate days or splitting the day between them.
5. Dismissing part-timers.
6. Short-time working.
7. Temporary lay-offs.

Voluntary redundancy

Asking for volunteers — with a suitable pay-off — is one way of relieving the number of compulsory redundancies. The amount you offer to persuade people to go is a matter of judgement. It clearly has to be more than the statutory minimum, although one inducement for your employees to leave early may be the belief that they will get another job more easily than if they hang on until the last moment. And you can try to help to place them elsewhere.

One of the disadvantages of voluntary redundancy is that the wrong people might go, ie your good workers who are best able to find other work. You may, in fact, find yourself going into reverse and having to offer them a special loyalty bonus if they agree to stay on.

Redundancy procedure

If you are forced into redundancy your problems will be reduced if you have an established procedure to follow. This procedure should have three aims:

1. To treat employees fairly.
2. To reduce suffering as much as possible.
3. To protect your own ability to run your business effectively.

These aims are not always compatible. You will want to retain your key workers. Trade unions, on the other hand, will want you to adopt the principle of last in, first out, irrespective of the value of each employee to the company.

A formal procedure may not be necessary in a very small concern. But whenever you have larger numbers to contend with or are dealing with trade unions, it is as well to have a standard method of dealing with the problem. The points you should include are:

1. Early warning and consultation with unions and staff: you are required by law to inform the union and the Department of Employment if 10 or more employees are to be made redundant; you must give at least 30 days' notice if 10 or more employees are to be dismissed over a period of 30 days or less, and at least 90 days' notice if 100 or more employees are to be made redundant over a period of 90 days or less.

2. Means to be adopted to avoid or reduce redundancies, eg cutting back overtime and the use of temporary staff, short-time working, transfers to other jobs with an appropriate trial period (four weeks are required in law).

3. The basis of selection for redundancy. You may start with the principle of last in, first out, but you have to reserve the right to deviate from this principle where selection on the basis of service would prejudice operational efficiency.
4. The basis of compensating for redundancy, ie payments made by the company which are additional to the statutory minimum.
5. The help the company will give to redundant employees to find other work.

LABOUR TURNOVER

Labour turnover can be an expensive process. There are the prime costs of recruiting a replacement: a few hundred pounds for a secretary, several thousands for a key executive. In addition there are the secondary costs arising from the gap caused by the leaver, the expenses of training the replacement and the loss of efficiency during the learning curve period before the new employee becomes fully effective.

The rate of labour turnover needs to be monitored. Past records will show the norms — and some wastage is inevitable, even desirable, if it means ineffective employees leaving because they can no longer cope with their jobs. There are no acceptable standards. A rate of 10 per cent could be regarded as high in some organizations, others would feel they were fortunate if they would bring their rate down to 20 per cent. But it is important to look at trends so that you can analyse the reasons for higher losses and take whatever steps are necessary to contain them.

Measuring labour turnover

The traditional formula for measuring wastage is:

$$\frac{\text{Number of leavers in a specified period (usually 1 year)} \times 100}{\text{Average number of employees during the same period}}$$

Thus a firm with an average of 150 employees which loses 30 in a year will have a labour turnover rate of 20 per cent. This formula is simple to use but it can be misleading. The turnover percentage may be inflated by the high turnover of a relatively small proportion of the labour force, especially in times of heavy recruitment. The figure may also be suspect if the average number of employees upon which the percentage is based is unrepresentative of recent trends because of considerable increases or decreases in the number employed during the period.

An alternative and more analytical method (because it can concentrate on particular categories of staff) is the survival rate. This measures the proportion of employees who are engaged within a certain period who remain with the firm after so many months or years of service. Thus if 20 clerks are recruited in a year and five leave in the following year the survival rate is 75 per cent. This index can be used to compare different types of staff and to assess the rate at which replacements may have to be made in the future.

Action checklist

1. What are the causes of wastage? They may include one or more of the following:
   - Uncompetitive rates of pay
   - An inequitable pay structure
   - Lack of opportunity
   - Feelings of insecurity
   - Poor relationships between management and staff
   - Competition from other employers
   - Poor selection
   - Inadequate training
   - Poor working conditions.

2. What steps can be taken to deal with causes of wastage?
   (a) Conduct surveys on market rates of pay and, so far as you can afford to, adjust rates where relatively low pay is clearly causing recruitment or wastage problems.
   (b) Look at your pay structure to see whether there are any inconsistencies between pay and level of responsibility. If necessary, apply some form of job evaluation.
   (c) Think about the way in which people are promoted or given opportunities to widen their experience. Can anything be done to make them feel that they will be able to progress, if they deserve to have the chance?
   (d) If people are worried about their future, can you reassure them in any way in meetings or by newsletters?
   (e) What are the causes of any poor relationships that exist between management and staff? What can you do about them?
   (f) Review your methods of recruitment and selection, check not only on wastage rates but also on survival rates (ie how long people remain with you after they have started). If wastage and survival rates show adverse trends, identify and correct

any faults in the recruitment procedures that may have caused them.

(g) Look at your training methods, especially induction training, and make improvements where it can be shown that people are leaving (or are being sacked) because they have not been given a proper chance to learn their new job.

(h) Identify any areas where working conditions are clearly unacceptable, and do whatever you can afford to put them right.

STATUTORY SICK PAY AND MATERNITY PAY

Statutory sick pay (SSP)

This is paid at three levels depending on earnings. The arrangements are summarized below.

1. To receive payment, eligible employees (see paragraph 6 for definition of non-eligibility) must have been sick for a spell of four or more complete days in a row. This forms a period of incapacity for work (PIW) and all complete days of sickness, including Saturdays, Sundays and holidays, count as part of this period.
2. PIWs which are separated by eight weeks (56 calendar days) or less are said to be linked, which means that they count as one PIW from the point of view of the requirement for incapacity to work for four days or more.
3. SSP is not paid for the first three days of sickness, which are termed 'waiting days'.
4. The qualifying days on which SSP is paid (excluding the three waiting days) are the days of the week on which employees are required to work, eg Monday to Friday inclusive.
5. To obtain SSP, the employee must notify his illness to the employer on the first qualifying day. The employer then requires the employee:
   (a) to follow this notification up with evidence of incapacity by signing a self-certificate for spells of four to seven days;
   (b) to produce a doctor's statement (sick note) for periods after the first seven days (doctors will not normally provide this statement for periods of less than seven days). Employers cannot require notification in writing more frequently than once a week during sickness.
6. The following categories of employees are not entitled to SSP:

(a) Those who have exhausted their claim to a state benefit such as sickness benefit and whose PIW starts within eight weeks of the end of the claim to state benefit. The local social security office send claimants in this situation a form known as a 'linking letter' which the employee has to give to his employer.
(b) Those over pension age.
(c) Employees whose contract of employment is three months or less.
(d) Employees whose earnings are less than the lower earnings limit.
(e) Employees who are pregnant during the 'disqualifying period' which begins with the eleventh week before the expected week of confinement and runs for 18 weeks.
(f) Employees who are abroad outside the EEC on the first day of the PIW.
(g) Employees who are in legal custody on the first day of the PIW.
(h) Employees who are on strike at the beginning of the PIW.

7. Employers must issue an 'exclusion form' to the social security office if an employee is not eligible for SSP for any of the reasons set out above.
8. The maximum liability to pay SSP is 28 weeks.
9. Employers can recover the SSP payments they make to their employees plus the proportion of employers' National Insurance contributions attributable to the value of the SSP payment. Recovery is achieved by deducting the SSP and UK payments from the National Insurance contributions made to the Collector of Taxes.
10. Employers must keep the following records of:
    (a) dates of sickness reported by their employees lasting at least four consecutive days;
    (b) any days within PIWs for which SSP was not paid, with reasons;
    (c) the qualifying days in each PIW;
    (d) linking letters (see paragraph 6a) issued to or received from employees.

Statutory maternity pay (SMP)

From April 1987 employers must pay their female employees statutory maternity pay when the latter stop work to have a baby.

The statutory maternity pay is payable for 18 weeks. A woman is entitled to SMP from her employer if she satisfies the following conditions:

1. She has been employed for a period of 26 weeks;
2. Her average weekly earnings have been greater than or equal to the lower earnings limit for National Insurance contributions;
3. She is pregnant or has been confined.

If these conditions are satisfied then the woman is entitled to the lower rate of SMP for 18 weeks. If conditions based on service and hours normally worked by the woman are satisfied then she is entitled to the higher rate of SMP for the first six of the 18 weeks.

The woman can choose to some extent when to receive her 18 weeks' payment. She can start no earlier than 11 weeks before the expected week of confinement and no later than six weeks before. There will always be a common 'core' of 13 weeks covering the period six weeks before the expected week of confinement, the expected week and six weeks after that week.

Employers will be able to recover payments of SMP from the payments of National Insurance contributions made to the Inland Revenue.

HEALTH AND SAFETY

Health and safety legislation

You cannot afford to ignore health and safety matters within your organization. If an accident occurs on your premises because of negligence on your part you are answerable both to your conscience and to rigorous requirements of the law. Trade unions and staff may legitimately demand that more attention be paid by management to the maintenance of a healthy and safe working environment. The law provides the framework within which you should act and the provisions of the Health and Safety at Work Act 1974 are summarized below.

General duty of employers
It is the general duty of every employer to ensure, so far as is reasonably practicable, the health, safety and welfare at work of all his employees.

Particular duties of employers
In particular, employers must, so far as is reasonably practicable:

(a) Provide and maintain plant and systems of work that are safe and without risk to health.

(b) Ensure safety and absence of risk to health in connection with the use, handling, storage and transport of articles and substances.
(c) Provide such information, training and supervision as is necessary to ensure the health and safety at work of employees.
(d) Maintain any place of work under the employer's control in a safe condition and without risks to health and ensure a safe means of access to and egress from that place.
(e) Provide and maintain a working environment for employees that is safe, without risks to health and adequate as regards facilities and arrangements for their welfare at work.

Principles of health and safety management

There are six basic principles which should determine your approach to health and safety management:

1. Accidents result from many factors, but these can be traced to their root causes, which are usually poor management and supervision, insufficient attention to the design of health and safety into the system, an unsystematic approach to the identification, analysis and elimination of hazards, and poor safety training.
2. The most important functions of health and safety programmes are to identify potential hazards, provide effective safety facilities, and to take prompt remedial action.
3. Health and safety is the concern of top management.
4. Managers and supervisors must be made fully accountable for health and safety performance in the areas they control.
5. All employees should be given thorough and continuous guidance in safe methods of work.
6. All employees should be given thorough training in safe methods of work and should receive continuing education and guidance on eliminating health and safety hazards and on the prevention of accidents.

5

TRAINING AND STAFF DEVELOPMENT

Michael Armstrong

INTRODUCTION

The head of an advertising agency once said, 'All my inventory goes up and down in the passenger lift.' He knew that his most important resource was his staff.

Putting it in the crudest terms possible, your staff are an investment from which you want a quick and increasing return. They also want the opportunity to acquire skills and knowledge and to grow with you.

These needs do not conflict. They can both be satisfied by paying a reasonable amount of attention to training and developing the people in your organization.

TRAINING AND DEVELOPING

Aims

Your aim in training and developing people should be to:

1. Shorten learning time so that new recruits reach their peak of efficiency as quickly and economically as possible.
2. Improve the performance of existing staff.
3. Help people to develop skills and knowledge so that you can meet some, if not all, of your future manpower requirements from within your organization.

Systematic training

The methods you choose should be cost-effective. They should provide a substantial return on the expenditure of money and time incurred in training. You should adapt the systematic training approach which involves developing training programmes which are specifically designed to meet defined needs. Systematic training is planned and provided by people who know how to train, but it need not be elaborate or costly. A systematic approach to training involves you in:

1. Defining training needs (discussed in a separate section).
2. Deciding what sort of training is required to satisfy these needs.
3. Implementing training programmes with clearly defined objectives.
4. Following up and evaluating training to ensure that it has been effective (see *Identifying training needs,* page 137).

Deciding what training is required

Less complex jobs
For manual and clerical jobs where the knowledge and skill requirements are not too complex, job instruction techniques should be used. These should be based on job analysis, which breaks the job into stages listing at each stage the operations that have to be performed and the skills and knowledge required. The key points to be learned should be emphasized, including special points of difficulty, safety factors and exceptions to the normal routines.

Managerial and supervisory jobs
For managerial and supervisory jobs these techniques are obviously not

so appropriate. The skills are more complex and most of the knowledge required is likely to be developed by experience rather than by training. The exceptions will be professional and technical jobs, and some specialized management techniques such as quantitative or financial analysis.

At this level, formal training courses have a necessary but no more than a supplementary role. Most training should take place on the job, using the techniques discussed in a later section.

Implementing training

Objectives

Your first step should be to make quite sure that you know what your objectives are. You should decide what you expect the trainee to be able to do after the training that he could not do before. This could be expressed in such terms as 'on completing this training programme the trainee will know a, b and c and will be able to x, y and z'.

Training programmes

Your second step should be to decide who is going to do what to whom. In other words, who will do the training, what is to be learned, what techniques are to be used, over what period does the training take place, and who is going to be trained. It may be necessary to draw up formal training programmes setting out objectives and listing these points.

But elaborate training schedules are no substitute for a real understanding on the part of your managers and supervisors of what they have to do and how they should do it, together with real commitment to getting it done.

Providing trainers

If your organization is large enough it may be necessary to employ a full-time training officer to help managers devise training programmes and to train managers and supervisors in how to coach and instruct. In a smaller organization you will have to rely on line managers and supervisors, although if you have large intakes of trainees in one department you could consider giving one supervisor the specific responsibility for training. If necessary that supervisor should be able to call on employees experienced in training to give instruction.

You could also consider appointing one person to take on the additional duty of coordinating training throughout the organization.

Training the trainers
Managers and supervisors and anyone else involved in training should know how to:

1. Identify training needs.
2. Prepare the material programmes and materials.
3. Present the material in such a way that the trainee knows what he has to learn.
4. Use coaching techniques.
5. Explain the 'why' as well as the 'how' to trainees.

IDENTIFYING TRAINING NEEDS

Training programmes are too often shots in the dark. If they are not relevant to what is required by the organization, then they are pointless. The only way to ensure relevance is to carry out a systematic training needs analysis exercise as an essential starting point in developing a training programme.

The analysis of training needs aims to define the gap between what is happening and what should happen. It can then be used to prepare relevant training programmes.

The gap may consist of the difference between:

- how the company or a function within the company is performing and how it should perform;
- what people know and can do and what they should know and do;
- what people actually do and what they should do.

Training needs analysis

Training needs analysis covers corporate, group and individual needs.

Corporate training needs should come from the analysis of company strengths and weaknesses as part of the corporate planning process. The company manpower plan will also indicate the numbers and types of people required in the future.

Group needs are identified by analysing functional or departmental manpower plans or by conducting special surveys using questionnaires and interviews. Job analysis can be used to determine the knowledge and skills required in specific jobs and this information can be supplemented by analysing the results obtained from the assessment of individual needs.

Individual training needs are identified by using the techniques of job analysis, skills analysis and performance appraisal.

EVALUATION OF TRAINING

Training is always said to be an investment, and rightly so. The danger, however, is that expenditure is often incurred in training without ever knowing whether or not it has paid off. There is always scope for improving the effectiveness of training but you will not be able to achieve specific improvements unless you follow up to find out what has happened and, on that basis, decide what has or has not worked in the training programme and what modifications are required.

Approach

It is at the planning stage that you should determine the basis upon which each category of training is to be evaluated. At the same time, it is necessary to consider how the information required to evaluate courses should be obtained and analysed. You are then in a position to decide what feedback information you need on the effects of the training programme so that you can assess the value of training.

Evaluation leads to control which means deciding if the training was worthwhile (preferably in cost/benefit terms) and what improvements are needed to make it even more cost-effective.

Evaluation is an integral feature of training. In its crudest form it is the comparison of objectives (criterion behaviour) with effects (terminal behaviour) to answer the question of how far training has achieved its purpose. The setting of objectives and the establishment of methods of measuring results are, or should be, an essential part of the planning stage of any training programme.

Evaluation is difficult because it is often hard to set measurable objectives and even harder to collect the information on the results or to decide on the level at which the evaluation should be made.

Evaluation levels

1. *Reactions.* The reactions of trainees to the training experience itself: how useful or even how enjoyable they feel the training is, what they think of individual sessions and speakers, what they would like put in or taken out, and so on.
2. *Learning.* Evaluation at the learning level requires the measurement of what trainees have learned as a result of their training — the new knowledge and skills they have acquired or the changes in attitude that have taken place. This is the terminal behaviour that

occurs immediately after the training has finished.

3. *Job behaviour.* At this level, evaluation attempts to measure the extent to which trainees have applied their learning on the job. This constitutes an assessment of the amount of transfer of learning that has taken place from an off-the-job training course to the job itself. If the training is carried out on the job there should be little difference between learning and job behaviour.
4. *Organization.* Evaluation at this level attempts to measure the effect of changes in the job behaviour of trainees on the functioning of the organization in which they are employed. The measurement might be in such terms as improvements in output, productivity, quality, morale (if that can be measured), contribution, or sales turnover. In effect, the question answered by this type of evaluation is not simply what behavioural changes have taken place, but what good have those changes been for the unit or department in which the employee works.
5. *Ultimate value.* This is a measure of how the organization as a whole has benefited from the training in terms of greater profitability, survival or growth. But it might also be defined in terms of the trainee's personal goals rather than those of the organization which sponsored him. This could be a legitimate company goal for training if it is believed that what is good for the individual is good for the organization, or if the company feels that it has a social duty to educate and train its employees to the maximum of their capacity. Fundamentally, however, evaluation at this level is related to the criteria by which the organization judges its efficiency and its success or failure. The difficulty is assessing how far training has contributed to the ultimate results.

The five levels are links in a chain: training leads to reactions, which lead to learning, which leads to changes in job behaviour, which lead to changes in the organization, which lead to changes in the achievement of ultimate goals. But the chain can be snapped at any link. A trainee can react favourably to a course — he can 'enjoy it' — but learn nothing. He can learn something, but he cannot, or will not, or is not allowed to, apply it. He applies it, but it does no good within his own area. It does some good in his function, but does not further the objectives of the organization.

Evaluation can start at any level. Ideally, some people might say, it starts and finishes at levels four and five; organizational and ultimate value. This is all that really matters, they claim. But it may be difficult, if not impossible, for you to measure backwards to find out what went wrong at earlier levels if the ultimate benefits arising from training are inadequate.

MANAGEMENT DEVELOPMENT

Management development is a systematic process which helps you to ensure that the organization has the effective managers it requires to meet its present and future needs. It is concerned with improving the performance of existing managers, giving them opportunities for growth and development, and ensuring, so far as possible, that management succession within the organization is provided for. The objectives of a typical management development programme are to improve the financial performance and long-term growth of your company by:

1. Improving the performance of managers by seeing that they are clearly informed of their responsibilities and by agreeing with them specific key objectives against which their performance will be regularly assessed;
2. Identifying managers with further potential and ensuring that they receive the required development, training and experience to equip them for more senior posts within their own locations and divisions within the company;
3. Assisting managers throughout the company to provide adequate succession and to create a system whereby this is kept under regular review.

Management development activities

Management development activities can be divided into seven areas:

1. Organization review
2. Manpower review
3. Performance review
4. Management by objectives
5. Training
6. Succession planning
7. Career planning.

Organization review

Management development activities should be founded upon a review of the objectives, plans and structure of your organization and the implications of present weaknesses and future demands on managerial requirements.

Manpower review

The organization review leads naturally into a review of your manpower resources. This is the manpower planning aspect of management development and, where the circumstances permit, it implies an analysis of the present resources and future requirements in terms of numbers, types and knowledge and skills. This is a general review, and individual and management succession needs would be analysed separately, although performance reviews will provide information on strengths and weaknesses that affect the overall plan.

It may be impossible to prepare precise forecasts of future requirements, but it is still desirable to give some thought to the general considerations that will affect education and training, career planning and succession planning.

Performance review

Performance review or appraisal systems are used to identify development needs by highlighting strengths and weaknesses and, so far as this is possible, potential for promotion. They are also a basis for the counselling and coaching activities which should form the most important part of an individual's development within your company.

Management by objectives

Management by objectives has in some quarters been regarded as the key activity in a management development programme. Perhaps it has been oversold as the universal panacea for all management development problems, but it can have a part to play in an integrated programme and its basic philosophy is relevant to anyone concerned with the management of people.

Management by objectives is essentially a method of managing organizations and people and of improving the performance of managers. The basic processes are as follows:

- Subordinates agree with their managers the objectives of their job, expressed as targets or standards of performance for each key result area. The individual objectives are in line with unit and organizational objectives, and are defined in a way which emphasizes the conbribution they make to achieving departmental and corporate plans. So far as possible, the objectives are quantified, 'job improvement' plans (in Humble's phrase) are jointly developed to indicate what the manager should contribute to the unit's and the company's plans for better performance.
- Performance is reviewed jointly by the manager and the subordinate to compare results with the defined objectives and standards.

- The manager and subordinate agree where improvements are required and how better results can be achieved and, as necessary, re-define targets and standards.

Management by objectives has often developed into a range of elaborate systems and techniques — too elaborate many people say — but it is based upon a fundamental philosophy with which it is difficult to quarrel.

Management training

Management development is sometimes seen as primarily a matter of providing a series of appropriate courses at various points in a manager's career. But, as Hawdon Hague suggests, the best definition of training is the 'modification of behaviour through experience', which means that managers will develop best if they receive their training in the 'real' situation, ie in the normal course of their work through coaching, projects and guided self-analysis.

The principal method by which managers can be equipped is by ensuring that they have the right variety of experience, in good time, in the course of their careers. This experience can and should be supplemented, but never replaced, by courses carefully timed and designed to meet particular needs.

Management succession planning

The aim of management succession planning is to ensure that as far as possible suitable managers are available to fill vacancies created by promotion, retirement, death, leaving or transfer. It also aims to ensure that a cadre of managers is available to fill the new appointments that may be established in the future.

The information for management succession planning comes from organization and manpower reviews and assessments of performance and potential. This information needs to be recorded so that decisions can be made on promotions and replacements, and training or additional experience arranged for those with potential or who are earmarked for promotion.

Career planning

Career planning has two aims: first, to ensure that men and women of promise are given a sequence of experience that will equip them for whatever level of responsibility they have the ability to reach; second, to provide individuals with potential with the guidance and encouragement they need if they are to fulfil their potential and remain with the organization. Career planning involves you in:

1. Management succession planning – assessing future losses of managers through retirement, promotion or natural wastage and deciding who is available who can replace them;
2. Counselling individuals on their possible career paths and what they must do to achieve promotion;
3. Providing whatever experience and training is appropriate to prepare individuals for greater responsibilities.

Trends in management development

The most important trend in management development is the increased emphasis on improving individual performance by means of guided experience and self-development. Do-it-yourself training is now regarded as the best way of obtaining new knowledge and skills within an organization. While it is useful to plan ahead for management succession, there is a limit to how much can be worked out in advance. Many companies are concentrating more on ensuring that managers are given the opportunity and guidance needed to improve in their present job than on making elaborate plans for a future that may not happen.

ON-THE-JOB TRAINING

Robert Townsend in *Up the Organization* has a simple approach to training: 'The only way I know to get somebody trained is on the job.'

This statement expresses a fundamental truth. People learn best by doing. Training off the job is too often irrelevant and there is always the problem of transferring what is learned on a course back to the workplace. Effective transfer of learning is possible if the off-the-job training simulates working conditions with a reasonable degree of precision. But this is difficult, although for managers and supervisors the problem can be tackled by using action-centred learning techniques on courses which attempt to involve trainees directly in real problems at work against a background of stimulation and guidance by external course tutors.

Training off the job is, however, appropriate is some circumstances; for example, it is often quicker and cheaper to train fitters and machinists in their basic skills in a separate workshop. And some knowledge, for example, of how to operate a new machine may only be obtainable outside the organization.

Managers can benefit from the broadening effect of an external course which enables them to reflect and build upon their own experience and, more importantly, meet and talk to other managers. Don't worry if they come back and say they learned more in the bar than in the classroom. It is what they learn that matters, not how they learn it. The three main techniques used in on-the-job training are discussed below:

Do-it-yourself training

The best form of development is self-development. People learn most effectively when they find things out for themselves rather than having information forced down their throats. Do-it-yourself training recognizes this by:

1. Starting from a definition of what someone needs to know and do to perform a job.
2. Establishing where the information required is available.
3. Giving the trainee an outline of the information he has to obtain and where and from whom he can get it. He may be given questions to answer or mini-projects to complete.
4. Briefing those concerned (mainly the trainee's boss and his colleagues, but also people in other departments) on the help they should give the trainee.
5. Preparing a timetable for the learning programme.
6. Arranging for someone (the trainee's boss or the executive responsible for training) to monitor his progress. This should include periodic meetings to check on what has been learned and provide extra encouragement and guidance.

Coaching

The best way to learn to manage is to manage, under the guidance of a good manager. Coaching is an informal but deliberate way of providing this guidance. It should be linked to performance appraisal and the counselling that takes place as part of the appraisal procedure.

But coaching is a more continuous process. Every time you delegate a task to someone and discuss the outcome you are presented with a coaching opportunity. When you delegate you can provide guidance on how the job should be done. When you discuss progress with your subordinate or when he reports back to you, you can ask questions on how well he has thought through what he is doing, suggest alternative ways of looking at a problem (do not provide the solution) and provide constructive criticism if things are not going right.

You can help to develop people by discussing higher-level problems with them, involving them in your decisions and increasing their understanding of how to tackle a job senior to the areas for which they are responsible.

Every contact you have with a subordinate provides you with a coaching opportunity. Without making too much effort, you can contribute significantly to his improvement and growth by making the most of the chances offered to you.

Planned experience

People learn mainly through experience. Surely, therefore, it is worth spending a little time planning the experience of anyone with potential for development.

Planning someone's experience means giving him extra tasks to do which provide a challenge or extend him into a new area. It could be a project which he has to complete himself or he could be included in a project team looking at a new development or problem which cuts across organizational boundaries. Projects which enlarge experience in unfamiliar areas, for example a marketing executive in finance or vice versa, are particularly useful. Planned experience will work better if it is accompanied by coaching so that those undergoing it can receive the maximum benefit from expert advice.

ACTION LEARNING

Action learning, as developed by Professor Revans, is a method of helping managers to develop their talents by being exposed to real problems. They are required to analyse them, formulate recommendations and then, instead of being satisfied with a report, actually take action. It accords with the belief that managers learn best by doing rather than being taught.

This approach conforms to the principle on which all good training should be based, ie it is problem-based and action-orientated. It recognizes that the most perplexing task managers face is how to achieve change, how to persuade their colleagues and others to commit themselves to a different way of doing things. An action-learning programme therefore concentrates on developing the skills which managers need to take action effectively, without ignoring the need for knowledge of relevant techniques.

The concept of action learning is based on five assumptions:

1. Experienced managers have a huge curiosity to know how other managers work.
2. Learning about oneself is threatening and is resisted if it tends to

change one's self-image. However, it is possible to reduce the external threat to a level which no longer acts as a total barrier to learning about oneself.

3. People only learn when they do something, and they learn more the more responsible they feel the task to be.
4. Learning is deepest when it involves the whole person — mind, values, body, emotions.
5. The learner knows better than anyone else what he has learned. Nobody else has much chance of knowing.

DISTANCE LEARNING

In distance learning, the individual uses training material supplied from another source when and where he wants to use it. Interaction with the teaching source can take place by letter, or periodical meetings, or courses.

Essentially, distance learning is like a correspondence course except that there are many alternative forms of communication (audio or video cassettes, radio or TV programmes as well as conventional written material) and more sophisticated teaching material is used such as those available in *computer-based training* systems, *programmed instruction* and *interactive video*. Much more has been learned over the last few years about methods of instruction and involving the learner with his teacher. The work of the Open University has been particularly important in this respect.

Advantages and disadvantages

The advantages of distance learning are that:

1. High quality, specially prepared material for this purpose can be made available to people who would otherwise not have access to it;
2. Individuals are not tied down to attending regular block, or day release or evening sessions;
3. Individuals can work at their own pace.

The disadvantages are that:

1. The continuing interaction between the teacher and learner that takes place in face-to-face learning methods does not happen which means that the teacher has no chance of responding quickly to the changing needs of his students;
2. People can learn from each other as well as their teacher, and there is no scope for this in distance learning;

3. Some people need the discipline of having to attend regular courses of instruction; without this, they may begin to drift and finally give up their course.

Methods

Distance learning as it has evolved makes extensive use of the technology mentioned earlier such as computer-based learning, audio and video cassettes. This can improve the effectiveness of the learning process considerably above what could be achieved by the old-fashioned correspondence course.

Distance learning can be used within large or dispersed companies to reach people who might not otherwise be able to benefit from training. A tutor from within the company can run the programme, or tutorial resources can be made available from the organization which provides the training material. Packages can be obtained from such centres as Henley or Cranfield, or a company can develop its own programmes, making the maximum use of training aids. In circumstances where it is difficult to get people to attend training centres, the advantages of distance learning considerably outweigh the disadvantages.

COMPUTER-BASED TRAINING

Computers can be used for training in the following ways:

1. To simulate actual situations so that trainees can 'learn by doing'. For example, technicians can be trained in troubleshooting and repairing electronic circuitry by looking at circuit diagrams displayed on the screen and using a light-pen to measure voltages at different points in the circuit. When faults are diagnosed, 'repairs' are effected by means of a light-pen, this time employed as a soldering iron.
2. To extend programmed learning texts to provide diagrammatic and pictorial displays in colour and to allow more interaction between the trainee and the information presented on the screen.
3. To provide a data base for information which trainees can access through a computer terminal.
4. To measure the performances of trainees against predefined criteria.
5. To provide tests or exercises for trainees. The technique of *adaptive testing* uses a program containing a large number of items designed to test a trainee's comprehension of certain principles. But it is not necessary for him to work through all of

them or even to satisfy them sequentially in order to demonstrate his understanding. His responses to a limited number of questions will show whether or not he has grasped the appropriate concepts to satisfy given training objectives. The process of testing can thus be speeded up considerably and prove less frustrating for the trainee.

MSC TRAINING INITIATIVES

The Manpower Services Commission has taken a number of initiatives recently to open doors to employment, training and enterprise. The principal programmes are summarized below:

Youth Training Scheme

YTS provides training and planned work experienced for up to two years to equip young people for working life. It has been expanded and developed to give 16-year-old school-leavers two years of training and 17-year-old leavers one year, with special arrangements for disabled young people and some other groups.

The new two-year programme will involve at least 20 weeks off-the-job training (in a college or training centre) in addition to on-the-job training and planned work experience. The second year will build on the first year's foundations by providing specific skill training, leading to vocational qualifications.

Job Training Scheme

The Job Training Scheme, a successor to the Training Opportunities Scheme (TOPS), provides a wide choice of training for unemployed people who are over 18 and who have been away from full-time education for at least two years. It can add to the skills they already have or, equally important, develop the new skills that local employers particularly need. Opportunities in the technician and new technology fields are features of the training offered.

The Job Training Scheme includes special provision for disabled people — for example, individual training with an employer for between four weeks and a year, after which the disabled person is normally employed for at least a short period.

Wider Opportunity Training Programme

The Wider Opportunity Training Programme helps people get back to work with a range of modular full- and part-time courses at various levels, closely matched to local employment needs.

Some courses include an introduction to setting up a small business. Courses vary in different areas but most begin by helping trainees decide what they want to do and giving them a chance to try out a range of skills — crafts, clerical, commercial, working with new technology. Some might be interested in taking their training further under the Job Training Scheme.

The main five programmes are:

1. For those with narrow and outdated skills: training and assessment in broad-based occupational skills (including new technology and self-employment).
2. For those needing general preparation for work: courses focusing on work-related literacy and numeracy, developing job-getting skills and enhancing occupational skills.
3. For speakers of English as a second language: work-related language training linked to instruction in occupational skills.
4. For women wishing to return to work: training to update skills and provide better knowledge of the labour market and the job-finding process.
5. For unemployed managers and professionals: courses to help them assess their skills and present them more effectively to employers.

The emphasis of the training offered is on flexibility and choice, providing a wide range of skills at times which suit the trainee.

Open Tech Programme

The Open Tech Programme allows people to learn at their own pace and at a time and place that suits them, whether at home or at work. It is designed to widen adult career and job opportunities at technician and supervisory management levels of skill.

The programme provides pump-priming funds to over 120 projects of broadly two types:

1. *Operational*: concerned with developing new open-learning materials and with their use by trainees.
2. *Supporting*: through the provision of services such as an information database and advice to project staff.

INDUSTRIAL TRAINING BOARDS

Industrial training boards were first set up in the 1960s and soon became a major force in what came to be known as the training revolution. Their achievements were considerable. They preached, with great success, the gospel of systematic training and translated this overall philosophy into a large number of specific training approaches which have done much to improve the quality of apprentice, technical and management training in the United Kingdom.

Specifically, the training boards:

(a) introduced module training which encapsulated the specific skills to be acquired to master a particular aspect of a job, using skills analysis techniques to ensure that the training was based on a full understanding of what the trainee had to learn;
(b) emphasized the need for job and skills analysis to ensure that training is relevant;
(c) encouraged the use of definitions of what the trainee will have learned and be able to do having completed the training (criterion behaviour) thus providing clearly defined objectives which can be used to structure the programme and against which the results achieved can be evaluated;
(d) improved the quality of basic training provided in the early years of apprenticeship, thus paving the way for the virtual disappearance of the old rigid five years' apprenticeship and its replacement by more concentrated training over a period of two or three years;
(e) the broadening of technician training to include manufacturing processes, and to supply and to equip trainees to keep abreast with new technology;
(f) conduct extensive research on training techniques, the results of which were incorporated in training modules and schemes;
(g) demonstrated to their industries in the boards' own training establishments how training should be conducted;
(h) emphasized the importance of follow-up and evaluation;
(i) spelt out the pay-off that can result from good training;
(j) built up a massive data-bank of training information on which employers could draw;
(k) encouraged in general a total strategic approach to training.

There were some negatives. A few boards became over-bureaucratic and some indulged in esoteric research programmes whose relevance to their industry was not obvious. Many employers resented paying levy when they felt either that they could do it better themselves (at less total cost) or that their money was being wasted.

Eventually, the government decided that in many industries the training boards were not fulfilling a useful purpose and in 1983 16 of the

23 boards were wound up. In a spirit of 'privatization', industries without boards were encouraged to develop voluntary training organizations based mainly on employers' associations.

The remaining seven boards cover the clothing, construction, engineering, hotel and catering, offshore petroleum, plastics processing and road transport sections. About 30 per cent of the country's working population is now within the scope of these statutory arrangements, compared with over half before the changes.

The Manpower Services Commission keeps a watching brief over the remaining boards which operate broadly on the same basis as before except that the maximum levy they can make is 1 per cent of payroll. The boards continue, therefore, to offer advice on training, to provide training facilities, to carry out research and to feed to their industry new or improved approaches to training.

6

ADMINISTRATION AND OFFICE SERVICES

Hano Johannsen

INTRODUCTION

The way that a business deals with much of the day-to-day administrative workload has changed almost beyond recognition during the past decade. Computers, word processors, facsimile machines, electronic mail etc have all made a significant impact on the way that many administrative tasks are now being undertaken.

It is clear is that dramatic changes are under way not only in the equipment now being used, but in the way that office activities are being re-examined and organized. In many areas stand-alone equipment and systems are giving way to systems which seek to link and integrate the processing and analysis of information and at the same time improve communications and closer management control.

The traditional responsibilities of the office function include responsibility for the building, maintenance and cleaning, security, office equipment, stationery purchases and stocks, mail room and reprographic services etc. In some cases it may also include responsibility for productivity and O & M services, records management, communication systems and so on.

In spite of the many technological changes affecting the administration and office fields, there is a real danger that businessmen become so absorbed (and increasingly dependant) on computer hardware and software and the like that many key basic 'old-fashioned' activities tend to become neglected. Many essential tasks remain which have little or nothing to do with computers!

TOWARDS OFFICE AUTOMATION

Although the much-heralded age of information technology and so-called office automation still has a long way to go before it becomes a reality in most organizations, few can doubt that moves in that direction are well advanced. Government encouragement in this direction has come from the series of reports commissioned by the then Department of Industry in the early 1980s.

Office automation implies the application of modern technology to handling information in the office including data input via ordinary speech, images and numeric data. It is essentially a systems approach which views the whole organization as an entity rather than a collection of loosely related elements. This has been reflected in the shift of emphasis away from an often narrow office function – perhaps carried out departmentally – to a broader range of activities often now described as 'support' or 'administrative' services.

While office automation involves the use of a range of electronic machinery it is primarily about developing an integrated system for handling information, access to databases, internal and external communications etc.

Research findings suggest that office automation can be got off the ground by:

- Establishing the nature of the information needed by managers and staff
- Identifying potential applications
- Simplifying and improving existing procedures before attempting to automate them
- Briefing staff involved
- Developing training materials and programmes
- Providing counselling and advice during the changeover period
- Supervising implementation
- Liaising with suppliers and contractors
- Monitoring new systems.

EFFECTIVE COMMUNICATIONS

Communication in business is all about the regular flow and exchange of information between individuals and groups. The term has become so widely used and often abused in recent years that the essential elements can easily be overlooked. Identifying the reasons for many so-called communication problems is not easy. In some organizations it may be the organization structure itself which is not conducive to the smooth interchange of information between senior management and subordinates. In others, poor communication may be due to the lack of trust between different levels of staff and employees. Research suggests that in some cases it is the methods of communication themselves which are inadequate and at fault.

Communication should not be seen as a way of 'talking at' or 'to' employees. It is essentially a two-way process involving not only the provision and dissemination of information, but also the reception of information and feedback from others. Developing and encouraging an effective flow of relevant communication between all levels of employees seems like common sense to many, but in practice it is often hampered for a number of reasons:

1. Lack of clarity

It can be argued that ambiguous communication is often worse than no information at all. Whatever the reason for the lack of clarity - a simple misunderstanding or the jargon used etc - the aim should be for the communicator to stand back and ask himself whether the tone and content of his message will be understood by those on the receiving end!

2. Insufficient information

Whether it is pressure of work or simply inability to express themselves clearly, many managers appear to pass on only part of the story or instructions they intended. It is therefore not surprising that subordinates can be in the dark when it comes to carrying out tasks or understanding why (say) a certain new procedure is being introduced. Insufficient information can so easily lead to unfounded rumours and staff anxieties.

3. Insufficient communication

This simply implies keeping people in the dark about what is going on. Whether by oversight or lack of sensitivity, it makes for poor staff morale and a lack of involvement and commitment by the workforce. If it relates to an isolated issue it may not be critical since not everything *has* to be communicated. Yet while some matters may indeed need to be kept confidential or confined to a few individuals only, the general aim should be to have an 'open' style which implies that employees receive regular and relevant communications and are involved in discussions and consultation on matters which affect them well *before* rather than *after* events take place.

For many companies improving communications can be a matter of recognizing the need for developing sound communication channels which can be brought into play quickly. Many rumours and misinformation can be scotched provided that meetings are arranged so that the staff are given information promptly and before the grapevine has had a chance to do any damage. Occasionally leaked information may have its uses, but there is no substitute for official communications coming from the management direct. The face-to-face meeting, whether one of a regular series or called for a special purpose, not only enables information to be properly presented but also allows for a dialogue and question-and-answer sessions.

Noticeboards, internal memos, newsletters and even loudspeaker announcements all have a useful role to play in the dissemination of information but should ideally be seen as supplementing direct communication via personal contact or at meetings and briefing groups etc.

If you feel you have a communication problem check where the weaknesses may lie. For example ask yourself:

- Does the way the business is organized inhibit good communications?
- Are there difficulties between managers and supervisors and their staff?
- What channels and media do you use to communicate?
- How do managers and employees currently receive information about their work and the business?
- Does information only travel up and down the reporting ladder or does it also travel between departments etc?
- Is there an air of secrecy surrounding the free exchange of information? Is this justified?
- Are some areas of the business starved of key information?
- Which? What are the reasons?

MEETINGS AND PRESENTATIONS

Meetings – either formal or informal – are called for many reasons. Some simply seek to get a group of people together for a discussion: others focus on collecting or disseminating information. Sometimes meetings may be called to help tackle a specific problem (eg the reorganization of a department) or to promote new ideas.

Whatever the reason for calling a meeting, experience shows that many can so easily turn into ineffective time-wasters. Before calling a meeting ask yourself, for example:

- Is a meeting really the best way of communicating?
- What are the alternatives?
- Who should attend? Why?
- Are the location, date and timing convenient?
- Have you done your homework on the agenda topics?
- Have you established the order of subjects and the time to be set aside for each item?
- How will the meeting be managed?
- How long will it last?
- Are any papers or background data to be circulated in advance?
- Have you carefully considered what you hope to achieve?

The success or failure of meetings and presentations depends not only their structure, content, audience etc, but also on the time devoted to ensuring that the physical arrangements are satisfactory. Comfortable seating, sensible room layout, good lighting, heating and ventilation and the professional use of visual aids can all make or break meetings. Often it is the little things which cause frustration to both the speaker(s) and audience. Really successful events depend on attention to detail and setting enough time and effort aside for the planning stage.

In checking on the arrangements ask yourself:

1. Is the room the right size for the size of audience?
2. What is the best form of layout (eg classroom, U-shape, round or square table)?
3. Does the room have pillars: is it too narrow or too large?
4. Are the walls or partitions sound-proof?
5. Can the ventilation, heating and air-conditioning be controlled?
6. Is smoking allowed?
7. What are the sound qualities of the room? Are microphones and so on called for?
8. Is the lighting satisfactory? If visual aids are to be used, have the equipment and aids been checked thoroughly? Check location of switches, sockets etc and ability to darken the room?
9. What can you do to avoid interruptions and noises off-stage?
10. Will you need to provide note paper, handouts, pencils, water, name cards, ashtrays, flip charts, blackboards etc?
11. Will you provide refreshments? When?

Visual aids can make or break meetings and presentations. If they are to be used make sure:

- They really are used to help you to get your message across.
- Seek professional help in their preparation: visual aids need to be bold and memorable.

- Spend time on rehearsing the use of equipment and aids.
- Check that the audience can see them clearly.

REPORT WRITING

Reports also have a very important role to play in the communication process. They come in all shapes and sizes and may report on sales performances, laboratory tests, management proposals, meetings, projects and survey results and so on.

Whatever the purpose, all reports should seek to observe the mnemonic *PAPER* which highlights the five key stages in getting a report ready for reproduction.

1. *Preparation.* Collecting relevant information and facts and figures.
2. *Assessment.* Checking whether all the necessary information for planning and writing the report is available.
3. *Planning.* Sifting the data and arranging it under sensible headings.
4. *Expression.* Choose the appropriate style and length, bearing in mind the target readership. Draft the actual report.
5. *Review*: Edit the first draft and producing a final text ready for reproduction.

Good reports should not only be concise and readable, but be written with a specific audience in mind. Ask yourself, for example, whether you:

- Are clear about the purpose of preparing the report?
- Do you know enough about the readership?
- Have you given yourself enough time to collect the background data and plan the structure of the report?
- Have you chosen the right headings and chapters?
- Will you make recommendations?
- Is the final text easy to read and understand?
- If you are using tables, charts, and so on, are they really relevant?

BUSINESS LETTERS

Business letters, like meetings and reports, need planning if they are to be effective. Beware of allowing them to happen rather than receiving the attention they deserve.

A simple mnemonic, *WEAP*, standing for

*W*hat?

*E*laboration
*A*ction
*P*oliteness
'highlights the four key sections' which should be covered by most business letters.

1. *What?* To attract attention letters need to start by indicating what they are about and why they are being written. The aim is to set the scene.
2. *Elaboration.* Normally the second stage is to develop the subject matter and possibly raise some issues and questions.
3. *Action.* This section of the letter should, for example, deal with the action to be taken or the solution suggested.
4. *Politeness.* Try to be friendly and end on a courteous note.

While some business letters will always call for special one-off replies because of the nature of the subject matter, many dealing with routine matters can be handled by developing a range of standard paragraphs or letters. If standard paragraphs or letters are not being used at present, consider their introduction after undertaking a simple analysis of the areas in which they could most readily be applied. The widespread use of word processors makes it simple to store a range of standard paragraphs or complete letters which can be selected when required.

MAIL ROOM

All businesses need to establish basic procedures for handling incoming and outgoing mail. Even the smaller organization is likely to centralize these activities to ensure that internal distribution is systematically organized and outgoing mail is handled by someone who is familiar with all the complexities of the postal and courier services available.

Post room information and machinery

1. The *Post Office Guide*, revised every two years, is an indispensable source of information for anyone using postal services. Available from all main post offices at a small charge, it gives a detailed description of the range of Post Office services and explains the conditions applying to, for example, packing, special services, bulk rates, Freepost, household delivery services etc.
2. Postcode directories available from the Post Office are very useful for checking mailing codes and can also be used to sort bulk mailings which qualify for postal rebates. Postcodes can also help to identify sales territories and plan deliveries.

3. Those responsible for the mail-room function should be familiar with the special stationery etc used for services such as recorded delivery, airmail post, Datapost, proof of posting and the host of others. Someone needs to be responsible for keeping adequate stocks (and reordering) basic postal stationery including forms, franking machine labels and so on.
4. Ensure you have current leaflets on postal rates and details of local and international courier services and the rest.
5. Keep up-to-date details of frequently used addresses, contacts, and useful telephone numbers on a noticeboard.
6. Make contact with your local postal services representative (attached to main post offices) for further information and bulk contract rates etc.
7. Ensure that someone is reponsible for the maintenance of the key post-room equipment such as franking machine, postal scale, inserting, addressing and folding machinery.

FILING

Storing and retrieving correspondence, reports, statistics etc are clearly important to all businesses but systems can easily get out of hand. The aim of filing should *not* be to store all paperwork but rather to keep *only* material which is really significant. The well-organized business will seek to establish rules on retention periods. A simple but effective system is to indicate with a code the importance of all letters at the time they are produced. Such simple procedures should ensure that important documents are kept but that ephemeral material is kept for shorter periods and then discarded. Check with the company secretary, accountant and legal adviser to ensure that any retention schedule devised meets legal requirements. Make sure that all contracts, agreements and the like are safely stored and readily retrievable. The original documents should be kept by the company secretary or other responsible executive.

Remember that all filing uses costly staff time to sift and store and takes up valuable space and equipment. Consider what you can do to cut down on filing work, for example:

- Do not create unnecessary copies of your own correspondence and reports for circulation.
- Normally, do not file all circulars, statistics and reports unless they are really essential to your work. Copies can always be obtained from the originator if really necessary.
- Keep papers of a temporary nature out of the filing system.

- Establish a 'weeding out' procedure and develop a policy for retaining vital documents.

The choice of filing method lies between:

1. *Alphabetical filing*, the most common system, but make sure you follow basic rules: see British Telecom directories for ways of handling less common names. If it is a question of allowing room for a cross-section of surnames, remember that B, C, H, M, S and W are the most frequently used letters (over 7 per cent each) while I, Q, U, X, Y and Z are the least frequent (less than 0.4 per cent each).
2. *Geographical filing* is sometimes adopted to deal with filing by place names, counties, regions or countries. If there are more than, say, 50 names you will also almost certainly need an alphabetical index to record what is filed where. This applies, for example, if dealing with branches or retail outlets by county.
3. *Subject indexing* is common, but in all but the simplest of systems, rules must be made and recorded so that a common procedure is adopted at all times.
4. *Numerical filing* is popular, especially for larger systems. This procedure also calls for keeping a systematic index which links numbers to names and it is therefore often called a numer-alpha system.

How effective is your filing system?

- Is it easy to decide where to file new papers?
- How quickly can existing documents in the system be found?
- If you have a centralized system, how well does it work?
- Is there a clear distinction between what files are kept centrally and departmentally?
- Can the system cope with protecting important legal, technical, etc documents?
- What happens to confidential material?
- Can files be found quickly if secretarial staff are absent?

RECORD STORAGE AND RETRIEVAL

Even the smaller organisation eventually requires a policy for 'weeding', storing and ultimately retrieving the vast quantity of information which it acquires and generates in the course of time. Much obviously depends on the nature and size of the business: three main types of storage can be identified:

Original documents. Box files, lever-arch files, drawer filing, suspended filing, mechanized systems etc.

Visual and graphic materials. Microfiche sheets, microfilm, aperture film cards etc.
Coded and magnetic data. Punched cards and tape, computer discs and tapes etc.

The choice of appropriate systems should take into account:
Space conservation
Cost of the equipment
Security and physical protection against fire and deterioration
Ease of storing and retrieving information
Simple processing systems and procedures
Minimum maintenance
Economic supplies.

TELEPHONE AND TELECOMMUNICATION SERVICES

Though British Telecom is by far the largest provider of a variety of services for the business user, a number of alternative and ancillary services are now being actively marketed by other companies, especially for the larger user.

British Telecom services include:

- Fixed-time calls
- Person-to-person calls
- Calls to be put through to a person at a specified number (say in a hotel) but charged only for the call (not the waiting) time
- Transfer-charge calls
- Phone cards enabling a predetermined number of units to be used in public call boxes
- Telephone credit cards enabling authorized users to make operator connected calls using a special credit card
- Cheap rates: telephone rates are levied in three time bands. The most expensive time is between 9.00am and 1.00pm. It is cheaper between 1.00 and 6.00pm and cheaper still after 6.00pm to 9.00am; weekend calls are also cheaper.
- Directories: while telephone subscribers receive free copies of directories for their area, the many other directories published can be ordered at a small charge (or consulted at main reference libraries).

The range of telecommunication services available has increased considerably over recent years. Key services include:

- Telemessages. A quick way of sending messages via British Telecom's telephone or telex services up to 8.00pm for delivery by first post on the following day.
- Teleprinters offer fast and effective means of sending information (eg share movements, news etc) to distant linked printer equipment.
- Telex. An international communications system consisting of teleprinters linked to telephone dialling equipment. The telex directory lists all subscribers using a special answer-back code. Once connected you can type out a letter or message which is charged on a time basis.
- Nowadays the telex system can also be accessed (and messages sent and received) by anyone with a micro terminal using appropriate communications software and a modem. This sytem uses one of the online systems such as Prestel's Telexlink, BT Gold, Easylink or One-to-One.
- Computer-linked facilities include electronic mail and bulletin boards. They too involve the use of micros (with modems and appropriate software) for gaining access to electronic mailboxes where computer-generated data can be 'dumped' (for access by other authorized users or for retrieval later by the subscribers themselves). A growing number of data bases can now also be accessed via micros connected to free or subscriber-only based 'bulletin boards' and information services: see Chapter 16 for further details.
- Datel is a British Telecom service for transmitting punchtape data via a computer to distant locations.

  Intelpost provides facilities for the facsimile transmission of documents worldwide.
- Confravision. This is a video and telephone service provided by British Telecom enabling 'meetings' to take place when the participants are dispersed in different locations. This service enables people to see and talk to each other as though they are together in one room.

REPROGRAPHY

Electrostatic copies have largely replaced many of the spirit or stencil duplicating machines which were once a familiar sight in most offices. Electrostatic copiers can now produce excellent copies - often as good or better than the originals - from a wide variety of masters. Nearly all coloured inks copy well these days. Using cheap plain paper, many can also copy in a range of colours, reduce or enlarge the text, or copy on both sides of the paper. The larger machines can produce transparencies, labels etc, and some can also collate papers into sets. The only chemical required is a powder toner. The larger machine can handle about 60 copies per minute.

Laser copiers

These printers can accept output direct from word processors and computers. They use photocopying and laser light technology and although relatively expensive, such printers provide a means of manipulating information before printing. A variety of different typefaces can be used and font sizes can be varied via the software and micro terminal. Such systems are very flexible, and are able to accept graphics including charts and logos; they mark a move towards so-called desk-top publishing which enables pages to be designed and made up and finished copies of leaflets, reports etc to be produced in the office itself.

Stencil and spirit duplicating

Though still widely used these processes have in recent years taken second place to electrostatic copying. Nevertheless for some tasks they can produce acceptable quality copies especially if existing machinery is available and economy is important.

MAINTENANCE

Maintenance of buildings, offices and equipment tends to be a neglected field especially in the smaller company. The old-fashioned solution is simply to respond to breakdowns or call in outside help when a problem arises. The modern approach is to identify all major pieces of equipment and plant and list all the key features of the building itself and draw up a schedule for lubricating, cleaning, servicing, replacing, painting and so on. One should be able to identify those items which may be borderline cases. This implies weighing up whether ongoing repairs and maintenance are justified: replacement may be a cheaper option. It also calls for a programme of preventative maintenance. This implies, for example, that *all* fluorescent tubes are replaced at regular intervals rather than replacing individual tubes as and when they fail.

Maintenance also involves decisions about the pros and cons of owning equipment (and having responsibility for repairs) or leasing items (such as cars) and leaving repairs etc to the leasing company.

Experience shows that over a period of time a pattern to breakdowns can be discerned. Frequency distributions of breakdowns for a range of components or machines make it possible to predict the probability of failures with a high degree of accuracy.

SECURITY

All organizations need to be prepared for potential risks and loss caused by theft, fire, explosion, flooding, criminal damage, loss of key records or information and disruptions caused by strikes or for other reasons.

While risks can be covered by insurance - at a cost (see Chapter 13) all reasonable precautions need to be taken to reduce exposure to risks to a minimum. The areas at most risk will obviously vary according to the nature of the firm's products or services, its location, size and its susceptibility to damage as a result of technical processes, industrial action and major disasters such as fire.

Even the smaller business can benefit from analysing its key operations and highlighting possible exposure to risk. Such an audit might, for example, cover:

Research and development
Production processes
Stores for materials and finished stock
Security of key information and records
Computer systems and records
Security for cash handling
Personnel records
Transport and distribution etc.

List the major risks against each activity and identify who is responsible.

Security is not just a question of security guards or the use of security services for handling cash. It is about involving all the workforce in safe working practices and vigilance. It is about anticipating the unexpected and leaving as little as possible to chance. The aim of a security policy should be to minimize potential dangers and take all reasonable (and cost-effective) ways of reducing the chances of arson, theft, fraud and the like.

7

MARKETING AND SELLING

Stephen P Morse

INTRODUCTION

Marketing should be seen as encompassing the whole business — and the whole business should be seen from the point of view of the customer; this means that everyone in the organization needs at least a working knowledge of what marketing entails and what functions are involved. In Drucker's words 'concern and responsibility for marketing must permeate all areas of the enterprise'.

The chapter which follows outlines the discovery of what the customer wants, how the specifying of the product to fit the customer's need is managed, and how promotion and selling distribute the product to the customer at a profit — which is the basic purpose and mainspring of the enterprise.

THE MARKETING CONCEPT

Background

There are a number of claimants to be the true originators of the marketing concept. General Electric is perhaps the best known for suggesting that the whole relationship of the company with the customer, from product innovation to after-sales service should be managed as a unit. Since the excitement of the 1950s and 60s in the discovery that if one was to be successful in an increasingly choosy market-place then one should recognize that customers' requirements should be the basis of decisions, there have been a number of major developments both in philosophies and practical changes.

First came the recognition that market research is essential to marketing; then that marketing thinking should influence company planning (see Theodore Levitt 'Marketing Myopia', *Harvard Business Review*, July-August 1960). Later came the recognition that planning of the 'marketing mix' was a separate and essential function; currently there is a considerable argument about how best to segment the market, so that one can not only find a worthwhile collection of customers, but can serve them with profit. Currently, perhaps the most acceptable (because of its brevity) definition of the marketing concept is that of the Du Pont company 'marketing is the focusing of strategic planning and resources toward the satisfaction of customer needs, against competitive thrusts, at a profit'.

The Institute of Marketing has adopted the following definition: 'Marketing is the management process responsible for identifying, anticipating and satisfying customer requirements profitably.'

These definitions have implications for the whole company — whether a manufacturing company of goods for consumers or for industry or a provider of services — for strategy and planning and for parts of the organization other than marketing.

Strategic decisions of the company which are influenced by the marketing concept include the choice of markets (groups of relatively homogeneous customers), methods of satisfying customers in the type of product to be manufactured, channels of distribution chosen to put the product or service into the hands of the customer, and levels of profit to be expected from these activities.

Where other parts of the organization are concerned it is the responsibility of the chief marketing executive to alert his colleagues in finance, administration, production or personnel to the need for customer orientation.

There is a further result of the development of the marketing concept within all kinds of companies (and it is now influential in manufacturing companies, distribution and marketing companies, services such as banks and insurance companies and organizations such as consulting engineers and architects) — and that is the differentiation between the concept and the function. The function of marketing of course varies within the organization of which it forms part, and with the purpose and objectives of that organization both in size and importance. Nevertheless two things should remain constant: (a) all the activities relating to the customer should be under the management of a chief marketing executive; and (b) the functions which need to be performed hardly differ except in size and scope between one type of business and another.

The activities can be divided into reconnaissance, planning, operations and control. Figure 7.1 developed by Urwick Management Centre indicates the scope and relationships of the different activities. These are developed further in the remainder of this chapter.

MARKETING ORGANIZATION

The organization of the marketing functions is subject to the same general considerations that influence other parts of the company, namely the jobs which need to be done to achieve corporate (and therefore marketing) objectives, and the different factors influencing the way in which the structure is assembled.

Organization structures imply three things:

1. that results are established; for example, customers need to be visited if the company is to get orders from them;
2. that responsibilities are clear; for example, that sales people, advertising and sales promotion people all have responsibility for the persuasion of customers or the maintenance of the company's 'image';
3. that relationships are understood; for example, that the advertising manager has only an advisory relationship with the manager of a product division.

A number of organization principles have become accepted over the years, which help to provide guidelines in the designing of structures: they can be covered under three headings:

- *Authority*. Clear lines running from top to bottom of the organization, matching responsibility and delegation;
- *Job definition*. For everyone in the structure, showing to whom he or she is accountable, and who are his or her subordinates;

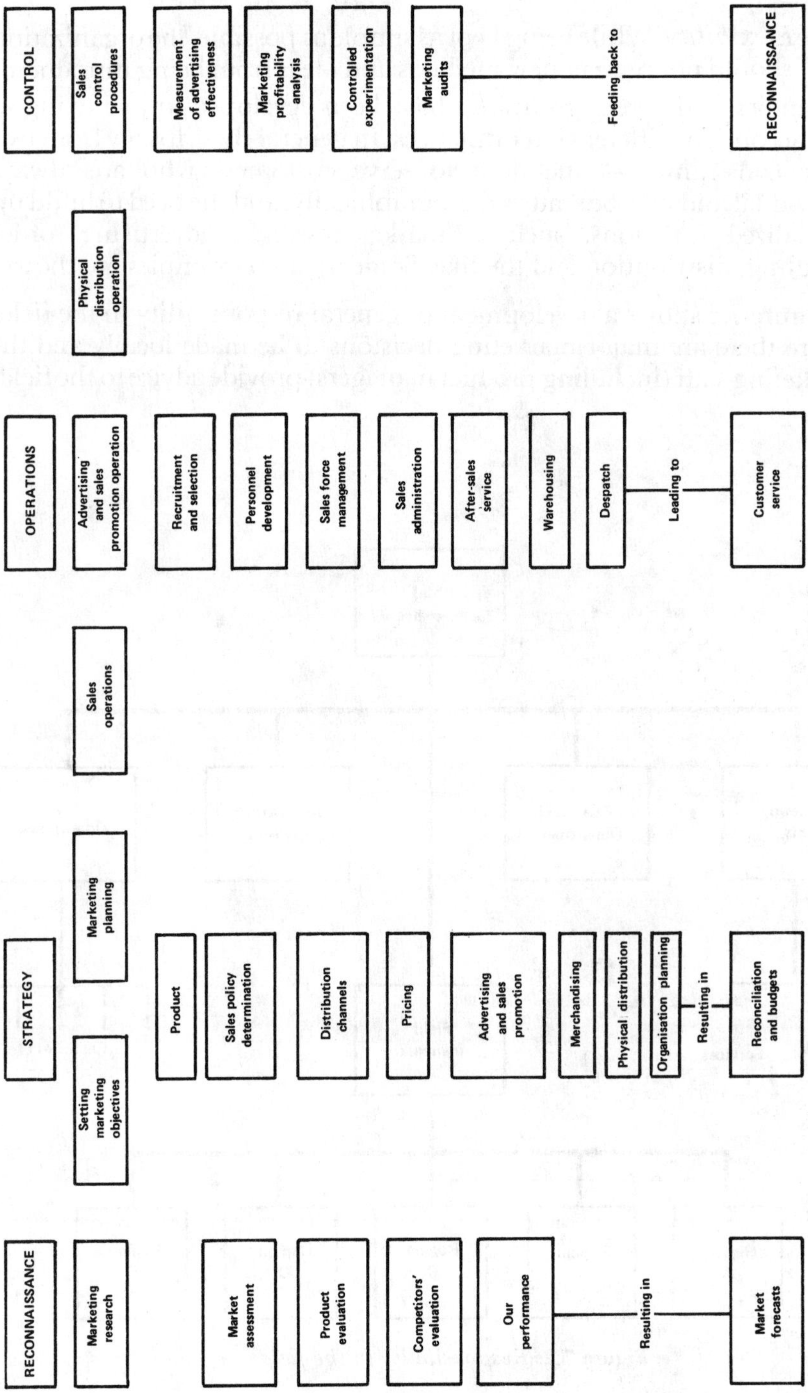

Figure 7.1 *Marketing activities*

- *Flexibility*. While being kept as simple as possible, the organization should not prevent new methods and ideas from being introduced.

A number of different groupings have been developed in marketing to take account of different circumstances. In general these follow from two basic constraints — the need to serve customers who are always individual and may be scattered geographically, and the need to build up specialized functions, such as market research, advertising, order handling, distribution and the like. Some modern examples are shown:

Figure 7.2 shows a development of general responsibility in the field, where there are major marketing decisions to be made locally and the marketing staff (including product managers) provide advice to the field.

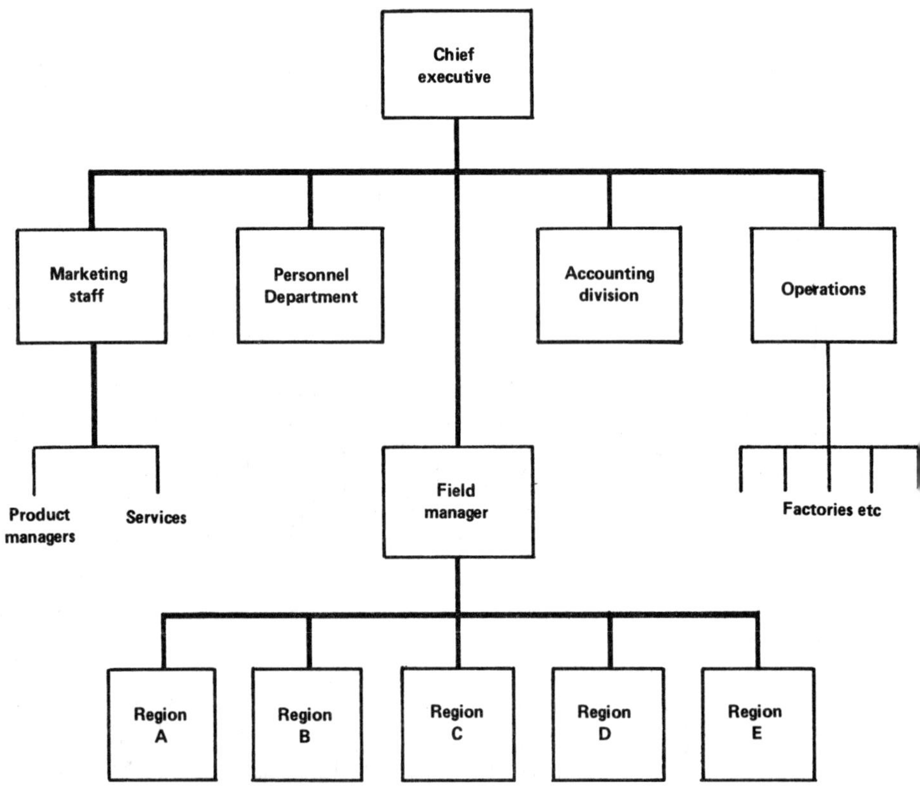

Figure 7.2 *Responsibility in the field*

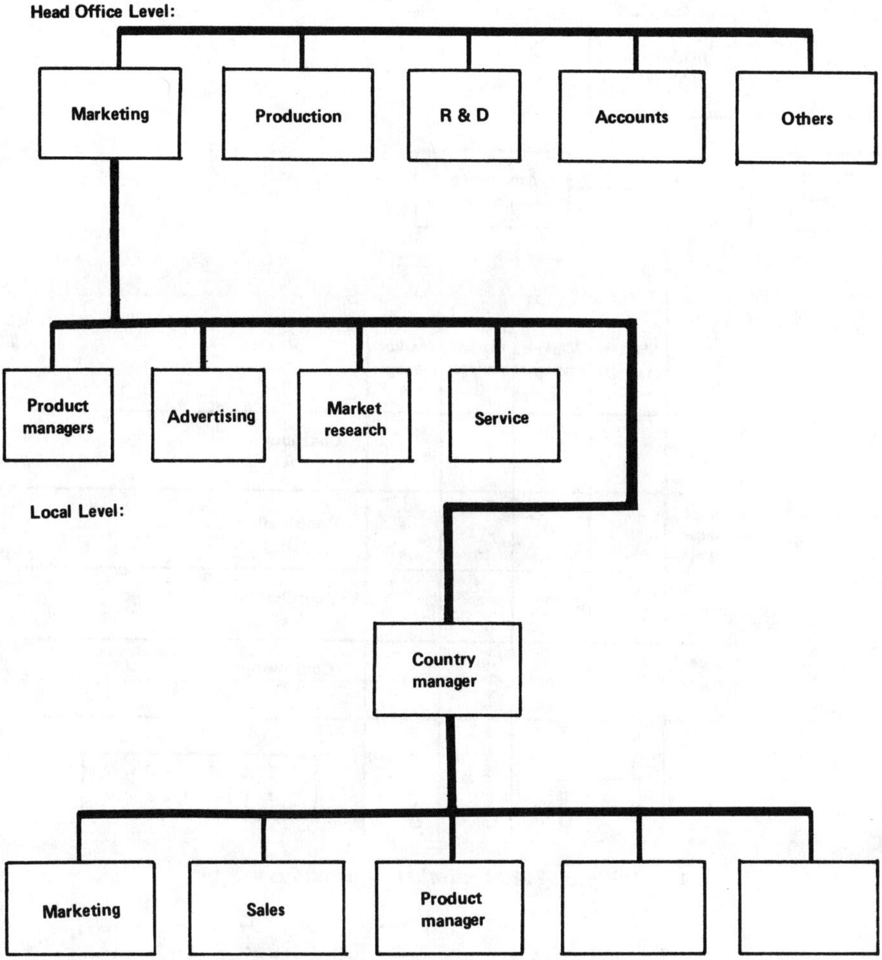

Figure 7.3 *A multinational organization*

Figure 7.3 shows a multinational organization which has staff both centrally and locally, which can produce problems of relationships unless great care is taken.

Figure 7.4 illustrates the situation where there are a number of products or product groups, and a number of different market groupings or geographical areas which have different requirements for these products. The matrix organization shown can work if, at the planning stage, market managers and product managers agree on the course of action needed to maximize the contribution of each.

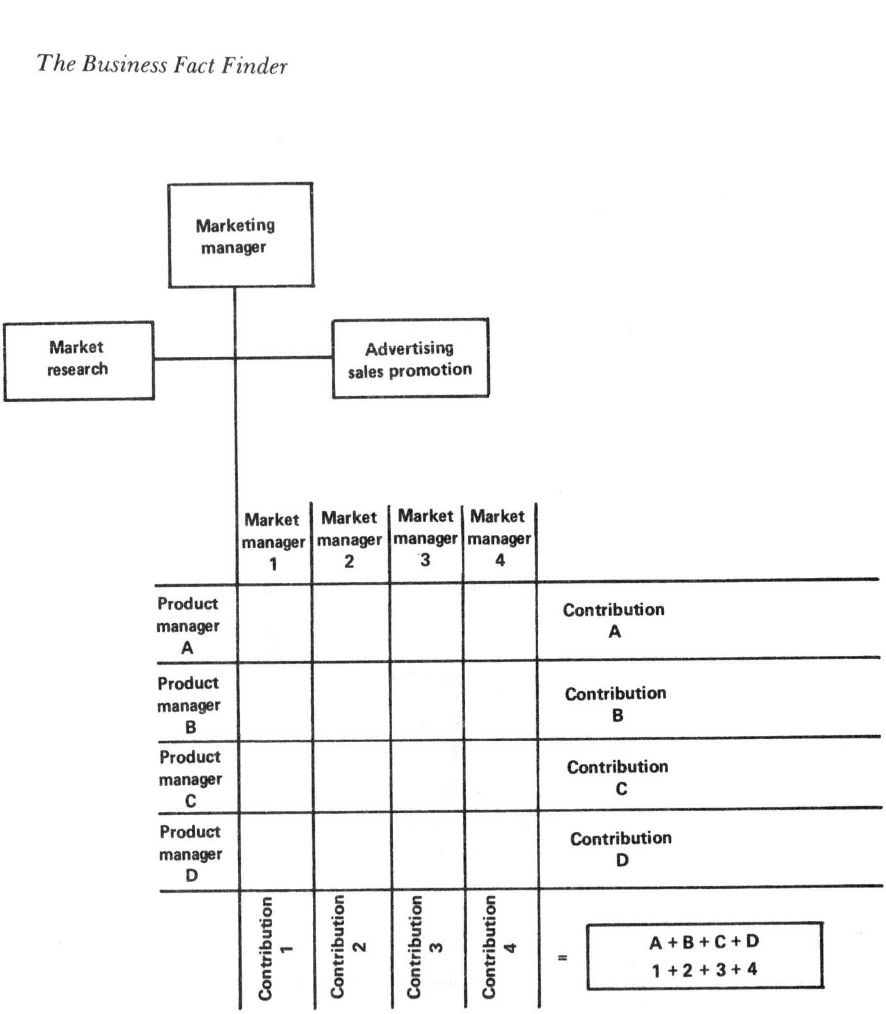

Figure 7.4 *A number of products*

Figure 7.5 demonstrates the most effective 'model' of a customer-orientated organization structure. It shows that marketing services are under a grouping separate from the 'business building' activities of sales, but that together they belong under the total authority of a chief marketing executive. The principle involved here is to separate the 'planning' activities from the 'action', to their mutual benefit.

MARKETING RESEARCH AND MARKETING INFORMATION SYSTEMS

1. The first major task of the chief marketing executive is to know about markets and customers. For that purpose there is a need for

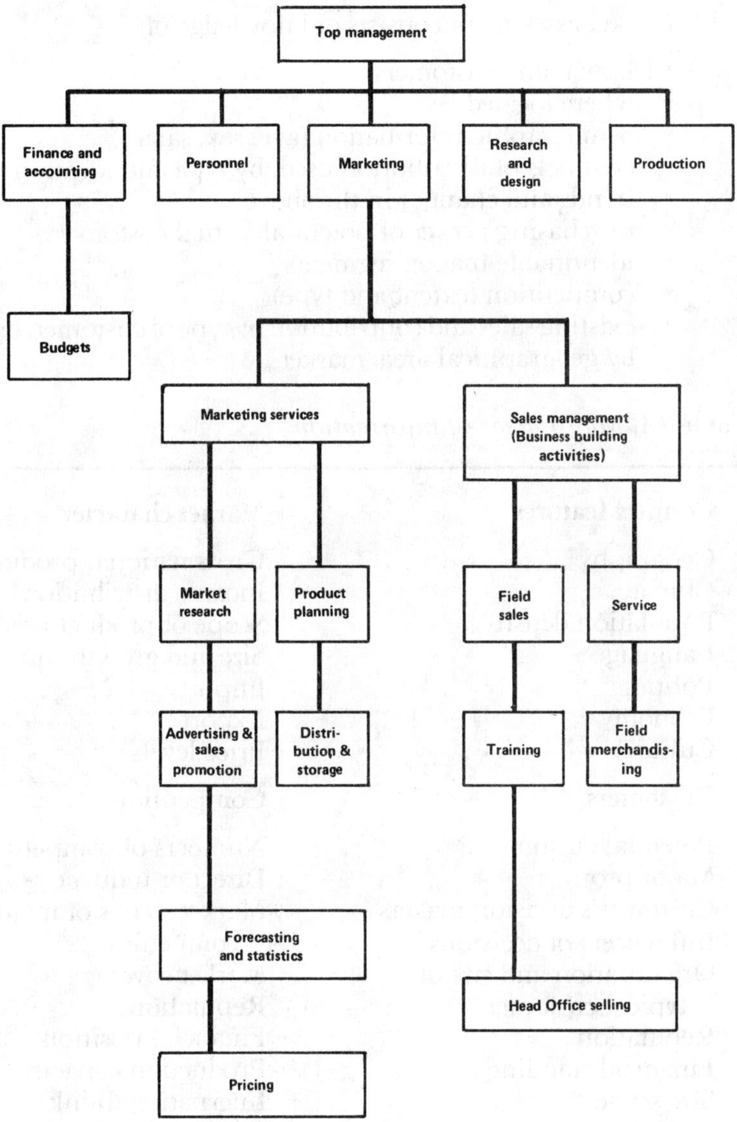

Figure 7.5 *A customer-orientated organization structure*

an intelligence service which can provide that information on a regular and ongoing basis. The kind of information required can be divided into two parts:

- market assessment
- product evaluation

2. Market assessment consists of knowledge of:
   - how many customers
   - where located
   - demographic information (age, sex, salary)
   - channels of distribution used, by type and location
   - trends and changes in the above
   - purchasing power of potential/actual customers
   - identifiable market segments
   - competition (extent and type)
   - existing sales and contribution by type of customer, by channel, by geographical area/market.

Table 7.1. *Major areas of information*

Country features	**Market character**
Geography	Gross national product
Climate	Income distribution
Population density	Scope of product used
Language	Size and growth (units)
Politics	Import
Economy	Export
Culture	Price levels
Customers	**Competition**
Potential customers	Numbers of competitors
Major projects	Direct or indirect
Customer's decision makers	Market shares of major competitors
Influencers of decisions	Market coverage
Organization and size of typical customer	Reputation
Reputation	Financial position
Financial standing	Production capacity
Size scatter*	International links
	Vertical links in the system

*Proportion of large, medium and small users.

3. Product evaluation is concerned with detailed information on:
   - Sales per product line per market
   - Trends in sales, and market share

Table 7.2. *Technical aspects: necessary knowledge when approaching new markets*

Organization and regulation of trade	Importing	Marketing and distribution	Legal	Finance
Trade associations	Licensing	Distribution channels	Patents	Banks
Wholesalers	Duties/quotas	Salesmen and agents	Trade-marks	Finance available
Governmental requirements	Certificates needed	Profit margins	Local legal assistance	Payment terms
	Taxation	Advertising media	Product liability	Credit levels
	Currency	Exhibitions		
	Profit repatriation	Language etc*	Labelling etc	
		Shipping internally		
	Transport costs Customs costs	*Including cultural problems		

- Competitive products and shares
- Prices, and price structures
- Product attributes
- How the product compares with others in terms of features, price, service etc.
- What the image of the product is in the mind of the customer
- Product features and benefits.

4. Before undertaking market research a number of questions should be asked:
   - What will be done with the information obtained?
   - How far will it be reliable?
   - What will it cost?
5. Methods of assessing markets:
   - Desk research from published sources of information
   - Field research through questioning samples of the population

by means of personal interview, postal questionnaire, observation, panel response
- Motivation research, in-depth interviews with small groups.

6. Market coverage and market penetration:

   - Valuable indices on share of channels of distribution (eg A C Nielsen)
   - Indicators of retail stock levels
   - Identification of competitors' physical success ('exposure')
   - Assessment of methods of reaching customers
   - Identifying market segments.

7. Product evaluation covers questions such as:

   Where does the product fit into the consumption system?
   What is the pattern of use?
   What is the pattern of replacement?

   Each product should be evaluated against the following criteria:

   (a) Knowledge of its existence
   (b) Its acceptability as a substitute for competitive products
   (c) Specific requests for the product
   (d) Unwillingness to accept a substitute
   where (d) is the most important and valuable category.

8. Differences between consumer and capital goods markets. In capital goods markets:

   (a) There is normally no large homogeneous group of customers.
   (b) Products usually enter the manufacture or assembly of other products before reaching the ultimate purchaser.
   (c) Products are often bought to specification.
   (d) Purchasing managers are generally more expert than the mass of consumers, and there are fewer of them.

   The anatomy of the capital goods market is less complex but the investigation of the market is more complicated as each customer tends to have different requirements.

9. It is equally important to have an ongoing marketing information system providing data and information regularly to decision makers. This is concerned with the collection of information which originates from both the customer and the other outside sources — and from within the marketing organization itself —

and with how this information is used throughout the organization.

It should:

- Identify sales performance of accounts, products, territories
- Identify new accounts, dormant accounts/customers
- Identify necessary changes in distribution structure or trade channels
- Monitor pricing, discount or allowance structure
- Establish norms of customer service:
    - (a) sales and service calls
    - (b) product availability
    - (c) guarantees
    - (d) minimum order/shipping quantities
    - (e) delivery performance
- Allow fair and profitable territory planning
- Relate promotion and advertising activities to what is required in the market
- Identify product life cycle, need for new products, task for test marketing
- Allow resources to be related to effectiveness of various parts of the marketing mix.

Thus there is a need to:

collect
analyse
present
and store } information to plan, act and control marketing

Internal information

To be collected:

1. Sales:
   per product, per customer, per territory per day/week/month/quarter
   in volume and value
2. Salesmen's productivity and coverage
3. Advertising and promotion cost:
   per product, per territory, per outlet type

4. Deliveries
5. Payments — receivables

External information

Covers four aspects:

- Product research
- Sales research
- Customer research
- Promotional research

Product research

Concerned with:

- Design
- Development
- Testing of new products
- Improvement of existing products
- Forecasting of trends in customer preferences such as styling, functional qualities etc
- Pricing
- Packaging
- Product line/Product mix
- After-sales service
- Comparison with competition

Sales research

Concerned with: selling activities — per outlet or territory, so that results can be compared with published data for the industry, including share of sales and coverage of outlets.

Customer research

Concerned with: investigations into buyer behaviour, at both trade distribution level and eventual user level.

- Preferences for brands, pack sizes in a particular market, attitudinal studies
- Comparison of 'image'
- Rating of critical aspects such as design, packaging, price, delivery,

accounting procedures, sales representation, product range etc as compared with competitors

And particularly important in overseas markets.

Promotional research

Testing and evaluating the effectiveness of the various methods used in promoting a company's products or service.

Pre-testing
Post testing - recall and recognition

'Learning and recall of factual information from mass communication does occur. However, recall and intention measures seem, at best irrelevant to the effect desired, the *changing of attitudes and behaviour.*'

Analysis, presentation and storage are outside the scope of this section.

Publishers of market surveys
AGB Research plc
Economist Publications
Euromonitor Publications
Extel Statistical Services
Financial Times Business Information
Inter Company Comparisons
Market Location
Mintel Information Services
A C Nielsen
The Times Publications
Also, clearing banks, merchant banks and stockbrokers

Industrial marketing, location of key sources
Anbar Publications
The AZ of UK Marketing Information Sources, Euromonitor
Bill of Entry Service, HM Customs & Excise
Building Research Establishment, Department of the Environment
Business Statistics Office
The Central Statistical Office
Current British Directories, CBD Research
Dun & Bradstreet
Her Majesty's Stationery Office
The Industrial Market Research Association
Institute of Marketing

Kompass Sales Information Services
Marketing Surveys Index
The Market Research Society
The Market Research Sourcebook, Headland Press
Monopolies and Mergers Commission
National Economic Development Council
Science Reference Library
Statistics and Market Intelligence Library

CONSUMER BUYING BEHAVIOUR

There is a need for the business to understand how consumers are likely to respond to marketing stimuli. A good deal of research, taken over from academic psychiatrists and psychologists, has gone into the attempt to understand how buyers' minds work. Models have been created in order to assess the rationality or irrationality of behaviour. In general, many conflicting conclusions have been reached, though most researchers would agree that consumers are influenced by cultural, social, personal and psychological characteristics.

Cultural factors include learned values and ways of doing things, which may stem from nationality or tradition, geography or socio-economic grouping. The generally accepted social groupings in the UK, originally set up by the National Readership Survey, are as follows:

Grade	Social Status	Head of Household
A	Upper middle class	Higher managerial, administrative or professional
B	Middle class	Intermediate managerial, administrative or professional
C1	Lower middle class	Supervisory or clerical, and junior managerial, administrative or professional
C2	Skilled working class	Skilled manual workers
D	Working class	Semi-skilled and unskilled manual workers
E	Those at lowest levels of subsistence	State pensioners, widows, casual or lowest grade workers

Social factors include the reference groups to which consumers belong both formally and informally (and perhaps also aspire to), family, both older and younger generation, and the role the consumer plays in each group — wife, daughter, brand manager, local youth leader etc. (Additionally there has recently been developed in the UK a concept called ACORN (Classification of Residential Neighbourhoods) based on the 1981 census information about the areas where people live which splits the whole population into 39 classifications.)

Personal factors include, most obviously, age and life-cycle stage (largely affected by arrival, upbringing and departure of children), occupation and economic circumstances; less obviously in terms of life style, expressed as a pattern of living (more particularly Stanford Research Institute's concept of Values and Life Styles, VALS).

Psychological factors include motivation, perception, learning and beliefs, each of which affects the purchase decision to a greater or lesser degree. Understanding motivations can help both advertisers and salesmen in their efforts to persuade buyers to purchase their product. How people perceive companies and their products or services can help strategic planning. The changes brought about by the learning process need to be monitored by continuous market research. Beliefs and attitudes are the building blocks on which producers can develop their brand and corporate images.

Buyer behaviour patterns (or models) need to be established for products or services so that marketing activities can be aimed at the point where the maximum impact will be made.

INDUSTRIAL BUYING BEHAVIOUR

It is often thought that, because industrial purchasers are professional, they are in some way insulated from normal human feelings and do not behave like consumers. This is evidently not true, but there are additional considerations to be taken into account when trying to influence 'industrial', 'professional', or 'capital goods' purchasers.

In particular, two ideas have been much explored in recent years — the *decision making unit* and the *buying situation.* Indeed, attempts have been made to put them together. The decision making unit (DMU) can consist of any or all of the following:

the user
the decision maker
the influencer
the buyer
the gatekeeper

and their approach to the purchase (of goods or services) will probably be different. At an early stage in any marketing approach it is therefore necessary to identify to whom the message is to be directed (by mail, phone, advertisement, sales call etc) and who the members of the DMU might be. In the case of government or local authority purchase a committee might well contain all of these functions.

The buying situations, which also need to be planned for, are as follows: *straight rebuy*, where the purchaser simply reorders without modification, a routine operation; a *modified rebuy*, where the purchaser desires to change the specification or price or terms, or seeks a second source; and *new purchase*, where a product or system or service is being purchased for the first time and the purchaser is seeking to minimize his risk in a situation where he feels in greatest uncertainty.

The aspects of risk and risk perception are a third area where industrial purchase decisions have been researched. Risks which the buyer tries to avoid are:

- wrong specification
- relationship to production process
- competitive offers
- technology changes
- delivery dates
- price levels
- standards of vendor

and marketing activities of vendors need to be adapted to the reduction of risk and uncertainty.

PRODUCT DEVELOPMENT

The development of products for consumers and products for industrial purchasers takes different paths. For consumers the process is one where, starting from an hypothesis, based on existing products or market research, the product goes through a series of screening processes in the course of development, and finally is test marketed either in a particular location or on a pilot scale. If the result of this effort is successful then the new product is fully launched on to the market.

In the case of the industrial product much more use is made of customer relationships in the development process — in some instances a product may be developed at the request of a customer group — and thus the risk of failure is probably reduced.

What seems to be required if persistent failure is to be avoided is a systematic approach to the development of new products which starts with a situation analysis assessing the need for a new product (eg what problems do customers have? Who is aware of the problems? Where have the needs arisen? Is a totally new product required or a modification of the existing product?) and collecting the appropriate facts. Then the objectives or criteria can be established and a 'screen' devised to separate out good from bad product ideas, which have been produced from the various sources – brainstorming, R & D personnel, search among patents, foreign licences etc.

This would be followed by a process of selection, and the identification of the resultant snags or problems which might arise. Finally a plan should be drawn up showing:

- Steps to be taken
- By whom
- Time limits, deadlines
- Control system to ensure deadlines are met
- What happens if it fails or it is the wrong solution.

Products ideas screening

Opportunity or Constraint	**(Max 20) Weight A**	**Fit with company 0–10**		**(Max 10) Rating B**	**Score A × B**
		Low (0)	*High (10)*		
Selling		New organization needed	Fits existing sales force		
Marketing		New market to be approached	Appeals to existing market		
Competition		Entrenched and strong	Ample unfilled demand		
Company image		Diminishes it	Major boost		
Reputation in same field		None	Dominant		
Product's attributes		Very complicated and difficult	Simple and straightforward		
Packaging		Complete repacking needed	No change needed		
Supply		Unreliable in unsuitable quantities	Regular in right quantities		

Purchase		New field	Knowledge and contacts		
Distribution	More space needed. Differ-ent transport needs	Use present warehouse and transport			
Distribution channels		New channel	Present channels		
Profitability		Below average	High volume and margin		
Personnel		New staff needed	Present staff can cope		

Only with such an approach can new products be developed either for consumer goods markets or industrial markets.

The organizational problems of new product development can also provide headaches. A great deal has been written recently about 'entrepreneurship', developing entrepreneurs inside the business, and about the need for championing new developments from the top of the organization if they are to succeed. In general, it seems to be accepted that one person should be charged with the responsibility for pushing the new product through the system, though he or she needs at every stage assistance and support from all the other major planning and development personnel in, for example, manufacturing, market research, pricing, advertising, distribution etc.

MARKETING PLANNING

The *purpose* of marketing planning is to enable desired objectives to be identified more clearly and the path to them to be more plainly set out.

The objectives of undertaking marketing planning are threefold:

- to assess the position of the enterprise in the various markets in which it finds itself
- to look at the strengths and weaknesses of the enterprise in relation to the markets, both in terms of products and marketing factors
- to establish objectives and goals, to allocate resources to meet these, and to set out a programme of action.

It is part of the attempt to create a more efficient marketing organization that continues to be responsive to the needs of the customers even though the enterprise itself may be becoming increasingly large and complex. There are a number of reasons, therefore, why a detailed written marketing plan must be produced by the marketing organization, namely:

- to discipline thinking
- to develop consultation
- to improve communication upwards and downwards
- to identify key factors and priorities
- to improve the basis of the measurement of performance.

The aim of the *process* of marketing planning is to produce a written marketing plan which is split up so that we can look at it analytically and make improved decisions at each stage.

There is always a temptation to start with the product and work outwards to the market but it has been found that more is gained by first looking at the environment in which the enterprise (or 'business unit') is operating. An examination of the product's strengths and weaknesses can then be undertaken. Only when that first stage is completed can objectives be established and resources allocated.

Stage 1. Market assessment

The first section of the marketing plan consists of:

- A general assessment of the market for the product or service and its likely future
- The market segmentation; namely which segments of the total market have been chosen (and which have been rejected), how they are described and their size and growth expectations
- The major competitors who are currently (or may in the future be) serving our customers' needs; our share of the market and how this compares with the rest of the market structure.

However, in order to acquire *the information* on which to base the first section of the plan, it will be necessary first to establish sources of information which are appropriate to the product/service offered.

Stage 2. Segmenting the market

Establishing the market segments on which to concentrate is one of the most important aspects of the planning process.

- *Geographical segmentation.* The simplest and easiest form of market segmentation is geographical. Assuming the market to be homogeneous, a division is made between different geographical areas - such as region, counties, cities, densities of population, topography etc.
- *Segmentation by type of industry.* In industrial goods selling a second form of segmentation is by industry (or type of industry), using the same product. In services, markets are often segmented by types of people served, divided by age groups, income groups or social groups.
- *Segmentation by market characteristics.* Markets can be segmented by their characteristics. Since these characteristics tend not to change much the markets do not seem to move rapidly and growth is slow. However, segmentation on this basis is good enough for most purposes.

If, however, one is to select and concentrate on market segments which can provide a really satisfactory turnover then it is important to look not only at 'characteristics' but also at 'motivations'. A matrix is constructed to show characteristics on the horixontal axis (X) and motivations on the vertical axis (Y).

Characteristics

MOTIVATIONS ↓

	OEMs *TV*	**OEMs** *Electric*	**Access Makers**	**Distributors**	**Small mfrs**	→
Quality						
Reliability						
Status						
Price						
Regular						
Delivery ↓						

OEMs = Original equipment manufacturers

It is then necessary to try to assess the potential in each of the 'boxes' and to concentrate on 'attacking' or 'serving' or 'finding' the segment described by the matrix. The process thus involves making an hypothesis about the interest of a particular market segment ('box') and then doing more detailed market research to establish the size and growth and potential of that segment.

- *Segmentation by elimination.* Market segmentation can also be made through 'elimination'.

  The technique involves making an 'elimination algorithm', eliminating at each stage of the decision tree those parts of the market which seem less likely to produce sales *at the right profit margin.*

Stage 3. Developing marketing information systems

The first section of the marketing plan requires a data base which can later be turned into a fully fledged marketing information system. This data base will provide the information for the annual Marketing Plan. (See page 174.)

Stage 4. Product range

The information which we seek about the product range can be divided into three sections: strategic, usage and competitive.

1. Strategic information can be derived from answers to a few pertinent questions. For example:
   - Where does the product fit in the user's consumption system?
   - Will the product/service retain its importance for buyers over the next five years?
2. Usage information results from asking 'How exactly does the customer use this product/service?'
3. Competitive information starts by ranking competitors in order of importance, either by image or market share. With such information it is possible to create an analysis matrix.

   Such a matrix demands that each product in each segment is rigorous compared with two or more competitors and conclusions drawn as to what action needs to be taken to bring the product (and its marketing) up to scratch.

Stage 5. Objectives and priorities

The planner is now ready to set objectives and to underline priorities. ('Now that we know where we stand this is what we expect to do about it.')

Objectives can be of two kinds:

1. Specific quantitative objectives such as sales or market share expected, or price change
2. Descriptive marketing objectives such as the intention to enter a new market, to launch a new product/service, or change the distribution system.

Checklist of marketing objectives

1. *Contribution/volume objectives*
   - by product
   - by market segment
   - by customer group
   - by customer/order size
2. *Margin/price change objectives*
   - by change of price
   - by change of channel
   - by change of terms and conditions
3. *Product objectives*
   - new products to be launched
   - range size (and changes)
   - packaging
   - level of service (including stock levels, delivery speed)
   - products phased out
4. *Sales force objectives*
   - coverage
   - new customers
   - customer size
   - order size
   - recruitment and training
5. *Advertising and promotion objectives*
   - awareness levels
   - image objectives
   - displays demonstration
   - leaflets, sharecards etc
   - exhibitions — (gimmicks?)
6. *Distribution channel objectives*
   - development of a new channel
   - adding/cutting distributors
   - improvement of distributors' performance

7. *Supporting staff objectives*
    - market intelligence
    - campaign to be set up
    - sales office service
    - complaint handling
    - after sales service levels

8. *Cost levels objectives*
    - absolute levels
    - variances accepted
    - cost centre controls

They will naturally vary from one type of business to another but the checklist above covers the objectives which might be established.

The setting of objectives should not be considered as immutable. They must be subject to the agreement by those responsible for reaching them that they are achievable. If the aim of marketing is *'to maximize the number of favourable buying decisions'* then at this point there is a need to examine the effectiveness of each of the factors under the control of the enterprise in bringing about buying decisions and to rate them:

- against each other
- in terms of budgets
- for each different market segment.

Before establishing a firm programme it is necessary to look again at each factor and ask what weight it carries in relation to the buyer's decision making.

All the planning activity outlined in the above sections should be contained in a series of action plans which demonstrate:

- Resources to be used
- Programme/timetable/checkpoints
- Controls, statistics etc.

The plan should be published to all the 'action takers' who are affected by the marketing plan.

Marketing plan

The final written plan should have the following chapters:

1 Introduction and Summary
2 General Assessment of the Market
  - past history
  - present position
  - future expectations

3 Market Segmentation
  - size and growth
  - share, competitors
  - problems and opportunities
4 Product Range
  - current range
  - strengths and weaknesses analysis
  - new product to be launched
5 Objectives and Priorities
6 Marketing Mix
7 Programme for the Year
8 Budgets
9 Control and Review Systems

PRICING

An element in the 'marketing mix' which varies in importance from industry to industry. A major distinction is between the theory of pricing and the day-to-day practice, and between the pricing of new products and the pricing of existing products.

Before establishing the price of any particular product the company needs to decide its pricing strategy and therefore needs to consider four main factors:

- Its marketing objectives
- Likely consumer response to price changes
- Cost considerations
- Competition.

Marketing objectives cover elements such as profit, sales volume and growth rate, and result from decisions over the type of business and the market segments the firm should be exploiting, which in turn determine whether it is desirable to 'lead' or to 'follow' in pricing. Consumer response to price changes is unlikely to follow conventional economic theory and needs to be checked with market research. Costs must be covered in the long run. Arguments about marginal or absorption costing are beyond the scope of this section, but marketing executives should understand the relevance of these concepts to pricing, and recognize that the relevance of different cost concepts can change. The competitive structure of the market has a bearing on whether prices can be influenced to restrict entry or not, and whether pricing is aimed at fighting competitors or making profit.

There are a number of practical approaches to pricing (for further discussion see *Pricing: Principles and Practice* by André Gabor) which can be considered under three headings:

- *Cost-oriented pricing,* which would include pricing based on adding a mark-up percentage to the cost, or trying to price products to achieve a specific rate of return on assets. This is the most widely used approach.
- *Competition-oriented pricing,* which includes pricing at the 'going-rate', pricing with discounts or premiums, pricing following the lead of the largest company, and competitive bidding. This is an area where firms try to recognize market influences while still attempting to control costs and margins.
- *Customer-oriented pricing,* focusing on the sensitivity of demand to price changes, expected pricing, and the use of promotional or psychological pricing.

Each of these aspects of pricing can be appropriate in given market or competitive conditions. Thus it is essential to analyse the market situation carefully before deciding on a pricing strategy. It is additionally important for both buyers and sellers to remember that the 'price' is not the sole reason for buying or rejecting a product!

DISTRIBUTION CHANNELS

The means of getting the product from the manufacturer to the consumer have usually been underestimated. However, in recent years the main aspect has been the considerable changes which have occurred, particularly in the area of fast moving consumer goods.

- Garages are now selling confectionery and soft drinks alongside their more conventional offerings for the motorist
- Newsagents are selling pop records, and a greatly expanded range of cards
- Chemists are selling wine; Boots have indeed become a mini supermarket in many places
- Food supermarkets have expanded into furniture and DIY.

A major change which is only slowly being recognized and exploited is the development of the 'one stop shopping' hypermarket, and the parallel and perhaps reactive development of the 'convenience store' ('8 till late'). Further developments are seen in the specialist fashion shop catering for a particular and very specific market segment — in many cases creating a niche for itself.

If a firm decides to sell through retail outlets it has a choice (much too wide for analysis here) of the following:

independent stores
voluntary groups
multiple stores

chains
department stores
cooperatives
supermarkets
cash and carry
discount stores
mobile retailers
van salesmen
door-to-door selling
garages and filling stations
franchising (McDonalds, Prontaprint etc)
party plan selling (Tupperware, jewellery, lingerie)
mail order (catalogues)
direct response (magazines and newspapers).

The selection of which to use must depend on three considerations:

- The type of consumer aimed at
- The status of the outlet
- The level of margin expected

(eg a product aimed at a middle level consumer should not be found in a lower level outlet - the consumer simply will not purchase items which have a particular status level in the 'wrong' outlet). Thus careful research is needed before decisions are taken — both at home and overseas.

Industrial channels of distribution tend to be simpler to operate: choice of distributor is a purely economic decision depending on whether the distributor has contact with the potential users. The function of the wholesaler in such markets — breaking bulk and distributing to smaller outlets — is usually long established and well understood. However, it is worth considering always how to work with distributors so as to improve their sales activity, how to improve the quality of sales agents, how to increase the effectiveness of service given by importers/distributors, and when once chosen continuous monitoring of their performance is vital.

Selling to distributors or resellers also requires the principal to think through what he has to offer. Selling to distributors of agricultural chemicals or foodstuffs needs careful consideration of the *benefits to the reseller* of the product or service, not simply a parroting of the benefits to the user.

PROMOTION

The different factors of promotion will be used in different ways and to different degrees. Three important factors are selling (and sales management), advertising and public relations.

Selling

Successful selling requires three things:

1. An understanding of the buying process
2. A satisfactory collection of qualities — and an understanding of oneself
3. A sales technique or framework.

If we look first at the buying process, it can be described mechanically, by outlining the 'inputs' (of price, quality, availability, style etc), the channels by which these inputs reach the buyer (eg advertising, observation, family acquaintances or salesmen) and the 'outputs' which appear (choice of product, brand, quantity, frequency, and so on).

Or we can see it more simply as the process by which a need or requirement is turned, via information gathering and assessment, into a decision and an order.

What happens in the buyer's mind is influenced by two major psychological aspects – the characteristics of the buyer and his particular emotions or drives.

We are, unfortunately, not entirely and always rational human beings; our behaviour is dictated both by the sort of people we are (characteristics) and by the kinds of 'drives' (emotions). Our reasoning ability is often used to discover an appropriate means of satisfying these emotions. But not all drives are to do with personal satisfaction.

Selling is a process of 'social interaction' and the salesman's effectiveness is also influenced by the buyer's perceptions of the salesman's behaviour as well as by his personal and social needs.

If the buyer is impressed by the salesman, then we need certain qualities in a man or woman selected for such a task. One must ask what we look for in selection, performance appraisal and promotion in the way of qualities, eg empathy, perseverance, confidence, verbal communication ability, motivation, professionalism etc.

The sales process itself really becomes a needs-satisfaction process, which must cover the following phases:

- Preparation, identifying needs or requirements
- Presenting the product in terms of its benefits
- Answering the possible objections raised by the customer, getting a decision and analysing the result.

Each stage needs to be treated separately, though in practice they overlap. Particular importance is to be attached to the preparation and planning stage, establishing what is known about the buyer and what result is expected.

The second stage covers the approach, gaining the potential customer's interest and investigating his requirements, business and personal. The third covers how the offer is to be presented to meet those requirements — the whole area of benefits and their 'factual support'.

Objections may be raised at any point in the interview and the sales person must possess not only the answer to them, but also an ability to come at the real obstacle and to 'sell through' the objection.

There are a number of techniques which can be used to make easier the process of getting a decision.

In analysing successes and failures the foundations for improving performance are laid.

Sales management

The changes which have affected the sales force:

- Fewer customers
- More negotiation at high level
- Increased telephone selling
- More brand selling and private label competition
- Competition from imported goods

have meant that the role of the sales manager in improving sales force performance has also had to emphasize different things. He has to concentrate on:

- establishing clear objectives
- discussing performance standards with sales people
- helping in the planning of journeys and work patterns
- exercising control, through review and appraisal meetings
- training and development of sales staff.

His role in the company management is to provide market information and to assess the 'contribution' to be expected from each customer (group). His task is to agree a sales action plan with the chief marketing executive covering:

- Market position
- Segments chosen and objectives per segment
- Resource allocation
- Sales tasks
- Controls to be used.

Advertising

As a marketing tool advertising should be used where it is more efficient than personal selling (in terms of cost per customer reached). Millions of words are produced annually both by and about advertising, so a full description is out of place here. The marketing man needs to know:

- What it can do
- How it does it
- How to establish advertising budgets
- Where advertising agencies fit.

1. Advertising can inform, increase awareness, change perceptions (of a company or a product), help readers to develop favourable views, and sometimes sell (in, for example, classified ads and 'direct response' advertising in glossy magazines). Measurement of results is best achieved if the objectives of the advertising are clearly defined in advance (ie 'increasing awareness among a defined group by 5 per cent').
2. It accomplishes its objective by placing, where the potential customers are likely to see or read it, information about the product/service which will interest, intrigue or inspire them — by describing the benefits of owning or using the product/service. In this context the advertiser develops a creative approach to using colour, sound, words or pictures in the service of his message.
3. Establishing advertising budgets is not a question of adding 10 per cent to last year's, but of starting from the objectives or goals of the advertising and working out carefully how much it will cost, relating that to the expected sales and reckoning that for the most part (in spite of what accountants may say) advertising expenditure is an investment rather than a cost.
4. Advertising agencies exist to provide professional help and advice in the design, creation and placing of ads. They are (still) generally paid by means of a commission from the medium where the ad is placed (eg 15 per cent from newspapers) — but more and more they are becoming more like consultants and being paid a fee for the advice given and the work done. The Advertising Association and Institute of Practitioners in Advertising can provide further help in selection.

Public relations

The responsibility of PR within a company is for maintaining good relations between an organization and its various publics, such as customers, shareholders, employees, local community and trades unions. Its concern is to develop and maintain the company's image — its 'public face' — and its growth in recent years has been at a phenomenal 30 per cent a year. It has naturally attracted a whole range of PR consultants who can provide specialist advice for companies who do not have the expertise to deal with the various media for their trade.

For good public relations, whether done in-house or through a consultant, there is a need to set clear objectives which march with, but do not overlap advertising objectives, and which can be accomplished using PR means:

- Company publications
- Editorial publicity (news stories in suitable papers and magazines)
- Corporate advertising
- Exhibitions, shop windows
- Staff training (particularly in service companies).

INTERNATIONAL MARKETING

A number of different approaches to international marketing are practised and researched today. The major concern of international marketing is that markets are not simply dumping grounds for surplus goods, nor are they areas where 'we can export our products'. Indeed 'global marketing' is a currently fashionable discussion subject, as people try to decide whether the same product can be sold in the same way in all markets.

The three approaches are:

- identifying relevant similarities in markets
- limits to standardization
- market portfolio analysis.

J Leontiades suggests that there are five categories of international market where the *relevant similarities* are such that the marketing strategy towards each category can be clearly established. They are:

- Pre-market — primitive market for sophisticated goods
- Less developed markets — low volume and slow growth
- Take-off markets — rapid growth but not yet mass markets
- Early mass markets — high volume
- Mature mass markets — highest level of development.

This analysis seems most suitable for consumer and consumer durable products.

The *limits to standardization* approach insists, like Leontiades, on the enormous production and other cost benefits of standardization but demonstrates that four major factors must limit it. These are:

- *Market characteristics,* such as physical environment, economic and social development and culture
- *Industry conditions* — the position of the product in its life cycle, and the strength of competition
- *Marketing systems* — the strength of wholesaling, use of agents and distributors, direct mail etc
- *Legal standards,* in such matters as trademark laws, sales restrictions, patents, tariffs and taxes.

These factors must be taken into account when exporting to any market is considered.

The third approach, *market portfolio analysis,* assesses markets in terms of rates of growth and market share in the same way as the better known product portfolio analysis, and not only positions the firm's products in the market but also establishes where competitors may be. This method of analysis can prove helpful in deciding where and whether to invest further in international markets.

Finally, the process of customer satisfaction at a profit to the provider is 'marketing', and this definition therefore applies to customers outside national boundaries. No one considers him or herself an 'export customer': everyone lives in a market surrounded by its culture and values. Thus 'marketing' is universally applicable.

CONTROLLING MARKETING EFFECTIVENESS

1. The costs of marketing are increasing rapidly and creating a demand for more effective means of measuring the contribution which marketing activities make to company profit. Studies in the USA have indicated that over 50 per cent of consumers' expenditure on products is absorbed by marketing costs. In the individual company total marketing costs frequently exceed 50 per cent of annual expenditure but, while capital expenditure and production costs are subject to increasingly sophisticated forms of assessment and control, measurement of the contribution made to profitability by marketing activities is often haphazard and incomplete.
2. In marketing there is a frequent tendency to limit the function of control to the identification of whether activities are being performed according to plan. Such evaluation is appropriate in the short term when resources have been committed to an activity, but all too frequently managers in marketing neglect the need for longer-term controls which measure the real contribution which the activity produces.

In the longer run, the emphasis of evaluation should be directed to:

- Achieving the optimum advertising budget
- Balancing the contribution of £10,000 spent on market research against, say, the return from £10,000 spent on new machinery
- That distribution of sales effort between the regions which maximizes profit.

3. Given the necessity to base decisions on marketing expenditure on evaluation of what the different marketing activities contribute to the business, the first task is to define those activities and costs which constitute 'marketing'. Evaluations limited to only a part of marketing can result in sub-optimization in the deployment of company resources. A comprehensive study of alternatives, on the other hand, might include assessment of the anticipated profitability from such alternatives as:

   - Extending a product's range with two additional sizes or hiring two more salesmen to sell the present range
   - Selling the product in its present form to a new geographical market compared to the probable pay-off from spending the money on research and development of a better product
   - £100,000 spent on a pack which increases the product's appeal to distributors against the same amount spent on additional consumer advertising
   - Extending credit terms versus a price reduction.

Only appreciation of the full range of marketing options, including such examples as these, will lead to really effective marketing control. Thus, control of marketing effectiveness should include comparative assessment of the contribution of *all* marketing activities including each item of expenditure involved in:

(a) The development of a competitive and profitable product range.
(b) Persuading intermediate and final customers to buy, including sales force operations, advertising and promotion and merchandising.
(c) Servicing customers to maintain their favourable attitude, including sales office activities, after-sales service etc.
(d) Physical distribution, including inventory service and product availability.

4. More could be done to assess the profit contribution of marketing

by the more intelligent use of marketing profitability analysis to determine the costs of performing specific marketing activities. The costs incurred after production are often lumped together as overheads, to be allocated to different products in an arbitrary manner. Natural classification of expenditure totals should be subdivided into functional cost groups, so that marketing costs can be assigned and effective management decisions made. A simple example of how expenditure can be attributed to functional activities and to products is given in the following table. The process illustrated is one of taking the natural accounts expense classifications, defining the method by which these could be identified with functional cost groups and then determining the unit on which functional costs should be assigned to particular products.

Natural expense classification	**Means by which natural expense items are attributed to functional activities**	**Basis of assignment to products**
Salesmen's salary and expenses	Work study of the selling job	Time devoted to selling individual products
Advertising	For specific product advertisements — direct assignment. For umbrella advertisements — management definition of the degree by which different products benefit from this general support	
Warehousing wages and expenses	Work study of the operation	Unit of handling or of weight
Office expenses	Work study (O & M)	Order, or invoice, or invoice line
Salary and expenses of servicemen	Study of the demands on servicemen's time made by different products	Time devoted to individual products
Transportation	Study of weight allocation of transport to different products	Weight of despatches

5. *Methods of measuring marketing effectiveness*

(a) Basic requirements

Marketing profitability analysis to establish the current marketing costs and profitability of individual products, regions, customer groups, distribution channels, order sizes etc is one of the basic requirements of effective marketing control. The other basic requirement is the definition of specific objectives for each marketing activity and the spelling out of clear standards of performance for each manager in the function. These objectives should, wherever possible, be set in terms of output (achievement) against input (resources) and these output/input relationships should reflect a considered corporate view of the optimum use of company resources. Thus, for example, objectives should be expressed not just in terms of required sales volume, but also as expressions of the required added profitability resulting from the marketing activities. Similarly, advertising objectives should be expressed in terms of defined communication goals against defined costs.

Marketing objectives expressed in these terms permit *prior* calculation of the estimated costs of their achievement. These estimates of input to defined output can be compared to alternative uses of the company's resources.

(b) Budgets

Sales volume, marketing cost and profitability budgets are instruments for the control of marketing performance against current expectations of marketing efficiency. They are useful management tools, but do not necessarily help in assessing whether current expectations could be improved.

(c) Sales control

A framework of sales controls for the management of sales operations is essential. Documentary controls linked to active personal sales supervision are marketing controls over sales force performance.

(d) Store audits

Store audits (eg Nielsen, Attwood etc) are methods of control over marketing effectiveness in selling into and selling out of the distributors. The increase in industrial goods sold through distributors will demand similar distributor audits in engineering merchants, factors etc.

(e) Measurement of advertising and promotion effectiveness

The measurement of advertising and promotional effectiveness against defined communication goals has reached the stage of practical use both in the USA and the UK. Description of the methods is beyond the scope of this chapter, but as advertising and promotion increase their share of the marketing mix control of their effectiveness can no longer be neglected.

(f) Buyer surveys

Buyer surveys are controls over the effectiveness of promotional strategies and over the effectiveness of the salesmen and publicity they employ. Buyer surveys of reactions and attitudes can also be used as marketing controls over the effectiveness of strategies and resources employed in product development, pricing, distribution channels, physical distribution etc.

(g) Marketing audits

Recent years have seen the development of the marketing audit as a control of marketing effectiveness and efficiency. A marketing audit is a systematic examination of all or a part of a company's marketing activity, covering objectives, strategies, implementation, organization and 'pay-off'. The audit has as its purpose to:

- Determine more clearly what is being done
- Appraise the effectiveness and efficiency of the activities, and
- Make recommendations on how to improve marketing's profitability.

Where marketing audits are carried out they can be executed by managers within the function, specialist control departments or outside consultants. The requirement is analytical ability, marketing expertise and objectivity.

Marketing will always remain an area of business where judgement and creativity play a major part. However, the development of effectiveness in marketing is responsive to the same logical approach as the development of effectiveness in other areas of the business.

8

PHYSICAL DISTRIBUTION MANAGEMENT

A G Slater

INTRODUCTION

Physical distribution management is the planning and control of the resources employed in the storage and movement of goods from the point of generation to the user. The physical distribution process may be specific to both the product and the company. Thus the storage and movement of a raw material (for example, timber) will be very different from the storage and movement of a processed consumer product (for example, meat pies).

However, in all cases the objectives of physical distribution management will be to:

- provide the right product
- at the right time
- in the right quantity
- in the right condition; and
- at the right cost.

Each of these objectives may be clearly defined in terms of meeting a customer's order, and a combination of these is termed the 'customer service level' and may include:

- delivery of the product required
- on or before the day required
- in the correct quantity
- properly identified and in a condition fit for use; and
- at an acceptable cost to the customer and supplier.

The real measure of success in physical distribution is determined by the number of occasions out of the total that the defined objectives are achieved.

In order to attain these objectives several essential stages may have to be undertaken including: factory storage (primary storage), factory to warehouse movement (primary movement/trunking), warehouse storage (secondary storage), and warehouse to retail store movement (secondary movement/customer delivery).

In the majority of physical distribution systems a large number of stages are involved, and each stage incurs a number of separate but defined costs. The distribution management task is to identify, control, and where possible reduce these costs, while maintaining an acceptable level of customer service.

This task is not easy: first, because of the complexity of a system which includes many detailed individual operations; second, because decisions cannot be taken in isolation (for example, a decision to increase the size of the outer packaging of a product may increase both the storage and movement costs); and third, because any decision which affects costs automatically affects profitability of the company if the distribution costs are not charged to the customer on an as incurred basis.

DISTRIBUTION STRATEGY

The physical distribution process can be defined as the process and identification of the elements involved in the formulation of a distribution strategy.

If, for example, consideration is given to the formulation of a distribution strategy for an established consumer product manufacturer then the basic knowledge that would be required to define the bounds of a physical distribution system would be:

- an established produce range
- established production facilities
- a definition of market location and size
- a definition of the service level required by the customer.

In a complex situation products, markets, locations, and customer types may have to be categorised into a number of groups in order to provide reasonable definitions upon which to build a distribution strategy.

The outline distribution system is built up by identifying: first, the number of separate stages through which the products will have to pass, and second, the number of products and the nature of the handling and transportation methods to be adopted at each stage in the process.

The simplest physical distribution system is direct from the manufacturer to the user; for example, mail order of textiles direct from the manufacturing point to the customer by parcel post. This system has many advantages, particularly:

- Both orders and stock may be consolidated at a single supply point thus providing maximum flexibility to meet customer demand while minimising stock holding costs
- Orders may even be consolidated until an economic production quantity is obtained before production begins thus eliminating stockholding
- The use of parcel post as direct transport from the factory to the customer minimises packaging, handling and transport charges; and
- The direct interface between the customer and the factory is inexpensive to manage (in terms of order processing and credit control) and provides valuable information about the marketplace.

Unfortunately, not all manufacturers may supply their product direct from the factory to the customer, either because their product is physically or economically unsuitable, or because the volume moving from one or more sources of supply is vast and economies of scale may be gained by consolidating product into warehouses and retail stores.

In these circumstances a manufacturer may use one or more of a number of different intermediate stages (see Figure 8.1). The combination of a number of individual stages is known as a supply chain. Each stage has an independent role to play in the physical distribution process, and although some of the elements undertake similar processes, the main difference is which organisation in the supply chain owns the goods and controls the system.

The function of the main stages in a supply chain are:

Manufacturer's central warehouse

May be co-located with the production site, or linked by an intra-factory transport system (often called a trunking system) because the operation is large volumes on fixed routes. The function of the central warehouse is to act as a buffer between the economic production quantities and the smaller quantities demanded by the market. Central warehouses are also used as the single reception, quality control and break bulk point when product is imported. The central warehouse may deliver large orders direct to customers to avoid duplication of handling costs.

Manufacturer's regional warehouse

Will be located to serve customers in a particular geographical region (in exceptional cases a limited product range to particular customers). The regional warehouse will be supplied by a transport system either from the factory or from a central warehouse (generally known as a primary transport operation). The regional warehouse will undertake local deliveries to customers through what is called the secondary transport operation. Some customers may choose to collect from the regional warehouse.

Retailer's central warehouse

Has the function of acting as a buffer between the economic order quantity (bulk) and the potential order quantities at the individual retail stores. Retailer's central warehouse deliveries are either direct from the factory (particularly in the case of 'own label' or 'brand name' goods), or from the manufacturer's central warehouse. The retailer's central warehouse may have a secondary transport system to deliver to the stores.

Retailer's regional warehouse

Also has the function of acting as buffer between the economic order

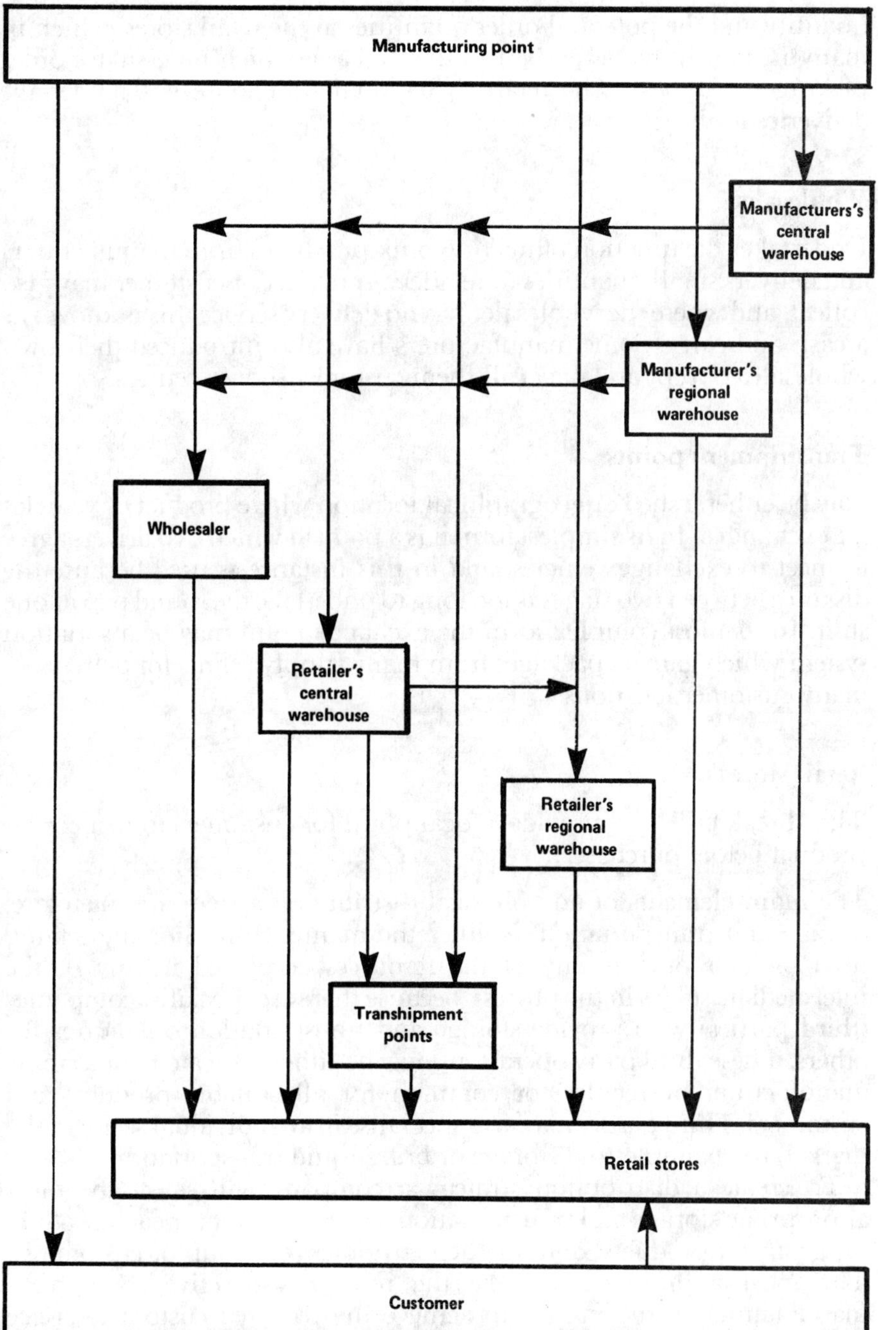

Figure 8.1 *Alternative physical distribution systems*

quantity and the potential order quantities at the retail stores, which in many instances may even be less than a case (which necessitates order picking in singles). The retailer's regional warehouse will undertake deliveries to the stores.

Wholesaler

Undertakes the function of making bulk purchases from manufacturers and delivers small quantities to retailers. A retailer or customer may also collect, and where the wholesaler has no delivery service this is known as a cash and carry. Some manufacturers have also introduced their own wholesale concept and may call them customer service centres.

Transhipment points

May be either a shed or geographical location where product or vehicles are exchanged. In its simplest form it is a point at which two drivers agree to meet to exchange vehicles, and in this instance is used because the distance between two stages is too long to undertake the round trip in one shift. In its most complex form the exchange point may be a sortation system which gathers packages from many supply points for delivery to many customer locations.

Retail stores

They break bulk and provide a focal point for customers to inspect the product before purchase.

The main elements of any physical distribution system are, therefore, storage and transportation. Neither the manufacturer nor the retailer need own or operate any of the resources employed in any of the intermediate stages in the process, because there are specialist companies (third parties) who provide storage and transportation operations for others. These third party operations may be either dedicated (for a single manufacturer or retailer) or common for all suitable products and customers. Third parties may also specialise in an individual sector of the market, for example cold storage or bulk liquid transportation.

To create a distribution strategy a company will select the most appropriate storage and transportation stages to adopt for each product (or group of products) and for each customer (or group of customers). The most appropriate will be the most cost-effective route from manufacturer to the market to achieve the required customer service levels.

The selection of a distribution strategy should be reviewed every two or three years because products change, markets change, and the operating environment changes. For example, ten years ago a manufacturer would need no fewer than ten regional warehouses to provide a three-day service level from order to receipt to 95 per cent of the UK cities and towns; but now, with improved motorways and new vehicles, the same manufacturer could obtain the same service level with only six warehouses.

STORAGE AND HANDLING

At some stages in the physical distribution process the product will be stationary, and it will then incur storage costs. In order to place product in storage and obtain product from storage, handling costs will be incurred. The storage location is usually a warehouse, which may have the following functional areas:

- *Inwards goods area,* where goods are received, counted and checked for physical damage; they may also be checked for quality but this is often a separate function. The goods may be placed upon a pallet or into a special container.
- *Bulk storage area,* where the majority of the product is stored and from which full pallets may be taken when the product is required for an order; this is known as bulk picking.
- *Order picking area,* where bulk pallets are manually broken down into requirements for individual customer orders.
- *Order assembly area,* where customers' orders are assembled or delivery vehicle loads consolidated (when the vehicle driver picks the customer's order at the point of delivery).
- *Despatch area,* where orders are checked and loaded on to delivery vehicles.
- *Maintenance area,* where mechanical handling equipment (fork-lift trucks) are held (and electric ones charged) when not in use.

In addition some warehouses may have some specific tasks to perform, for example, re-packaging or initial packaging of product, and in these cases specific areas will be allocated to these tasks.

The basic routine tasks of a warehouse, however, normally include the following:

- Identification, unloading, quantity checking and recording of the receipt of goods.
- Consolidation of receipts into a bulk load suitable for movement and storage (for example, pallet, cage or tray).

- Movement and recording of the consolidated load into the bulk store.
- Identification, selection and recording of the movement of a consolidated load from the bulk store to the order picking area.
- Identification, selection, recording and movement of customers' orders from the order picking location.
- Checking the number and physical condition of product in both the bulk and order picking areas.
- Preparation of individual customer orders into vehicle loads, checking and assistance with loading.
- Unloading product which is returned, checking, recording and returning to the order picking area if appropriate.

The above list clearly identifies the main tasks as identification, checking, recording, movement, selection and consolidation; these tasks imply both physical strength and numeracy as the main requirements of warehouse staff.

In order to obtain both maximum use of the cubic capacity of the warehouse and maximum productivity from the staff, a number of storage and material handling methods and techniques may be adopted.

The storage techniques may include:

Block stacking

Where flat-top cases are stacked on flat-bottomed pallets, and these may then be stacked directly on top of one another.

The advantages are: a good use of square footage, flexibility of layout, low equipment costs and rapid throughput.

The disadvantages include: height of stacking limited by weight and strength of loads, most pallets are not directly accessible, and there is a limited risk of damage. Thus only flat topped, uncrushable and stable product is suitable.

Post pallets

Pallets with both a base and sides. These stack securely on top of each other without transferring any of the load to the product.

The advantages, in addition to those of block stacking, are that they are suitable for crushable and unstable product.

The disadvantages are that they are more expensive than flat pallets, take up more space (particularly when empty), and that if block stacked most post pallets are not directly accessible. However, the box and cage versions of post pallets give simple storage and transportation of small loose items, unstable loads and irregularly shaped goods.

Pallet converters

Supports fitted to flat pallets enabling them to be stacked without the goods bearing the load.

They have similar advantages to post pallets and in addition may be collapsed to occupy a limited space when empty.

The disadvantages are that they are more expensive than flat pallets, and again, if used in a block stack the majority of the pallets will be inaccessible.

Overhead storage area (mezzanine floors)

The construction of a modular steel-structured second-floor level within a warehouse.

The advantages are: the use of the headroom for increased storage space, no additional rates, and an extremely useful way of segregating valuable items.

The major disadvantage is that pallet handling is restricted. Mezzanine floors require detailed planning which should include consultation with the local authority planning department, the fire officer and the insurance companies responsible for both the building and the contents.

Adjustable pallet racking

A combination of steel uprights and cross members into which pallets are stored by general purpose fork-lift trucks (either reach or counterbalance types) which move between the aisles.

There are many advantages including: every pallet may be moved individually without moving other pallets, the system is suitable for most products and the load support beams may be easily moved to new levels to accommodate new load sizes, throughput and handling are relatively rapid, the headroom of the warehouse may be used to the full, and the product is protected from compression and other damage.

The disadvantages include: special high reach trucks are required above 25 ft, the density of storage is less than with other systems because of the amount of aisle (gangway) needed for the trucks to manoeuvre, and the layout should be regarded as fixed for a reasonable period. Other than block stacking, adjustable pallet racking is the simplest system to operate and is economical with capital. It may also be quickly changed by dismantling and reassembling as required.

Narrow aisle pallet racking

Similar to adjustable pallet racking except that the aisles are restricted to being only marginally wider than the specially designed trucks or stacker cranes which operate within the system. The trucks and cranes used may operate within the aisles on fixed paths within guide rails and do not turn in the aisle; instead they pick up and deposit product at a position at the end of the aisle (known as a P and D station). Some of these installations use computer controlled equipment to make some or all of the operation automatic.

The advantages of narrow aisle pallet racking are: high density storage, individual access to each pallet, rapid throughput, may be operated to great heights, and may be fully automatic (computer controlled and without operators).

The disadvantages are that it requires special handling equipment, the racking must engineered to tight tolerances, and the trucks or cranes are virtually captive to work within the racking.

Double depth racking

Similar to either adjustable pallet racking or narrow aisle pallet racking except there are two pallet spaces, one directly behind the other, and the system requires a special truck with telescopic forks to reach the rear pallet space.

The additional advantage is that greater storage space is available.

The disadvantage is that more time is required to place and retrieve the rear pallets, a task which may only be done when the front pallet space is empty.

Drive-in drive-through racking

Consists of a continuous block of pallet racking not divided into aisles. Either reach or counterbalance fork-lift trucks may drive into the centre of the block, between any uprights, to select any of the front faces to either pick up or deposit a pallet. This system differs from other racking in so far as it uses continuous cantilever rails attached to the uprights to support the front-to-back edges of the pallet. This design principle allows the truck to move freely up and down one row.

The advantages of this system are: high density storage, no crushing or damage to goods, and standard trucks may be used.

The significant disadvantage is that it is only possible to place into and select from the first front pallet space on each row for each level.

This system is best suited to situations where the product range is small, the movement pattern is predictable, and where individual pallet selectivity is not important. This system is often used to store seasonal goods.

Powered mobile racking

Individually power-driven racks which close together on steel rails so that one aisle may be used for up to 12 individual racks. Control is either by a central console or by push buttons at the end of each rack, and there are built-in safety devices to avoid both operators and product from being crushed between the racks.

The advantages include: maximum use of available storage space, direct access to all items, standard trucks may be used, and improved security of product.

The major disadvantage is that throughput is slow because there is access only to two rack faces at once.

Live storage

A number of gravity conveyor lanes ranged side by side and one above another so that pallets are loaded at the upper end and travel down to the lower end. The upper end is the input face and the lower end the picking face. When a pallet is removed from the lower picking face the remainder of the pallets move forward slowly under the control of a braking system.

The advantages are: excellent use of space, automatic stock rotation in each lane, and standard trucks may be used.

The disadvantages include high cost and some loss of flexibility.

Shelving

May be found in many different forms the most notable being short-span, long-span, cantilever, high-rise, multi-tier, and mobile shelving. Shelving is particularly versatile and suitable for many products, shelves may be divided into small compartments with dividers and there are many types of accessories to make shelving easier to use and more secure. In general, shelving gives good access, good visibility, it is easily adjusted, allows easy stock rotation and provides high density storage. Shelving is most suitable for those products which are small and would be unsuitable for pallet racking.

Carousels

May be either vertical or horizontal and are a series of shelves or trays connected to rotating chain; in the case of the vertical carousel the shelves are pivoted so that they remain upright in all positions. The systems may be enclosed and operated electrically to present the required shelves at an aperture.

The advantages include: high density storage for small items, labour productivity in the order picking operation, rapid access to stock and good security.

The major disadvantage is that these systems are expensive even without the optional extra of computer control.

The selection of one or more storage systems will depend upon a combination of factors including product characteristics, annual throughput, stock turnover rates, and customer service level required expressed in terms of order to delivery time. Generally the rule is the greater the mechanisation the lower the unit storage and picking cost but the less flexible the operating system.

Associated with each storage method there will be one or more product handling techniques. Some complex handling techniques are designed specifically for the product or the packaging (for example, handling of chemical drums requires specific equipment or special attachments). The most common handling equipment include:

Fork-lift trucks

Small power-operated vehicles which have an attachment to secure pallets and to move them in both vertical and horizontal planes. These vehicles may be powered by battery, gas, diesel or petrol. There are many different types of truck, including reach truck, counterbalance truck (usually fitted with large wheels), stacker trucks (often confined to lifting applications), and order picking trucks (usually for use in narrow aisle pallet racking). The fork-lift truck is the general purpose vehicle for the movement of unit loads (pallets) both inside and the immediate outside of the warehouse; specialist varieties and accessories have been developed to accommodate both the need of product requirements and specific storage system limitations. If used on the public highway the vehicle must be registered and insured.

Low lifters

The collective name for equipment designed to move pallets over the floor from place to place. There are a number of different types of low lifters, particularly hand pallet trucks, powered pallet trucks, pedestrian pallet trucks, stand-on pallet trucks and sit-on pallet trucks. The choice of which low lifter is suitable will depend upon load weights, frequency of movements, distance to be moved and type of terrain/floor upon which the movement is to made. Low lifters cost less than fork-lift trucks and where only a horizontal movement is required they are faster and more flexible.

Automatic guide vehicles

Powered, unmanned low-lift trucks which are guided by electric wires in the floor which are inductively sensed by the trucks as they move. The main advantage of automatic guided vehicles (AGVs) is that manpower is eliminated, and they are, therefore, most suitable for regular material flows (for example, between the inward goods bay and the bulk storage). They need a computer system to program and control their movements, and are normally linked with computer controlled bulk storage, or sortation systems.

Cranes

Consist of a motorised platform containing a mast to which telescopic forks are attached; the whole mechanism may either run on ground rails, or be suspended from a running beam bolted to the racking or the warehouse structure. The crane is designed to work in high rise warehouses (approximately 40 ft) with long aisles. The crane will only work in one aisle at a time, and may need a transfer car to enable it to change aisles. Cranes are very expensive and are normally used in support of a fully automatic computer controlled warehouse.

Conveyors

Means of moving packs, cases and pallets on belts, wheels or rollers. Conveyors may be either gravity systems or powered systems. The advantages of conveyors are they are particularly applicable for long distance movements, involve relatively low capital cost, minimum manning and maintenance requirements, may function continuously and will improve productivity. Complex conveyor and sortation systems may be designed to accept bulk product at the inward goods area, and sequence the movement of the product in such a manner that the despatch area is fed with items in the correct sequence for despatch.

Configuration of equipment

From the combination of alternative storage and handling techniques it is possible to determine the most appropriate configuration of equipment:

- *A simple warehouse configuration* may consist of:
  (a) Inward goods area
    - Hand pallet truck to unload vehicles
    - Block and single stacks of product
    - Fork-lift truck for movement
  (b) Bulk storage area
    - Fork-lift truck for movement in and out
    - Block stacking area
    - Adjustable pallet racking
    - Long span shelving
  (c) Order picking area
    - Adjustable pallet racking
    - Short span shelving
    - Hand pallet trucks
  (d) Despatch area
    - Block and single stacks of product
    - Hand pallet trucks to load vehicles
    - Small powered conveyor for loading vehicles.
- *A complex warehouse configuration* may consist of:
  (a) Inward goods area
    - Hand pallet trucks/fork-lift trucks
    - Powered conveyors
    - Automatic guided vehicles
  (b) Bulk storage area
    - High bay with narrow aisle pallet racking
    - Carousels for small items
    - Cranes (fully automatic)
  (c) Order picking area
    - Powered conveyors
    - Powered pallet trucks
    - Adjustable pallet racking and mezzanine flooring
    - Sortation system
  (d) Despatch area
    - Powered conveyors
    - Live racking for load assembly
    - Fork-lift trucks.

A further item of equipment which is an essential part of the handling system is the item on to or into which product is consolidated; for example, the pallet, the cage, the tray, the bin or the basket. It is the physical nature of the product which will determine which container to adopt, and the choice of container may have a significant impact upon the selection of the main elements of the storage and handling system.

In addition to the equipment required both systems will need a stock location and operational control system. The operator of the simple warehouse configuration is likely to use a manual system which is a combination of section control sheets and pallet cards. The operator of the complex warehouse system will have little choice but to use computer control systems for both stock location and operational control of both equipment and manpower.

TRANSPORTATION

Transport is the link between each stage in the supply chain, and is normally the responsibility of the owner of the goods. Thus in the case of food products the manufacturer will be responsible for transportation to the retailer's warehouse (or direct to store), the retailer responsible for transportation from its warehouse to the store and the customer responsible for the movement from the store to the home (or point of consumption).

Transportation is usually the most expensive distribution function, because it is normally both labour and capital intensive, and there are few opportunities to exchange capital for labour.

There are five basic modes of transport: road, rail, air, water and pipelines. The majority of product moves by road either for the full distance from manufacturer to consumer, or for part of the distance. Many products, however, use two or more transport modes in their journey from the manufacturer. For example, a consumer electronics product sourced from the Far East to be sold in Scotland may pass through the following transport methods:

- Road from the factory to the dockside at the port of departure
- Sea freight from departure port to arrival port
- Road from arrival port to a central warehouse in the South of England
- Road from central warehouse to freightliner (rail) terminal
- Rail from South of England to Scotland
- Road from freightliner terminal in Scotland to local delivery depot
- Road from local delivery depot to retail store
- Road from retail store to customer.

In comparison with road, other modes of transport may often be slow, expensive or inflexible; but each mode of transport has its advantages.

Rail

Has the ability to transport most products from parcels to special full train loads weighing up to approximately 2000 tonnes. Rail has the capability to transport large loads over long distances at very low cost, with the additional advantage of little additional environmental damage. In the UK British Rail offer a number of services including: full train movements (where the customer may own the diesel engine and rail wagons), single wagon movements (where the customer may own the wagon), freightliner service for moving containers between fixed terminals, a groupage service for large loads, a parcel carriage service, and an express parcel and package carriage service. In addition some European rail systems offer the movement of road vehicles complete with a load.

Within the UK rail is really only a cost-effective operation for the carriage of low-value large bulky loads (coal, iron ore, timber) or for product which needs to travel distances in excess of 100 miles in bulk and without any real time constraints. Rail is ideal for the movement of seasonal products from North to South or vice versa, because rail is cheaper than road, and slower, so the wagons act as a moving warehouse.

Under the Railways Act 1974 the government have offered grants of up to 50 per cent of the total cost of building or improving rail sidings at manufacturing plants. Unfortunately, few applications are made and this grant is in danger of lapsing.

Air

Becoming a popular means of transport, particularly for low volume high value goods. Air is often used as an alternative to seafreight to move single products (samples) or large consignments required urgently. Air cargo rates are generally expensive because they are charged on a weight basis up to a volume of 335 cubic inches above which the charge is based upon a volumetric weight. However, consignment charges depend upon: type of product, volume carried, distance, and both point of departure and destination. Where it is possible to use a special unit load (igloo or container) the rates are more favourable. Air freight is used as a standard method of movement for some products because the supplier obtains the combined benefits of: rapid delivery, low inventory and capital costs of goods in transit, minimal packaging costs, low insurance cost for theft and damage and a guaranteed customer service level (order to delivery time). Air freight for regular shipment is only economic where the alternatives are sea freight or long rail movements.

Water

May take the form of sea freight, roll-on roll-off ferries, coastal seaways and inland waterways. The main advantage of water transport is the ability to move extremely large shipments in a cost-effective manner. The main disadvantage is speed, which is very slow. Thus the only economic use of water is long distances, linking the UK with the continent of Europe, or where the commodity is suitable for bulk transport (powder, rock or granular) and both the source and destination are adjacent to a waterway.

Pipeline

Has limited applications because of the high capital cost involved but is used economically for the movement of liquids and gases.

Road transport is the most common and normally offers the greatest scope for potential improvement. On the one hand, vehicle costs have increased with fuel rises and changes required to ensure the operations remain within the mounting volume of legislation; and on the other hand, vehicle design has increased the overall efficiency often making road transport more competitive than other modes. Road transport operators have five main issues to consider: source of finance for the vehicle, vehicle specification, vehicle maintenance, vehicle routeing and fleet control.

ROAD TRANSPORT OPERATIONS

Finance

At an early stage in the planning or re-evaluation of a vehicle fleet it will be necessary to establish whether the fleet will be wholly or partly owned or financed in some other manner. This decision usually depends upon such factors as the extent of the capital required, the cost of capital, and the size of the organisation. The evaluation of alternative methods of finance is a matter of evaluating all the options over a comparative time period and undertaking financial calculations to determine the most appropriate. The basic alternatives are:

1. *Outright purchase* involves not only the provision of capital, but if the vehicles are above 3.5 tonnes maximum permissible gross weight then an operator's licence is required ('O' licence), and this in turn requires a suitably qualified person (professionally competent) to be employed by the company to administer the vehicle fleet.

2. *Hire purchase* involves a hire charge for an agreed period of time during which the vehicle is not the property of the operator; however, at the end of the hire period the payment of a nominal sum will secure ownership. No capital tax allowance apply because the vehicle is not owned by the operator. In a similar manner, to purchase outright the operator must have an 'O' licence if required by law.
3. *Leasing* involves regular payments over a fixed period of time and the vehicle never becomes the property of the operator. No capital allowances are obtained. However, the operator must have an 'O' licence if required by law.
4. *Contract hire* involves regular payments over a fixed period of time and the vehicle never becomes the property of the operator. No capital allowances are obtained. The difference from leasing is that there are a number of alternative schemes including:
   - contract hire of vehicle only
   - contract hire of vehicle with maintenance
   - contract hire of vehicle with driver and maintenance.

   In those cases of contract hire of vehicle with driver and maintenance the 'O' licence is the responsibility of the contract hirer
5. *Short-term hire* involves regular payments over a short period of time and the vehicle never becomes the property of the operator.

Vehicle selection

The selection of the most appropriate vehicle for a particular task is extremely complex and requires detailed knowledge of the technical specifications of: the chassis cabs, bodywork design, and ancillary equipment. The technical specification of any vehicle is subject to the regulations laid down in the Motor Vehicles (Construction and Use) Regulations 1978 which specify the legal requirements to be observed by vehicle designers, manufacturers and body builders. However, the choice of the right vehicle is critical and the basic requirement is that the vehicle carries its load safely and economically. There are a number of different classifications of commercial vehicles including:

- *Light vans* – basically car derivatives
- *Medium and heavy vans* – special purpose light load carriers
- *Rigid vehicles* (up to 16.2 tonnes) – with two axles and up to 11 metres maximum length
- *Rigid vehicles* (up to 24.3 tonnes) – with three axles and up to 11 meters maximum length

- *Rigid vehicles* (up to 30.4 tonnes) – with four axles and up to 11 meters maximum length
- *Articulated Vehicles* (up to 24.3 tonnes) – with a two-axle tractive unit and single-axle trailer and up to 15 meters maximum length
- *Articulated vehicles* (up to 32.5 tonnes) – with either a single-axle tractive unit and a two-axle trailer or a two-axle tractive unit and a single-axle trailer both up to 15 meters maximum length
- *Articulated vehicles* (up to 38 tonnes) – with either a three-axle tractive unit and a two-axle trailer or a two-axle tractive unit and a three-axle trailer both up to 15 meters maximum length
- *Draw-bar trailer combination* (up to 32.5 tonne) – with a maximum length of 18 meters

Vehicles must be designed and operated within the maximum gross weights (vehicle and payload), the maximum lengths and a maximum width of 2.5 meters. There is no restriction upon maximum height, although a vehicle must be stable and most are designed to go underneath the motorway bridges. The vehicle height, however, must be clearly displayed in the cab, in a position visible to the driver.

The vehicle bodies should be built to suit the needs of the individual operator. The basic types of vehicle body include the flat platform, the box van, the drop body, the tanker and the tipper.

Maintenance

Operation of a vehicle implies maintenance for safety and economic reasons. There are various legal requirements for vehicle maintenance contained in the Road Traffic Act 1972 (annual vehicle test and inspections), Motor Vehicles (Construction and Use) Regulations 1978 (standing operating conditions for vehicles) and the Transport Act 1968 (conditions relating to vehicle maintenance and the issue of an 'O' licence).

Good maintenance planning and procedures will lead to the economic operation of a fleet by extending the life of vehicles, reducing vehicle downtime, maintaining the value of the vehicle, improving the fuel consumption and maintaining the engine and drive line (clutch, gearbox and axles) efficiency. If third party maintenance facilities are used, under the 'O' licence regulations the operator is still responsible for the provision of the vehicle in a mechanically safe condition (even if defects are discovered which are due to a repair).

Route planning

The main effect upon vehicle costs and efficiency is the day-to-day route planning operation. Good route planning minimises vehicles (therefore minimises the fixed costs) and minimises mileage (therefore minimises the variable costs of fuel, maintenance and tyres). Traditionally, vehicle route planning has been done by the supervisor or foreman, who was previously a driver, and understands what should be an average day's work. However, the vehicle routeing operation may be brought down to a mathematical calculation to fill the available vehicle capacity and driver's time; as a result, operations research techniques have been applied to create vehicle scheduling methods which may be undertaken by a clerk. These manual systems have been improved and computers are now used to calculate mileages, driving times and vehicle loads accurately. Some of these computer systems may be purchased complete with hardware for under £20,000 which is a fraction of the annual costs of a single vehicle and driver.

Legislation

Control of the fleet operation is a difficult and complex task because the resources available are normally fixed in terms of drivers and vehicles, which need to be controlled in relation to both legislation and trade union agreements; and the demands on the system are made by customers' orders which are a variable element. The main elements of transport operations covered by legislation include:

- Road traffic regulations
- Operator's licences (both national and international)
- HGV licences - for vehicle types above 7.5 tonnes, and people over 21 years of age
- Goods vehicles drivers' hours regulations
- Goods vehicles drivers' records
- Excise duty payments
- National type approval legislation
- Vehicle lighting and marking regulations
- HGV plating and annual testing regulations, and light vehicle testing regulations

The following legislation may also be applicable in certain circumstances:

- Abnormal and projecting load regulations
- Chemical and hazardous load regulations and codes of practice

All these regulations are in addition to the standard health and safety at work legislation and employment regulations which are currently enforceable. One particular element of transport law that is important is that the payment of productivity bonuses and incentive payments to boost drivers' potential earnings is prohibited under EEC Regulation 543/69 which forbids the use of any payment scheme which may encourage a driver to either exceed the statutory driving time limits or overload the vehicle.

THIRD PARTY DISTRIBUTION

The ownership of product does not necessarily mean involvement in the physical distribution process, because there are many specialist distribution firms who will either store, move or arrange the storage and movement of product. The use of third party distribution services may be economic in the following circumstances:

- When the customer stipulates a nominated carrier
- When it is more economic to use third parties rather than in-house resources
- When seasonal or peak demands occur
- When there are a number of stages in the physical distribution cycle to undertake which are special to a few products or a few customers
- When capital or skilled labour is scarce
- When the physical distribution requirement is one which does not meet the company's patterns of work (for example, the need for night driving)
- When specialist skills are needed
- When there is a need to mix in-house and third party operations to keep the costs of in-house operations down.

CONCLUSION

The physical distribution management task is the organisation, planning and control of the resources employed in the storage and movement of goods from manufacturer to user. This task is complex because of the large number of elements involved in the overall process and the need to undertake the operations in a cost-effective manner, within the current laws, and to the customers' satisfaction. Distribution management must select the correct resources to employ to effect the distribution process efficiently; the selection of these resources is a real risk because customers, products and the environment will change during the forecast life of many of the resources employed.

9

PURCHASING AND SUPPLY

John R Gammon

INTRODUCTION

It is sometimes considered that buying, stock control, contract purchasing and distribution in industry and commerce may be treated as straightforward, routine tasks. Knowing the risks involved, responsible management would certainly not subscribe to this attitude.

Whatever its shortcomings, commerce in civilized societies provides a relatively high standard of consumer satisfaction. Shop-counters are usually well stocked and new car models come out regularly each year. When a water-main bursts or the electricity supply fails, the repair team puts matters to rights fairly speedily. The levels of performance in manufacturing industry, the public services and business in general depend heavily upon the quality and effectiveness of purchasing and supply management.

The function of purchasing and supply has been defined as 'the management of all tasks and activities concerned with the procurement of materials, equipment and services and control of items purchased, until added to the inventory, consumed or resold'. Its task begins with the identification of a requirement and ends with the satisfaction of that requirement, thus completing the 'supply chain'. But the chain can be long and, like its material counterpart, will be no stronger than its weakest link. The job of designing that chain, setting it up and ensuring that it fulfils its purpose, requires a complex of skills.

THE SUPPLY CHAIN

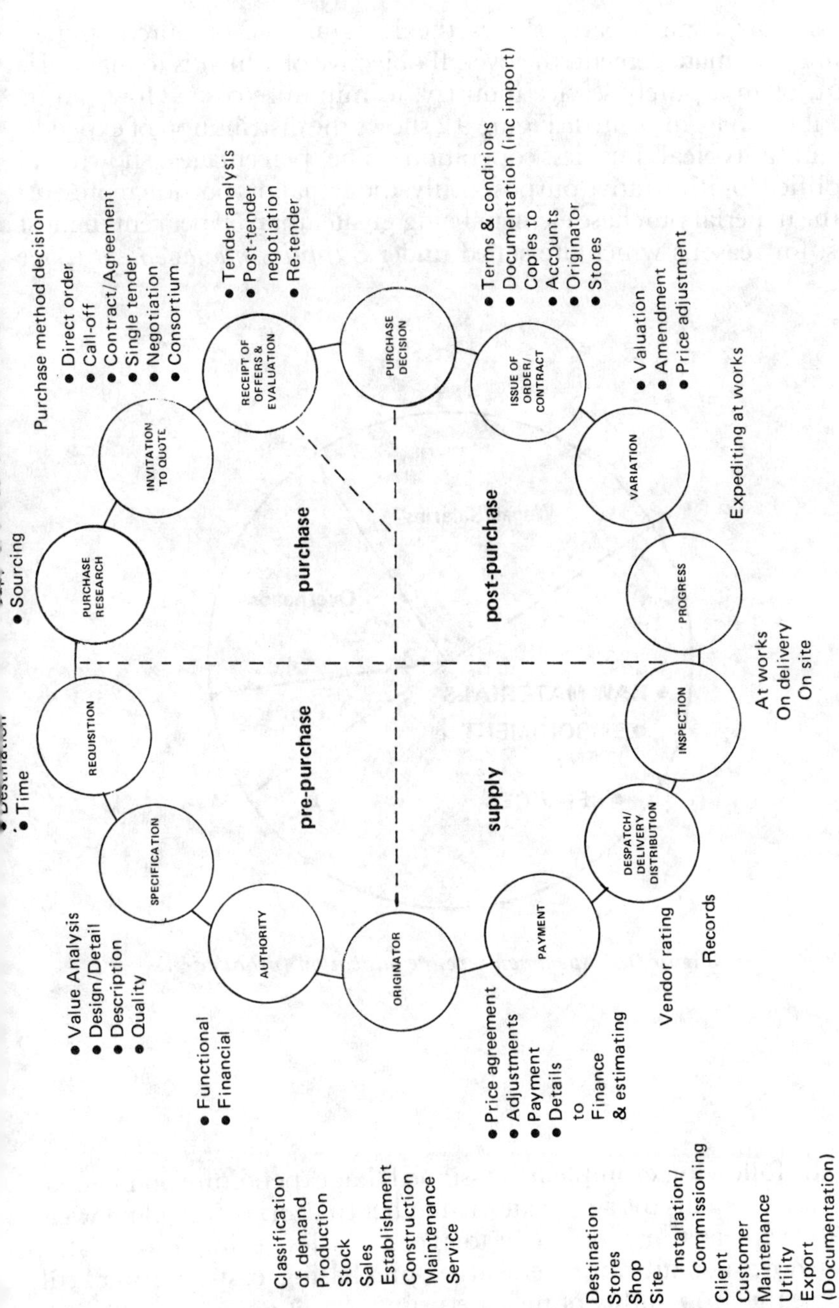

Figure 9.1 *The supply chain*

PURCHASING FOR PROFIT

The supply chain clearly shows the integral role of purchasing in commercial management, the overall objective of which is to maximize profit, or in a purely service industry, to minimize costs. How can its contribution be measured? Figure 9.2 shows the distribution of expenditure in a typical business operation. The percentages shown are simplified for illustrative purposes only, the actual proportion representing the material purchase element being greater than 50 per cent in most cases, for reasons which are stated under *Supplies management* (page 232).

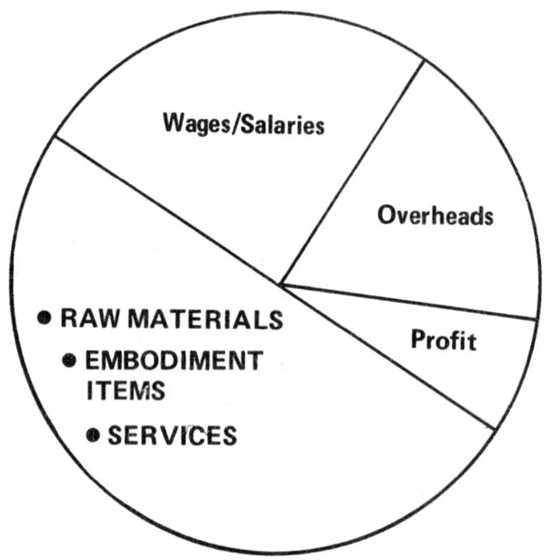

Figure 9.2 *Specimen revenue allocation (production)*

In the following example it is assumed that expenditure on materials and services equals the aggregate of all other categories, including wages and all overheads, making up the total cost of sales. A simple calculation shows how a small improvement in purchasing costs can markedly improve the profitability of the enterprise.

	Situation A	Situation B
	£	£
Purchase costs of materials and services	50,000	48,000 (saving of 4%)
Labour costs	30,000	30,000
Other oncosts (on sales)	20,000	20,000
Total cost of sales	100,000	98,000
Total sales	110,000	110,000
Profit	10,000 (10%)	12,000 (12.25%)

In Situation B the profit return is some 22.5 per cent greater than in Situation A, because the materials cost 4 per cent less. A similar increase in profit due to turnover only would require a sales figure in excess of (£110,000 x 1.225) = £134,750. (It must be borne in mind that higher sales also attract higher manufacturing, management and selling costs and the attendant risks, which means that there is no certainty that increased sales would produce a corresponding percentage increase in profit.)

Reverting to the examples set out above, it may alternatively be decided to *reduce* the selling prices to 109,000, producing a modest £1000 extra profit, but improving competitiveness. The profit margin would still be £1000 (11.22 per cent) better than that achieved in Situation A.

The purchase costs of materials can vary considerably, depending on the skill with which the function is operated, without requiring additional staff or adding to purchasing expenses. In some cases prices quoted for the supply of goods and services might vary within a range as wide as 100 per cent, according to the source selected. When a keen purchasing operation is combined with efficient stores and distribution management the organization will be fortunate in having a significant profit-making centre in its purchasing and supply department.

JOB TITLES

There is a profusion (and confusion) of job titles for people in the purchasing and supply function. Although purchasing and supply management has become widely recognized as a profession in its own right no single, comprehensive job-descriptive title has yet emerged for those who practise it. This is for a number of reasons:

- Purchasing and supply embraces a wide span of functional activities.
- Employing organizations determine their individual operational

and management structures which may *not* show a separate supplies function.
- The functional emphasis will vary according to the main purpose of the organization.

Thus, we might come across the following job titles in the corresponding environments:

Civil Engineering	: Contracts Officer
Military Establishments	: Controller of Supplies
Retail Trade	: Warehouse Manager
Merchandising	: Chief Buyer
Health Service	: Supplies Officer
Local Government	: Purchasing Officer
Production	: Materials Manager
Civil Service	: Assistant Secretary (Procurement)

The actual jobs may nevertheless have a great deal more in common than their titles suggest.

For the purpose of this chapter we shall concentrate on a limited set of departmental and job titles:

SUPPLIES DEPARTMENT

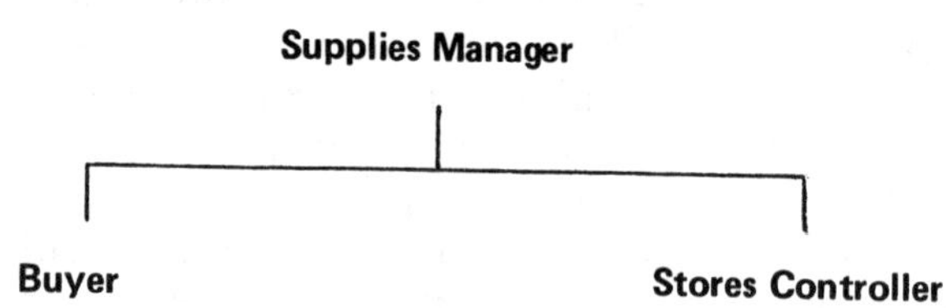

If the firm is too small to have a separate department, or buyer, then the functions described must be performed by whoever is responsible for ensuring the successful administration of the commercial activity.

SUPPLIES MANAGEMENT

Materials purchases

In recent years the proportion of industrial costs represented by materials purchases has gradually increased and the average probably exceeds 60 per cent of total costs. This trend has been largely due to the following factors:
- Labour rationalization;

- The substitution of human workers by electro-mechanical robots in the factory and micros in the office;
- The increase in imported finished products.

In consequence, management attention has been focused more intensely on the area where greater savings and better value can be achieved for each pound spent, that is to say, in supply management.

Management tasks

The principal duties of the person responsible for managing the supplies function may be summarized as follows:

- Contribute to the organization's overall objectives by procuring materials and services, cost-effectively, as and when required;
- Maximize the function's contribution to profitability;
- Achieve maximum cooperation with other functions and departments within the organization;
- Develop satisfactory relationships with vendors and other external bodies;
- Advise general management of developments and trends in relation to supply matters which affect corporate objectives;
- Optimize levels of stockholding and inventory investment;
- Direct and control the identification, handling, storage, safe custody and movement of all stores and materials in and from storehouses and stockyards, from the point of delivery to user points;
- Minimize inventory losses due to deterioration, obsolescence, theft or other causes;
- Keep records of all transactions and movements of stock and be accountable for the same;
- Train and motivate staff.

The above list of the principal functional tasks could be used to draft a comprehensive job description. One should add that, apart from skills, integrity of the highest order is essential and it is particularly important that the supplies manager should set the necessary standards for his staff by example.

SIZE OF ORGANIZATION

Proprietors and managers of smaller companies, which comprise the vast majority of industrial concerns, might question the justification for engaging a highly skilled professional in what seems to be a relatively limited role. In such a case it would still be necessary for someone in a senior position to be made responsible for managing the function. It is important to remember that, when competing with the buying power of larger companies and their financial capacity for stock investment, the odd percentage improvements in production costs can make a great deal of difference to the amount of business gained. This may determine the profitability and, ultimately, the viability of a smaller concern.

Detailed studies to evaluate how management time is spent in a representative group of small and medium-sized companies have produced some surprising results. In some cases it was established that as much as 25-30 per cent of the managers' time was spent in dealing with supplies matters. This implied that:

- only 70–75 per cent of managers' total time was occupied with their principal duties (eg design, production, sales);
- 25–30 per cent of the managers' salaries bill would have easily funded the cost of a supply section, leaving something to spare.

As an organization grows it requires specialist staff in many functions, including supplies. A manufacturing firm with up to 50 operatives would almost certainly need a buyer who would also deal with stores. At 100 strong there would probably be a small supplies unit. The function must be managed properly and the attendant staff overheads should be more than offset by the resultant gains in cost-efficiency. If supplies operations are dealt with unsystematically in the early stages, and carried out by anyone who happens to want the goods, it may be difficult to dislodge (possibly undesirable) practices when the company grows; section heads would tend to be reluctant to surrender control of buying, to the detriment of the business as a whole. It is therefore desirable to designate areas of responsibility and specify procedures as soon as possible. Evolution and growth will then not be as painful for those concerned with the problems of managing change.

DEFINING THE DEMAND

When it is established that *something* is needed it might seem a short next step to deciding *what* is to be made or purchased. This is not necessarily the case. For example, a production manager may be working to a design in which two parts of an assembly have to be attached to each other by hinged fastenings. The type of hinge and fastening, their dimensions, weight and the materials from which they could be manufactured might be decided from a wide range of alternatives. Which will be best for the job — cheapest, most attractive, most reliable — will present an equally challenging choice of criteria. Manufacturing to standard patterns or simply buying proprietary items 'off the shelf' every time a demand arises is relatively easy. But it may not be the best way to do the job. It is worthwhile taking stock from time to time, challenging established practices, questioning sources of supply and the range of products, with the object of checking whether we are specifying what we *want* rather than what we *need.* Lateral thinking can work wonders!

VALUE ANALYSIS AND VALUE ENGINEERING

Value analysis is one of many commonsense concepts which have evolved into widely recognized techniques of supply management. The term originated in a construction setting at the end of the last war, in describing part of a programme of cost reduction in the United States navy. It is often used in conjunction with 'value engineering'. Their respective applications are as follows:

Value engineering	**Relating to**	**Objective**
Monitoring, testing and investigation of details during the design, prototype and pre-production stages; before the specification is finalized; and subsequently when modifications are under consideration.	Materials, components, techniques and services used in the production process.	Achieving the optimum production cost in meeting the design requirements.
Value analysis		
Examination and review of the finished product-in-use.	Quality, reliability, life cycle, maintenance.	Minimum cost; and satisfying performance criteria.

Because of their sequential relationship it is often convenient to merge assessment criteria into a common matrix. The matrix is constructed on the framework of all the functions and characteristics of the device or service, and its market. For instance, if one is designing an electric motor, characteristics might include:

- Occupation of space
- Weight
- Noise
- External appearance.

If the appliance is intended for quarry work these characteristics may not be too significant, but in a domestic liquidizer they would be most important. When all the functions and characteristics have been written down each is given a positive or negative value and plotted on the matrix. This will provide the analyst with comparative data from the initial design stage through to the point of use or marketing.

A typical check-list might be as follows:

1. *Function*

   - What are its basic functions?
   - Does its use contribute value?
   - Are all its functions necessary?
   - Is there another way of performing the necessary functions?

2. *Design*

   - What design features could be left out without detriment?
   - Can dimensions be reduced?
   - Are the tolerances too tight?
   - Are specifications too high?
   - What are the effects of all the above on total cost?

3. *Manufacture*

   - Can manufacturing methods be simplified?
   - Can standard techniques/tools/jigs be used?
   - Can machine operations be combined?
   - What are the manpower implications?
   - Can prefabricated parts be used?

4 *Materials*

   - Can materials be standardized?
   - Are alternative materials more suitable?
   - What materials waste factors are involved?
   - What packaging/protection is required for finished product?

5. *Performance*

   - What is the product's life?
   - What will the maintenance costs be?
   - What power will the product consume in operation?

Value analysis and value engineering are intended to optimize those aspects of design, manufacture and end use which produce the best results, measured by the criteria listed above. They should not be confused with cost reduction techniques, which relate to the elements of cost of manufacturing an existing product.

PURCHASING: THE FIVE 'RIGHTS'

The principal aims of effective purchasing are 'the five rights'. These are to secure goods or services

of the right QUALITY
in the right QUANTITY
at the right TIME and
at the right PRICE,
delivered to the right PLACE.

To this a sixth is sometimes added: 'from the right source'. Sourcing will be dealt with later (page 260), but the author takes the view that, if all the remaining five rights are satisfied, then the sixth becomes a corollary, rather than a separate objective.

Quality

When used in a purchasing context, this is not a term describing excellence for its own sake, but a measure of suitability for the intended purpose. To take a simple example, we all have experience of using the humble table fork in different situations. In four-star hotels we would probably handle good quality silver cutlery; at roadside cafes the base-metal type, just about strong enough to tackle a steak-and-kidney pie, and at picnics a plastic fork of the throw-away variety. Each would be suitable for its particular purpose and place but would be inappropriate when provided in a different setting. As with so many other aspects of supply management, it is sometimes difficult to define 'quality'. Nevertheless, if it is to have any real meaning, it is essential to adopt a common language for descriptive purposes. Fortunately, the British Standards Institution (BS 4778) comes to our assistance in providing a schedule of definitions relating to quality.

Quality. The totality of features and characteristics of a product or service that bear upon its ability to satisfy a given need.

Quality control. A system for programming and co-ordinating the efforts of the various groups in an organization to maintain or improve quality, at an economical level which allows for customer satisfaction.

Conformity. Agreement between the defined and verified quality of a product or service.

Certification. Act of licensing by a document formally attesting the fulfilment of conditions.

Inspection. The process of measuring, examining, testing, gauging or otherwise comparing the item with the applicable requirement.

Reliability. The ability of an item to perform a required function under stated conditions for a stated period of time.

Specification. The document which prescribes in detail the requirements to which the supplies or services must conform.

Test. An inspection process in which a functional requirement is measured or observed and usually in which stress or energy is applied to the item.

Being able to refer to a handy set of definitions does not, however, solve all the problems concerned with determining the right quality. In a retail situation, for instance, it is as a *vendor* that the proprietor must assess the quality of the products which he buys for resale. In this case the supplier or manufacturer of the goods will have set the quality level which the ultimate customer will either accept or reject according to choice. In the case of very large organizations in the retailing field, such as Marks and Spencer or British Home Stores, the merchandiser has enough buying power to be able to specify quality standards to the nth degree. Thus the manufacturers of shirts and underwear, or producers or processors of food items to be sold through these stores must meet exacting standards set by the purchaser. In this context the purchaser is called the 'buyer' or 'merchandiser'.

The individual small retailer has less influence on the manufacture or production standards for the items he wishes to buy. This is why many groups of retailers have formed themselves into consortia for the purpose of aggregating their buying power with manufacturers and wholesalers. Not only does this improve their capacity to negotiate more favourable pricing terms, but it is of considerable value in influencing and regulating merchandising quality standards over a wider field of demand. These associations of retailers have made a significant impact in the retail market, though none of these groups can be compared by size or market share with the giants of the distributive trades.

In manufacturing industry the designer obviously makes a significant contribution to the setting of quality standards. Here the overall appearance of the product will probably count for less than its efficiency in use, convenience, durability and size, and specification becomes a key factor in determining the quality level.

Most components procured for production do not involve the preparation of specifications. Those in common demand are readily available from merchants or may be obtained without difficulty by reference to suppliers' catalogues. Fixings and fastenings provide a simple example, usually being purchased 'over the counter' from wholesalers. Even here, however, where there is a range of choice from say, importers, merchants or home manufacturers, buyers must exercise a degree of discernment and judgement. The quality of products varies greatly according to origin and, within limits, grades usually correspond with prices. Buying in small quantities, on an ad hoc basis, is the least efficient way of doing business. The buyer will soon learn another important axiom: if he accepts a passive (or 'order-clerk') role in satisfying the demands of the technical staff both he and his company will experience the worst of all worlds and none of the 'rights' will be achieved. A cheap component may prove to be unsuitable for its intended purpose, causing the product to fail in service or use. This would involve extra cost of rectification or replacement, probably offsetting any nominal profit on the original sale. Worst of all would be the effect on the customer. Goodwill and reputation take time to build, but are quickly dismantled.

The role of the buyer in satisfying the quality criteria should not be understated or overlooked. He should always be associated, from the outset, with project or design teams, and be prepared to make a positive contribution, based on his knowledge and skills on prices and availability of materials and components. To do this without treading on his colleagues' toes from time to time is perhaps not easy. It is an occupational hazard of the buyer which should be treated with occupational tact and diplomacy.

1. *Specification*

Some items are described by brand name. These may be manufactured for a particular function or application (eg a timing device for the regeneration process in water-softening equipment) and a suitable alternative may not be available. Registered designs or patents may preclude competition. Customer demand (particularly in fashion and style) often limits the retail buyer's choice of bought-in materials intended for making up and resale. Consumer preferences are often localized. Yorkshire ladies may favour a range of dress patterns quite different from those sought after by shoppers in Cambridge. At one and the same time a buyer for a retailer of domestic appliances found it necessary to order large quantities of electric storage heaters with *bronze* finish for sales in Cornwall and approximately the same number finished in *cream* for sale in Devon, across the Tamar bridge. If the retail buyer of materials and merchandise fashions is not responsive to taste, fashion and up-to-date improvements in style, his company is likely to be left with unacceptable levels of unsaleable stocks, and consequential losses.

2. *Standardization*

While standardization offers many benefits it should be applied with caution. The pros and cons may be summarized as follows:

	Possible advantages
• Fewer stock items	simplified vocabulary and improved control
• Lower stock levels	reduced financial charges
• Stock concentration in stores	reduced inspection, stores and handling costs
• Service from suppliers	less need for progressing
• Larger item quantities	improved purchasing terms
• Deliveries scheduled according to requirements	
• Simpler documentation	reduced purchasing costs
• Fewer orders	
	Possible disadvantages
• Less flexibility	supply shortages arise when production is interrupted
• Resistance to changes/ improvements	discourages innovation in design
• Commitment to regular supplier	complacency in relationships
• Pricing	cheaper suitable alternatives may become available during currency of contracts

Other factors for and against the principle of standardization may occur to the reader but, on balance, the benefits usually outweigh the risks.

3. *Standards*

Standardization, dealt with above, should not be confused with *standards*. The former is a term usually applied to regulation of the range of items obtained for the company's internal needs, for manufacture, conversion or resale, and is closely related to the term 'variety reduction'. 'Standards', on the other hand, has a wider application relative to quality. The concept of common standards has historical origins, and evolved from the efforts of trade guilds (and later associations) to create a logical code or schedule of measures and descriptions upon which all might agree and use to their individual and mutual benefit. As industry progressed, this service was provided by the British Standards Institution

(BSI). This service operates nationally, but not in isolation. It is connected with foreign institutions with similar terms of reference and objectives, eg Deutsche Industrie Normen (DIN), the European Standards Committee (CEN) and the International Standards Organization (ISO). It is to be hoped that the shortcomings traditionally associated with large-scale international bureaucracies may be offset to some extent by the benefits derived from being able to communicate in terms upon which all its members can agree.

4. *Other determinants of quality include*
   - *Market grades.* Generally in relation to primary materials (eg cotton, timber, barley). Though the grades themselves do not provide precise definition of standards they are mutually understood by purchasers and vendors within the trade.
   - *Brand.* By quoting names of manufacturers or makes which are well known and which serve as adequate descriptions of type, design, grade and level of performance in use (eg motor vehicles, vacuum cleaners, proprietary medicines).
   - *Sample.* By agreement on a typical specimen of the item required which would be difficult to describe satisfactorily in any other way (eg shape, appearance, colour or taste).
   - *Performance.* Where no clear specification of the item may be available at the initial stage, but its purpose is described within narrow limits (an instrument to measure crushing resistance of materials, or a centrifuge for separating uranium isotopes). This type of case often arises in research and development work but is less frequently encountered in standard production.

5. *Quality control and measurement*

Two further topics which are of direct concern to the supplies manager are:

- *Quality control.* The system applied to the regulation of a supply, product or service in order to achieve the required quality.
- *Quality assurance.* The technique for checking and measuring the extent to which the quality criteria have been met.

The first of these — *control* - relates mainly to the manufacturing, construction or process stage and is the responsibility of the producer. He will be provided with the necessary guidance

- in the original enquiry, the order specification;
- before work begins; and
- during the contract itself.

He will often be requested to provide samples during production (the latter stage also being part of *quality assurance* procedure).

Quality assurance is of more particular interest to the purchaser, because final acceptance of and payment for the product supplied or service rendered will usually be dependent upon the outcome. The procedures for ascertaining that the required standards have been met will include:

- inspection at manufacturer's premises
- production sampling
- inspection on delivery
- testing on installation and commissioning
- independent inspection and quality assurance (eg BSI 'Kitemark' endorsement; Textile Institute; Timber Trades Association).

6. *Quality circles*

Many areas of manufacture in this country have attracted widespread criticism by home and overseas customers because of:

- shoddy workmanship
- irregular production performance
- lack of reliability of finished product
- inconsistency in delivery performance
- poor 'back-up' service
- and so on.

Confronted with similar problems two generations ago, Japanese industrialists adapted a concept, first expounded in America in the 1930s, into a management philosophy based on the formation of 'quality circles'. These consist of small groups of individuals drawn from all functions and levels of the establishment, not necessarily production or management. These persons act independently, on a voluntary basis and within a collective framework, with the objects of improving:

- Design and quality of the product;
- Efficiency of the production process, including procurement and use of materials;
- Labour efficiency;
- Interdepartmental relations;
- Worker-management communications;
- Company competitiveness and other aspects involving service and delivery performance.

Reducing/eliminating:

- Waste;
- 'Down' time;
- Worker-turnover.

Results can be measured by the proven satisfaction of customers, happier relationships within organizations — and continual growth in market share. The subject is seen from the personnel management point of view in Chapter 4.

The right quantity

The question 'how much to buy?' is by no means as simple as it may sound. Even in relation to a single requirement, such as a machine tool, or a fork-lift truck, it will raise a number of supplementary issues involving the availability of essential spares, and the quantities which it would be prudent to order at the same time as the main item. But when purchases are made to meet recurring demands, however regular they may be, the determination of quantities is far from straightforward.

It is important to recognize that buyers never work in isolation. Everything they do in their provisioning role will be influenced by considerations and factors operating elsewhere within the supply chain. For instance, in a manufacturing unit:

Production planning will determine *what* materials are required, and *when*. These will consist of:

- Raw materials — for machining within the company;
- Piece parts manufactured within the company;
- Bought-out parts, for incorporation into the manufacture;
- Processed materials — manufactured within the company and processed by outside manufacturers for incorporation in the finished product.

for Production

- Plant and equipment;
- Jigs, tools;
- General items, eg hand tools, cleaning materials, lubricants, protective clothing;
- Timber, packaging.

for Operations

The above categories would be subdivided further into:

- Capital requirements;
- Major/Minor items for production;

- Continuity of need (continuous or non-recurrent).

Supplies department will be responsible for setting up and operating the necessary systems of stock control and purchasing, viz:

which items	are available from should be held in should be purchased for	stock
how many	should be purchased for	• Capital inventory • Direct input to production line • Operations/maintenance • Spares

and *when*.

Quantities requisitioned by Production or Stores are not necessarily the same as the quantities which will be ordered by the buyer. For instance, decisions regarding capital plant purchasing will usually originate at top management level. In respect of requisitions for production etc materials, the supplies manager will be responsible for co-ordinating withdrawals from stock with the necessary purchasing action.

1. *Stock levels*

Overall stockholding policy is based on maintaining a judicious balance between the needs of production and material supplies in the form of stock. Stockholding will be restricted to avoid

- tying up working capital unnecessarily;
- incurring heavy stockholding costs.

(a) *Minimum stock level.* This is the point at which new supplies should be imminent (also called safety or buffer stock level).

(b) *Reorder level.* The quantity above the minimum stock level to cover usage requirements during the production/delivery period.

Example:

Usage — 250 per week
Production/delivery period — 12 weeks
Safety/Buffer period — 3 weeks

Given the above data the stock levels are calculated as follows:
Minimum. Weekly usage x safety period: 250 x 3 = 750
Reorder. Minimum stock + (weekly usage x production/delivery period)

= 750 + (250 x 12) = 3750

(c) *Maximum stock level.* This level cannot be determined by a simple calculation, and will depend upon a variety of factors, eg:

- Available working capital
- Average rate of stock turnover
- Store capacity
- Shelf life of perishable stores
- Stockholding and administration costs
- Availability of supplies (eg possible importation problems)
- Economic purchase terms (eg attractive quantity discounts).

While the above example is based on a representative *production* situation, the considerations which will determine the right quantity will be similar in other business environments, though possibly not quite as complex. Nevertheless, since the ultimate objectives of profitability or the containment of service costs are the same, the buying considerations will not be very different.

In retailing it is crucial that merchandise should be

- available in quantities necessary to meet customer demand, eg by styles, fashions, colours, sizes, shapes and tastes;
- turned over as rapidly as possible;
- economic in terms of storage capacity;
- purchased in quantities to guarantee maximum profitability;
- disposed of immediately as demand falls;
- replaced, in sufficient quantities, by orders placed for new merchandise.

In the service industries and public utilities the ratios relative to stockholding for regular call-off and emergencies will show considerable variations from the above examples. For instance, in the extractive industries (particularly oil drilling and coal mining) energy (gas, electricity, water), the stockyards and store houses hold very high proportions of emergency and maintenance supplies with a relatively slow turnover rate. Calculations of minimum stock and reorder levels must accordingly be based on separate data, unique to each separate category.

2. *Classification of supplies, stocks and orders*

At this stage it may it may be considered a slight diversion to refer to an Italian sociologist, Vilfredo Pareto (1848–1932), who investigated the 'wealth' profile of his country's population during the nineteenth century. Not surprisingly, he found that the majority owned the least wealth and the minority the most, and he went on to evaluate the relationships of the parts. What is now popularly known as 'Pareto's Law' can be applied to other situations such as supplies management. This demonstrates that something like 20 per cent of the items bought by typical organizations account for about 80 per cent of the total purchase costs, and that 80 per cent of the purchases by value are acquired from 20 per cent of their suppliers. Thus, Pareto's Law is sometimes called 'the 80/20 rule'. It must be emphasized that this 'rule' is far from invariable and should be regarded more as a general principle only. In relation to different types of industry it will certainly vary in detail. For instance, extractive industry will obviously show weightings different from those one would expect to find in retailing.

Pareto's Law, as applied to stocks, is used to classify categories of stores by usage, relative volumes held, and for ordering purposes. This is

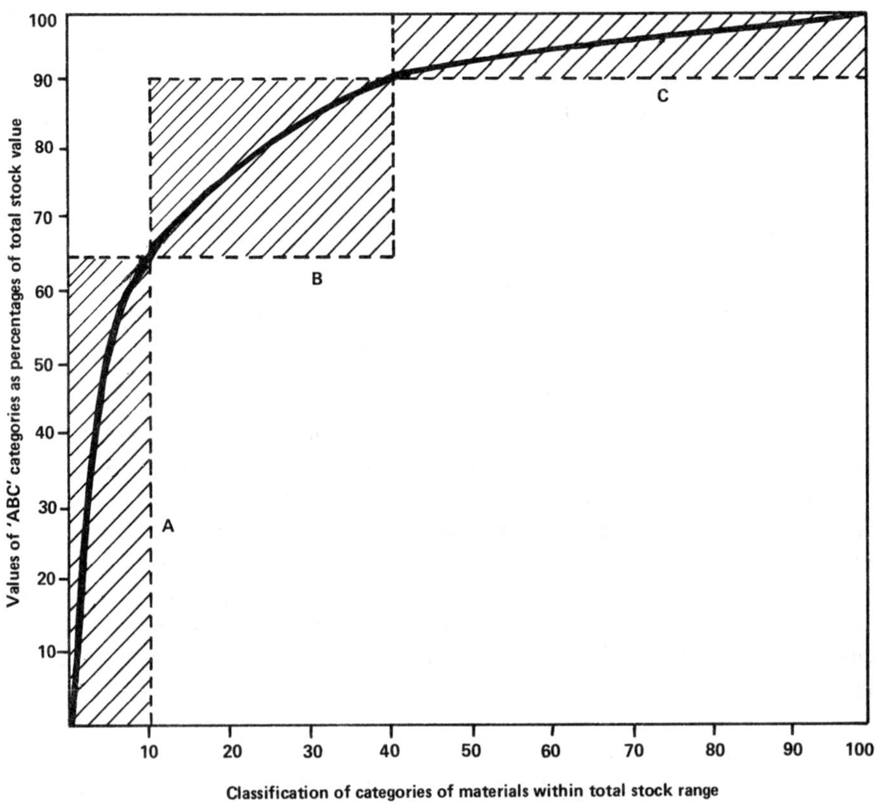

Figure 9.3 *'ABC' analysis: the Pareto curve*

usually called the 'ABC analysis'. Each type of enterprise has its own ABC profile, which relates to the characteristics of the environment in which it operates. A representative profile might be as follows:

Category	**Percentage of commodity range**	**Percentage of total values over a period**
A.High value	10	65
B.Medium value	25	25
C.Low value	65	10

from which would be plotted the following Pareto curve (adapted from BS.5729) which also illustrates the relevance of the 80/20 rule. BS.5729 represents the characteristics of demand patterns in different types of enterprise.

3. *Quantity to be ordered*

When dealing with this subject it is easy to be confused by graphs and formulae. The greater part of industry consists of medium- or small-scale operations which are subject to a considerable range of variants. This renders over-formulation in ordering policies of doubtful value. Having said this, the Economic Order Quantity (EOQ) formula, well known to supplies managers, is capable of achieving lower stocks, fewer orders and, consequently, lower costs. But it must be applied intelligently and economically. Simple methods for determining ordering quantities based on experience and common sense may often prove more reliable than formulae, however well tried, which may be more appropriate to situations other than one's own.

The basic EOQ formula is as follows:

$$\text{EOQ} = \frac{2 \text{ x annual usage quantity x ordering cost}}{\text{unit cost x stockholding cost}}$$

$$\text{eg EOQ} = \frac{2 \text{ x } 80 \text{ x } £5}{£50 \text{ x } 0.2}$$

$$= \text{(about) } 9$$

This formula can be varied to account for the number of weeks' or months' supply to cover with an order, how many orders to place in a year, or to cater for weekly or monthly demand rather than annual demand.

Note.

1. The EOQ formula is useful when applied to large quantities of small items in general demand on a range of products.
2. This formula is of less value
   - in periods of price fluctuation

- where demands fluctuate
- where lead time is indefinite
- where acquisition costs vary.

In these circumstances its application may be unreliable.

The right time

The five rights cannot be set out in a league table of priorities. They are interdependent and each will take its turn in demanding most attention, according to circumstances. When, due to poor planning, an item is urgently required at short notice, immediate delivery will be a more important consideration than the best price. As we saw in the previous section, timing and frequency of deliveries are crucial factors in determining ordering quantities and stock levels. Delays in availability of supplies may lead to production hold-ups, lost sales or public emergency. (During the Windscale incident in 1957, an emergency arose because of the immediate need to prevent the escape of radioactivity. This called for the immediate supply of extraordinary quantities of specialized protective clothing. The demand could not be met from emergency stocks or the limited quantities being produced by existing manufacturers. Extra capacity was created without delay, supplies were rushed to the scene and public safety was restored. Thus a potential nuclear crisis became a supply problem, in the solving of which time was of the essence.)

Other factors which may affect the buyer's ability to secure deliveries when they are needed are:

1. *Stock control policy.* Whether levels are being reviewed continuously (possible where limited ranges and quantities are involved, or where online facilities with appropriate signals are available), or only periodically;
2. *Possible shortages due to international conditions,* eg effect of sanctions on supplies of rhodium from South Africa;
3. *'Glut' conditions.* Immediate availability because of, eg 'dumping' of oil; arrival of banana boat with perishable cargo;
4. *Seasonal demand.* Christmas toy sales.

The experienced buyer is all too familiar with the high proportion of 'urgent' requisitions which land in his in-tray, particularly on Friday afternoons and before holiday breaks. This is mainly due to lack of foresight on the part of the originator, and bad planning back along the line. H K Compton, in his excellent book *Supplies and Materials Management,* stresses the importance of what he describes as 'supplies horizons', in coming to terms with the time factor in supplies management.

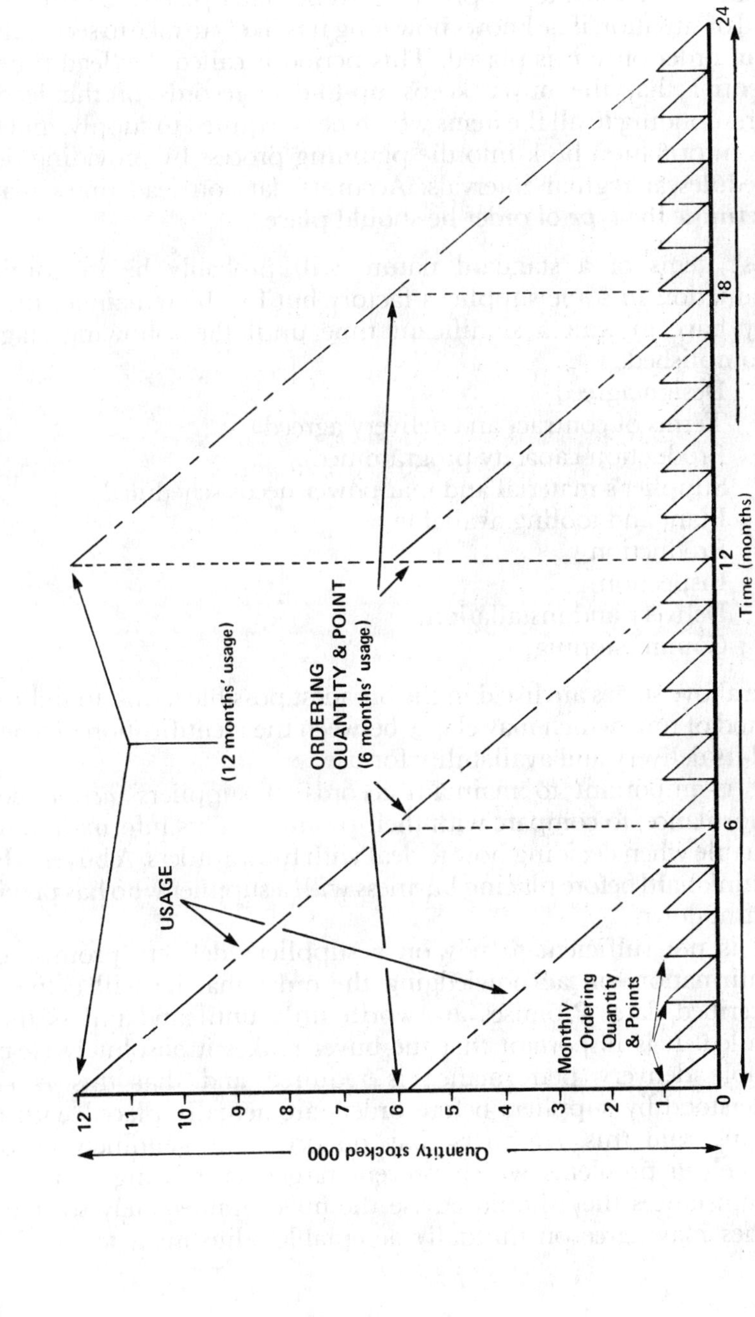

Figure 9.4 *Stock usage levels and reordering time points and quantities*

Whatever the reasons for hold-ups along the line, the buyer must be in constant readiness to meet demands at short notice. Inevitably, blame for delays or non-delivery will be concentrated on him since he is the last one to have been asked to supply. He will be better placed to deal with this kind of situation if he knows how long it is likely to take to secure delivery of an order once it is placed. This period is called the 'lead time'. It is essential that the buyer keeps up-to-date records of the lead time corresponding to all the items which he is required to supply, and to feed this information back into the planning process by providing detailed schedules at regular intervals. Accurate data on lead times may also determine the *type* of order he should place.

Most items of a standard nature will probably be in continuous production in some supplier's factory but for the remainder the buyer may have to wait a significant time until the following stages are accomplished:

- Design agreed
- Terms of contract and delivery agreed
- Production capacity programmed
- Supplier's material and manpower needs scheduled
- Plant and tooling available
- Production
- Inspection
- Delivery and installation
- Commissioning.

The above stages are listed in the broadest possible terms, to indicate the period of time which may elapse between the identification of a demand and its delivery and availability for use.

It is important to maintain records of suppliers' *actual* delivery performance, to compare with their promises. This information will be valuable when deciding how to deal with future orders. A buyer is bound to think hard before placing business with a supplier who has previously let him down.

It is not sufficient to rely on a supplier's delivery promise or his 'confirmation' on acknowledging the order that he will deliver by a prescribed date. Promises are worth little until and unless they are fulfilled. It is important that the buyer makes it absolutely clear that reliable delivery performance is required and that this is clearly understood by suppliers before orders are actually placed with them. Having said this, suppliers may on occasions genuinely encounter unforeseen problems which prevent target dates being met. In such circumstances they should advise the buyer immediately so that both parties may agree on mutually acceptable adjustment to the delivery

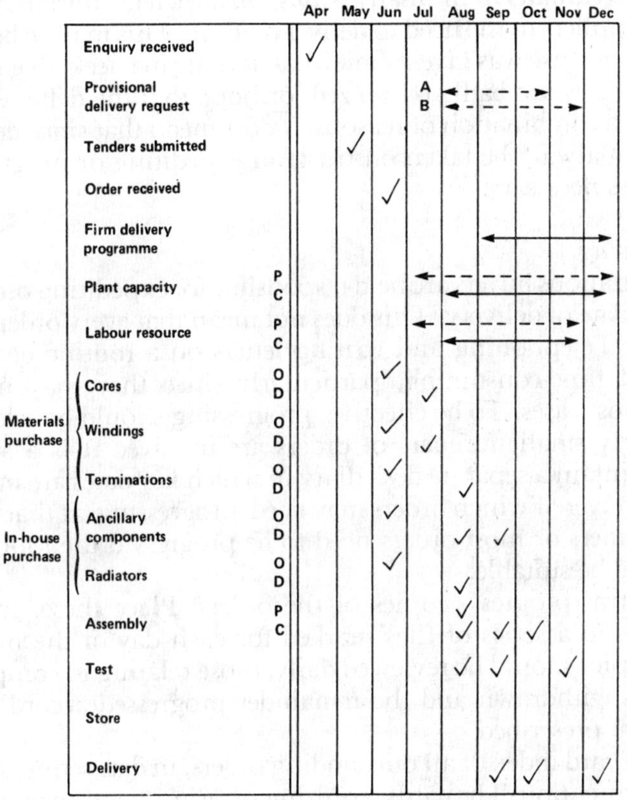

A simplified matrix for Materials Requirements Planning (MRP)

A 500 kVA
B 750 kVA
} Distribution Transformers

Key:
P Provisional
C Confirmed
O Ordered
D Delivered
✓ Stage achieved

Notes:

1. A similar matrix should be prepared for each product range.
2. The example shows MRP within context of an overall production planning schedule for a single contract. For clarity only selected material items have been shown. In practice the matrix should be divided into ABC categories.
3. For continuous production the schedule would normally provide for purchases for and issues from stock.
4. The matrix could be adapted for construction and contracting work. (For instance, in the electricity supply industry the process has been described as Job Organization, Planning and Progressing or JOPP.)
5. The system can easily be computerized, and suitable software should be readily available.

schedule. Unfortunately, in many cases, insufficient importance is attached by suppliers to the need to deliver on time. This may be because their original promise was given somewhat 'tongue in cheek' to gain the order, because they are badly organized, or hope that the delay will be overlooked, or a combination of reasons. It does mean that since delivery on time cannot always be taken on trust, an expediting or progressing system becomes necessary.

1. *Progressing*

In most organizations buyers are held responsible for expediting orders to the point and date of delivery. This does not mean that every order must be progressed. Telephoning and writing letters on a routine basis are expensive and time-consuming, particularly since they may not be necessary in most cases. To be effective, progressing should be selective. Where relatively small numbers of orders are involved it is a simple practice to maintain a separate desk diary in which key dates are marked to remind the buyer of which orders may need 'progressing' at that stage.

If large numbers or most orders need to be progressed the following methods would be suitable:

- Make extra (progress) copies of the orders. Place these, in date sequence, in a series of files marked for each day of the month. These copies should be reviewed daily, those relating to completed deliveries withdrawn and the remainder progressed according to the system prescribed.
- Prepare a card index of all outstanding orders, in date sequence, for progress attention. The cards requiring priority attention would be marked with coloured tags and these would be looked at first when the cards are checked each day for progress action.
- Feed the order details into the computer which would be programmed to indicate the delivery position each day. Appropriate action would then be taken.

Progressing is not something which is done only when deliveries become overdue. It is then often too late to take alternative measures to secure supply. The production line may come to a standstill, or a customer will be let down. The experienced buyer or progress-chaser will come to recognize situations which require special attention, particularly those which they know have critical time factors. It is prudent to *check* progress before completion dates and important to get the true facts on how things stand. If the supplier appears evasive, or if the regular contact 'is not available' when a call is made, these are tell-tale signs that all is not quite right. The buyer must then take positive action and, if necessary, visit the supplier to ascertain the position.

If it is confirmed that the delivery requirement will not be met the buyer must agree with the requisitioner what alternative action is necessary. It must be remembered that in some instances liquidated damages may be claimed against delays. If the buyer's organization is the main contractor in a project it will become liable for such payments. Furthermore, the company will jeopardize its own reputation for reliability if it is seen to be incapable of asserting its authority on the subcontractors who cause the delay.

Progressing is not only an activity relating to outside suppliers and subcontractors. Quite often delays take place *within* the primary organization: supervisors and managers concerned with shop floor activities and frequently under pressure, usually concentrating upon a small area of activity. A progress unit in the supplies department can be of considerable help in ensuring that all the checks and expediting that may be necessary to maintain continuity in the movement of internal material, resources and services are carried out. At the same time its assistance will have a co-ordinating effect in relation to:

- Material control and availability;
- Store
- Toolroom and tool stores;
- Transport and materials handling;
- Maintenance — notification of breakdowns;
- Sales and distribution.

2. *Network analysis and planning*

Good planning is essential to supplies as to any other other function of management. Consequently, many of the techniques used elsewhere in industry and commerce can be usefully applied to the control of ordering and phasing of deliveries of goods and materials. One of these techniques is network analysis, which traces the 'critical path' from initiation to completion of a sequence of actions. In the case of material purchasing planning the network would closely relate to the production schedule, the critical path making its way through a pattern of sub- or contributory paths to the ultimate (delivery) objective of the supply chain.

3. *Buying and time*

In this section we have briefly touched on some of the more important aspects of time in supplies administration. There are other, more complex areas which demand specialization of the highest order which can only be mentioned here, such as commodities and futures buying. The reader requiring further information should refer to:

Lee and Dobler, *Purchasing and Materials Management*
G W Aljian, *Purchasing Handbook*
G L Rees, *British Commodity Markets*
Watling and Morley, *Successful Commodities Future Trading.*

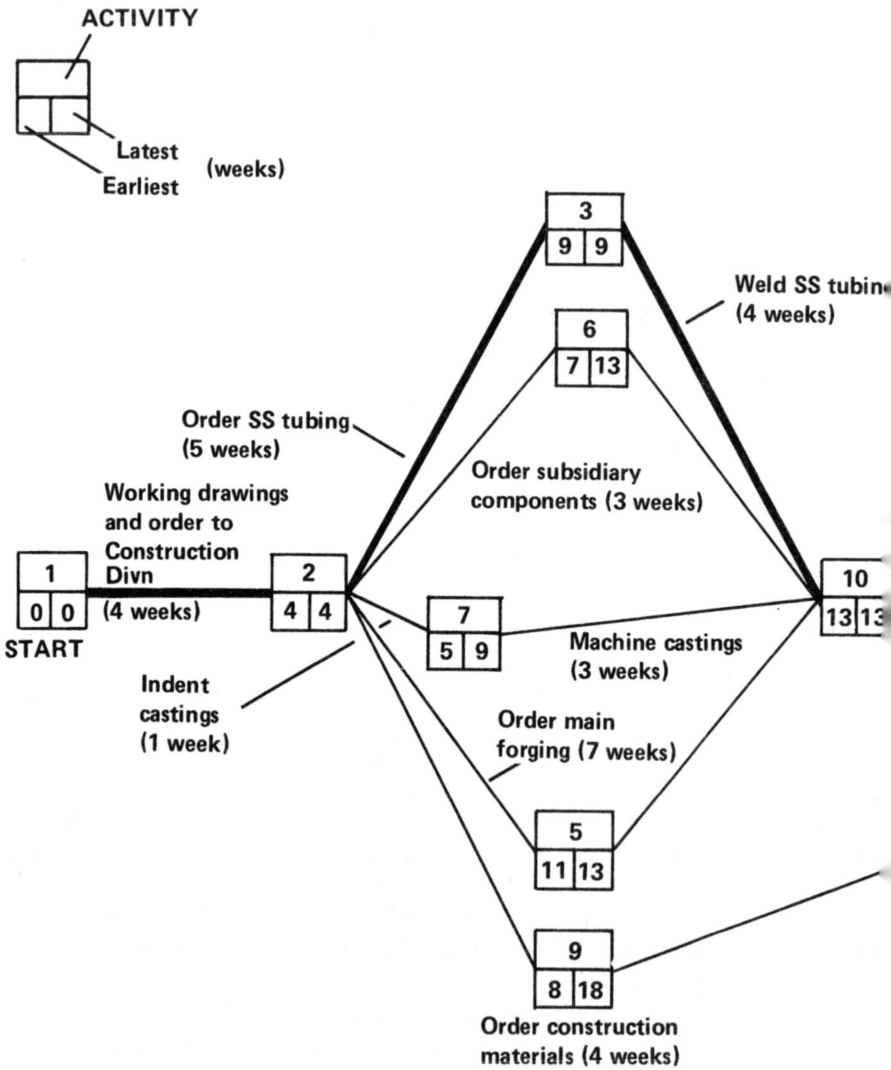

Figure 9.5 *Activity network – pressure tubing assembly*

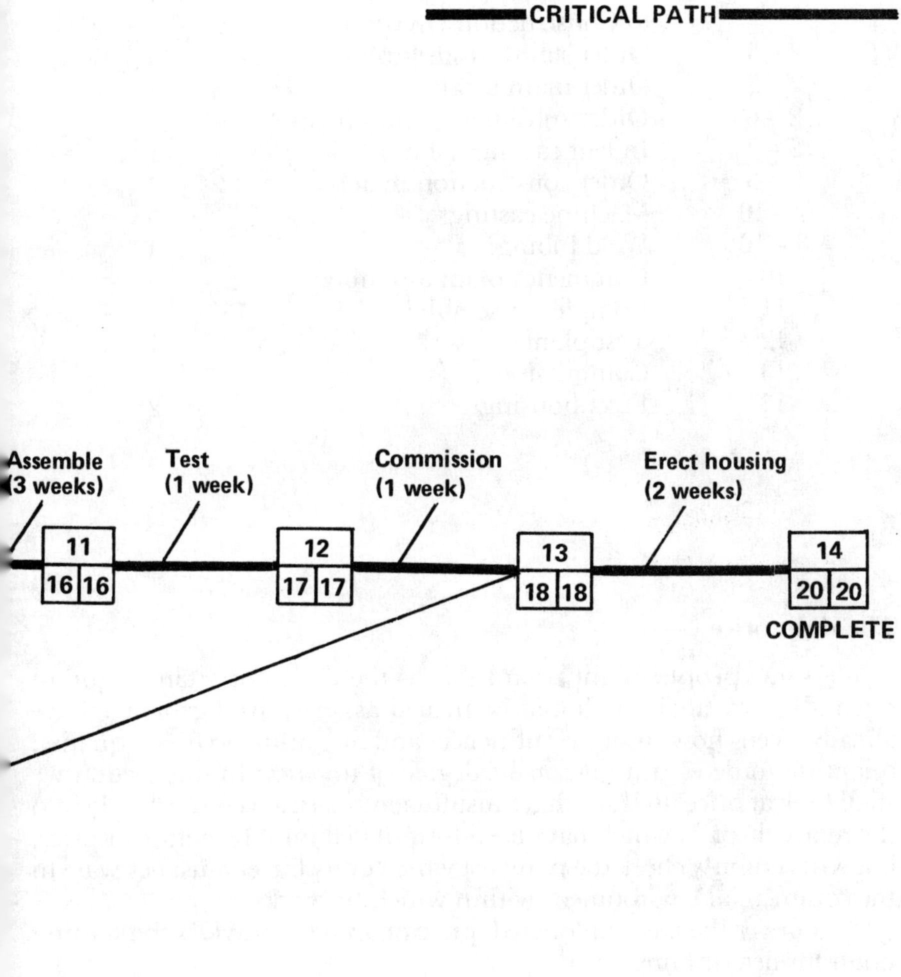
CRITICAL PATH
Assemble
(3 weeks)
Test
(1 week)
Commission
(1 week)
Erect housing
(2 weeks)
11
16 16
12
17 17
13
18 18
14
20 20
COMPLETE

Activity No		Duration (weeks)
	START	-
1 - 2	Working drawings and order to Construction Division	4
2 - 3	Order stainless steel tubing	5
2 - 5	Order main forging	7
2 - 6	Order subsidiary components	3
2 - 7	Indent castings (store)	1
2 - 9	Order construction materials	4
7 - 10	Machine castings	3
3 - 10	Weld tubing	4
10	Commence plant assembly	3
11	Complete assembly	
12	Test plant	1
13	Commission	1
14	Erect housing	2

The right price

While some people might regard this as the most important 'right' of them all, once again it should be treated as a relative factor. We have already seen how it may influence and be influenced by quality, quantities ordered, timing, or the degree of urgency. In this section we shall look at price itself. We have insufficient space to venture deeply into the many theories which have been formulated into the nature of price, but will certainly check the points of which every buyer must be aware in the commercial environment within which he works.

To a buyer the basic or 'offered' price of an item provides the starting point for determining

- the price he will eventually pay;
- the total *costs* of buying the item;
- the value in use of the item, compared with other items on offer.

The price the buyer eventually pays will depend on a number of *external* factors, including:

- The actual cost of producing the item
- Supply/demand in the market place at a particular time
- Market forces (eg competition)

- Pricing strategy (eg loss-leadership)
- Seller dominance or price leadership
- Monopoly situation
- Special relationship with seller
- Continuity of manufacture for future orders
- Reliability of supply for future orders
- Accessibility of manufacture
- Inflation/currency trends.

The price paid will also be balanced against a number of *internal* factors, including:

- The purchase strategy (eg competition, single tender or negotiation)
- Flexibility in time-scale for delivery
- Life-cycle costs
- Type of order (fixed price, or price subject to variation)
- Contribution of own organization (eg capital assistance, installation, erection, maintenance)
- Terms of payment agreed (eg stage payments, progress payments, financing costs)
- Resale price strategy (eg profit margins).

Before proceeding to the second and third determinants (total purchase costs and value in use) it would be useful to provide more detail to some of the points already listed.

1. *Cost of producing the article*

It is of immense value to the buyer to know as much as possible about the actual cost make-up of the article he is seeking to purchase. This knowledge may be based on:

- his own experience;
- previous history from which data is available;
- figures from his estimating department;
- information provided by the potential seller;
- comparative information received from competitors.

Armed with this type of information the buyer can test the reasonableness of the offer price and undertake subsequent negotiations from a position of strength. Cost investigations should aim to establish details within the following framework:

Direct costs (Production cost)

Labour
Materials
Bought-in terms

Conversion costs
Cost-centre overheads
(eg location, shop,
machine, inspection)

Indirect costs

General factory charges (eg power, lighting, repairs, cleaning)	Factory cost
Administrative and financing charges and overheads	Establishment cost
Warehousing, sales, distribution	Selling cost

Profit

It will be noted that many items listed among the external factors are greatly influenced by the nature of the market at a particular *time* (eg market forces, supply/demand, loss-leadership to attract initial business, monopoly situations, currency trends), which again underlines the interrelationship between the 'rights' of purchasing. Other external factors (eg continuity of manufacture and reliability of supply) are concerned with future, as well as with present needs.

The *internal* factors governing the price to be paid which most directly concern the buyer are his purchase strategy and the type of order or contract which he decides to place. In respect of strategy his choice is limited to two alternatives:

Competition — by 'open' or selective tendering
Single sourcing — by single tender or by negotiation

It is usually considered advantageous to seek competitive quotations depending on the nature of the items required, and the range of approved and capable suppliers. It is best to avoid issuing a specification which restricts selection to a proprietary or branded article to the exclusion of others which may be equally suitable for the intended purpose. However, where competition may not be available because only one specialist firm is capable of undertaking the work, the buyer will have to take single tender action or enter into negotiation with that firm.

Note. Negotiation is not excluded from the competitive process. Nevertheless, if introduced, it must be conducted with the utmost consideration of the interests of all competing parties as well as those of the purchaser.

The least desirable situation occurs when the buyer is virtually obliged to take single tender action merely because there is insufficient time to seek competition — on the grounds of urgency. This places the buyer at a disadvantage when it comes to price agreement.

In exceptional cases the supplier may be given an 'instruction to proceed' with the work (again on the grounds of urgency or because the purchaser cannot specify in sufficient detail what he actually wants) before a price can be agreed. These instances usually arise where supply or the work to be carried out is of an original or development nature. It must be made clear to the supplier that price agreement must be on the basis of full disclosure of costing information, to enable both parties to negotiate a fair and reasonable price on equal terms.

2. *Price in different types of purchase order*

- *General order.* This is the type in common use for most normal transactions and includes the price at which delivery will be completed.

- *Running contract.* Frequently used by government departments, based on specified suppliers' catalogues, and subject to pre-agreed discount rebate and payment terms. No quantity commitment.

- *Forward supply arrangement.* A quasi-contract placed for a period or specifying approximate quantity parameters; setting out terms on which individual withdrawal orders will be priced. Prices are normally quoted in the covering document; subsequent variations being subject to prior agreement.

- *Withdrawal order.* See *Forward supply arrangement* above.

- *Blanket order.* Usually for higher-value items, covering a fixed supply period. This constitutes a commitment to draw off a quantity of items according to a schedule, at prices determined at the outset.

- *Cost-plus contract.* This is associated with work which cannot be priced at the outset, because of the development or research nature of the project. Payments are made on production of evidence of reasonable costs, a 'non-risk' profit percentage being added.

- *Technical costed contract.* Similar to cost-plus. In this case the client's costing officers value the work and payment is made accordingly, with the addition of a 'semi-risk' profit percentage.

- *Fixed price.* Relevant to civil engineering and building projects where the price at which the work specified will be carried out is established at the outset. This may not cover subsequent variations to the project for which separate pricing agreement may be necessary.

- *Firm and fixed price.* When this is determined, no change is allowed.

- *Schedule rate.* This also normally applies to civil engineering works, in which prices are agreed according to a schedule (not necessarily a bill of quantities).

- *Lump sum.* The contractor undertakes the work set out in drawings and specification for a fixed sum, come what may. Any subsequent alteration to the client's requirements would be subject to separate negotiation.

- *Price variation.* In times of price uncertainty (eg inflationary periods) price variation clauses are included in contract terms to enable adjustments to be made according to predetermined formulae.

The above list is not exhaustive, but covers the main types of pricing arrangement encountered in buying practice. Readers wishing to have more detail should refer to the books mentioned in Chapter 16.

3. *Total buying cost*

It should be borne in mind that in many cases the costs of tendering, negotiation, financing, handling, importation and a proportion of the overheads of the supplies department have to be added to the basic purchase price of the item concerned. These factors should always be taken into account when weighing the advantages of certain methods of purchasing and also when comparing different offers.

The value in use of the item purchased may also be relative to (almost a consequence of) the price paid for it. Price itself will be less significant than such factors as quality, reliability and durability when long-term use is required. The well-known Yorkshire expression sums up the situation admirably: 'You don't get owt for nowt' 'and you won't get much for a mite more'.

The right place

It should be obvious to the buyer that if an item of plant, for instance, is to be delivered to a building site, then it must be clear to the supplier *where* it must be set down. Delivery will not be effected at the site entrance if the construction or materials are required in a particular location on the site. Delivery at works will not necessarily be fulfilled if the goods arrive at the store, some distance away. Precise instructions as to the required destination must always be included in order documentation.

Sourcing

When introducing the five 'rights' of purchasing we indicated that if all the other criteria were satisfied it could be considered that the right supplier had been selected. This does not necessarily mean that the same supplier should be used every time a particular demand arises. Market conditions are constantly changing and the buyer must be constantly on the look-out for alternative sources of supply. This is likely to sharpen competition in terms of price and in the range of selection of similar products. The supplier may not be changed at regular intervals but if he knows that he is subject to continual comparison evaluation, he will be keener to satisfy the buyer. Otherwise complacency will eventually set in. From the buyer's point of view it is no good sitting back with a fixed attitude to supply sources, relying solely on the loyalty factor of his relationships with particular companies, or buying where he is told to buy. This is typical of the 'order-clerk' syndrome. Positive purchasing calls for a dynamic approach to the question of supplier selection.

Subject to the foregoing observations, the buyer would follow Figure 9.6 to establish sources of supply. Much of the required sourcing details will be obtainable from past records. New data resulting from further enquiries and tender action should be added to the existing information 'bank' for future use.

When determining sources of supply, the buyer should also consider

- dealing through wholesalers through whom, in many instances (eg electrical equipment, building and contracting materials, stationery, food products) better terms can be obtained;
- obtaining the product by in-house manufacture (see *Make or buy*, page 265) or inter-group transaction;

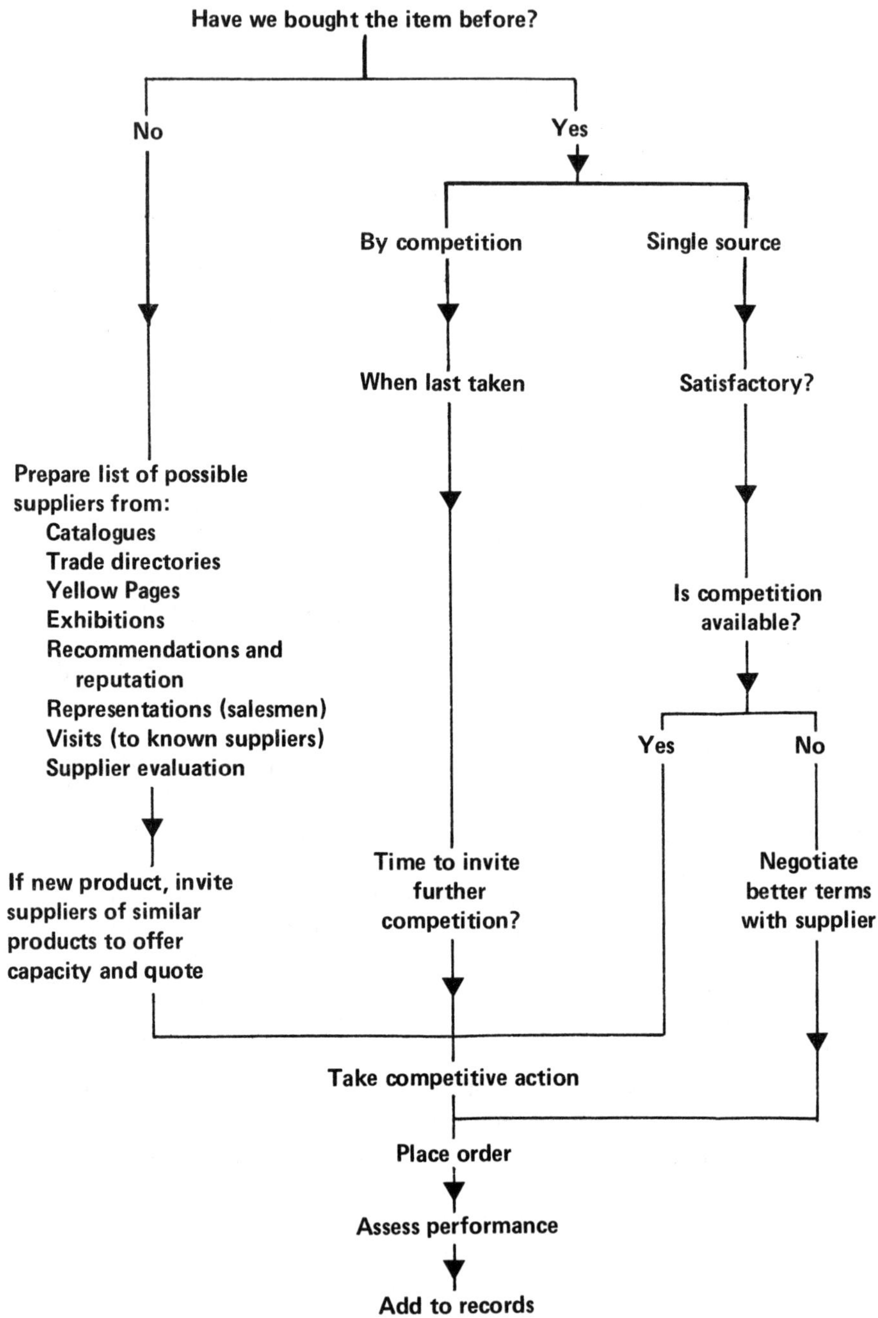

Figure 9.6 *Establishing sources of supply*

- importing (see *Buying from Abroad*, page 266);
- reciprocal trading;
- approach to manufacturers' agents.

1. *Supplier evaluation*

Having produced what may be a long list of possible suppliers the buyer will wish to reduce the number to manageable and sensible proportions. Before issuing enquiries to, or entering into negotiations with, new suppliers it is preferable to begin with the number capable of being properly assessed with the resources at his disposal. If time permits it is best to visit the suppliers concerned. The buyer should first prepare a questionnaire on the lines suggested below, which he will complete during and after his visit.

SUPPLIER EVALUATION REPORT

Name of supplier:

Address:
Product range:

			Weighting	*Rating*
Plant:	Layout			
	Capacity			
	Maintenance			
	Condition			
	Housekeeping			
		Sub-Total		
Machinery & Tools	Origin			
	Age			
	Capacity			
	Capability			
	Condition			
	Maintenance			
	Safety			
		Sub-Total		
Workforce:	Operatives			
	Operator skills			
	Supervision			
	Inspection			
		Sub-Total		

Design, Research & Development:	Direction	
	Staff	
	Computers	
	Laboratories	
		Sub-Total
Planning & Production Control:	Direction	
	Estimating	
	Methods	
	Order book	
		Sub-Total
Quality Control:	Management	
	Systems	
	Equipment	
	Materials	
	Inspection	
		Sub-Total
Stores:	Capacity	
	Handling	
	Equipment	
	Staff	
	Systems	
		Sub-Total
Administration:	Direction	
	Specialisms	
	Performance	
	Conditions	
		Sub-Total
Supplier Relations:	Purchasing staff	
	Sales staff	
	Stocks	
	Delivery	
	Performance	
		Sub-Total
Finance:	Capital invested	
	Reserves	
	Liquidity ratio	
	Credit rating	
		Sub-Total
Overall:	Management	
	Morale	
		Sub-Total Total Rating:

The reader will obviously be anxious to add or substitute his own categories, priorities and ratings for those shown in the above example. The list of possible items to be checked when evaluating suppliers is virtually endless and will vary according to the buyer's interests.

2. *Vendor rating*

Armed with the information collected from his sorties into suppliers' territory, the buyer will not only be better placed to assess their potential, but he will have improved his own education immeasurably in respect of contemporary conditions in business. When the order has been completed by the selected supplier the buyer should review his initial assessments. At this stage he will revise his 'markings' where appropriate, and maintain records of performance, thus constituting a comprehensive system of vendor rating.

3. *Make or buy?*

It may not be necessary to seek capacity outside the organization. When components or parts are required for production, management must decide whether they can or should be manufactured in-house or bought elsewhere. The decision will depend on a number of factors, and the buyer must be closely involved in evaluating the alternatives. Where time is of the essence to maintain the production line, the prime concern of the production manager will be immediate availability and if the buyer has not been given adequate notice of the requirement he will be under great pressure to secure the items without delay. In these circumstances he may be placed at a disadvantage in securing deliveries at reasonable prices.

If in-house manufacturing capacity is available at the time there should, on the face of things, be no problem. The item would be made, instead of bought.

A typical situation such as that described in the previous paragraph may appear to represent a simple statement of the principles applied to 'make or buy' decisions. However, it should be perceived that:

- the decision might be made at different levels:
  (a) *Top management.* Where new plant is required to manufacture in-house;
  (b) *Middle management.* In assessing costs of in-house production for long-run requirements by comparison with purchase;
  (c) *Routine.* Cost-comparisons for short-run requirements.
- the buyer is involved in each situation.

Decision-making may be further complicated by the following circumstances:

- Where the company had traditionally produced components in-house and market conditions have changed, making in-house production uncompetitive;
- Where the firm has been taken over by an organization within which suitable production facilities are available at lower cost.

In such cases long-term policy decisions would need to be made which will have industrial relations and real-estate implications. Every time the question 'make or buy?' arises, the answer may well be 'what we did last time'. In consequence, it is easy to see that, as conditions change, however gradually, the time will come when a different line of action would be more appropriate. It is important, therefore, to undertake continual reviews of supply areas in which make or buy situations occur.

4. *Buying from abroad*

It may be necessary to use overseas sources of supply for one or more of the following reasons.

Reasons	*Examples*
• Non-availability of product from home sources	Brand (eg Tobler chocolate) Design (eg Mercedes car) Raw material (eg Rhodium) Absence of expertise/know-how
• Lack of home production capacity	Foodstuffs Decision of home-based manufacturers to cease production.
• Quality	High technology Machine tools which do the job better Style, having more customer appeal More durable finishes
• Price	Competitive with or cheaper than equivalent home-produced items Exchange rates may offer temporary advantage
• Delivery	Better geared to production/sales requirements
• Reliability	After-sales service Availability of spares

• Conditions of purchase	Design rights in dispute v availability of equivalent off-the-shelf
• Reciprocity	Government- or company- level trade agreement; relations between holding/subsidiary companies
• Second sourcing	Providing back-up in event of failure of home source.

The buyer will recognize from the above list of examples many of the criteria which make up the five principal 'rights' of good purchasing practice.

Buying from abroad will involve certain problems which are not encountered when sourcing at home, such as language differences, tariffs, exchange controls, customs procedures, documentation, payment, insurance and freight, communications and distance. An experienced buyer should be able to deal with problems of this kind but, if difficulties arise, there are many places and people from whom he may receive advice.

Information on sourcing from abroad may be obtained from:

Trade journals. Up-to-date copies are available from trade associations and may be found in most good public libraries.

Chambers of Trade and Commerce. Membership subscriptions are good value. These organizations are in regular direct contact with their opposite numbers overseas.

Trade directories. These are readily obtainable from the publishers. Among the most useful are Kemps, Kompass, Jaeger and Waldman.

Embassies/Trade consuls. Most large cities have trade consuls representing overseas countries.

Professional institutes. The Institute of Purchasing and Supply Yearbooks, monthly and weekly publications, provide helpful sourcing information. The International Federation of Purchasing and Materials Management has member Associations in most overseas countries.

Trade fairs and exhibitions. Numerous events are held each year both at home and abroad. (The buyer and his company must include travel and subsistence costs in his profit/loss equation for potential deals.)

Representatives. Enterprising selling concerns will ensure that potential buyers are visited at intervals.

Other buyers. There is usually helpful disposition between people who have similar business interests and between whom professional relationships may be of mutual benefit.

5. *Enquiries to foreign suppliers*

It is important that requirements be clearly defined in the simplest terms consistent with being precise. Points to be resolved include:

- *Language.* While English is in common use in trading circles it should not be assumed that recipients are familiar with or *fluent* in our native tongue. Having resolved the technical detail to its essentials the buyer should, if necessary, consult with an experienced translator or translation agency. Clarity at this stage will avoid unnecessary correspondence about questions of fact.
- *Specification.* It is helpful to refer to the appropriate standard recognized by both parties to the projected deal.
- *Law and currency.* The country under whose laws the transaction is to take place should be stated at this stage, and similarly the currency in which payment will be made.
- *Delivery.* The buyer's requirements must be expressed to ensure that all quotations are made on the same basis, eg to include carriage, insurance and freight (CIF); to be placed free on board ship (FOB); free alongside ship (FAS), etc. (See table on page 269).
- *Price.* There must be clear and mutual understanding between buyer and tenderer regarding the elements of the quoted price. Among the more important of these are:
  (a) Currency rate base
  (b) Net price of product
  (c) Separate costs of packing (if applicable).
  In addition, the buyer will require details of:
  (d) Payment terms
  (e) Freight charges
  (f) Duty
  (g) Other costs to the delivery point.

Should the buyer himself decide to handle procedures following despatch from the supplier, he must assume responsibility for the tasks shown in the table opposite; and, of course, he must bear the costs associated with them.

Range of tasks	**Buyer's responsibilities**	
	Terms of sale	Tasks — Numbers
1. Load on carrier ex-supplier's works 2. Provide/pay for inland transport	A. Ex-works	1 to 2 inclusive
3. Pay for insurance 4. Pay for demurrage	B. Free on board (FOB) seller's works	2, 3, 5 to 26 inclusive
5. Obtain export documents 6. Deliver to port of exit 7. Unload at port of exit	C. FOB seller's works freight allowed	2, 3, 5, 7 to 26 inclusive
8. Pay port dues 9. Name vessel	D. FOB seller's works freight prepaid	3, 7, to 26 inclusive
Give notice of 10. Sailing date 11. Loading berth	E. FOB vessel port of export	3, 9, to 12 inclusive. 16 to 26 inclusive
12. Required delivery time 13. Load on ship	F. FOB vessel port of import	3, 18 to 26 inclusive
14. Pay loading charges 15. Provide bill of lading Air waybill 16. Provide insurance	G. Free alongside ship (FAS) port of export	3, 9 to 26 inclusive
17. Pay for shipment 18. Unload at port of entry 19. Pay unloading charges	H. FAS port of import	3, 20 to 26 inclusive
20. Pay port dues 21. Pay customs dues 22. Pay demurrage costs	I. Carriage, insurance and freight (CIF) port of import	3, 18 to 26 inclusive
23. Prepare import documentation 24. Provide/pay for inland transport 25. Receive	J. Carriage and freight (C&F) port of import	3, 16, 18 to 26 inclusive
26. Unload	K. FOB buyer's works	3, 25, 26

PROCESSING THE DEMAND

Having identified a requirement, a number of points have to be satisfied before quotations are invited:

- How much is the item likely to cost?
- Are sufficient funds readily available?
- Has approval to spend been given at the right level?
- To what cost category will the expenditure be charged?

1. *Requisition*

It is usual to obtain the signature of each person whose authority is required to validate the demand on a single document. This is called a requisition, and should provide all essential details relating to the demand, including:

- Reference
- Originator
- Date raised
- Items required by catalogue/part number/description
- Quantity
- Required delivery date and location
- Special instructions (eg packaging, mode of transport or handling)
- Commodity code identification (where applicable). This indicates stock location and facilitates stores accounting.
- Job to which purchase is to be charged
- Present stock (if relevant)
- Evidence of *financial* sanction for expenditure
- Suggestions as to source(s) of supply
- Signature of senior person authorizing *purchase order*
- Purchase order reference number (added by buyer when action is taken)

The requisition is prepared in duplicate:

Top copy — to buyer (attached to order in due course)
Carbon copy — retained by originator

Both copies will be retained for record and audit purposes.

Should additional copies be required provision should be made when the requisition sets are designed. It is good practice to restrict the circulation of copies to those persons or sections who really *need* to know the details at any particular stage.

'Travelling' requisition. For routine requirements in regular demand a 'travelling' requisition may be found useful. This document should be in

card form, to withstand repeated handling over a period. It enables paperwork to be reduced and, provided the card is not mislaid, should prove quite adequate for the purposes of action, control and record.

2. *Indent*

Another type of formal request for goods or materials (usually for withdrawal from *stock*) is called an indent, which is a simplified form of requisition. The items in question are likely to be identifiable by a unique commodity code, rendering lengthy descriptions unnecessary. The document should show:

- the name of the originator
- authority to indent
- cost allocation.

All documentation should be prepared with sufficient information for the purposes of:

- stores and stock accounting and valuation
- reconciliation
- recharge
- reordering
- record.

3. *Request for information*

Details of availability and prices may be needed before a firm requisition is raised. These may be for budgetary purposes or to assist in preparing a specification. When communicating the details to potential suppliers or contractors the buyer should make it quite clear that only information is required and that no contractual commitment is intended or implied at that stage.

4. *Inviting quotations*

Buyers working for local authorities, nationalized industries and government departments are subject to very strict regulations in the handling of tenders and quotations and in placing orders and contracts. This is because the requirements of public accountability have to be satisfied, having regard to the immense spending power of the sector. This does not mean that the public sector differs in any other respect from the rest of the business world in the manner of dealing with commercial transactions.

Whether or not he or she is subject to the constraints of public accountability, in any environment the buyer is in a position of trust and he should undertake his responsibilities with the utmost integrity. The interests of his employers are paramount, consistent with even-handed treatment of the companies with which he acts on their behalf in business relationships.

When inviting quotations it is recommended that standard forms of enquiry be used and that suppliers be asked to return their tenders by a common fixed date. This practice will ensure that tenderers have equal opportunity to consider their offers, and provides the buyer with a definite time schedule for dealing with them. It is also more likely to avoid an extended 'horsetrading' period during which tenderers may try to circumvent the disciplines imposed by tendering. Most buyers are wedded to the principle of competition, which is the process most likely to achieve the best results in the longer term.

5. *Placing the order*

When it has been decided where the business should be placed, the successful tenderer should be informed that his offer has been accepted, preferably in writing. All terms of the agreed contract should be written into a document and issued to the supplier. This will reduce the scope for dispute at a later stage. It is as well to secure an acknowledgement from the supplier that he has, in fact, received the document though even if he does not do so, this would not alter the force of the contract.

6. *Post-contract action*

Copies of the contract or order should be sent to

- the originator
- receipt point
- accounts

} these copies need not be priced, if confidentiality is required.

When the goods have been delivered or work completed, payment being due, the supplier's invoice should be passed to the accountant for action. Any queries, amendments and claims should be dealt with by the buyer who will take such advice as may be appropriate from the client or originator.

BUYING FOR RESALE

Stock range

What, when, and how much to buy or stock for resale are crucial questions for the retailer. If he is a sole trader or partner, profits and losses are transferred to his personal account. He is in competition with the 'big guns' of the retail trade who will easily be able to outbuy and outsell him. The axiom for the smaller trading unit must therefore be:

- buy as well as possible

- stock as little as is needed to sustain target sales
- keep overheads to a minimum.

A range of purchasing and supply problems will confront the trader taking up retailing for the first time, possibly having purchased a going concern.

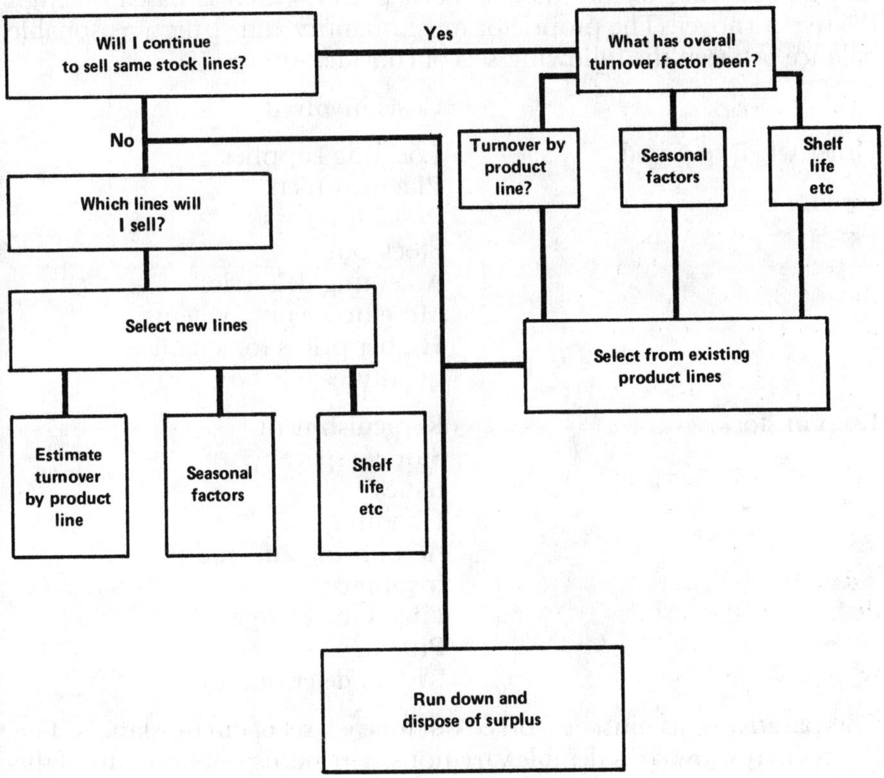

Figure 9.7 *Stock range*

Having decided which items to sell, the retailer must determine how much he should hold in stock, each product line being separately identified for this purpose according to the nature of the business:

- Perishables
- Fashions
- Seasonal lines
- Varieties (general store)

While values per item, sub-range and range of stock may vary widely it would be prudent to budget for a reasonably consistent total average value of stock to be held throughout the trading period. This will obviously minimize difficulties which are caused by erratic cash flow. It also makes sense to formulate a stock policy which is based on high relative turnover. The proprietor must quantify and strike a reasonable balance between the following sets of considerations:

	Costs involved
Order when required:	Locating supplies Placing orders Possible delays Stock-outs Accepting deliveries More frequent payments Higher prices for smaller quantities
Keep in stock:	Replenishment Storage space Issues Handling Accounting and audit Insurance Financing charges Pilferage Risk of deterioration

Comparative costs must be worked out for each set of circumstances. The figures may show considerable variations, depending on the nature of the business concerned, but retailers should be warned that the total cost of holding stocks can easily reach 20 per cent of the average value of the goods stocked. A high relative sales turnover is therefore necessary to achieve a reasonable profit margin.

Wholesalers and distributors

Fortunately, smaller retail businesses are not left entirely to their own resources in regard to stockholding. Most of their problems can be solved by the 'middlemen' of the wholesale and distribution industry. These provide a very important service to retailers by supplying and delivering ranges and quantities of goods on a selective basis to individual outlets. This service is available on a regular basis in most areas. Regularity of delivery will depend on the product: daily for food perishables and perhaps once a week for DIY items, for example. The two key components in the distribution chain are:

- the manufacturer anxious to distribute } as economically
- the customer wishing to buy } as possible

Individual manufacturers with a limited range cannot hope to supply a multitude of outlets separately and individual customers cannot deal with scores of potential suppliers, economically. The wholesaler provides the answer for both parties. It would, in any event, probably cost a retailer more in time and trouble to go to a 'cheaper' source than it would to have quick and reliable delivery from a local source.

LEGAL ASPECTS

Law is an area in which most people try to avoid entanglements. Nevertheless, those engaged in purchasing and supply management would be well advised to develop an intelligent appreciation of the legal implications of the actions taken by themselves and their suppliers in the course of everyday dealings. In any contract the seller seeks to protect his interests to the limit and the buyer must also seek complementary safeguards for his company. There is every reason why the buyer should take the initiative by preparing his company's terms and conditions for purchasing, rather than waiting to see what is in the vendor's 'small print'.

It is essential that the basics of contract law are understood, to avoid confusion or doubt. These are as follows:

- There must be offer and acceptance (and the acceptance must relate to the offer and not comprise a counter-offer).
- There must be a mutual intent to create a legal relationship.
- The parties must be capable of making a contract.
- A consideration must pass between the parties.

Special care should be taken in the following problem areas:

- Performance obligations (including contract programme, damages for delay, retentions and spares availability)
- Guarantees

- Patent and design rights
- Sub-contracting

though there are many other contract conditions which contain traps for the unwary.

Many textbooks deal explicitly (and interestingly) with commercial law, and Chapter 15 covers the subject in greater detail. The supplies manager should familiarize himself with the following legislation:

Supply of Goods and Services Act 1982
Supply of Goods (Implied Terms) Act 1973
Unfair Contract Terms Act 1977
Fair Trading Act 1973
Consumer Protection Act 1987
Consumer Safety Act 1978
Competition Act 1980
European Communities Act 1972, as well as the relevant areas of transport and industrial law, current legislation and case law.

POSITIVE SUPPLIES MANAGEMENT

The leading enterprises amply demonstrate that advanced business skills can be translated into profitability and success, but not all the rewards come solely from the marketing and sales departments. No one sells anything until someone else buys it.

We have seen how purchasing can also be an important profit centre and that effective stock management can have a dramatic impact on financing and overhead costs. Good supplies management is an essential element in a healthy enterprise and a properly trained and professional supplies manager can be one of its most valuable assets.

Employers who expect their supplies staff to spend most of their time in an office dealing with paperwork, making and receiving telephone calls, are not getting the best out of them. Individual skills are not likely to develop much where an 'ivory tower' attitude prevails. Much potential talent will be wasted where it could be used to make a positive contribution to the company's growth and prosperity. It is important that buyers venture into the market-place themselves. That is where a high proportion of business is done. It should not be left to the highly motivated salesman to visit the buyer to seek orders. The buyer knows what is wanted and he is likely to achieve more if he 'shops around' and negotiates with suppliers than would be possible in studying catalogues and issuing enquiries to traditional suppliers who will respond to his lack of enterprise by taking him for granted. When visiting exhibitions or attending presentations of new production lines the buyer is bound to meet his opposite numbers from other organizations. Buying can be as competitive as selling. When new products become available, or when supply shortages occur, the buyer must be on the spot at the right time to look after his company's interests. He should never miss an opportunity of widening his perspective of the business world and sharpening his commercial instincts.

Training is available in most parts of the country. The principal colleges, as well as many polytechnics, provide first class facilities for students studying for the professional qualifications of the Institute of Purchasing and Supply, which is probably the premier organization of its kind in the world.

Highly professional supplies departments are established in all major concerns throughout industry and commerce. Contacts with buyers in these organizations can be of considerable value, particularly to buyers in smaller companies, since they provide opportunities to:

- Learn more about buying and stores control practices than is possible with the limited resources available within their own companies. When it comes to sharing knowledge on professional aspects of their jobs, explaining operational procedures or merely discussing problems, senior people in purchasing and supply are generally pleased to meet and assist buyers from other organizations.
- Examine products, see production processes and assess supplier performance.
- Foster business relationships, including the possibility of reciprocal trading. Visits to other companies invariably widen the scope for identifying areas of common interest.

Versatility, creative thinking and self-confidence are essential attributes in a supplies manager, as with any other person occupying a position of responsibility. The basic educational requirements will usually have been satisfied before he joins the organization. His skills will be developed in company-based projects, by training on the job and external courses. His potential will be measured as he gains experience and takes on wider assignments. His actual achievement will be measured by the positive contribution which he and his staff make to the profitability of the organization.

At all stages the attitude of the company itself is crucial. Where top management recognizes the potential value of effective supplies management they are more likely to maximize their profit margins. They will also attract managers and staff of the calibre which will demonstrate proof of the maxim that 'you get what you pay for'.

Within the limitations imposed by any book dealing with a wide range of management disciplines it is impossible to give more than cursory treatment to many important aspects of purchasing and supply. No mention has been made of *inter alia* engineering and construction contracts, hiring, leasing, discounted cash flow techniques, use of agents, warehousing (see Chapter 8), inventory control and distribution management, all of which are links in or attached to the supply chain. Some of these topics are dealt with elsewhere in this book, as indicated, but the reader is also recommended to refer to the books listed in Chapter 16.

10

MANAGEMENT TECHNIQUES

Hano Johannsen

INTRODUCTION

Management techniques come in all shapes and sizes. Many areas of business activity have developed their own specialized methods and techniques for dealing with a range of day-to-day and longer-term operational problems. Some of these techniques are little more than a range of relatively simple, informal steps which help to achieve some predetermined objective or provide a means of handling routine tasks. Some would argue that they are little more than applied common sense and could perhaps more accurately be termed knacks or tricks of the trade which have been developed and proved over time: many are confined to specific industries or services.

On the other hand, there is a broad range of techniques involving operational research, statistical and mathematical analysis and financial and management accounting know-how. Most require varying degrees of expertise and detailed knowledge which are primarily the province of specialists. Some offer solutions to a widespread range of topics while others are of relevance only to specific sectors of business activity.

Between these two extremes there are a host of techniques which can help to solve many everyday business problems. These techniques are applicable to most business sectors and some — at least in their basic form — can be applied by anyone able to master the essential procedures. Often it is a question of understanding the principles and adapting them to help solve specific business problems. If it involves, say, complex mathematics, a colleague or expert can usually be found and called in to help.

A few techniques have already been mentioned or discussed in previous chapters. The focus here is on just a few of the many techniques available: the choice has had to be very selective as there are hundreds of techniques which justify inclusion. Those described here have been selected primarily because they can be applied 'across the board' to most types of business. They can all help to provide a framework for analysing situations, give help in planning and scheduling projects, aid decision making and problem solving and provide ways of improving performance etc.

Further information

There is a vast range of literature on techniques, much of it dispersed and concentrated on specific disciplines or functions. A useful concise analysis and introduction on the nature and scope of a wide range of management techniques is given in *Concise Encyclopedia of Management Techniques* (F Finch) and *A Handbook of Management Techniques* (M Armstrong). See Chapter 16.

DECISION TREES

These are a very useful means of representing a range of decision making choices available in a simple diagramatic form. They enable a set of circumstances involving alternative courses of action, risks etc, to be put down on paper so as to highlight the key decision stages inherent in a given situation.

Decision making often involves a series of interrelated stages where each is dependent on earlier decisions taken. Decision trees enable these choices and the likely effects of each to be recorded. While a number of conventions for drawing decision trees have been developed — especially for the more complex problems — in essence one need only show the sequence of alternative courses of action as in the example.

It is important when drawing the tree to remember that the aim is to 'see the wood for the trees'. Narrative should be cut down to the bare minimum so that the 'labels' attached to each item are clear and unambiguous. Remember, too, that although trees are normally thought of as growing upright from the ground, decision trees are usually represented sideways from left to right. Some advocate the use of different symbols to distinguish between key decision points and chance events. Whatever style is adopted, the resulting diagram should seek to be as clear as possible: a decision tree which is too cluttered with symbols and words only confuses!

When laying out a decision tree remember to:

- Identify the key decision points and the relevant alternatives at each stage
- If appropriate show the costs and benefits of alternatives in financial terms
- Examine all the alternatives so that a preferred course of action can be chosen.

Further information: Moore, P G and Thomas, H, *Anatomy of Decisions*

80/20 RULE

This simple but very useful technique (also known as Pareto's law of distribution and as the ABC method) — though perhaps strictly speaking more of a concept than a technique — can be summarized as the 'law of the trivial many and the critical few' and is based on work by a nineteenth-century economist who used it specifically to describe the distribution of incomes and wealth. His research concluded that only a very small minority of the population owned most of the wealth or received most of the income: the vast majority were poor in terms of capital resources and income.

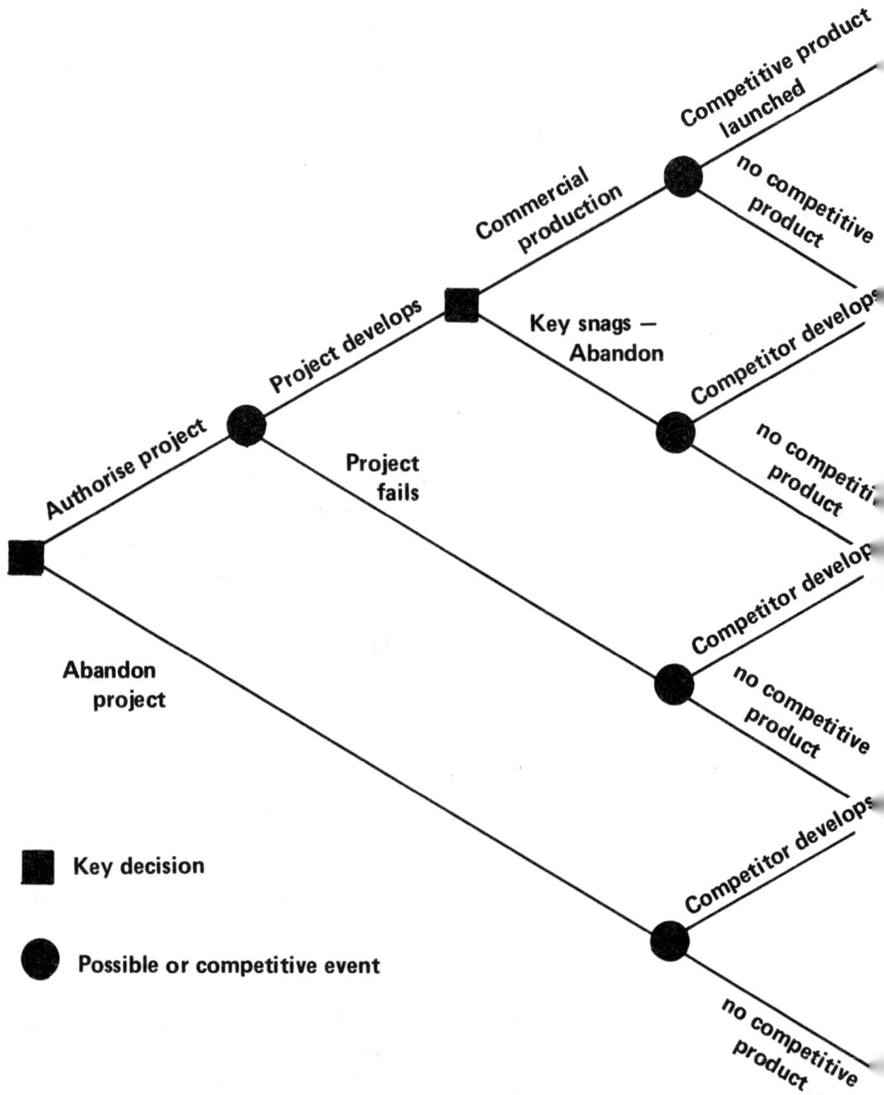

Figure 10.1 *Example of a simple decision tree*

This uneven (skewed) distribution has since been observed and proved by statistical analysis to be relevant to many types of business data. It appears that there is often an inverse relationship between the percentage of items in a particular category or group and their importance.

While the Pareto distribution can be expressed in mathematical terms in the form of a distribution frequency, this is rarely used in business.

What matters is the basic idea which simply means, for example, that in many businesses the majority of orders are received from the minority of customers. The same phenomenon can be observed, for example, with sales revenue (or profit) which is typically generated by about 20 per cent of the customers. Similarly in stock levels approximately 20 per cent of the total inventory often accounts for about 80 per cent of the total value of inventory. A simple graph can be drawn to check whether this holds true in a given set of circumstances.

Although it is difficult to provide a valid theoretical explanation for this tendency, empirical observations in many fields indicate that it holds true in a wide range of business circumstances. The concept's importance lies in the fact that it is a powerful means of focusing attention on what really matters.

Example

In the case of stock levels and values, management time and effort should be properly focused on monitoring and controlling the 20 per cent of stock which accounts for 80 per cent of the stock value. Such an analysis is likely to indicate that there is considerable scope for reducing stock levels, reviewing reordering procedures and introducing a variety of cost saving measures. There is little to be gained by applying the same level of control or effort to the 80 per cent of stock which in financial terms accounts for only 20 per cent of the value.

The message is clear: devote effort and time in proportion to the likely benefits and give little, if any, time to trying to cure minor problems for you may spend more than you can save; put like that it seems little more than common sense!

The so-called ABC method is really only a simple refinement of the Pareto concept. Instead of focusing attention on just one group or category which really matters, the analysis is taken a step further. For example, an analysis of customers is likely to reveal that 20 per cent account for 80 per cent of sales revenue; then these customers can be further analysed and broken down into three groups: A, B and C.

A = Key customers one cannot afford to lose under any circumstances
B = Important customers which, although significant, would not lead to major problems if they were lost
C = Customers who account for less than, say, 1 per cent of turnover.

It can also, for example, be applied to the purchasing and supplies function. All components or raw materials purchases may be categorized A, B or C. A could cover major items of expenditure (say over £50,000) which could be the responsibility of the senior management; B items might fall within the responsibility of the purchasing function, while C might cover all other purchases up to say £50 and be handled departmentally. Similarly, sales territories or different types of customers (distributors, wholesalers etc) could be grouped into A, B and C categories.

Both the Pareto approach and the ABC method are closely allied with another basic concept, ie management control by exception. This implies that *only* when there are significant deviations from the plan or norm should managers get involved. For example, trying to establish why sales or stock levels are 1 per cent down on plan or budget is most unlikely to be a worthwhile exercise. However, finding out what 'went wrong' when last month's forward orders were down by 30 per cent compared with budget does justify management attention. The 'management by exception' principle demands that parameters or deviations from the norm are established and that management information does not come in the form of yards of computer printout but in short summarized reports which focus *only* on the significant exceptions.

Further information: Carson, G B, *Production Handbook*; Juran, J M, *Quality Control Handbook.*

ACTIVITY SAMPLING

This is a straightforward and useful technique for examining the use of resources, say staff time, machinery or facilities. There are many situations where one wants a reasonably accurate but quick answer to questions such as:

- How often and for how long are specific pieces of equipment or machinery used?
- How much office staff time is devoted to specific tasks, eg telephoning, handling customer complaints etc?
- How many calls do the sales staff make?
- How much time do salesmen spend on travel compared with face-to-face customer contact?

Accurate answers to such questions could only come from detailed and costly investigations carried out over time. Activity sampling provides a short-cut approach by applying simple statistical sampling. Instead of undertaking a detailed study to establish all the facts one accepts that, say, 95 per cent accuracy will suffice for all practical purposes. The method therefore involves setting up a procedure for making a large number of observations (say 30) over a period of time (say a month). Each observation records what is happening at that point of time and the percentage of observations recording a particular activity (or non-activity) is a reflection and measure of the percentage of time devoted to that activity. To be reasonably accurate one needs to adopt a time-scale which covers peaks and troughs in workloads and activities etc throughout the period so that these are fairly reflected in the data collected. The kind of activity being studied should determine an acceptable time-scale to take account of this.

Example

If the work under review covers several busy periods at the beginning and end of the month with relatively quiet periods in between, then observations over a typical month will be necessary. If, on the other hand, there is little fluctuation in the workload or range of activities, then observations taken at random over, say, three days in the week may suffice.

The use of statistical sampling will enable one to establish the number of observations to be made in a given set of circumstances and calculate how accurate and representative the sample is. You can work out that the data collected is accurate to within, say, plus or minus 4 per cent which is likely to be more than adequate for most practical purposes.

The technique is also sometimes known as work sampling, snap reading method or random observation technique.

Further information: Barnes, R M, *Work Sampling*; Grillo, E V, *Control Techniques for Office Efficiency*.

BRAINSTORMING

Brainstorming is closely associated with creative and lateral thinking and is a powerful and practical technique for generating ideas from a small group of people.

There are five main stages in running a brainstorming session:

1. Appoint a leader and get a group (between five and 15 is ideal) together for about an hour. The leader explains the purpose of the

meeting and outlines the topic to be explored. The object is not to give a detailed presentation but to provide background information which enables participants to understand what the problem or issue is. Too much detailed information at this stage is likely to inhibit members from actively participating and lead to confusion: this is particularly true if any complex technical details are involved.

2. The second stage is for the group to stand back from the stated problem and see whether it can be refined, clarified or simplified. The chances are that the initial issue can be seen in a new and perhaps wider context than was originally conceived. The group seeks to redefine the problem and one or two restatements are selected as the theme for the main part of the brainstorming session itself.
3. After a short dummy run to get people familiar with the process, the participants are encouraged to come up with as many ideas and suggestions as possible. It is important that all the ideas are recorded. As the session progresses the ideas are displayed around the room. At this stage no attempt is made to evaluate or criticize them. The aim is to generate the maximum number of ideas in, say, 20 to 30 minutes. Although some ideas may appear silly, complex, humorous or obvious, all should be recorded. The golden rule is to encourage the free flow of ideas and suspend judgement on them until later. In a successful exercise one could typically expect to generate perhaps 100 to 150 ideas.
4. The fourth stage is optional but is often introduced in practice when the main flow of ideas has dried up. The aim is to select the most off-beat or apparently wildest idea that came up in the main session and attempt to re-examine it in a new light to see whether it can be turned into something really worthwhile.
5. The final stage is to examine and sift through all the ideas and evaluate them. Normally it will be necessary to group the ideas under a number of broad generic headings. This stage may be undertaken by all the original participants or by a smaller team made up of the leader and, say, two or three participants.

Brainstorming has been widely used by many business organizations. It can, for example, be used to generate ideas for cost-cutting exercises, improving packaging, reorganizing systems and procedures or developing new products and services etc.

Further information: Rickards, T, *Problem Solving through Creative Analysis*; De Bono, E, *Lateral Thinking: A Textbook of Creativity*: Rawlinson, J G, *Creative Thinking and Brainstorming*.

FORECASTING

Forecasting is an essential ingredient of the planning process for most businesses. Although it can never be an exact science, the application of basic statistical techniques goes a long way towards providing a systematic approach to quantifying what the future is likely to hold in store. The aim is to enhance planning and decision making by trying to narrow down areas of uncertainty about the future. Forecasting is, as the word suggests, not an insight into the future. It assumes that, by analysing past patterns and cycles of behaviour and adding external and internal information, one can gain a reasonably reliable picture of the future. How reliable and accurate it turns out to be will depend in large measure on the factors which are incorporated in the forecast and the overall views (optimistic or pessimistic) which are built into the data. Always remember that forecasting is both art and science.

The starting point is to collect together relevant facts and figures about past performance, be it home sales data by products, areas or similar data for exports etc. How much detailed data needs to be collected and analysed will depend primarily on the purpose of the forecast, the kind of activity under review and the time-scale to be covered. A forecast to be used as a basis for working out next year's budget is likely to require more detailed inputs than a forecast of raw material requirements for next week's workload.

The major requirement in all forecasting is the availability of key data which is reliable, up to date and in a form which can be readily used. It implies ready access to external statistical data and internal management information which makes it possible to obtain breakdowns of data which are meaningful for the purpose in hand.

While 'hard' facts and figures are important, few realistic forecasts rely on them alone. There is always room for making adjustments to statistical evidence by bringing experience and management judgement to bear on them.

In shorter-term forecasts (say up to six months) which are commonplace in business for sales, machine loading, stock levels etc, there are often three key elements:

1. An overall trend (up, down or static)
2. Seasonal variations which reflect peaks and troughs
3. A random residual quantity.

Three methods are commonly used. The simplest technique (often adequate for simple forecasts) is to calculate the moving average.

For example, a forecast of sales in the fifth month is simply the total sales for the first four months divided by 4.

$$\frac{\text{Jan 10 + Feb 20 + March 30 + April 20}}{4} = 80.$$

So May = $^{80}/_{4}$ = 20.

A refinement is to calculate the 'weighted moving average' which gives higher 'weighting factors' to the more recent months, eg:

Month	**Weighting %**	**Sales**	**Weighted sales**
January	10	10	1.0
February	20	20	4.0
March	30	30	8.0
April	40	20	6.0
May forecast	100		19.0

The exponential smoothing or weighted moving average method is a third alternative. It is getting more complex but works out as:

This month's forecast = Last month's forecast + α [Actual — Forecast for last month.]
α = an arbitrary factor with a value ranging from 0 to +1.

In longer-term forecasting one is likely to want to rely less on the past performance and trends and allow for a variety of 'what if' questions. For example, 'What would be the effect of a price increase or a change in advertising expenditure? What if the methods of distribution were changed? What if the sales promotion budget were increased or reduced by 20 per cent?' These and similar questions are likely to require the use of model building for which the popular computer spreadsheets provide a very useful tool.

The basic steps in short- and medium-term forecasting involve:

1. Collecting and organizing figures on past performance covering (say) three to four years.
2. Analysing the data to uncover any seasonal variations or patterns which recur regularly year (or period) after year.
3. Having established the seasonal patterns, make appropriate adjustments to the figures to eliminate them.

Further information: Anson, C J, *Profit From Figures*.

VALUE ANALYSIS

It is argued that value analysis should be an integral aspect of the design function and therefore does not justify treatment as a 'separate' technique. Though this may be true in theory, it has been found in practice that it is by no means universally adopted by designers. Furthermore, value analysis is often seen as a technique extending well beyond the design function itself.

It is often seen as a useful analytical approach which critically examines the materials, components, designs and procedures used in manufacturing products or providing services. There are no hard and fast rules on how value analysis should be conducted or applied. It may take the form of ad hoc project groups drawn from a variety of allied activities — such as design and purchasing — examining specific products or services or an ongoing panel which systematically reviews all key products and components over the long term.

However the group is composed and whatever methods may be employed (brainstorming, checklists etc), a broad range of information needs to be collected and many questions asked. For example:

- What is the function of the item under review? Is it essential or can it be cut out altogether?
- What are the present costs?
- Can designs be simplified?
- Can the same or improved performance be achieved by the use of cheaper materials?
- Is it really necessary to use so many non-standard parts?
- Are the materials and components available from a number of sources?

These are just some types of issue involved: much will depend on the item under review.

The technique has been widely used to examine alternative raw material and component purchases, the critical review of product designs, the use of standard parts rather than 'specials' and decisions concerned with making or buying components.

Further information: Miles, L D, *Techniques of Value Analysis and Engineering.*

NETWORK ANALYSIS

Network analysis is a generic term used to describe a group of similar techniques used for planning, controlling and subsequently monitoring major civil engineering, research and development (R & D), maintenance and repair, new product marketing and promotion projects.

There are two major types of network:

1. *Critical path* method is used when the timetable for completing each activity can be measured or predicted accurately. It is then

possible to identify the critical path and establish precisely how long the total project will take.

2. *PERT* (an acronym for programme evaluation review technique) on the other hand is used when time-scales are not accurately known or predictable. The PERT network provides an overall plan of:
   - all key events
   - all the key activities required to accomplish each 'event' and
   - enables the critical path to be established for the project as a whole.

Normally the plan includes three time estimates for each activity (an optimistic, 'most likely' and pessimistic forecast). As the volume of data and the possible variables is extensive, a PERT network can be computer simulated using one of the many software packages available for this purpose.

The aim of all networks is to represent in diagrammatic form the many interrelated stages involved in achieving a goal and highlighting the duration of each activity and the relationship between them. 'Network' describes the complex diagram of lines and circles which emerges when the sequential relationships between all the activities are committed to paper. The critical 'path' shows the optimum 'route' through all the stages and those activities which are critical and need to be completed before proceeding to the next stage and finally completion of the whole project.

Further information: Battersby, A, *Network Analysis for Planning and Scheduling*.

ERGONOMICS

The only reason for including this rather obscure subject in the selection of management techniques is that it focuses attention on an important, and often neglected, subject. It covers a range of disciplines concerned with matching the workplace and equipment used with individual employees so that work is done efficiently and with the minimum of strain and fatigue. It cannot be easily applied in detail by the businessman but the principles involved are important at the workplace. It is a question of ensuring that the whole working environment — the equipment, controls, machinery design, lighting, workplace layout etc — provides the best possible working conditions conducive to high performance.

Ergonomics research focuses on the capabilities and limitations of people at work and is particularly relevant when designing complex

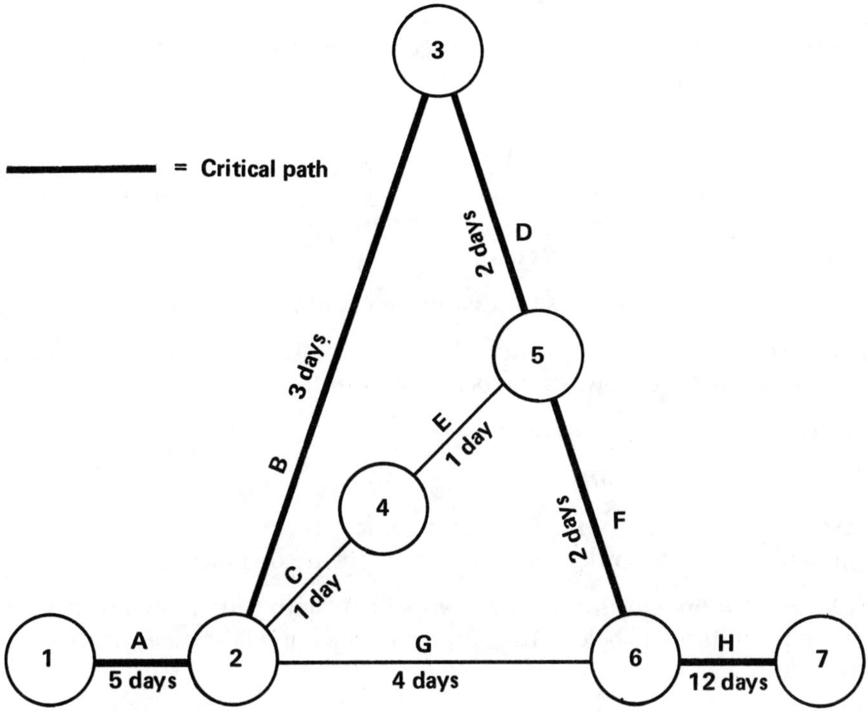

A Prepare drawings
B Site preparation and clearance
C Fell woodland
D Excavate foundations
E Transport major building materials
F Set up scaffolding
G Prepare for public services
H Major building work

Figure 10.2 *Example of simple network showing critical path for building work*

machinery, control panel and systems. It has applications too in job analysis, training methods, computer communications etc.

Further information: Hammond, J, *Understanding Human Engineering;* Murrell, K F H, *Ergonomics.*

QUEUEING THEORY

Although queueing theory involves complex mathematical and probability theory and simulation techniques which are outside the scope of this book, the aims of queueing analysis are essentially practical and relevant to many areas of business activity. For example, customer queues at retail shops, banks or airports, hold-ups of lorries at loading bays or aircraft ready for take off on airport runways etc are all cases where there is a mismatch between demand and supply or customers requiring more than a given facility or service can provide. As a result of these and similar queueing situations, delays are caused leading to poor customer service, frustration, 'bottlenecks' etc.

In queueing situations there are four main variables:

1. The rate and pattern of arrival of 'customers'
2. A timetable of when the services or facilities are available
3. The nature of the queue which develops
4. The kind of services etc on offer.

Commonplace procedures for dealing with queues include:

FIFO (First in, first out: while the fairest system from the customers' viewpoint, it is not always the best from the supplier's)

SIRO (Service in random order)

LIFO (Last in, first out)

PSPO (Pre-emptive service priority order: if an important customer suddenly places an order, other prior orders are displaced)

NNPS (Non pre-emptive priority service). As with PSPO, but an existing order is dealt with before the important customers' orders 'jump' the queue.

In practice queueing theory can help to provide optimum solutions to all types of congestion problems. The aim is to come to a decision about the most cost-effective use of resources. It is a question of minimizing delays and yet not allowing expensive facilities to be provided which are only used at peak times.

Further information: Greenwood, W T, *Decision Theory and Information Systems.*

LONG RANGE PLANNING

Although few techniques have received so much attention in management circles as long range planning in the late 1960s and 70s, the business climate in more recent years has developed a healthy realism and scepticism about the subject.

Few deny the importance of planning generally, or indeed the validity and value of longer range planning which seeks to outline in varying degrees of detail how a business should be developing in the future. As a general rule, the longer term the plan and the larger the organization, the greater are the number of variable factors which have to be examined and included in the plan. It is also generally true that longer-term plans have to be made incorporating many assumptions and forecasts which, however carefully prepared, are bound to be inaccurate. These factors do not invalidate the planning process itself, but they do underline the need to interpret long-term plans carefully. Ideally, they are about key strategic objectives which spell out where the business would like to be in the future. Long-term planning is an attempt to ensure that a business is 'going somewhere' rather than merely drifting. The degree of detail a plan includes is a matter of taste, the resources allocated to the task and the management philosophy and style.

What is primarily at issue is how long range planning should be organized, how it can become integrated into the existing company and management structure, who is to be responsible for developing, updating, implementing and monitoring the plan, how to maintain flexibility and ensure that 'the plan' does not merely become a theoretical document to which little more than lip service is paid.

At the heart of the long range planning dilemma is defining what it means. There is no generally understood definition. Financial or management accountants and departmental managers tend to regard any plans extending beyond the current financial year or budget period as 'long term': these are usually described as operating or divisional plans.

'Proper' long range planning at the corporate level, however, usually means strategic planning which focuses on the business as a whole. It might include the development of existing and new products or services, opening up new markets at home and abroad and perhaps spell out an acquisition policy etc. They usually cover a longer time-scale: perhaps three, five or even ten years and beyond and seek to show where the business as a whole wants to be in the coming years.

Long range planning involves specifying:

- The personnel to be involved
- Who is to lead and co-ordinate activities
- Time-scales and timetables
- Defining the key financial and corporate objectives
- What company resources and top management involvement and support are to be committed
- That the planners will have ready access to company information and statistics.

There are few hard and fast rules about what areas should be included in a long range plan: much will clearly depend on the type and size of business etc. They might, for example, include:

Marketing objectives. Market share, product planning, pricing, distribution and customer profiles etc.

Competition. Major competitors, their and 'our' strengths and weaknesses etc.

Economic environment. Trends and developments, exchange rates, inflation levels, the employment situation etc.

Manufacturing and service. Future capacity and capability, plant and machinery, labour requirements, suppliers, raw material and components etc.

Financial implications. R & D expenditure, new equipment and plant, budget forecasts, cash flows, raising finance, return on capital etc.

Organization. Management structure, review functions and responsibilities etc.

Others have stressed that the key elements should be:

- Establishing key financial objectives
- Developing new sources of earnings or redirecting present resources into more profitable activities
- Appraising internal strengths and weaknesses
- Examining which elements of the business offer growth opportunities and how these can be exploited
- Asking whether there are parts of the business 'milking' the rest of the company. Can they be revived, restructured or disposed of?
- Which new ventures should be developed and encouraged? etc.

Further information: Argenti, J, *Practical Corporate Planning.*

RATIOS

Ratios — usually expressed as percentages — are useful for comparing performance or measuring change over time *within* a business as well as providing yardsticks for *external* comparisons with other organizations. Some useful ratios have already been mentioned in the separate chapters. In practice there are dangers from drawing too many conclusions from ratios. The key problem is to ensure that the factors summarized by a ratio are being consistently defined and measured. In this regard ratios produced in-house are usually less of a problem than those quoted by other organizations or for other industrial or service sectors.

In recent years inter-firm comparisons have been conducted among small groups of companies in the same sector and considerable care has been taken to agree which ratios are really significant and how each should be defined and measured. Provided this type of care is taken, ratios can be valuable guides to financial and management performance across a wide range of areas, but many ratios are not necessarily applicable to all types of business activity.

The main categories of management ratios include:

Financial ratios

Tests of liquidity such as current assets to current liabilities; the acid test ratio which compares cash and quickly realizable assets with current liabilities; the conversion of credit sales into cash which measures the average number of days of debt collection etc.

Performance ratios

These include the rate of return (net profits to capital employed); net profit to sales (or gross income); gross profit to sales (or sales income) etc.

Measures of solvency

These include the ratio of capital to liabilities.

Personnel ratios

There are numerous ratios in this field including those measuring staff turnover, absenteeism and sickness levels.

Stock market ratios

Again there is a wide selection. The key ratios include: Earnings per share; market price: earnings per share; market capitalization: earnings per share; Dividend yield.

Further information: Westwick, C A, *How to Use Management Ratios*; Helfert, E A, *Techniques of Financial Analysis*.

11

TAXATION

Joe Horner

INTRODUCTION

Individuals are liable for *income tax* on their income and for *capital gains tax* on many capital profits. They are not normally liable to pay tax on any gifts they receive (although there are circumstances where they may be) or on most 'windfall' additions to their finances such as gambling winnings or insurance proceeds.

Companies resident in the UK are liable to *corporation tax* on both their income and their capital gains. *Companies outside the UK* may be liable for *income tax* on income arising in the UK or for *corporation tax* if they carry on a trade through a branch or agency in this country.

Trusts are liable to *income tax* and *capital gains tax*.

Many *unincorporated bodies* such as clubs, societies and associations may also be liable for *corporation tax* on their income and capital gains.

Most businesses are liable for *value added tax*.

Individuals must also pay *National Insurance contributions*. These are theoretically not taxes but they have much in common with taxes and to a large extent are collected through the tax collection system. *Employers* must also pay *National Insurance contributions* (NIC).

Businesses are required to act as tax collectors. In addition to the tax on their own profits they must deduct tax from the wages of their employees and pay it to the Inland Revenue. If they fail to deduct it or if they deduct an inadequate amount they may have to suffer the extra tax themselves. There are also other areas in which a payer of money must withhold tax and pay it to the authorities.

Inheritance tax is due on property passing on death and on certain gifts and other disposals within seven years before death. This tax was previously called *capital transfer tax* and covered a wider range than the present tax.

INCOME TAX

The income tax year runs from 6 April until 5 April. Each person who is liable for tax must make a declaration of his income for a year when called upon to do so by the tax inspector. He must make the declaration on the approved form. Many employed people do not receive a form each year. This creates no problem as long as the Inland Revenue have been notified of the employment and have instructed the employer about what tax to deduct from earnings. However, anybody who does not receive a form and who is liable for tax and who does not suffer tax by deduction from his income has a legal obligation to make himself known to the Inland Revenue. Failure to do so can lead to penalties being imposed.

Income can take many forms. All types must be declared and the statutory amount stated. This can be difficult because the way income is calculated differs according to the type of income. Sometimes it is difficult to know whether something is income or not. In all such cases it is advisable to notify the tax inspector and to discuss with him whether it is income. He will not always know. Sometimes he may believe it is and the taxpayer may believe it is not. There are ways of settling such disputes.

Having listed each source of income and agreed the taxable amount from each source the next stage is to decide what deductions should be made from the total. The main deductions available are: mortgage and certain other interest payments; payments for approved superannuation and retirement provisions; relief for losses; relief for Business Expansion Scheme investments; and capital allowances. In many cases the taxpayer has a choice about what deductions to claim. It is not always sensible to claim the maximum available. There are also time limits for claims.

Having ascertained the income from all sources and deducted the appropriate deductions we will know the net statutory income for the tax year. The next step is to deduct the personal allowances (ie the amount of income which can be enjoyed tax free) which will depend upon the personal circumstances of each taxpayer; see Table A, page 357. The balance is chargeable to tax. For most people this balance is chargeable at the standard rate (29 per cent in 1986–87 but 30 per cent for several years past) but people with large incomes will be charged at higher rates on parts of their income; see Table B, page 358.

The tax calculated in this way is compared with the tax suffered (or deemed to have been suffered) by deduction. If more tax is due the inspector will raise an assessment and indicate when and where the tax should be paid. Delay in payment may mean that interest is payable in addition to the tax.

Where the tax suffered by deduction exceeds the tax due the inspector will invite a request for repayment. However, the tax 'deemed' to have been suffered by deduction is frequently not available for repayment. This is a curious anomaly of UK tax law. Because the people whose amount due is less than the amount deemed to be deducted will usually be people with low incomes, it really amounts to a subsidy from poor people to wealthier people.

The most common types of income are:

Working for an employer
This includes being a director of a company. If it is a small family company the directors may in fact regard the business as their own business but the legal reality is that the company has its own identity; the business belongs to the company; and the directors are servants of the company. Tax for employees is deductible from their earnings under Pay As You Earn (PAYE) and it is the employer who is responsible for paying it to the Inland Revenue; see pages 308–313.

Pensions
State pensions are taxable but they are paid in full. The amount is normally less than the personal allowance to which the pensioner is entitled so the question of payment of tax does not arise. Pensions from a former employer have PAYE tax deducted in the same way as income from an employment.

Self-employment
The proprietor of a business is required to keep records of all matters which might affect the profitability. He pays his tax on business profits in two half-yearly instalments. For the tax year 1986–87 the first instalment was due on 1 January 1987 and the second on 1 July 1987; see pages 313–323.

Partnership
The position is very much the same as self-employment but one assessment is made on the partnership. The amount of personal allowances and the rates at which tax is charged are calculated by apportioning the assessment among the partners according to the basis on which they share profits. In most partnerships each partner will contribute his own appropriate share of the tax but if the tax is not paid the Inland Revenue can take steps to recover the whole of the partnership tax from any one of the partners; see page 316.

Rents from property
The correct amount to assess is the net rents arising in the tax year after

deducting approved expenses paid in the year. The tax for 1986–87 was due on 1 January 1987. This of course is before the tax year has ended. The law therefore says that the tax inspector will originally base his assessment on the rents of the previous year and that the tax shall be paid on that assessment. After the year end the true net rents are agreed and the assessment is revised upward or downward. Further tax becomes due or a refund is made; see pages 324–325.

Bank and building society interest
Basic rate is 'deemed' to have been deducted from the interest before payment. Thus if the interest credited is £71 it is treated as though it as £100 less £29 tax. If the account holder is liable for tax at, say, 45 per cent, the inspector must make an assessment to collect tax on £100 at 16 per cent. On the other hand, if the account holder is not liable for tax no part of the deemed £29 can be repaid.

Dividends from UK companies
When a company pays a dividend it pays 'advance corporation tax' to the Inland Revenue. The amount is 29 pence for every 71 pence of dividend paid. The shareholder is credited with tax of the same amount. Thus if £71 is received it is treated as £100 less tax of 29 per cent. If the shareholder is not liable for tax on the full amount it can be repaid by the Inland Revenue.

Interest from companies, local authorities or government
With a few exceptions, tax of 29 per cent is deducted before payment is made.

Interest from other individuals
Tax is not deducted by the payer. The interest will be taxed by the tax inspector raising an assessment.

Income received under deed of covenant
The payer deducts tax of 29 per cent. This can be reclaimed by the recipient in most cases.

Income from trusts
In some cases tax is withheld by the trustees at 29 per cent. In other cases it is withheld at 45 per cent. In either case a refund can be claimed if the tax is excessive.

Husband and wife

The income of a woman living with her husband is deemed, for income tax purposes, to be the income of her husband. The exception is the year of marriage (unless the marriage takes place on the first day of the year, ie 6 April).

Tax is calculated on the joint income. If any of the earned income is earned by the wife, a 'wife's earned income allowance' is given in addition to the married man's personal allowance. The amount is equal to the amount of the wife's earnings up to a maximum of £2335 (for 1986–87). Where the maximum is due it is therefore equal to the single person's allowance.

Invalid care allowance has in the past been payable to single people and to married men. It has recently been decided to extend the allowance to married women and backdate the allowance to December 1984. The statute does not allow such an allowance to be treated as wife's earned income but legislation to allow it to be so treated is to be included in the Finance Bill 1987. In the meantime the Inland Revenue will treat it, by concession, as wife's earned income.

If a married woman is in employment the tax will be withheld at source under PAYE. If any of this tax is repayable it will be repaid to the wife. Apart from this, any repayment on the joint income will be repaid to the husband and any tax chargeable on the joint income will be charged to the husband.

In many cases where a married woman gives business assistance to her husband, it is thought convenient to limit her wages to just below the amount of the National Insurance threshold (£38 per week for 1986–87). This saves having to deduct PAYE or NIC.

If the wife owns substantial capital assets used in the business, for example a share in land and buildings, it may be preferable for capital gains tax and capital transfer tax reasons that she should be a partner in the business and her share of income would then be taxed under Schedule D Case I.

When a married man who is entitled to the higher personal allowance dies, the income of his wife from the previous 6 April until the date of death is treated as his, but the widow is assessable on her own income from the date of death and is therefore treated as a separate individual entitled to the lower personal allowance. If she has a qualifying child resident with her she will also be entitled to the additional personal allowance; see Table A, page 357.

Separate assessment

Either the husband or the wife may elect that each spouse should be assessed separately. An election will not alter the amount of tax they must jointly pay but it will divide the joint liability by reference to the individual incomes and by reference to the basis on which they each support dependants or make certain other payments.

Separate assessment gives a certain amount of privacy as each spouse makes a separate tax return, but it can create complications in checking assessments and it can also cause delay in settling tax matters. If the husband and wife can come to an amicable agreement about how tax bills or refunds should be shared it will usually be easier to do that than to have formal separate assessment. In general, separate assessment is only recommended where the question of privacy is of importance to either the husband or the wife.

An election for separate assessment must be made within six months before 6 July in the year to which it is to apply. The election will then continue in force for future years until it is revoked. Notice to revoke must be made within six months before 6 July in the year for which it is no longer required.

Option regarding wife's earnings

A quite different matter from separate assessment is an option that a married woman shall be regarded as a single person for the purpose of assessing her earned income. If this treatment is required it must be elected for by both spouses. The election must be made within 12 months after the end of the tax year for which it is to apply. It will then continue in force until both spouses revoke it. Notice to revoke must be made within 12 months after the end of the year for which it is not wanted. Election or revocation must therefore be made by 5 April 1988 for the year 1986–87, although the Board of Inland Revenue have power to extend these time limits in some cases.

If the option is chosen the tax on the wife's earnings is calculated as though she were a single person. Tax on her other income is calculated in conjunction with the husband's income, but the husband cannot claim the higher personal allowance normally available to a married man. The wife does not make a separate tax return.

Neither spouse can claim age allowance or additional personal allowance.

Where the joint income is high enough to be taxed at higher rates there will be a saving in taking the option. There will also be a loss because of the unavailability of the higher personal allowance to the husband, who will receive only the lower personal allowance. (The husband will also lose the wife's earned income allowance, but this will be compensated for by the wife receiving a single person's allowance, which is the same amount.) An individual calculation is necessary in all cases to see if the saving outweighs the loss. The point of advantage will vary from couple to couple depending upon the total income, the make-up of this income and certain deductions to which they may be entitled.

Table C on page 358 gives an approximate guide to the point of advantage for the years 1985–86 and 1986–87. Column 1 shows the total income of the couple and column 2 shows the minimum amount of income which should be on each side of the divide (ie wife's earned income on one side less qualifying interest and annual payments which she makes and wife's other income plus husband's income less qualifying interest and annual payments which he makes on the other side).

Separation and divorce

Payments under a court order which are to be paid weekly or monthly and which do not exceed specified amounts are known as *small maintenance payments* and are paid in full. The payer may claim to deduct them from his income and the recipient is taxable on them. The maximum amounts are £48 per week or £208 per month to a divorced or separated spouse and £25 per week or £108 per month for any child under 21.

If the court order does not come within the above limits or if maintenance payments to a divorced or separated spouse are made on a regular basis under a deed or other enforceable agreement, the payer is entitled to deduct tax when making the payment. He should give the other party a certificate annually showing the payments made and the tax withheld.

If a court orders that payments (by the spouse who does not have custody of the child) are made direct to a child rather than to the divorced or separated spouse, such payments become income of the child and not of the spouse. If the payments do not exceed £48 per week or £208 per month they are *small maintenance payments* and may be paid in full. If the payments exceed these figures the payer is entitled to withhold tax at 30 per cent from the payments.

Difficulties can arise where school fees are paid under a court order. To enable the fees to be treated as income of the child, the contract for the child's education should be between the child (ie *not* his guardian) and the school and the fees should be paid to the school as appointed agent for the child. The Inland Revenue have approved a form of contract which can be used in such cases.

Settling tax disputes

There are many areas of tax law and practice on which it is quite reasonable to hold different opinions and where the tax inspector's view is likely to be different from that of many traders. Examples might be:

whether certain costs should be classified as repairs and maintenance (which is tax deductible) or as improvements (which isn't); whether something falls within the meaning of 'machinery and plant' or not; whether a payment is wholly and exclusively for business; where there is mixed use (of a car, for instance) what the business/non-business split should be; what value should be placed on stock or work-in-progress in certain cases; and many, many other issues.

In the main such matters are settled by negotiation between inspectors and accountants. The courts have come to decisions in the past and new cases are continually being heard. Inspectors and accountants who specialize in tax are familiar with many of these precedents. The particular issue to be decided may not be identical to a previous court case but similarities and differences can be discussed and some agreement reached.

If it is impossible to reach agreement the problem can be referred to Commissioners of Taxes. There are two categories of Commissioners: the Special Commissioners and the General Commissioners. Some matters can only be considered by the Special Commissioners but in most cases the taxpayer can choose which body he wishes to to appeal to. In most cases this will be the General Commissioners. These are people who are appointed to act in a certain area of the country. They are not paid and they act rather like magistrates. They will have a Clerk who will probably be a solicitor but the Commissioners themselves might have no specialist knowledge of tax law or other law. They are prominent members of the local community and what they are supposed to have is good sense and experience of life and a high regard for justice. They listen to the arguments on both sides and decide whether to support the inspector's or the appellant's view. Sometimes it is possible that they partially accept both views and make what is seen as a compromise decision. On very rare occasions they may make a decision which differs from both parties but is not in between. It is more extreme in one direction or the other.

If either party is dissatisfied with a decision of the Commissioners he can ask for a case to be stated for the High Court. If such a case goes ahead it will normally follow that the party who loses in the court will incur heavy legal costs. Further appeals are possible to the Court of Appeal and to the House of Lords. These of course are rare and are even more costly for the losing party.

It can be a very difficult matter to decide whether to accept an inspector's view or to argue a matter of principle before the Commissioners. The problem for the taxpayer is that if he wins the decision but the Inland Revenue decide to appeal to the courts he risks not only a reversal of the decision but also costs which might be more than the tax involved. It is often said that tax inspectors use this fear to 'blackmail' people into accepting their view. This is usually an unjust interpretation of the inspector's attitude, but nevertheless the system does have a built-in inequity to the taxpayer's disadvantage.

Tax planning, tax avoidance and tax evasion

There is often confusion about these terms. Tax evasion is the deliberate failure to declare taxable income or gains in the correct figures and the message to readers is quite simple - *don't do it.*

Tax planning can range from matters which have specific official approval (eg investing in Business Expansion Schemes; supporting children at university or supporting charity by deeds of covenant) to matters which do not have such approval but are legally permissible. The advice here is to be aware of what legal options are available and what commercial risks and costs are involved. For most people this will only be possible with experienced professional help.

It can be argued that there is no such thing as tax avoidance. Either tax is due, in which case a failure to declare the source and the amount is evasion; or tax is not due because of the way affairs are conducted, in which case there is no tax to avoid. However, in reality there are ways of trying to organize financial matters tax-efficiently which transgress an undefined boundary of what is reasonable. The Inland Revenue and the courts go to some lengths to frustrate 'schemes' which carry out transactions in an artificial manner in order to minimize the tax consequences.

There are laws under which the income of one person can be deemed, for tax purposes, to be the income of another person or under which capital receipts can be taxed as income. Among the most important are:

1. Taxation of certain capital gains on land and buildings as income.
2. Income arising to a person abroad being attributed to a UK resident in certain cases.
3. Profits on certain shares and securities being treated as income if the transactions cannot be shown to be carried out for bona fide commercial reasons.
4. Dividends and interest being attributed to a person other than the person who receives them where shares or securities have changed ownership in certain circumstances.
5. Capital arising to an individual from sale of income derived from personal activities to be taxed as income.

In addition, judicial interpretation of the law makes it clear that in some circumstances where a series of transactions takes place for tax avoidance purposes some of the transactions can be disregarded and the substance of actions can be taxed without limitation by the form in which they were carried out.

Neglect, wilful default and fraud

If a taxpayer is guilty of neglect (or worse) and it is discovered he will have to pay the tax underpaid by his transgression and he will also become liable for the payment of interest and the imposition of penalties. The law permits the penalty to be higher than the tax lost. In the most extreme cases the penalty could be over twice the tax lost.

In practice the Inland Revenue seek to settle what they refer to as 'back duty cases' by negotiation with the taxpayer and his accountant. They try to persuade the taxpayer to make an offer of settlement which includes some penalty but usually this is much less than the maximum envisaged by the law.

Interest and penalties are charged even when the irregularity is voluntarily disclosed by the offender. However, the penalty will be much reduced if the disclosure is truly voluntary (as opposed to an admission when the inspector raises questions).

Series delay is regarded as 'neglect'.

In many cases an inspector will believe returns and/or accounts to be incorrect and if he does so he can raise assessments in figures greater than those declared. He can often also raise further assessments for earlier years. If he wishes to raise an assessment for a year which elapsed more than six years earlier he must get the consent of Commissioners who must be satisfied that he has justifiable cause to suspect that the information given by the taxpayer is incorrect.

The taxpayer can appeal against assessments. If the inspector cannot be persuaded to cancel or reduce them the taxpayer can ask for the Commissioners to adjudicate. In effect, he will be required to prove that the inspector's view is wrong - rather than the inspector being required to prove that he is right.

Most back duty cases care settled by negotiation between inspectors and accountants. In cases where the amount involved is significant it is often advisable to have the services of an accountant who specializes in this sort of work in addition to the accountant who prepares the normal accounts.

Back duty cases can be very time-consuming and very expensive in professional time costs, as well as very worrying. The most obvious advice to avoid these distressing experiences is to take great care to declare things correctly and at the right time.

It is also advisable to consider what features (eg gross profit ratios) are normally to be expected in the sort of business you run. If your own business is out of line with a typical similar business, find out what has caused this and explain it to the inspector when accounts are sent to him. An explanation sent like this is likely to be more convincing than an explanation sent as a reply to a query raised by the inspector.

Sometimes a business can show quite acceptable profits but an inspector will still be suspicious because the drawings from the business seem to be too low to finance personal expenditure. If a trader does have low drawings it is sensible for him to point this out to the inspector and to explain how he manages. This could, for instance, be because there is money coming into the house which does not reflect in the tax return or accounts. It may be, for instance, the maturing of National Savings Certificates or a life assurance policy; a win on premium bonds or football pools; a legacy; or adult children living at home and contributing generously to household expenses.

If there are very low personal drawings; or a particularly low rate of gross profit or some other suspicious-looking feature in the accounts and an explanation cannot be offered to the inspector, the trader and the accountant should re-examine all the papers before they finish the accounts as it may be that there is some error which they had not spotted. It would be much better to adjust the accounts before sending them to the tax inspector (even if they had to make some adjustments which could not be proved) than to have to accept some adjustment after an enquiry by the inspector.

Income from employment

Tax is charged under Schedule E on the emoluments from any office (eg a directorship) or employment. The word 'emoluments' includes perquisites and all kinds of profits as well as such obvious remuneration as wages, salaries, fees, commissions etc; see *Benefits in kind*, page 309. Emoluments arising from the employment can be assessed even if they do not come from the employer. Tips, for instance, are assessable. Deductions can be claimed for travelling expenses necessarily incurred in the performance of the duties and also for other expenses incurred wholly, exclusively and necessarily in the performance of the duties of the office or employment.

In some cases (particularly close company directors) where emoluments fluctuate the Inland Revenue like to make assessments based on the emoluments for the employer's accounting year which ends in the fiscal year (eg an accounting year to 31 December 1986 is treated as if it is the fiscal year 1986-87). This basis is only adopted if it is acceptable to the taxpayer. It will not be used for the first and last years for which assessments are due. The effect of using this basis is that in the first two years a part of the remuneration is assessed twice but at a later date there is some remuneration which escapes assessment. The rising trend of remuneration usually ensures that the amount which escapes is more than the amount which is doubly taxed and therefore over a period of years this practice will generally give a small benefit to the taxpayer.

Schedule E tax is normally deducted by the employer under PAYE but in some cases the taxpayer will be asked to pay direct to the Collector of Taxes. If remuneration which is assessable for one year is not received in that year (and therefore PAYE is not collected) the assessment will show that the individual has underpaid tax at the end of the year. The Inland Revenue will not usually ask the taxpayer to make payment of such an underpayment to the extent that they estimate the PAYE system will collect it in the following year.

It is sometimes difficult to know whether a person who does some work for a business is an employee or is a self-employed person doing some subcontract work. There are special provisions dealing with this problem in the building and construction industry but the problem can arise in any type of business. If there can be any doubt it is essential to notify the tax inspector of the arrangements and to get his agreement to the treatment proposed. It will normally be very easy to get him to agree that the person should be treated as an employee and taxed under PAYE (with both employer's and employee's National Insurance contributions also being payable). It may be a lot harder to get him to agree that the person is self-employed and should therefore receive his earnings in full. Despite the difficulty it is dangerous to adopt this treatment without the inspector's agreement. If the Inland Revenue eventually come to the conclusion that the person should have been subject to PAYE and NIC the 'employer' can become liable to pay the tax himself and have no practical way of recovering it from the 'employee'. He may even find that he has to pay a penalty in addition to the tax. The difference between an employment and a self-employed status is sometimes very difficult to define. In theory the inspector is not the final judge of the matter but in practice the cost of trying to prove him wrong might be higher than the cost of accepting his decision.

Benefits in kind

In addition to payment in money an employed person will be assessed on other emoluments arising because of his employment. Types of emolument assessable are:

1. Vouchers for cash, goods or services.
2. Provision of anything which is convertible into money. Assessed on re-sale value.

3. Settlement of a debt or liability incurred by the employee.
4. Provision of living accommodation (but not where it is necessary for the job or where there is a special security risk or where it is desirable and customary in that type of occupation). For houses which cost up to £75,000 the amount assessable is the annual value less any rent paid. For houses costing over £75,000 the amount assessed is the annual value plus 12 per cent of the excess cost of the property over £75,000. If the property was acquired by the employer more than six years before occupation by the employee the cost is deemed to be the market value at the date of first occupation.

Directors and higher paid employees
Higher paid employees and company directors (but not full-time directors who have less than a 5 per cent interest in the company, unless they are also higher paid) may also be assessed on a wider range of emoluments. A higher paid person is anybody whose emoluments exceed £8500. In deciding whether a person's emoluments do exceed £8500 all the items listed below (as well as those listed above) are taken into account. Expenses paid to or for him are also treated as emoluments. The wider range of emoluments comprises:

1. *Cars which are available for private use.* Tables G and H (pages 360 and 361) show the amount assessable as a benefit in most cases. If the employee makes a payment for his private use it is deducted from the amount shown in these tables.
2. *The cost of provision of a chauffeur.*
3. *Beneficial loans.* Assessment is by reference to the difference between interest paid by the employee and interest at a prescribed rate, which has been 12 per cent since 6 October 1982. If the difference is below £200 it is disregarded. If it is above this figure the whole amount is assessed. If, had the employee paid a full rate of interest, relief would have been claimable under any of the circumstances described on page 332 no assessment will be made.
4. *Loans written off.* The amount written off is treated as remuneration unless it is written off following the death of the employee or if it is written off in pursuit of an arrangement made before 6 April 1976 and relating to a share incentive scheme where the shares have fallen in value (a 'stop loss' arrangement).
5. *Expenses connected with living accommodation.* If the occupation is necessary for the job; or is because of a special security risk; or is desirable and customary in the particular occupation, the assessment to cover heat, light, cleaning, repairs and use of

furniture shall not exceed 10 per cent of the emoluments (after deducting any expenses, capital allowances and pension contributions).

6. *Other assets made available for the use of the employee.* The assessment is on 20 per cent of the original value less any rent paid if the asset was first provided after 5 April 1980. For assets first provided before that date the assessment is on 10 per cent of original value less any rent paid.
7. *Assets given to the employee.* The assessment is on the market value at the time the asset is given, if it was originally made available for the benefit of the employee before 6 April 1980. For assets first made available after 5 April 1980 assessment will be on the market value at the time first made available less any amounts already assessed as benefit.
8. *The acquisition of shares at an undervalue* (other than under an approved profit sharing scheme).
9. *Medical insurance (eg BUPA).* The assessment is the cost to the employer. No assessment on premiums to cover travel abroad on business.
10. *Scholarship income.* On any scholarship, bursary or similar endowment paid after 14 March 1983 to a member of the family of an employee by reason of his employment, the employee may be assessed. There are exceptions where over 75 per cent of the payments made by the scholarship fund cover children of people who are not employees and also in some cases where the original award to a student was before 15 March 1983.
11. *Other benefits provided for the employee.* The assessment is on the cash equivalent.

In addition to the above, a director or higher paid employee may be assessed on all expenses paid to or for him. He will be entitled to claim a deduction for travelling expenses necessarily incurred in the performance of his duties and also for other expenses incurred wholly, exclusively and necessarily in the performance of his duties. If he has been assessed on the provision of a chauffeur's services he may claim a deduction for the part of those services attributable to necessary business journeys.

Payments on retirement or removal from office or employment

Tax under Schedule E is chargeable on all emoluments from an office or employment. This term includes some payments on leaving — usually where they are stipulated as part of the terms of the employment. In other cases, compensation or other payments on termination would not normally be within the meaning of 'emoluments' but they are taxed by special legislation. The impact of the tax in such cases is modified. If the payment is in connection with the death, injury or disability of the employee it will be exempt.

Since 4 June 1986 a payment of up to £25,000 has also been exempt. If a payment is for more than £25,000 the excess is taxed at a special rate. It is necessary to calculate (a) tax on total income including the excess termination payment; and then to recalculate it split into (b) tax on income excluding the excess termination payment; (c) tax on the 'slice' of excess termination payment up to a maximum of £25,000; (d) tax on the next slice, if any, up to a maximum of a further £25,000; and (e) tax on the balance, if any (ie where the termination payment exceeds £75,000). From the figure (a) is deducted one-half of the figure in (c) and one-quarter of the figure in (d).

It was intended that the figures in the preceding paragraph should have applied since April 1982. However, the wording of the legislation was such that the slice in (c) was £50,000 and that therefore (e) only applied if the termination payment exceeded £100,000.

The misunderstanding was publicized by the Inland Revenue on 4 June 1986 and the law redrafted to achieve the original intention. People fortunate enough to have received payments of over £50,000 between 6 April 1982 and 3 June 1986 benefit from the legal (but unintended) interpretation. If necessary they will receive a tax refund.

Occupational pension schemes

A company can contribute towards an approved fund for providing retirement and other benefits for its employees (including directors) and the ordinary annual contributions will be allowable expenses for tax purposes. Additional contributions can also be deducted but in some cases the deduction may be spread over a few years. A fund can be limited to certain classes of employees but it is not permitted to discriminate by sex.

The maximum benefits which a fund may provide are:

1. A pension of two-thirds of final pensionable salary after at least ten years' service (smaller fractions for shorter service).
2. A tax-free lump sum on retirement of up to one and a half times final pensionable salary after 20 years' service (smaller amounts for shorter service). If this is taken the amount of pension must be reduced.
3. A dependant's pension following death after retirement of up to two-thirds of employee's pension.
4. A lump sum on death in service of up to four times final salary.

5. A dependant's pension on death in service of up to four-ninths final salary.

A fund need not provide all of these benefits and need not go up to the maximum amounts.

Final salary can be taken as the highest remuneration for one of the five years preceding death or retirement. Alternatively, it can be the average of at least three consecutive years ending in the ten years before death or retirement. If the member is a director who can control at least 20 per cent of the company shares the latter definition must be used.

When making the calculations it is permissible to take the actual remuneration for any year except the year immediately preceding death or retirement and revalue it in accordance with the movement in the index of retail prices. Thus a person who has been well paid in the past but whose increases in emoluments have not kept pace with inflation may possibly be entitled to a pension of an amount higher than he has ever been paid while in service.

In addition to the employer's contribution the employee may, if he chooses, contribute amounts of up to 15 per cent of his salary and such contributions will be deducted in calculating the amount of income on which he will be taxed.

An approved fund is exempt from tax on the income generated from the investment of contributions received and is also exempt from capital gains tax. Directors of all close companies are strongly advised that they should consider whether they should be members of such a fund.

A pension fund is usually run for the company by a life assurance company. This, however, is not compulsory and it is possible for a fund to be run by independent trustees appointed by the company.

It is even possible for the fund to invest some of its resources in the company (for instance, by purchasing business premises and letting them to the company or by lending money to the company at a commercial rate of interest). In this way, a company which is soundly based, but which may have a poor cash flow, can provide a pension scheme for director/shareholders without having to find too much immediate cash.

An employed person in a non-pensionable employment can make arrangements for his own retirement and family protection in the same way as a self-employed person. See page 323 for details of *Retirement annuities*.

Income from self-employment

Calculation of profit

The profit for any period is arrived at by taking the gross earnings and deducting approved costs and expenses. The earnings are the full amounts earned even if they have not been received by the end of the period. Thus trade debtors at the end of the first trading period must be added to the amounts received in the period. In later periods the 'opening' debtors are deducted from receipts and the 'closing' debtors added.

The 'costs of sales' are the first deduction in order to establish the 'gross profit'. These will vary according to the nature of the business but probably the most common items are purchases of goods for resale or to be used in production and productive wages. The amounts deductible are the amounts which refer to the earnings of the period. In the case of stock purchased, therefore, it is not only the stock paid for which comes into account but also any stock bought but not yet paid for. Trade creditors must therefore be added to the purchases.

On the other hand, any stock not yet used must be deducted from the purchases (this is sometimes shown in the accounts by adding to the 'sales' or 'earnings' figure). If the stock has fallen in value the amount to be deducted is the reduced value, but otherwise it is the cost. A similar adjustment must be made for work in progress.

Other deductions are revenue expenses which are incurred wholly and exclusively for the business and which are not specifically prohibited.

The expression 'revenue expenses' excludes the cost of fixed assets and also the cost of alterations or improvements to premises or other fixed assets. In measuring the profitability of a business by normal accountancy standards depreciation of assets is a deductible cost but for tax purposes it is not. Accounts are normally prepared to show depreciation but it is then disallowed in a separate tax computation. However, the tax law provides a system for claiming 'capital allowances'. In recent years these have been very generous but they are not so now. Nevertheless they still normally give a little more flexibility than commercial depreciation.

An example of a genuine business expense which is specifically prohibited for tax is entertaining (except if it is entertaining an overseas customer or is staff entertaining). If any prohibited amount is included in the accounts — as it might quite correctly be for commercial purposes — it is disallowed in the tax computation.

Some expenses are partly for business and partly for other purposes. In the case, for instance, of car running expenses and telephone bills the Inland Revenue like to agree what proportion is applicable to business and what proportion is private and to adjust the tax computation accordingly. In other matters they take the view that if an expense has a joint purpose no part of it is deductible as it is not 'exclusively' for business.

Basis of assessment
It is customary but not compulsory, to prepare accounts to the same date each year. The following paragraphs show how the accounts are used to calculate the amount of income to be assessed. It will be seen that the profit for some periods is taken into account twice or more while the profit for other periods does not enter into the calculation for any tax year. Accounting dates should be chosen with care to try to take maximum advantage of this system.

Year in which business commences. Amount assessed is the profit for the period from date of commencement to the following 5 April.

First complete fiscal year for which business is carried on. Amount assessed is the amount of profit for the first 12 months of business.

Subsequent years.
(a) If there is a 12-month account prepared to a date in the previous fiscal year, and if this account started when business started or immediately after the accounts which were taken as the base of assessment for the previous fiscal year; and if there is no other account ending in the previous fiscal year; the amount assessed is the profit for those accounts.
(b) If the three conditions in (a) above are not all present the Inland Revenue may select any period of 12 months ending in the previous fiscal year and the amount assessed will be the amount of profit for that period.

Fiscal year in which business ceases. Amount assessed is the amount of profit from 6 April preceding cessation until date of cessation.

Taxpayer's option. The taxpayer may request that the assessments for the second and third years of assessment shall be based on the amount of profit for the actual fiscal years. The request must be for both the years. It can be made at any time up to six years after the end of the third year.

Inland Revenue option (1). Where an assessment for a 'subsequent year' is calculated under (b) above, the Board may also revise the assessment for the previous year to the amount of profit for a corresponding period. If the taxpayer is dissatisfied with the revised assessment he can claim such relief, if any, as is just. In practice, the Inland Revenue anticipate such a claim and limit the amount of the revision by using a complicated formula which tries to achieve a reasonable average assessment over a series of years in relation to the average profits of relevant accounting periods.

Inland Revenue option (2). For the two years preceding the year in which the business ceases the Inland Revenue may, if the aggregate profit for those two fiscal years exceeds the aggregate profits assessed, revise both years so that assessments are on the actual profit for the fiscal years.

Partnerships. If, after 19 March 1985, there is a change in a partnership; and at least one person is a partner before and after the change; and the law applies so as to treat the business as a new business from the date of change (see page 317), the above rules are modified.

The profit assessable for the tax year in which the new business is deemed to commence and for the next *three* years will be the amount actually earned in each of these years. For later years the procedure in 'subsequent years' above will apply.

The *Taxpayer's option* described above will apply for years five and six.

If it is necessary to know the amount of profit for any of the periods referred to above and accounts have not been prepared to coincide with that period it is normal to establish that profit by apportionment and/or aggregation of the profit for whatever relevant accounting periods accounts have been prepared.

An example of how *Basis of assessment* works is as follows:

Four people each commenced trading on 6 January 1985. Their books are kept in such a way that it is possible to see that in the first 18 months of trade (split into six quarters) they all earned identical profit, namely:

	£
3 months to 5 April 1985	500
3 months to 5 July 1985	2,000
3 months to 5 October 1985	3,000
3 months to 5 January 1986	6,000
3 months to 5 April 1986	1,400
3 months to 5 July 1986	800

'A' decides that he will prepare his accounts to 5 January each year as he started trade on 6 January. 'B' decides to prepare accounts to 5 April 1985 and stick to the same date each year. 'C' also chooses 5 April but does not have an account to 5 April 1985. He chooses instead to have a 15 month account to 5 April 1986. 'D' wants 5 July as his accounting date and decides to start with an 18 month account to July 1986.

The amounts on which each will be assessed are as follows:

	'A'	'B'	'C'	'D'
1984–85	2,875	500	2,580	2,283
1985–86	11,500	9,800	10,320	9,133
1986–87	11,500	12,400	10,320	9,133
1987–88				9,133

It can be seen that four very different results can come from identical starting figures. In fact, there are many more options in addition to these. In the case of 'D' we are able to say what his 1987–88 assessment will be as well as the other years. This is because in his case we have accounts which end in tax year 1986–87.

On the surface it seems that 'D' made the wisest choice. This may well be true but it is not necessarily true. Much will depend on what income each of them may have had from other sources in each year; what losses or other deductions are available in each year; and what profits may be made in the next few quarters.

Partnerships

A single assessment under Case I or II of Schedule D is made on a partnership, but for the purpose of deciding what allowances shall be given and what tax rates apply the amount of the assessment is apportioned among the partners. The assessment will not normally be on the amount of profit for the tax year (in most cases it will be on the amount of profit earned in the accounting year ending in the previous tax year), but the apportionment is made by reference to the way in which profits are divided between partners for the tax year.

Where there is a change in the membership of a partnership, either by one or more partners leaving or by one or more new partners joining, the business is treated as having ceased and a new business commenced. However, if at least one person is a member of the partnership before and after the change, and if all the partners before and after the change so elect, the business will be treated as continuing throughout. An election must be made within two years of the change. If an election is made it can be withdrawn within the same period.

Capital allowances

Although the depreciation of an asset is a proper cost of a business and should certainly be taken into account in deciding how profitable the business is, it is not part of the profit or loss for a trading period as measured for tax. Instead there is a system of 'capital allowances' for certain fixed assets.

The types of asset which attract allowances and which are likely to be of most interest to readers are (a) machinery and plant; (b) industrial buildings; (c) commercial buildings in enterprise zones; and (d) scientific research expenditure.

Machinery and plant. This covers a wider range of assets than is apparent from the title. It includes many types of fixtures, fittings, equipment, vehicles, and apparatus. In some circumstances it can include the cost of alterations to a building incidental to the installation of plant.

Movable office partitioning has been held by the courts to be plant. So has expenditure on decorating and lighting to create 'atmosphere' in public houses. Another item which would not be immediately obvious is a swimming pool.

There are some items which would not come within the meaning of plant but which are given parity of treatment for tax, principally thermal insulation of industrial buildings, and expenditure on fire safety to comply with the requirements of the Fire Precautions Act 1971.

In the past there have been high 'first year allowances' available on the cost of new machinery and plant but these are being phased out and the main allowance now is a 'writing down allowance'. This is 25 per cent of the cost or the written down value. If a trade is not carried on throughout the tax year the allowance is reduced proportionately to reflect the part of the year for which it is carried on. Thus if a person commences trading on 6 February 1987 and spends £2400 on qualifying plant, the allowance for tax year 1986–87 will be (£2400 x 25% x 2/12 =) £100. Assuming this is claimed it will reduce the value to £2300 and the allowance available for tax year 1987–88 will be (£2300 x 25%=) £575.

In the main all machinery and plant is 'pooled' together. New expenditure is added to the 'pool' and if an asset is sold the sale proceeds are deducted from the pool — unless the proceeds are more than the original cost, in which case only the cost is deducted.

If an asset is used partly for business and partly for other purposes it is kept out of the pool and treated separately. The allowances will be restricted according to the proportion of business to non-business use. Cars costing over £8000 are also treated separately.

A trader may also claim that any 'short life asset' (which, broadly, means an anticipated life of under five years) can be put into a different pool from the normal pool.

A trader can claim less than the full allowance available for a tax year or can claim no allowance at all. A reduced claim will of course mean that a bigger pool is available for the future. An example of when it would be sensible not to claim might be if the assessable profit before capital allowances was only £3000. If the trader was married and had no other income he could have a taxable profit of up to £3655 without paying tax. It would therefore be pointless to claim allowances and reduce the assessment.

If assets are sold and the amount realized exceeds the value of the pool the excess figure becomes a 'balancing charge' and is added to profit. A balancing charge is therefore in effect a withdrawal of allowances given in earlier years.

When a business ceases the market value of the machinery and plant is compared with the value of the pool. If the market value is bigger a balancing charge is added to the taxable profit. If the pool value is the bigger a balancing allowance is given.

Industrial buildings. An allowance is based on the cost of construction (or extension) of a qualifying building. There is no allowance for the cost of the land.

Broadly speaking, an industrial building is one in which some manufacture is carried on or in which goods or materials are subjected to a process. In addition certain storage premises may qualify and, rather strangely, so can a building which is used as a sports pavilion for the welfare of employees. There are also a few other definitions which are unlikely to apply to readers of this book.

When the building is constructed the person who can claim the allowance is not necessarily the person who will carry on the trade in it. It is the person who incurs the cost of construction or (if the cost is borne by a builder who then sells the building before it is occupied) the person who buys it from the builder. This of course may be the person who occupies it for trade but equally it might be someone who leases it to the trader.

The allowance is 4 per cent of the construction cost for each year until the twenty-fifth anniversary of the first use of the building. For buildings constructed before 6 November 1962 it was 2 per cent per year for a period of 50 years.

In the past 'initial allowances' have been claimable. The percentages have varied over the years. On some small buildings they have been as much as 100 per cent. On larger buildings the highest rate has been 75 per cent. The total allowances cannot exceed the qualifying cost and so the effect of claiming initial allowances has been that the period for claiming annual allowances has been reduced from 25 years (or 50 years). However, the period in which the claimant is vulnerable to a balancing charge would not be shortened.

The person who incurs the expenditure is said to have a 'relevant interest'. He may, for instance, own the land freehold or he may have a lease of it. If he disposes of this relevant interest within the period of 25 years (or 50 years for older buildings) he will cease to be entitled to continuing allowances. He may have a balancing allowance or a balancing charge depending upon how much he received for the disposal.

The new holder of the relevant interest will then be entitled to some allowances in future years. The amount will depend upon the price he has paid. The tax inspector will first ascertain the 'residue before sale' applicable to the vendor. This will normally be the original qualifying cost less allowances claimed but in a few cases where there may have been usage for a period for a non-qualifying purpose some other notional allowances may also be deducted. Any balancing charge is added to the residue (or any balancing allowance deducted) and this gives the 'residue after sale'. This figure is then divided by the number of years from the date of the transfer until the twenty-fifth (or fiftieth) anniversary of first use and the resultant figure is the annual allowance available to the new holder of the relevant interest.

Example. A trader spent £40,000 on the construction of a qualifying building in 1966 when the initial allowance was 15 per cent. The building was first occupied in April 1966 and the twenty-fifth anniversary will therefore be April 1991. For 19 years up to 1984–85 he claimed annual allowances of £1600 which therefore total £30,400. Together with the initial allowance of £6000 he had therefore had a total of £36,400. His residue before sale was £3600.

If he sold the building on 6 April 1985 for £30,000 (excluding price for the land) he would have a balancing charge of £26,400 and the residue after sale would be £30,000.

If he sold for £50,000 the balancing charge would be £36,400 because it cannot exceed the allowance given and the residue after sale would be the original cost of £40,000.

If for three years during the period he (or his tenant) had used the building for a non-qualifying period he would have received annual allowances for only 16 out of the total 19 years. Allowances would have been notionally written off for those three years so the residue before sale would be the same figure of £3600. However, the balancing charge would be limited to the figure of £31,600 (£6000 initial + 16 x £1600 annual). The residue after sale would therefore be £35,200.

As there are five tax years from 6 April 1986 to April 1991 the new owner can claim one-fifth of the residue (ie £6000 or £8000 or £7040 depending on which of the above assumptions we take) for each of those five years.

Commercial buildings in enterprise zones. Since 1981 various areas of the country have been designated as 'enterprise zones' and the government tries to stimulate economic activity in them. One of the measures taken is to give allowances based on similar lines to industrial buildings allowance to any commercial premises on which cost of construction is incurred within ten years of the zone being designated.

The old concept of an initial allowance is kept and the rate of allowance is 100 per cent so that a person can write off the whole construction costs in one year if he chooses. If he decides that he does not want the whole cost he can choose whatever smaller figure he likes and the balance goes forward to be written off in later years. In each later year he can claim an annual allowance up to a maximum of 25 per cent of original cost.

There are other advantages in enterprise zones, a major one being that premises are free of rates for the first ten years. Another is that planning ritual and regulations are relaxed.

Scientific research. One allowance which is often in danger of being overlooked is the allowance for capital expenditure on buildings and plant (but excluding land and houses) for trading activities 'in the fields of natural or applied science for the extension of knowledge'. It is not possible to give a comprehensive definition of what might come within this phrase but professional advice should be taken if significant amounts are about to be spent which seem as though they might come within it.

Where expenditure can be regarded as qualifying the allowance is 100 per cent of the expenditure.

Other capital allowances. Allowances are also available for capital expenditure on: agricultural buildings and works; certain dwellings let on assured tenancies; cemeteries and crematoria; mines, oil wells and mineral deposits; certain hotels built after 11 April 1978; patent rights; and know-how.

Business losses

There are several ways in which relief may be claimed in respect of losses incurred by an individual or a partnership carrying on a trade, profession or vocation. It is advisable to have experienced professional assistance when considering which method of claim is likely to be most beneficial.

For a loss to qualify for relief the business must be carried on on a commercial basis with a view to profit. For the 'new business' relief there must also be a reasonable expectation of profit. In a business of farming or market gardening relief may be refused in some cases if losses are made for more than five consecutive years.

In general, capital allowances may be taken into account in such a way as to increase the amount of loss or convert a profit into a loss. However, if the trade consists of leasing or includes leasing, capital allowances on the leased assets may not be included for the purpose of setting off against income, other than income from plant leasing, unless the trade is carried on for at least six months and unless the claimant devotes substantially the whole of his time to it.

If a partnership makes a loss each partner may, subject to certain conditions, decide which method of claim for relief he wishes to make for his share of the loss. There are now rules to restrict the tax losses of a limited partner to the actual financial loss suffered by the partner.

A broad summary of the options available is as follows:

1. *Same year set-off.* The loss may be treated as reducing total income of the year. It reduces the earned income of the person who suffers the loss and, if it exceeds that, it then reduces the unearned income. If the loss is still not fully relieved any balance reduces the earned income of the spouse and then the unearned income. In the rare cases where income from the business would be treated as unearned income (ie sleeping partners) the set-off is against unearned income in priority to earned income.

   A claim may be made to exclude the income of the spouse. Apart from this, it is not permissible to claim relief for a reduced part only of the loss. If same year set-off is claimed the losses must be used up to the amount of income even if some of that income, by virtue of personal allowances, would have suffered no tax.

   A claim for this relief must be made within two years.
2. *Following year set-off.* If the person still carries on the business in the year following the year of loss it may be deducted, in a similar manner to 'same year set-off', from the income of that later year. If a person claims this relief it is given in priority to 'same year set-off' for the year of claim.

   Relief must be claimed within two years of the later year (ie the year of claim).
3. *New business relief.* If a business incurs a loss in the year of commencement or in any of the three succeeding years the loss may be carried back and set against income of the three years preceding the year of loss. It will be set against the earliest year first and any balance not used will be set against the later years.

   Relief must be claimed within two years after the year of loss.
4. *Carry forward.* If losses have not been used in other ways a claim may be made to carry them forward and reduce the income of later years from the same business. Losses carried forward must be used as soon as possible even if they reduce income which, by virtue of personal allowances, would have suffered no tax.

   Claims must be made within six years.
5. *Transfer of a business.* If the trade in which losses have been incurred is transferred to a company in exchange for the issue of shares in the company the losses may be carried forward and set against income which the individual subsequently receives from the company. Losses can only be set against income for a year throughout which the relevant shares are owned and they will be set against earned income in priority to unearned income.

   Claims must be made within six years.

6. *Terminal losses.* When a person finishes in business, losses incurred in the final 12 months may be carried back and deducted from income from the business for the three previous years. The losses are deducted from the latest year first.

   Claims must be made within six years from the date of cessation of the trade.
7. *Certain capital losses.* If an individual has subscribed for shares in a qualifying trading company and after 5 April 1980 he subsequently makes a loss on the disposal of those shares he may claim to treat that loss as reducing his income for the year of disposal or the following year. It is treated as reducing earned income in priority to investment income and the provisions regarding spouses' income are similar to 'same year set-off'.

   The loss must be incurred in a disposal at arm's length for full consideration or in winding up or upon the value of the shares becoming negligible.

   Claims must be made within two years.
8. *Agricultural lettings.* If deductible expenses exceed assessable rent etc, the excess may be set against other income for the same or the next year. Alternatively it can be carried forward against future income from farming or ownership of agricultural land.

   Claims for set-off must be made within two years.

Retirement annuities (self-employed pensions)

Self-employed persons, partners, and persons in non-pensionable employment may provide for their retirement or family security by entering into contracts for annuities or death benefits. Within specified limits, premiums for these contracts are deductible in deciding the amount of taxable earned income and tax relief is therefore effectively allowed at the individual's highest rate.

The benefits obtainable will be related to the premiums paid and to the age at which the contract commences. The premiums payable are restricted to a percentage of 'net relevant earnings'. The net relevant earnings for any tax year are the assessable income from all trades, professions, vocations and non-pensionable employments after deducting capital allowances, losses, stock relief, and certain annual payments connected with the business.

1. Apart from a few specified occupations an annuity for the individual may commence not earlier than his sixtieth and not later than his seventy-fifth birthday. At commencement a part of the annuity may be commuted for a tax-free lump sum, but apart from this the annuity will be assessed as earned income. In the

event of death before retiring age, premiums together with interest may be returned to the surviving spouse, dependants or personal representatives.

2. An annuity for a widow, widower or dependants of the person may commence on his death.
3. A capital sum may be paid on his death before the age of 75. By creating appropriate trusts such a lump sum death benefit may be excluded from the estate of the individual and passed to any chosen beneficiary without suffering inheritance tax.

The maximum premium on which relief is allowed for contracts under 2 and/or 3 is 5 per cent net relevant earnings. The maximum for contracts under 1, 2 and 3 combined has varied over the years. The limits from 1980–81 are as set out in Table D on page 359.

An individual who pays a qualifying premium may, before the end of the fiscal year in which it is paid, elect that it shall be treated as having been paid in the preceding year. If there were no net relevant earnings in the preceding year he may elect that the premium is treated as having been paid in the preceding year but one.

If a person has not taken full advantage of the relief which he could have claimed for any year had he paid the maximum allowable contribution he can pay a premium (or an additional premium) within six years and claim the relief for the year in which it is paid in addition to claiming his normal maximum for that year.

Many insurance companies write contracts under which the contributor may borrow substantial amounts back again. This aid to cash flow may help the hard-pressed businessman fund the premiums. More importantly, as the contributions build up, the loan-back facility may be a useful source of finance for expanding the business, buying out retiring partners, or even paying inheritance tax.

Rents from property

Rents from land in the UK, including land let to a family partnership or company, are assessed under Schedule A on the full amount of rent receivable whether received in the year of assessment or later.

The amount assessable is reduced by amounts actually paid in respect of maintenance, repairs, insurance and management; the cost of services which the lessor is obliged to supply; rates or other tenants' burdens borne by the lessor; any rents, ground annuals etc paid by the lessor.

Where properties are let at a full rent and not on tenants' repairing leases any excess of expenses over rents on one property can be set against another property. Any excess of expenses on the combined such properties is carried forward to set against future rents. If a property is on a tenants' repairing lease it is treated by itself and excess expenses in one year can be carried forward against rents of later years. Similarly, a property which is let at less than a full rent is dealt with in isolation.

Premiums on leases

A premium is an amount paid in connection with a new leasehold interest. Thus, if a lessee transfers the residue of his lease for a capital sum, that capital sum is not a premium. If he creates a sub-lease for a capital sum, that capital sum is a premium.

A premium receivable for a lease of up to 50 years is taxable as income. If the lease is for a period of two years or more the assessment is on the premium less a reduction of 2 per cent for every complete year except the first. Thus on a 20-year lease the assessment will be on 62 per cent of the premium.

If a tenant is required to make improvements to the property the value of those improvements is treated as if a premium were receivable. Certain other receipts are also treated as premiums. These include payments in commutation of rents, payments for variation or waiver of the terms of a lease, and payments for the assignments of leases granted at an undervalue.

Where premises are occupied for business purposes the amount of premium (or other payment) treated as income of the landlord can also be treated as additional rent payable by the tenant. The figure is treated as spread over the period of the lease. For instance, in the above example, where 62 per cent of the premium for a 20-year lease is assessed, an amount equal to 3.1 per cent of the premium is treated as an additional deductible business expense in each of the 20 years.

Furnished lettings

Furnished lettings are normally assessed under Schedule D Case VI but a landlord may ask that the element of receipts relating to the property itself be assessed under Schedule A.

Furnished holiday lettings are taxed under Schedule D Case VI but the income is treated as earned income for the purposes of wife's earned income allowance; wife's earnings election, losses and retirement annuity relief (see page 323).

In addition the 'rollover relief' (see page 342) for replacement of business assets is available for capital gains tax. So also is 'retirement relief' (see page 343).

Business Expansion Scheme
The Business Expansion Scheme (BES) was introduced as an incentive to encourage individuals to subscribe new capital to companies. There is no restriction on the size of companies which may attract the new capital but they must not be quoted on the Stock Exchange or the Unlisted Securities Market so in effect they will tend to be smaller companies.

The company must be incorporated and resident in the UK. It must carry on its trade wholly or mainly in the UK. This does not mean that it cannot be an exporter. It means that at least half of its activities are carried on in this country. In measuring the activities the Inland Revenue will wish to know where employees actually work and where assets are situated.

If a company wishes to raise £50,000 or more of capital eligible for relief it must not hold more than half of its 'assets as a whole' by way of 'interests in land'.

'Assets as a whole' means the market value of all assets minus all debts and liabilities of the company and for this purpose paid-up preference capital is regarded as a debt.

'Interests in land' mean the market value of all land and buildings minus any debts secured on the land and building and minus also all unsecured debts falling due later than 12 months and the amount paid up in respect of preference shares.

There are some restrictions on the trade which the company may carry on but most manufacturing, wholesaling and retailing can qualify. Where items dealt in are of a kind which may often be held for investment purposes (eg antiques, fine wines) there are rules to exclude the trade unless it conforms to normal wholesale or retail standards. The types of trade which are excluded are financial services; leasing or hiring of assets; receiving royalties or licence fees; dealing in land; property development; dealing in commodities, shares, securities or futures; oil extraction; providing legal or accountancy services; or providing support services to any of the aforementioned activities.

The trade of the company must be conducted on a commercial basis and with a view to the realization of profit. Research and development from which a qualifying trade is expected to derive is treated in the same way as a trade.

Nature of capital subscribed. For an individual to obtain the benefit of this scheme the company must issue new shares to him. They must be ordinary shares. There must not be any arrangement under which they have any present or future right to preferential treatment in the matter of being redeemed or of having a preferential right to dividends or to preferential treatment on a winding up. If any rights come into existence within five years from the date of issue of the shares they will invalidate the shares.

The company must not have any issued share capital which is not fully paid up.

Benefit to the subscribing individual. The amount subscribed shall be treated as reduction of the individual's taxable income for the fiscal year in which the shares are issued. The maximum amount which may be treated as such a reduction for any individual is £40,000 for any fiscal year from 1983–84 onwards.

Husband and wife are treated as one individual.

An individual may invest in more than one company but the minimum amount in any company must be £500. This condition does not apply if his investment is made through an Approved Investment Fund (see page 330).

If a person has income on which the top £10,000 is taxed at 60 per cent and he invests £10,000 in qualifying shares his tax bill will be cut by £6000. So it is reasonable for him to say that the shares have really only cost him £4000. This might seem too good to be true and to some extent it is. The apparently simple arithmetic can be misleading.

A person's shares in a company can only qualify for relief if that person is not connected with the company. This means that he may not have more than a 30 per cent stake in the capital (ie the ordinary share capital or the share and loan capital combined) or more than 30 per cent of the voting power in the company. When testing to see whether these limits are exceeded the capital or rights held by his associates will be regarded as his. 'Associates' include partners, husbands, wives, children or other descendants, parents or other ancestors, and people with whom he is connected by virtue of trusts. It does not, however, include brothers or sisters, nieces or nephews, or remoter relations.

A claimant for BES relief cannot be an employee of the company. He can be a director but he must not be paid for these services. He can receive expenses so long as they pass the normal Inland Revenue test of being incurred 'wholly, exclusively and necessarily for the performance of his duties as a director'. If any small part of the expenses fails to pass this test it will be treated as remuneration and will disqualify him from relief.

The prohibition against receiving remuneration applies to his associates as well as to the claimant.

The result of this limitation of interest is that he is a minority shareholder who may have little chance to control the way the company is run and who may find it difficult to sell his shares at a later date if he should want to do so. Moreover, if he should come to sell his shares he may find that the price he could negotiate was much less than he had hoped for. It is well established that a minority holding in a non-quoted company may have very small value. A 20 per cent interest, for instance, is not worth anything like 20 per cent of the value of the whole company except in rare cases.

Having sounded a note of caution about the value of minority interests it would be wrong to suggest that in all cases it is unwise to make such investment. Such holdings can be excellent investments in well run and profitable companies. In particular, if no individual or family has over 50 per cent of the control in a company minority shareholders have extra influence.

Difficulties over the right to dispose of shares and the valuation of them on a disposal are reduced in cases where a company might eventually come to the stock market or Unlisted Securities Market; or in cases where some other company or persons may eventually wish to buy the whole company; or where a company prospers and later feels that it is desirable to reduce its share capital.

Prospects for acquiring minority interests should be viewed with caution and the personalities and business skills of the directors and managers of the company should be considered as well as the accounts and other figures. In many cases, despite all the risks, investment may prove to be rewarding. Remember that it is precisely because of the risks that small companies have difficulty in raising finance and that therefore the government has created this scheme. The BES is not designed merely to reduce the tax bill of high-rate taxpayers. It is intended to encourage them to put some of the money they would have otherwise paid in tax into businesses which otherwise might be in financial difficulty. By doing this the minority shareholders will be helping the economy of the country and will help to fight unemployment. If they unfortunately pick the wrong companies to support they should not lose too much and if they pick the right ones they will be amply rewarded.

The BES is not limited to high-rate taxpayers. A person who pays only 29 per cent tax may take advantage of it but clearly it is much more attractive to those on the highest rates.

Shares disposed of within five years. If they are not sold at arm's length all the relief will be withdrawn. If they are sold at arm's length and the money or other value received for them is less than their cost the relief will be withdrawn up to the amount of value received. If the value received exceeds cost all the relief will be withdrawn. On withdrawal, tax for the year in which relief was given is recalculated but for the purpose of charging interest the relevant date is the date of the disposal which caused the withdrawal.

Other events causing withdrawal of relief. Relief is withdrawn if within five years the individual receives value from the company. This can happen, for instance, if he borrows from the company; or if the company transfers an asset to him at less than full worth; if it repays or redeems any capital or makes a payment for giving up any rights; or even repays any debt it had to him before the shares were issued.

If the ratio of company's 'interests in land' changes within three years so that it comes to exceed 50 per cent of the 'assets as a whole' relief can be withdrawn.

Relief is also withdrawn if within five years the company ceases to carry on a qualifying trade; or if the claimant becomes connected with the company; or if the company otherwise becomes ineligible.

If any event does occur which required relief to be withdrawn the law requires the claimant and the company to notify the tax inspector within 60 days.

Shares disposed of after five years. Broadly, for shares issued up to 18 March 1986, it is almost as though the relief had not been given. The relief is not withdrawn. If the sale proceeds (or other disposal value in the case of a gift, for instance) are higher than the amount subscribed for the shares, a capital gain will be calculated in the normal way. However, if the proceeds are less than the cost a capital loss cannot be used in the normal way (ie it cannot be set off against capital gains).

If a person has some shares in a company on which relief has been claimed and also has other shares in the company there are special rules to identify each category for capital gains tax purposes.

Shares issued after 18 March 1986 on which relief is given and not withdrawn shall not give rise to any chargeable gain or allowable loss on disposal by the person who received the relief.

Making the claim. The company must first notify its own tax inspector and satisfy him that it satisfies the conditions for being a qualifying company. Then with his consent it will give certificates to new shareholders saying that the company and the trade qualify. The shareholder can then make a claim for relief to his own tax inspector and support it with the certificate. His own inspector will need to be satisfied that he is a qualifying person.

If the company has not yet started to trade or has only just started a claim cannot be made until the trade has been carried on for four months. If the company does not start to trade within two years of shares being issued no claim can be made for relief on those shares.

A claim must be made within two years after the end of the tax year in which the shares are issued. However, if the shares are issued before the company started to trade or within four months of commencement the two-year period for claiming does not expire until two years after the end of the fourth month of trading.

If a person can make his claim and have it accepted quickly enough the tax relief can be given under PAYE. In other cases if the relief will reduce tax demanded on an assessment he can ask for that tax to be held over until the claim is agreed. If the claim is not agreed for any reason the normal rules will apply for calculation of tax paid late.

If any tax is in arrear and a claim is made for relief after the tax became due the relief may be used to settle the overdue tax but it will not be treated as having been settled until the date the claim was made so that interest may be chargeable for the period before that date.

Other points to remember. Relief is not available unless the claimant is resident and ordinarily resident in the UK.

A person who is not otherwise connected with a company will be regarded as connected if he subscribes for shares under an arrangement which provides for some other person to subscribe for shares in a company with which the first person is connected.

Relief can be refused 'unless the shares are subscribed for and issued for bona fide commercial purposes and not as part of a scheme or arrangement the main purpose or one of the main purposes of which is the avoidance of tax'. This wording is rather imprecise and is clearly designed to frustrate any ingenious plans which people may devise to obtain relief without genuinely providing new capital for qualifying trades. Investors should therefore not be seeking for 'loopholes' but should abide by the spirit as well as the letter of the legislation.

Approved investment funds. Because of the risks involved in investment in unquoted companies; and because some people would like to spread investment over several companies but do not have the time or resources to examine prospective investments in detail, a number of 'approved investment funds' have been formed. It is likely that more will be formed in the future.

These funds accept investment money from a lot of individuals and then invest that money on behalf of the individuals in several companies. They treat each individual on a proportionate basis so that if, for instance, one person had placed £2000 with a fund and another had placed £20,000 the first person would receive shares in the same companies as the second but would only have one-tenth as many in each company.

An approved fund will have been approved by the Inland Revenue but the authorities take pains to point out that they cannot be responsible for the actions of the fund managers. The fund will obviously try to select companies to invest in which have good potential for profit and expansion but clearly their judgement can be wrong. Most people will feel that because investment is spread over several companies the risk of losing a lot by picking the wrong companies is minimized.

The funds may have to receive applications from many companies and spend a lot of time and money in investigation before deciding which companies are worth investing in. There are several ways in which they make charges to cover these costs and their own income.

Funds normally charge a commission related to the amount of the investment made. The amount varies for each fund. If, for instance, the commission is 6 per cent then on an investment of £5000 the investor would also have to pay a further £300 plus £45 VAT. These charges would not be regarded as part of the cost of shares for the granting of relief.

Funds have a target date for attracting investment money and a much later target date for investing it. In the interim period the money is kept on deposit and the interest may accrue for the benefit of the fund.

When investing on behalf of the people they act for, the funds may take an option which permits them to invest on their own behalf at a similar price but at a later date. This obviously gives them a chance to invest at very advantageous cost.

If a company applies to a fund for an investment of capital it may be charged with the investigation costs.

When a fund does invest on behalf of the people it represents it may ask that a member represents it in the board of the company and that member will receive director's fees.

There is some criticism that funds may be overpaid for the services they perform. Whether this criticism is justified or not must be a matter for the individual judgement of each potential investor. It can be very costly and time-consuming to examine a lot of companies and to sort the wheat from the chaff. If other forms of remuneration were not available it is possible that the funds would feel the need to charge much higher initial fees. The right to options is akin to charging a payment by results. If the fund wishes to exercise its option it will be because the company invested in is performing well so the people represented by the fund should not be dissatisfied. The right to keep the interest on investors' money may not disturb most of the people who invest. In the main they will be high-rate taxpayers so that if the interest accrrued to them it would be heavily taxed so the net interest they lose will be small. On the other hand, some people might argue that a fund which can have free use of uninvested money may deliberately be slow to invest.

The ways in which remuneration is taken must be made clear in the memorandum which the fund issues to potential investors (and which must receive Inland Revenue clearance) so investors have an opportunity to see all charges which will be made to them and to others and if these are not acceptable the investor should avoid the fund.

When placing money with a fund the investor should realize that the tax relief under BES does not arise at that time. It arises only on the occasions that the fund is issued with shares on his behalf. This may be in a later tax year than the one in which he pays money to the fund. Indeed it can happen that some of the money is not invested in shares and is returned to the investor and in that case of course no relief can be claimed on such money.

An investor may place money with different funds or may place some with funds and may make direct investment in other companies as well so long as he does not claim relief on more than the maximum of £40,000 which is permitted for any tax year.

Personal equity plans

Since 1 January 1987 an individual who is resident and ordinarily resident in the UK and who is over 18 has been able to enter into contracts with 'plan managers' (eg stockbrokers, banks, building societies etc) under which up to £2400 a calendar year can be invested. Provided that the individual leaves his investment in the plan to the end of the year and throughout the following year all dividends and profits will be free of income tax and capital gains tax.

The plan manager must use the investment to buy shares but a part of the funds may be used to buy unit trusts.

In the first year the tax saving will be small but a person who invests the maximum (or near to it) every year could, over a number of years, generate quite a significant tax-free income.

Relief for interest paid

When money is borrowed for the purposes of a business the interest may be deducted in calculating the taxable trading profit, under the normal business expense rules. This deduction will be available whether the money is borrowed by way of fixed loan or overdraft, but it is essential that the trading entity (ie the sole trader, partnership or company actually carrying on the trade) should be the borrower.

The normal business expense rules do not help where borrowing is not undertaken for the purpose of trade, profession or vocation or where the person borrowing the money is not the person actually carrying on the business (eg an individual partner borrowing money in connection with the partnership business, or a shareholder borrowing money for the company's business). In such cases, however, it is often possible for the borrower to obtain tax relief for the interest. It is important to realize that the borrowing must be by way of fixed loan rather than overdraft.

There is no statutory relief where money is borrowed by a partner to purchase land to be used by the partnership, or where a shareholder buys land to be used by a company. If the partner/shareholder actually lets the land to the partnership/company at a commercial rent, then tax relief may be claimed against the rent. In cases where the partnership or company pays interest on behalf of the individual the payment will be treated as a payment of rent. This may affect entitlement to 'retirement relief' from capital gains tax (see page 343).

The following chart gives a broad summary of the situations where interest can be deducted from income for income tax purposes.

Purpose	Conditions	Restrictions
Purchase or improvement of land or buildings (including caravans, mobile homes and houseboats) in UK or Republic of Ireland — see also *MIRAS* (page 335).	Property must be (1) used as the only or main residence of the borrower (or of divorced or separated spouse); or (2) acquired by person living in job-related accommodation and must either be used as a residence or be meant to be used eventually as the only or main residence; or (3) occupied rent free by a dependent relative of the borrower or his spouse; or	Relief is not allowed on loans totalling more than £30,000 for any person. However, interest can also be allowed on a bridging loan of up to £30,000 for one year (or even longer in special circumstances).
	Property must be let at a commercial rent for at least 26 out of any 52 weeks. When not so let it must be available for letting; be in the course of construction or repair; or be used as main residence.	Interest can only be deducted from rental income. If it exceeds the income in one year it can be carried forward.
Business purposes	Money borrowed must buy an interest in a partnership or be lent to a partnership in which the borrower is a member (but not as a limited partner); or	No relief on money borrowed to the extent that capital is subsequently recovered from the partnership.
	Money borrowed must acquire a share in, or be lent to, a cooperative in which the borrower is employed substantially full time; or	No relief for interest on money borrowed to the extent that capital is later recovered from the cooperative.

Purpose	Conditions	Restrictions
	Money borrowed must be used to buy close company shares (but not in an investment company, unless more than 75 per cent of its income is estate or trading income) or must be lent to a close company for use in its business. The borrower must, at the time the interest is paid, have at least a 5 per cent interest in the company or be engaged full time in the conduct or management of the company; or	If the company is an investment company, no property held by the company must be used as a residence by the individual. No relief on money borrowed to the extent that capital is subsequently recovered from the company.
	Money borrowed must be used to acquire shares in an unquoted employee-controlled trading company (within 12 months of its becoming employee-controlled) and the borrower (or spouse) must be a full-time employee. A company is employee-controlled if at least 50 per cent of the shares and of the voting power is owned by full-time employees or their spouses; or	If any employee holds over 10 per cent of shares or votes the excess is deemed to be held by a non-employee. If husband and wife are both full-time employees they may hold up to 10 per cent each. No relief to extent that capital is recovered from the company.
	Money borrowed must be used to buy plant or machinery for use in a partnership of which the borrower is a partner or, if he is an employee, for use in his employment.	Relief only on interest within three years after the end of tax year in which money borrowed.
Purchase of life annuity by person aged 65 or over	At least 90 per cent of money borrowed must be used to buy an annuity for the borrower or for the survivor of the borrower or for the survivor of the borrower and another person. The loan must be secured on the only or main residence of the annuitant(s).	Relief restricted to interest on £30,000.

MIRAS (Mortgage Interest Relief at Source)
The relief for interest on money borrowed to purchase or improve one's home (or the home of a dependent relative or former spouse) is usually given 'at source'. This means that instead of paying the full amount of interest due the borrower only pays 71 per cent of the amount (70 per cent when the basic tax rate was 30 per cent) and the Inland Revenue pays the balance to the lender.

In a few cases (eg where loans exceed £30,000 or where the lender is not an approved operator of MIRAS) interest is paid in full and the tax inspector gives the tax relief against an assessment or in PAYE coding.

If a person is liable for higher rates of tax MIRAS will give him relief at the basic rate only. The tax inspector will give the extra relief by extending the tranche of income which is taxable at basic rate. For instance, if the gross amount of interest payable is £2000, the amount of income taxable at 29 per cent goes up from £17,200 (see Table B, page 358) to £19,200.

Interest on tax

Interest on tax repayments
If the Inland Revenue make a repayment of tax to a person more than 12 months after the end of the fiscal year for which it was paid, and if the person was resident in the UK for that year, they will pay interest in addition to the tax. The interest is called a 'repayment supplement'. It is calculated from the end of the year following the year of assessment until the end of the tax month (ie a month ending on the 6th) in which the tax is repaid. From January 1980 to 5 December 1982 the rate was 12 per cent; from 6 December 1982 to 5 May 1985 it was 8 per cent; from 6 May 1985 to 5 August 1986 it was 11 per cent; from 6 August to 5 November 1986 it was 8½ per cent, and it is currently 9½ per cent. Interest is not payable on repayments under £25.

If the tax had not been paid by the person before 12 months after the year of assessment the interest only commences to run at the end of the fiscal year in which it was paid.

Interest on tax repayments is not treated as income for taxation purposes.

Similar provisions apply for companies, but the minimum repayment on which interest is paid is £100 instead of £25.

For companies, interest is calculated by reference to the date on which corporation tax for the relevant period would normally be due. If the tax was paid within 12 months after that date interest starts to run on the first anniversary of the date. If the tax was paid later interest starts to run on the next anniversary of the date following date of payment.

Interest on overdue tax

If tax is not paid on the due date interest becomes chargeable. The present rate of interest is 9½ per cent per annum. Interest so paid cannot be regarded as a deductible expense.

If an appeal is made against an assessment and the appellant has reason to believe that the tax charged is overstated he may ask that collection of the excess be postponed. If this request is granted collection can be delayed until the appeal is settled but if settlement is delayed beyond six months after the due date interest will be charged from the end of the six-month period. The six-month postponement does not apply to the second instalment of tax on trades, professions or vocations.

If an assessment is made late and the due date becomes 30 days after the assessment rather than the normal due date, the period of postponement free of interest can only run to six months after the normal due date.

When an appeal is made which might take a long time to resolve the appellant must consider whether he should withhold payment of the amount in dispute and risk being charged with interest if he should lose his appeal or whether he should pay the tax and then reclaim it if he wins his appeal.

The Board of Inland Revenue have power to waive a claim to interest on an assessment if it is less than £30.

For assessments issued before 1 August 1982 if on settlement of an appeal an increased amount of tax was due, interest would be charged from 30 days after the revised notice of assessment. For later assessments, any increased amount of tax is regarded as due at the normal date applicable to the original assessment and interest will be calculated from this date.

The Inland Revenue also have power to charge interest for a period before an assessment was made if the reason for it being made late was negligence (or worse) on the part of the taxpayer.

Certificates of tax deposit

A person can make advance provision for tax which will be payable in the future by buying certificates of tax deposit. The minimum deposit is £2000, which may be deposited with any tax collector. Additional deposits are in multiples of £500. The certificates can be used in payment of income tax (other than PAYE or the money which must be deducted from certain payments to subcontractors in the construction industry), corporation tax, capital gains tax, or inheritance tax.

Deposits earn interest from the date of deposit to the date they are used in settlement of tax, but subject to a maximum of six years. For the first two years it is the rate prevailing on the date of deposit. For the next two years it is the rate prevailing on the second anniversary and the next two it is the rate prevailing on the fourth anniversary. The rate varies from time to time. The rate in effect at 14 November 1986 was 10¾ per cent. If deposits are not used to settle tax, they can be encashed but a much smaller rate of interest will be given. Higher rates are available for deposits in excess of £100,000.

Settlements

A settlement (or trust) is created when one person (the settlor) places funds or assets under the control of trustees for the benefit of a person or group of persons (the beneficiaries). For taxation purposes the trustees have an identity separate from the settlor or the beneficiaries and separate from their own personal affairs.

The trustees are not liable for higher rate tax. They are not entitled to any personal reliefs. If the income of the settlement is to be accumulated or is payable at the discretion of the trustees there is a liability to surcharge of 16 per cent as well as basic rate tax.

When trustees release income to or for a beneficiary they provide him with a certificate showing that the income is the net amount after the deduction of basic rate tax or (in the case of an accumulation or discretionary settlement) basic rate tax plus surcharge. The income is then taken into account with the rest of the beneficiary's income for the year to see if any further tax or any repayment of tax is due.

In some cases the income of a settlement is deemed to be the income of the settlor. The circumstances in which this occurs are complicated and so rare as to need the help of a specialist.

Charities

An approved charity can claim exemption from income tax on investment income which is used for charitable purposes. It can also claim exemption on trading income if the trade is exercised in the course of carrying out a primary purpose of the charity or if the work in connection with the trade is mainly carried out by beneficiaries of the charity.

Exemption from capital gains tax is also available if the gain is used for charitable purposes.

If a trader seconds an employee to work temporarily for a charity he may still treat the costs of employing that person as a trading expense.

A group of individuals who raise funds to support a charity (by bazaars, jumble sales etc) are not statutorily exempt from tax on their trading income but by concession the Inland Revenue do not charge tax if the following conditions apply:

1. The organization is not regularly trading.
2. The trading is not in competition with other traders.
3. The activities are supported substantially because the public know that the profits are for charity.
4. The profits are given to a charity or applied for charitable purposes.

From April 1987 employers are able to join a 'Payroll Giving Scheme'. This enables any employee who wishes to join to make donations of up to £100 a year. The employer deducts the donations from pay before operating PAYE and passes the money to an approved agent who passes it on to the nominated charity or charities.

Individuals are encouraged to assist charities by means of deeds of covenant.

In normal circumstances no payment can be made under a deed of covenant before the deed is signed but by concession the Inland Revenue will often accept that a deed in favour of a charity can be backdated to cover payments before the deed is signed but in the same income tax year (eg weekly donations to churches).

In some circumstances if a person wishes to make an isolated donation to a charity the donation can be made more valuable by means of a 'deposited covenant'. Broadly, this means that the gift is treated as four separate payments due in four succeeding years but that money for the later years is loaned to the charity until such time as it becomes the absolute property of the charity.

NATIONAL INSURANCE CONTRIBUTIONS

Class I

Contributions for employed people must be paid by the employee (the employer deducting the contribution along with PAYE tax) and by the employer. If an employee pays contributions to an approved superannuation fund the employer only applies PAYE tax to pay after deducting the contributions, but he must base the National Insurance contributions on the pay before deduction of superannuation.

The employee's contribution is a percentage of gross pay up to a maximum (for 1986–87) of £285 per week. The rates vary according to income. It is important to realize that, having decided what percentage applies by reference to the gross pay, that percentage applies to the whole of the pay. Thus a person whose pay is slightly over one of the thresholds may find that his 'take-home pay' is lower than that of another person whose earnings are less. For example, a person who earns £94.50 per week will pay 7 per cent of £94.50 = £6.62, but a person who earns £95 will pay 9 per cent of £95 = £8.55. The extra 50 pence pay will therefore cost the higher paid person an extra £1.93 in contribution. As he will also probably have to pay an additional 15 pence in tax, his take-home pay will be £1.58 less than that of his lower-paid colleague.

The employer's contribution is also a percentage of gross pay and up to 5 October 1985 it was also limited to the first £265 of weekly pay but since that date it has applied to all earnings. The 'booby-trap' of paying people just over rather than just under one of the thresholds applies to employers' contributions in the same way as it applies to employees' contributions.

Classes II and IV

A self-employed person is required to pay a flat rate weekly contribution and also a contribution based on taxable income. This latter contribution is assessed by the Inland Revenue along with the income tax assessment under Schedule D, Case I or II.

See Tables I, J and K on pages 362 and 363 for the amount of contributions.

CAPITAL GAINS TAX (CGT)

A capital gain arises when a 'chargeable asset' is disposed of at a disposal value in excess of its acquisition value. Disposal value will usually mean sale price, but in some cases (eg the gift of an asset) it will be the market value. Acquisition value will usually be the cost price plus any later expenditure on improvements, but in some cases it will be market value at the time of acquisition.

There is deemed to be disposal when a capital sum which is not chargeable to income tax is received. This may apply, for instance, where a long lease of property is granted for a premium.

The date of disposal of an asset is the date of the contract for sale, unless it is a conditional contract in which case the date of disposal is the date on which the conditions are satisfied. If the disposal is made to a local authority under compulsory purchase powers the date of disposal is the date when the authority takes possession or, if earlier, the date when the amount of compensation is agreed.

If the asset was acquired before 6 April 1965 there are rules for excluding a part of the gain which is deemed to relate to the period before 6 April 1965. Sometimes the exclusion is by treating the 6 April 1965 value as the acquisition value. Sometimes it is by 'time-apportionment'.

Time-apportionment (which assumes that the rate of inflation was the same before and after 1965) often gives a particularly favourable result. It is important to note the dates of acquisition (eg a farm tenant who purchases the freehold may be able to claim time-apportionment from the grant of the tenancy, on the grounds that this was when he first acquired an interest in the land) and all subsequent capital expenditure. Time-apportionment is not available where the sale price of land reflects development or even hope value.

A disposal may result in a loss. Such a loss is deducted from gains arising in the same fiscal year on other assets to give the net gains for the year. If there is a net loss it can be carried forward to later years. See page 323 for one circumstance in which a capital loss may be treated as an income loss.

A loss arising in the year of death can be carried back against gains arising in the three previous years. Gains of later years are reduced in priority to gains of earlier years.

If a person makes a disposal to a 'connected person' and the disposal results in a loss, that loss may only be used to reduce gains arising on disposals to the same person.

Sales or gifts between husband and wife living together are treated as having a disposal value which gives neither a gain nor a loss. No tax is therefore charged, but on a subsequent disposal the gain or loss is calculated by reference to the whole period of ownership by husband and wife.

On the death of an individual, assets are deemed to be acquired by his personal representatives or legatees at their current market value as ascertained for capital transfer tax. Capital gains tax is not, however, chargeable on the death. Thus the increase in value of an asset between date of acquisition and date of death escapes capital gains tax.

Indexation allowance

The amount of a gain may be reduced where a disposal is made, after 5 April 1982, to take account of the rise in the retail price index. For 1982–83 to 1984–85 the reduction could only apply to an asset which had been held for over 12 months. The retail price index for the month in which the disposal was made was compared with the index for March 1982 (or, if this was later, with the index for the month which was 12 months after the 'cost' was incurred). The rise in the index was then applied to the cost — or, where costs were incurred at varying dates — to each element of cost, and the resultant figure was deducted from the gain. See Table E (page 359) for details of the Retail Prices Index.

For disposals from 6 April 1985 indexation allowance is available even if the asset has been held for less than 12 months and the comparison of the index for the month of disposal will be with the month of acquisition (or March 1982 if this is later).

Another very important change in the law is that if an asset was acquired before 31 March 1982 and is disposed of after 5 April 1985 the taxpayer may claim that the indexation allowance is based on the 31 March 1982 value rather than on the cost.

For disposals up to 5 April 1985 the indexation allowance could not be used to turn a gain into a loss or to increase the amount of a loss but from 6 April 1985 it can.

Rate of tax

The first slice of net gains is free of tax and the balance is taxed at 30 per cent. The tax-free figure for 1985–86 was £5900; for 1986–87 it was £6300.

A settlement for the benefit of a mentally disabled person is treated in the same way as an individual.

Any other settlement made before 7 June 1978 is entitled to a tax-free gain equal to half the amount available to an individual. For settlements made after 6 June 1978 the tax-free entitlement will depend upon how many other settlements the settlor has made. The allowance (half the individual's figure) is in effect shared between the settlements with a minimum for each equal to one-tenth of the individual's figure – ie £630 for 1986–87.

Losses brought forward from an earlier year are only set against gains which would suffer tax. Thus if a person had net gains of £6600 for 1985–86 and there were losses of £2600 brought forward, £700 of the losses would be set against the 1985–86 gains to reduce them to the tax-free figure of £5900 and the balance of £1900 would be carried forward again to 1986–87.

Exemptions

1. Ordinary private motor vehicles.
2. Betting, lottery etc winnings.
3. Premium bonds.
4. National savings certificates, British savings bonds.
5. Compensation or damages for a wrong or injury.
6. Compensation paid to agricultural and other tenants under statutory provisions.
7. Life assurance policies and deferred annuity contracts.
8. British government and some British government guaranteed securities.
9. Certain debenture and loan stocks issued by companies.
10. Principal residence, with up to an acre of land (or a larger area in some cases). A person with more than one residence can choose which one he wishes to regard as the principal. If some part of the

property has not been used exclusively as a private residence (eg if some part has been used exclusively for business purposes, or if the property is let for some period), the gain is apportioned by reference to time and/or separate parts of the property, and exemption applies only to the residential part and periods.

Exemption can also apply to a property if it, or a part of it, has been let for residential purposes. The amount of such exemption is limited to the lower of (a) the exempt gain on the owner-occupied part and (b) £20,000. In deciding for what period(s) a property is owner-occupied, any absence during the last two years of ownership is disregarded.

A person living in job-related accommodation can be treated as living in another house which he intends to occupy in the future as his only or main residence.

11. House occupied rent free by a dependent relative.
12. Chattels (tangible movable property) with a disposal value not exceeding £3000. If the value exceeds £3000 the gain is limited to 5/3 of the excess.
13. Chattels with a predictable life of 50 years or less (but this exemption does not cover commodities or business assets on which capital allowances have been claimed).
14. Interests under UK settlements (unless they were acquired for money or money's worth).
15. Assets given to charities, museums, universities etc.
16. Growing timber.
17. See also the sections on BES (page 326) and PEP (page 332).

Replacement of business assets (rollover relief)

If the proceeds of sale of certain business assets are used to acquire other business assets the gain can, subject to certain conditions, be deducted from the cost of the new assets so that tax is not paid at the time. In such a case, if the new asset is subsequently sold, the gain on the old asset as well as the later asset will materialize.

The relevant types of asset are: land and buildings, fixed plant, goodwill, ships, aircraft and hovercraft. The assets must be used for a business (including commercial forestry). If there is a part of the asset which was not so used or if the asset had for some period been used for a non-qualifying purpose, the gain is apportioned to see what part of it can be 'rolled-over'.

Part disposals of land

Complicated rules apply where part only of a piece of land is disposed of. The remaining part of the land has to be valued in allocating part of the cost to the piece of land disposed of. However, where the amount or value of the consideration does not exceed one-fifth of total value (in practice one-twentieth prior to 6 April 1986) the person making the disposal can claim that no assessment is made but what would have been the 'disposal value' is deducted from the 'cost' of the whole - thus leaving the possibility of a larger gain on any future disposal. This claim cannot be made if the sale proceeds (or value) are over £20,000.

Compulsory purchase of land
If land is disposed of to an authority exercising or having compulsory powers and if the vendor uses all or part of the proceeds to acquire other land (but not land that will be capital gains tax exempt as his private residence) the gain can, subject to certain conditions, be deducted from the cost of the replacement land. Tax on the gain is in effect deferred until the replacement land is disposed of.

Transfer of business to a company
If an individual transfers to a company a business as a going concern together with all the assets (or all the assets except cash) in exchange for shares in the company any gain on the disposal of the assets is calculated but not assessed. The cost of the shares for future capital gains tax purposes would normally be the value of the consideration (ie the business assets, including goodwill) given for the shares, but it is reduced to take account of the gain calculated on the assets. In effect, therefore, the gain on the disposal of original assets is deferred until the substituted assets (the company shares) are disposed of.

Beneficiaries of non-resident settlements
There is provision to treat beneficiaries of non-resident settlements as having made capital gains in certain cases if they receive capital payments from the settlements.

Retirement relief
A person aged over 60 may be entitled to a reduction in the amount of capital gain assessed if he disposes of a business or part of a business or certain business assets or of shares in a family company for which he has worked substantially full time. Full relief is available if the period of ownership has been ten years, and reduced relief is available for shorter periods of ownership with a minimum of one year.

Prior to 6 April 1985 the reduction was up to £20,000 for each year by which age exceeded 60 with a maximum of £100,000. For part years a fraction of the £20,000 was calculated.

From 6 April 1985 the full amount of £100,000 relief can be given from age 60. Moreover, the relief can also now be claimed by a person who retires earlier than age 60 on grounds of ill health.

The relief is restricted in so far as the gain refers to assets which are not 'chargeable business assets'. Thus, if a company owns business assets and also investments only the appropriate proportion of the gain on the company shares can be considered for retirement relief.

Relief for gifts ('Holdover relief')

If an individual makes a gift of a chargeable asset to another individual he is deemed to have disposed of it at its market value and the donee is deemed to have acquired it at that value. If both parties so elect the gain can be calculated but need not be assessed. The amount of the gain (after deducting any retirement relief to which the donor may be entitled) is deducted from the deemed acquisition value of the donee and may, therefore, eventually increase the amount of capital gain which he might make.

Where a gift is made and a claim is made under these provisions the law is anxious to ensure that a capital gain cannot be avoided by the recipient becoming non-resident and then disposing of the asset. If, therefore, the recipient becomes non-resident within six years after the year of gift he will be deemed to have made a capital gain equal to the amount of the held-over gain immediately before becoming non-resident. If he does not pay the consequential tax within 12 months the person who made the gift can be held responsible for it. If the reason for the recipient becoming non-resident is that he is employed abroad and if he becomes resident or ordinarily resident again in the UK within three years without having disposed of the asset, this provision will not apply.

Gifts made to a settlement can be similarly held over. In this instance the claim need only be made by the transferor.

Disposals by trustees to individuals can also be held over. In these cases the election must be made by both parties.

CORPORATION TAX

Chargeable profits

Corporation tax is assessed on the chargeable profit of companies resident in the UK and also on certain profits of some non-resident companies if they carry on a trade in the UK. For UK companies, 'chargeable profit' means the whole of the income (except any dividends receivable from another UK company) and also capital gains.

It is intended that capital gains should suffer tax at 30 per cent only and to achieve this the law provides that a fraction of the gains shall be assessed but that fraction shall be taxed at the full rate for the year. Losses on chargeable assets are deducted from gains before the fraction is applied and if losses exceed gains they are carried forward and deducted from gains in later years.

Trading losses

If a company makes a trading loss it may deduct the amount of the loss from any other profits (including the assessable fraction of capital gains) which it may have for the same accounting period. Alternatively, it may carry the loss forward and deduct it from subsequent profits of the trade in which the loss was incurred. In some cases the losses can be carried back to earlier years or can be surrendered to another company in the same group.

Income taxed at source

Some of the income which a company receives may have suffered deduction of income tax at source. Such income (eg some types of interest) is included in the corporation tax assessment but credit is allowed for the income tax deducted.

Rate of tax

The rate for 'large companies' for the year to 31 March 1986 was 40 per cent. For the year to 31 March 1987 it was 35 per cent. If an accounting period of a company is partly before 31 March 1986 and partly after the profit is split on a time basis and taxed accordingly.

Small companies

Small companies pay a lower rate of tax on their income (but not on their capital gains). In deciding whether a company is small its total profit is taken into account. Total profit means the chargeable profit assessable to corporation tax plus any dividends received from other UK companies (other than companies within the same group). If the profit is less than £100,000 the rate was 30 per cent for the year to 31 March 1986 and 29 per cent for the year to 31 March 1987. If a company has an associated company the figure of £100,000 is reduced to £50,000 for each of them. If it has two associated companies the figure is £33,333 for each of the three; and so on.

A company with profits too big to qualify as a small company may be entitled to some 'tapering relief'. The relief is a fraction of the amount by which the total profit falls short of £500,000 (or a fraction of £500,000 where there are associated companies). The fraction is multiplied by the income chargeable to corporation tax and divided by the total profit.

In many cases this formula can be simplified by saying that the first £100,000 (or £50,000 etc) for the year to 31 March 1986 would be taxed at 30 per cent and any excess in the 'tapering zone' at 42.5 per cent. For the year to 31 March 1986 the effective rate in the tapering zone was 36.5 per cent.

Advance corporation tax

When a company pays a dividend it must pay some tax known as advanced corporation tax (ACT) to the Inland Revenue. The ACT is an amount which 'grosses up' the dividend at the prevailing basic rate of income tax. The ACT therefore operates from 6 April to 5 April, although the other corporation tax figures apply from 1 April to 31 March.

For ACT purposes the year is divided into four, or five, parts. These are the periods ending 31 March, 30 June, 30 September, 31 December and the accounting date of the company if it is not one of these dates. If a dividend is paid during one of these periods the ACT must be paid within 14 days after the end of the period. ACT paid by a company on dividends paid during its accounting period is regarded as a payment on account of the tax for the period and is deducted from tax ultimately due on the assessment. The amount to be deducted cannot exceed tax at the ACT rate on income assessed. Thus if a company is assessed on income of, say, £30,000 the maximum ACT which can be deducted from the tax charged is £8700.

Surplus ACT is carried forward and credited against tax due in later years. Alternatively, it can be carried back to earlier years. For ACT in respect of distributions before 1 April 1984 the carry back is limited to two years. For later distributions it is up to six years.

In some cases the benefit of surplus ACT can be surrendered to other companies in a group.

In some groups of companies elections can be made which allow dividends to be paid within the group without the payment of ACT.

Close companies

A close company is, broadly, a company which is director-controlled or is controlled by five or fewer people. For this purpose certain relatives and associated persons are treated as the same person. Control usually refers to over 50 per cent of the voting power but there are also other meanings.

In order that individuals cannot avoid the higher rates of income tax by forming a company and letting all their income be taxed only at corporation tax rates the law empowers Inspectors of Taxes to apportion some of the income of a close company to its participators if the income is not distributed as dividends. Higher rate tax and/or investment income surcharge can then be assessed on the participators. If they fail to pay it the company may be called upon to pay.

It is not intended that this procedure should operate if profits are needed for the running or extension of the business. The law therefore lays down a standard for calculating the 'relevant income' which should be distributed.

In the past trading income entered into the calculation of the relevant income. At present, however, trading income can be retained in full.

The relevant income is therefore restricted to estate income (ie income from real property) and investment income. The net income after tax is considered. For estate income a minimum of 50 per cent may be retained and for investment the normal retention is a figure equal to 10 per cent of the estate or trading income up to a maximum of £3000. The balance is expected to be distributed. There are, however, many occasions when the anticipated distribution can be reduced even further.

Loans to participators

If a close company makes a loan to a participator it will be required to pay the Inland Revenue an amount which 'grosses up' the payment at the prevailing basic rate of income tax. At present that means that it will pay an amount equal to 29/71 of the amount advanced to the participator. When the participator repays the loan (or part of it) repayment of the appropriate amount can be reclaimed from the Inland Revenue. This treatment extends to indirect loans including the settling of debts of the participator or advancing money to a third party who in turn does something to benefit the participator.

Company buying its own shares

The 1981 Companies Act permits a company to purchase and cancel its own shares. Normally, if a company repays to a shareholder more than the amount originally subscribed for a share the excess is treated as a distribution (ie as income). The government wishes to relieve this treatment in certain cases but does want to encourage a situation where a company may in effect be paying out distributable profits to shareholders who then suffer only capital gains tax instead of income tax so the relieving treatment is conditional upon certain criteria being established.

A rough summary of the principal criteria is as follows:

- The company must be a trading company or the holding company

of a trading group. The trade must not be dealing in shares, securities, land or futures.
- The vendor must be resident and ordinarily resident in the UK.
- The vendor must have owned the shares for at least five years. If he acquired them under the will or intestacy of a deceased person the period of ownership by the deceased is taken into account.
- If the vendor does not part with all his shares his interest as a shareholder must be substantially reduced. Broadly, this means that his fractional share of the capital after the sale shall not be more than 75 per cent of his fractional share before the sale.
- After the sale the vendor must not control more than 30 per cent of the capital or the voting power in the company.
- The transaction must be made primarily for the benefit of the trade of the company and must not be part of a scheme of tax avoidance.

If all these conditions are met the sale will not be treated as giving rise to income but will come within the capital gains tax legislation. Some of the requirements may be relaxed where substantially the whole of the money received is used (within two years of a death) to meet an inheritance tax liability arising on death and where that tax could not otherwise be paid without undue hardship.

The precise conditions are complex and in some cases (eg the benefit of the trade) subjective. There is therefore an advance clearance procedure which should always be used.

Some examples of situations where it might be desirable for a company to be able to purchase its own shares are:

- A minority shareholder who is not involved in the running of the company may wish to realize his investment but may be unable to find a buyer among the other shareholders.
- The manager and majority shareholder of a company may wish to retire and sell his shares to those succeeding him in managing the company but they may not be able to afford to buy the shares.
- There may be a dispute between the shareholders about the management and future of the company and the best solution is for a dissenting shareholder to withdraw from the company.
- If a member of the management team who holds shares is leaving the company it may be appropriate for him to relinquish all his interest in the company.
- On the death of a shareholder his beneficiaries may wish to realize their investment for a variety of reasons, eg lack of commitment to the company or the need for cash to meet inheritance tax liability.
- On a divorce one spouse may wish to buy the other out of a jointly owned company but lack the resources to do it.

- The administration of an employees' share incentive scheme might be helped if the company can buy its shares back from an employee who leaves the employment of the company.
- It is difficult to attract outside equity capital into a private company because of the disadvantage of a shareholder being 'locked in'. The Business Expansion Scheme provides an income tax incentive to certain individuals to take up new shares in a company. The knowledge that there is a possible escape route in the future might help the attractiveness of such investments.

VALUE ADDED TAX (VAT)

VAT is a tax on the consumer of goods and services. The tax is collected at various stages in the production and supply processes. Every registered business must account for the tax on its sales (or 'outputs') and can recover tax suffered on its purchases (or 'inputs'). The effect is that, at each stage of manufacture or distribution, tax is paid on the value added to the product at that stage.

Registration

Businesses with an annual turnover below a certain figure do not need to register but may apply to do so if they wish. Above certain quarterly or annual limits registration is compulsory. The 1986–87 limits are £7000 for any quarter and £20,500 for a year.

Recovery of tax

Apart from the small businesses referred to above, the supply of certain services is exempt. An exempt business cannot recover the tax suffered on its inputs. This applies whether the exemption is by reason of the nature of the services supplied or because the business is below the registration limits.

The recovery of tax on inputs by businesses which are not exempt does not include tax on private motor cars or on business entertaining (unless the entertaining is of overseas customers).

A person who intends to make taxable supplies may apply for registration before doing so and, if accepted, may therefore recover tax on preliminary expenditure.

A company may treat as input tax any tax suffered on its behalf before its incorporation.

Rates

The rate of tax is 15 per cent. Some goods are, however, accorded a zero rate. Suppliers of these goods do not charge tax to purchasers but, unlike suppliers of exempt services, they can recover the tax suffered on their inputs.

Time of supply

It is important to know at what time a supply of goods or services is treated as taking place. This is the earliest of the following:

1. payment being received;
2. an invoice being issued;
3. in the case of services, the services being performed;
4. in the case of goods being removed from the vendor, the date of removal;
5. in the case of goods not being removed, the date when they are available to the purchaser; and
6. in the case of goods on approval or sale or return the date when the purchaser agrees to buy or 12 months after possession given if that is earlier.

The acceptance of a deposit by a retailer in consideration of keeping goods is not treated as the making of a supply. If, however, the deposit is merely the first payment for the goods the previous paragraph will apply.

If a business makes business gifts these are treated as supplies made at the value of cost of the goods to the donor. A gift to one person which cost under £10 is disregarded unless it is one of a succession of regular gifts to the same person.

Supplies at below market value

If supplies are made to connected persons at below market value, tax is payable as though they had been made at full market value.

Second-hand goods

Some second-hand goods are not taxed on their full disposal value. Only the amount of profit made by the trader is taxed. These are types of goods which are often sold by non-traders to traders. Without this special treatment such goods might suffer an excessive burden of tax if they changed hands frequently and tax was charged on outputs several times without credit being allowed for inputs. The items in question are used cars, motor-cycles, caravans, boats and outboard motors, aircraft, electronic organs, works of art, antiques and scientific collections.

Customer insolvency

Because tax is payable by a trader when an invoice is issued, it is possible that he may not recover the tax from his customer. If the customer becomes formally insolvent relief can be obtained in respect of the bad debt.

Groups of companies and partnerships

Where two or more companies are in a group or are controlled by one person or are controlled by persons carrying on a business in partnership they may elect to be treated as one taxable unit. Transactions between themselves are ignored. One representative member makes all returns of the outputs of all members and claims on the inputs of all members.

Exemptions

1. Sales, leases etc of land and buildings (but not holiday lettings, parking fees etc). The sale of a property used for taxable business is exempt but will not prejudice the right to reclaim input tax.
2. Insurance services.
3. Postal services.
4. Betting, gaming and lotteries.
5. Banking, discounting and certain other financial services.
6. Education services (but not correspondence, secretarial, language etc colleges or schools).
7. Health, dental, optical etc services. Approved nurseries and play groups.
8. Burial and cremation (but not flowers, gravestones etc).
9. Trade union and professional organizations.
10. Sports competitions.
11. Certain works of art.

Zero-rated items

1. Most human foods (excluding confectionery, food supplied in the course of catering and hot take-away food). Tea, coffee etc. Some animal foodstuffs. Many seed, bulbs etc.
2. Water (but not distilled water or mineral water etc).
3. Books, newspapers, music and maps (but not stationery items or diaries).
4. Talking books and radios for the blind.

5. News services.
6. Most types of fuel and power.
7. Construction of buildings (but not 'secondary buildings' within the grounds or garden of a private residence).
8. Protected buildings.
9. Services to overseas traders or for overseas purposes.
10. Most transport services (but not unaccompanied luggage).
11. Large caravans and houseboats.
12. Gold.
13. Bank notes.
14. Drugs, medicines and appliances supplied on prescription.
15. Transfers by a supplier from his UK base to his overseas base.
16. Sales etc by charities.
17. Children's clothing and footwear. Protective boots and helmets.

Car fuel. From 6 April 1987, where a business provides fuel in a vehicle and an individual (either the proprietor of the business or a partner in the business or an employee of the business) makes use of the fuel for private purposes and does not fully reimburse the business there will be a scale to determine the amount of fuel which shall be treated as non-business and on which VAT cannot be treated as an input. This will avoid having to keep detailed records of business and non-business mileage. The scale will be based on the cylinder capacity of the vehicle. See Table P (page 366).

VAT penalties

It has been estimated that 85 per cent of all VAT returns are submitted late. If there is any truth in this it is not surprising that the government found it necessary to introduce new penalties for businesses who are slow to make returns.

There are also new penalties for other offences. Some are already in force and some are to be phased in before 1988.

Late returns

- The first returns to be covered are those to 30 September 1986.
- The first time that a business submits a late return no action is taken.
- If any of the next four quarters' returns are late a 'surchage liability notice' is issued covering a period of one year, ie the following four quarters.
- If one of these subsequent four returns is late, there is an automatic surcharge of 5 per cent of the tax due (or £30 if greater), and the

surcharge period is extended for a period of one year from the end of the period for which the return was late. If another return is late in this period the surcharge becomes 10 per cent of the tax due and the period is extended yet again. Further late returns result in the surcharge going up in steps of 5 per cent to a maximum of 30 per cent, with the period being extended each time.

- Once a surcharge liability notice has been served the trader needs to submit four consecutive returns on time in order to avoid the imposition of escalating penalties.
- The same system applies if returns are on time but the tax is paid late.
- There is a defence if the trader can show that it was not his fault or that there was a reasonable excuse. Lack of funds or a failure on the part of an employee or agent is not an acceptable excuse.
- It is not sufficient merely to post a return by the due date. The trader must take reasonable steps to ensure that it is received by the VAT office by the due date. Customs & Excise have said that if the due date falls at a weekend or on a bank holiday it will be necessary to initiate payment so that it arrives by the last working day beforehand.

Serious misdeclaration

Penalties will be imposed where:

- A VAT return understates a liability, or
- A repayment to which there is no entitlement is claimed on a return, or
- An understated assessment is not brought to the notice of Customs & Excise within 30 days.

These penalties will apply where the loss of tax would be:

- 30 per cent of the correct tax due, or
- The greater of 5 per cent of the correct tax or £10,000, or
- 15 per cent of the correct tax if there have been two similar offences within the preceding four years.

The penalty will be 30 per cent of the tax which would have been lost if the matter had not come to light. There will be no penalty if the trader discovers the problem and brings it to the notice of Customs & Excise before they start making enquiries. A penalty can also be avoided if a reasonable excuse can be shown.

These provisions come into force in July 1988.

Breaches of regulations

Where there is failure to comply with various regulations, including notifying the cessation of taxable supplies; keeping proper records; furnishing information; and producing documents, penalties may arise.

Records have to be kept for six years and the penalty for failing to do so is £500. Otherwise the penalty accrues on a day-by-day basis and ranges from £10 per day for the first offence in a two-year period to £30 a day for third and subsequent offences.

Failure to register

Once a trader's turnover exceeds the annual or quarterly registration limit he is required to notify Customs & Excise within ten days of the end of the period in question. As from 25 July 1985 there is a penalty for late notification. It is 30 per cent of the VAT payable between the date when he should have registered and the date when Customs & Excise were actually notified. In small cases there is a minimum penalty of £50. The penalty is, of course, in addition to the tax.

Although the penalty will not be imposed if there is 'reasonable excuse' precedents have established that a mere lack of awareness that turnover had crossed the registration threshold is insufficient to avoid the penalty. It should also be noted that VAT tribunals have no power to reduce or abate the penalty no matter how much sympathy they may have for an offender. It is all or nothing (unlike the Inland Revenue where penalties are frequently negotiable).

Interest on VAT

Assessments to VAT are made if VAT has been under-declared or overclaimed or if a previous assessment proves to be too low. From 1 July 1988 interest will also be charged, running from the date the tax should have been paid. The rate of interest has not yet been announced. The interest will not be deductible for income tax or corporation tax purposes.

Since 1 October 1986, Customs & Excise have made a 'repayment supplement' of 5 per cent if repayment of VAT to a trader is delayed without good reason.

Civil fraud and criminal offences

There are more serious punishments than the above: attempting to evade tax dishonestly; being knowingly concerned in fraudulent evasion by oneself or others; accepting goods or services with reason to believe that tax is being evaded; or supplying goods or services in contravention of security provisions imposed by Customs & Excise. Punishments range from fines to imprisonment but it is hoped that these matters will be only of mild interest to readers and therefore no detail needs to be given.

INHERITANCE TAX (PREVIOUSLY CALLED CAPITAL TRANSFER TAX)

Transfers and exemptions

Inheritance tax is a tax on 'transfers of value' made during a person's life and on death. The expression 'transfers of value' covers gifts, sales at below market value, and the passing of property on death. It also covers indirect ways in which a person allows his wealth to be diminished and that of another person to be increased.

Before 18 March 1986 transfers were added to earlier transfers within a period of ten years prior to the date of transfer and were taxed at progressively higher rates. Since that date the cumulation period has been reduced from ten to seven years. It is also necessary to look at lifetime transfers and classify them into one of three categories.

Gifts with reservation

These are where possession and enjoyment of the property given is not bona fide assumed by the donee immediately; or where the property given is not enjoyed by the donee to the entire exclusion (or virtually the entire exclusion) of the donor; or the donor continues to benefit from the property. Such property is still regarded as the property of the donor until such time as the 'reservation' is removed. At that time it moves into one of the other categories. If the 'reservation' still exists at the time of death of the donor the property becomes part of the property passing on death.

Potentially exempt transfers

These are transfers from one individual to another or from an individual to an accumulation and maintenance trust or a disabled trust. No calculation of tax is made at the time of such transfer and it is ignored for the purpose of calculating tax on the cumulative basis on other transfers. However, when a person dies all such transfers within the previous seven years cease to be exempt.

Chargeable transfers

These are all other transfers (eg cash or other assets given to discretionary trusts) and tax is calculated at 50 per cent of the death rate on the cumulative basis. Table L (page 363) shows the rates of tax.

On death

On death the position for the previous seven years is reviewed. All potentially exempt transfers within the period are now treated as chargeable transfers and tax on each such transfer and each transfer which has already been treated as chargeable is recalculated on the cumulative basis at full death rate.

The tax on each transfer which was made more than three years before death is then reduced as follows:

Transfers three to four years before death: tax reduced by 20 per cent
Transfers four to five years before death: tax reduced by 40 per cent
Transfers five to six years before death: tax reduced by 60 per cent
Transfers six to seven years before death: tax reduced by 80 per cent

This reduction shall not operate, however, to reduce the tax already charged on transfers which were always chargeable (ie transfers within five to seven years before death) when the 50 per cent scale applied.

Some transfers are exempt from tax. Many people find it advisable to make regular gifts within these exemptions. The main exemptions are shown in Table M on page 363. As there is no tax on transfers between husband and wife it is often wise to try to balance the wealth of each spouse so that each is able to make the fullest use of the exemptions and of the lower rates of tax.

There is provision for beneficiaries under a will to make a deed of family arrangement within two years after death and thereby to redistribute the estate without the amounts disclaimed being regarded as further transfers.

Transfers and their value

Some business assets are valued for Inheritance tax at below their true market value. Table N on page 364 shows the percentage by which different types of asset are reduced in value.

For inheritance tax purposes the value of a transfer is based on the reduction in the estate of the donor, which is not necessarily the same thing as the value of the gift to the recipient. Perhaps the most marked demonstration of this difference is in the case of close company shares. If a person who owns 57 per cent of the ordinary capital of a typical company gives away 5 per cent his estate will have been reduced by the difference between the value of 57 per cent and the value of 52 per cent. If he then gives away another 5 per cent the reduction in the second case is the difference between the value of 52 per cent and the value of 47 per cent. This second transaction is likely to be much bigger than the first because he has lost control of the company and all his remaining shares have been effectively devalued. Each recipient will have 5 per cent of the shares and the value of this holding in their hands will normally be quite a lot less than the reduction in the donor's estate on each occasion.

For valuation purposes, property owned by the spouse is taken into account. Thus if a man owns 45 per cent of the shares in a company and his wife owns 15 per cent the value of his holding is three-quarters of the value of 60 per cent. Other related property taken into account in the same way is property transferred by him or his spouse after 15 April 1976 to a charity, political party etc in an exempt transfer.

Trusts

There is a charge on property held in trusts. The charge varies depending upon whether there is an interest in possession carrying a right to income or use of the property. If there is such an interest the tax is charged when it comes to an end or is transferred. It is calculated by reference to the previous transfers of the person who had the interest.

In a discretionary trust where there is no interest in possession, tax is charged at ten-year intervals. It is also charged on distributions of capital and when a person becomes entitled to an interest in possession. These rules are relaxed for maintenance and accumulation trusts for beneficiaries under 25 and for certain specialized trusts (eg trusts for the disabled; protective trusts).

TABLES OF TAX RATES ETC

(1987–88 rates, where quoted, are provisional. The chapter text is based on 1986–87 rates.)

Table A: Personal allowances 1987–88

	£
Higher personal allowance. This is for a married man living with or voluntarily maintaining his wife.	3,795
Lower personal allowance. This is for any other individual.	2,425
Wife's earned income allowance. This is the amount of the earned income of a married woman up to a maximum of:	2,425
Age allowance (married). This is available if either spouse is over 65 by 5 April 1987.	4,675
Age allowance (single). If the person is 65 by 5 April 1987.	2,960

(The age allowance is reduced by £2 for every £3 by which the person's income exceeds £9800. However, it will not be reduced below the normal (higher or lower) allowance and therefore it ceases to be effective for a single person with income over £10,768 or a married couple with income over £11,375.)

Additional personal allowance. This is for a person who is not entitled to the higher personal allowance but who has a qualifying child or children resident with him or her for at least part of the year. It is also available to a married man whose wife is incapacitated. 1,370

Widow's bereavement allowance. This is available to a widow in the year in which her husband dies and in the following year. 1,370

Blind person's allowance. If both spouses are blind the allowance is doubled. 540

Housekeeper allowance. If the claimant is a single woman. 145
Any other claimant. 100

Person dependent upon services of a son or daughter. 55

Table B: Rates of income tax 1987–88

Band of taxable income £	Rate of tax %	Total taxable income to top of band £	Total tax to top of band £
First 17,900	27	17,900	4,833
Next 2,500	40	20,400	5,833
Next 5,000	45	25,400	8,083
Next 7,900	50	33,300	12,033
Next 7,900	55	41,200	16,378
Remainder	60		

Table C: Wife's earnings option

1986–87		1987–88	
Column 1	Column 2	Column 1	Column 2
£	£	£	£
26,521	6,986	26,870	6,545
30,000	6,048	30,000	5,851
35,000	5,478	35,000	5,404

40,000	5,309	40,000	5,299
45,000	5,128	45,000	5,117
48,429 or over	4,894	48,541 or over	4,916

Table D: Retirement annuities

Year of birth	1980–81 to 1981–82 %	1982–83 to 1987–88 %
1907 or earlier	32½	32½
1908 or 1909	29½	29½
1910 or 1911	26½	26½
1912 or 1913	23½	24
1914 or 1915	20½	21
1916 to 1933	17½	20
1934 or later	17½	17½

Table E: Capital gains indexation

Retail price index (Base: 100 in January 1974)

	1982	1983	1984	1985	1986
January		325.9	342.6	359.8	379.7
February		327.3	344.0	362.7	381.1
March	313.4	327.9	345.1	366.1	381.6
April	319.7	332.5	349.7	373.9	385.3
May	322.0	333.9	351.0	375.6	386.0
June	322.9	334.7	351.9	376.4	385.8
July	323.0	336.5	351.5	375.7	384.7
August	323.1	338.0	354.8	376.7	385.9
September	322.9	339.5	355.5	376.5	387.8
October	324.5	340.7	357.7	377.1	388.4
November	326.1	341.9	358.8	378.4	391.7
December	325.5	342.8	358.5	378.9	

Table F: Official errors

Gross income £	% of arrears waived
Not exceeding 8,500	100

8,501-10,500	75
10,501-13,500	50
13,501-16,000	25
16,001-23,000	10
Exceeding 23,000	0

For taxpayers who are over 65 and in receipt of National Insurance retirement pension or widow's pension the income limits above are increased by £2,500. However, inspectors have discretion to go beyond the limits above in cases of extreme hardship.

Table G: Employed persons

Private use of motor car: assessable benefit: Scale for 1986-87						
Original value of car	**Business use 18,000 miles or over in year**			**Business use under 18,000 miles in year**		
	Car under 4 years old at end of year	Car 4 years old or more at end	Addition for fuel supplied also by employer†	Car under 4 years old at end of year	Car 4 years old or more at end	Addition for fuel supplied also by employer†
Original value of car up to £19,250*						
Engine capacity:						
1300cc or less	£225	£150	£225	£450	£300	£450
1301-1800cc	£288	£190	£288	£575	£380	£575
over 1800cc	£450	£300	£450	£900	£600	£900
Original value of car £19,251-£29,000 (with or without a cc)	£660	£438	£450	£1,320	£875	£900
Original value of car over £29,000 (with or without a cc)	£1,050	£700	£450	£2,100	£1,400	£900

† There will be no addition for fuel if the employee pays for all fuel used for private purposes.
* For cars with original market value up to £19,250 and not having a cylinder capacity the benefits are at the levels shown in the above section, but with these ranges of original market value being used instead of the cc rating: less than £6000; £6000-£8499; £8500-£19,249.

Where the business use of a car is under 2500 miles the scale benefit (but not the addition for fuel) is increased by 50 per cent. If a person has the use of more than one car this also applies to all cars except the first.

Table H: Employed persons

Private use of motor car: assessable benefit: Proposed scale for 1987–88						
Original value of car	**Business use 18,000 miles or over in year**			**Business use under 18,000 miles in year**		
	Car under 4 years old at end of year	Car 4 years old or more at end of year	Addition for fuel supplied also by employer†	Car under 4 years old at end of year	Car 4 years old or more at end of year	Addition for fuel supplied also by employer†
Original value of car up to £19,250*						
Engine capacity:						
1400cc or less	£263	£175	£240	£525	£350	£480
1401–2000cc	£350	£235	£300	£700	£470	£600
over 2000cc	£550	£363	£450	£1100	£725	£900
Original value of car £19,251–£29,000 (with or without a cc)	£725	£485	£450	£1,450	£970	£900
Original value of car over £29,000 (with or without a cc)	£1,150	£765	£450	£2,300	£1,530	£900

† There will be no additions for fuel if the employee pays for all fuel used for private purposes.
* For car with original market value up to £19,250 and not having a cylinder capacity the benefits are at the levels shown in the above section, but with these ranges of original market value being used instead of the cc rating: less than £6000; £6000–£8499; £8500–£19,249.

Where the business use of a car is under 2500 miles the scale benefit (but not the addition for fuel) is increased by 50 per cent. If a person has the use of more than one car this also applies to all cars except the first.

Table I: National Insurance contributions

Employed persons 1987–88: Weekly rates				Employee's Contribution (%)	Employer's Contribution (%)
Child under 16				nil	nil
Person earning less than £39.00 per week				nil	nil
Man over 65 or woman over 60				nil	as for other employees
Certain married women and widows				3.85	
Other employees	contracted out	pay £39.00 to £64.99	first £39.00	5.00	5.00
			balance	2.85	0.90
		pay £65.00 to £99.99	first £39.00	7.00	7.00
			balance	4.85	2.90
		£100.00 to £149.99	first £39.00	9.00	9.00
			balance	6.85	4.90
		pay £150.00 to £295.00	first £39.00	9.00	10.45
			balance	6.85	6.35
		pay over £285.00	first £39.00	9.00	10.45
			next £256.00	6.85	6.35
			balance	nil	10.45
	not contracted out	pay £39.00 to £64.99		5 (all earnings)	5 (all earnings)
		pay £65.00 to £99.99		7 (all earnings)	7 (all earnings)
		pay £100.00 to £149.99		9 (all earnings)	9 (all earnings)
		pay £150.00 to £295.00		9 (all earnings)	10.45 (all earnings)
		pay over £295.00		9 (of £295.00)	10.45 (all earnings)

Table J: National Insurance contributions

Self-employed persons 1987-88 (Men under 65; women over 60)	
Flat rate	£3.85 per week Nil if earnings are below £2125 in the year.
Profit-related (profit is the amount assessable after deducting capital allowances and adding balancing charges)	6.3% of profit between £4590 and £15,340

Table K: National Insurance contributions

Maximum contributions 1986–87
If a person has more than one source of employment or has employment and self-employment the maximum amount of contributions by him (ie excluding employers' contributions) is £1359.45. His maximum Class IV (self-employed, profit-related) contributions are limited to a figure which when added to Class I (employee) and Class II (self-employed; flat rate) contributions totals £852.06. If Class I and Class II exceed this amount the Class IV is nil.

Table L: Inheritance tax

Rates of tax (from 17 March 1987)

Value of transfer	**Rate of tax**	**Transfer on death**	
		Cumulative transfer to top of band	**Cumulative tax to top of band**
£	%	£	£
First 90,000	nil	90,000	nil
Next 50,000	30	140,000	15,000
Next 80,000	40	220,000	47,000
Next 110,000	50	330,000	102,000
Remainder	60		

Table M: Inheritance tax

Exemptions 1986–87		
Transfers to spouse	if spouse is domiciled in UK	no limit
	if spouse is domiciled elsewhere	£55,000
Small gifts during lifetime (amount each year to each recipient)		£250
	by parent of bride or groom	£5,000
Gifts during lifetime in	by grandparent or remoter ancestor or by a party to the marriage	£2,500

consideration of marriage		
	by any other donor	£1,000
Gifts to charities		no limit
Gifts to political parties	transfers on, or within one year of, death	£100,000
	transfers more than one year before death	no limit
Lifetime transfers in addition to the above (annual amount)		£3,000

In addition to the above certain other gifts to public bodies or for public benefit are exempt.

Table N: Inheritance tax

Business property relief	
Reduction in the valuation of certain business assets	%
A business or an interest in a business	50
Shares out of a holding which, immediately before the transfer, gave the transferor control of the company*	50
Other shares in unquoted companies*	30
Land or building, machinery or plant owned by controlling shareholder or by a partner and used for the business	30

The assets transferred must have been owned and used for the business for a period of two years before the transfer or must have replaced another asset such that the asset transferred plus the asset which it replaced had been owned for a minimum period of two years during the last five years.

* The relief does not extend to investment companies or to share-dealing or property-dealing companies.

Table O: Due dates for payment of tax

Income tax	Schedule D. Cases I and II and trades, professions or vocations assessed Case V	Half on 1 January in the year of assessment. The other half on the following 1 July
	Schedule A* Schedule B Schedule D, Cases III, IV and	1 January in year of assessment

	VI and Case V assessments other than trades, professions or vocations	
	Schedule E (to the extent that tax is not collected under PAYE)	14 days after application by the Collector of Taxes
	Higher rate tax on any income from which basic rate tax deducted at source or which carries a tax credit	1 December following year of assessment
Capital gains tax		1 December following year of assessment
Advance corporation tax and income tax deducted by companies from annual payments and interest		14 days after the end of the quarter (or period to accounting year end) in which the dividend etc was paid
'Mainstream' corporation tax		9 months after the companies' accounts year end. A longer interval (up to 21 months) for many companies which were trading before 1 April 1965
Inheritance tax	Lifetime transfers between 6 April and 30 September	End of April in following year
	Lifetime transfers between 1 October and 5 April	6 months after the end of the months of transfer
	Increase, following death, of tax paid on transfers with 7 years before death and tax on potentially exempt transfers	6 months after the end of the month of death
	Other tax on death	On delivery of their account by personal representatives

For inheritance tax there are provisions for payment by instalments in some cases.

* Schedule A: payment of tax. The tax is due on 1 January, but the amount of income to be assessed cannot be known until after the following 5 April. To get round this difficulty the law provides that the tax inspector shall make the assessment on the same amount as the final assessment for the previous year. The tax on this assessment is payable on 1 January, but the assessment is then reviewed after 5 April to see if it should be increased or reduced.

If there has been a change in the source of the income (eg if the property or one of the properties has been sold) the original assessment can be based on an appropriate fraction of the previous year's assessment.

Table P: VAT: Cars

Cylinder capacity	**Business use up to 4500 miles in a quarter**		**Business use over 4500 miles in a quarter**	
	3 month period £	**1 month period £**	**3 month period £**	**1 month period £**
14000 or less	120	40	60	20
1401–2000	150	50	75	25
over 2000	225	75	113	38

12

ACCOUNTING

James Turner

INTRODUCTION

Accounting is a complex, and some may even say mysterious, process concerned with recording and analysing the transactions of a business from a financial point of view. A company's policies and practices, its sales performance, stock levels, borrowings, staff costs and a host of other activities all have to be quantified, measured, interpreted and controlled in money terms.

The accounting function not only has to manage the day-to-day financial operations of the business but also contribute to budgeting, planning and monitoring costs and revenue, managing cash flow and dealing with VAT and taxation. It also has to provide regular and meaningful reports so that the management can keep a close control of all aspects of the business.

This chapter outlines the basic accounting activities and the way that balance sheets and profit and loss accounts are produced. The guide to further sources of information in Chapter 16 points the way to more detailed coverage of specific accounting topics.

BASIC PRINCIPLES

The fundamental necessity in accountancy and bookkeeping in any business is to keep records of:

1. Proprietors' capital introduced into the firm. This may be share or loan capital in the case of a company or cash introduced by a sole trader, or the partners in a partnership.
2. Money expended on purchase of assets, whether fixed, ie for the purpose of running the business such as equipment, motor vehicles, or current, ie raw materials, stationery and similar items such as stock in trade.
3. Expenditure on revenue items such as rent, rates, light, heat, telephone etc.
4. Money earned by sales or the provision of services.
5. Other monies earned such as sales of fixed assets, commissions, interest or dividends on investments.
6. The receipt and payment of monies and the balance of cash or bank account.

The last item ultimately should reflect the effects of the preceding items. In practice, unless the business is what is often described as a 'cash business', where all income is received immediately it is earned and paid when it is expended, the cash or bank balance will not by itself reflect the true results or happenings.

The reason for this is time. Even in the cash type business, which is nearly always small retail shops, there will be expenses, such as electricity, which, unless paid by meter, are incurred before payment is required or known. In reality these time differences are of considerable importance.

It is therefore necessary to keep records of sales made and separate records of money received for sales. Similarly, it is necessary to keep records of expenditure incurred and the payment made to the provider of the goods or services.

In practice, businesses do not keep expenditure records for items, often comparatively small, such as electricity or gas. They simply pay them when the bill arrives. Indeed, in some businesses where the expenditure is almost entirely paid at the time it is incurred, often service industries, the payments are the expenditure.

Most businesses, other than retail cash, do need to keep records of sales made and separate records of money received. The actual record may be quite simple; when there are but a few large items one of the most effective methods is to have two invoice files. A copy of each sales invoice is placed on file 1 when the invoice is despatched to the customer. When payment is received the invoice is transferred to file 2. Total sales can be ascertained by adding together the amounts received and the total of the invoices on file 1. This may be sufficient, but sometimes the effect of discounts, queries on amounts, returned goods or disputes over price can make it ineffective.

DAY BOOKS AND LEDGERS

The formal 'textbook' method of recording sales and purchase is to use a day book (or journal as it is sometimes called) and a ledger. The method of keeping these will vary with the size and complexity of the business; these days many are part of an integrated accounting system and maintained on computers.

The principle is to record the two aspects of each transaction: in the case of sales the provision of the goods or services and the creation of the obligation to pay for them.

Essentially, the day book is a list of invoices, in the case of the sales day book the sales invoices. Normally it will look something like this:

Date of invoice	Customer name	Total Amount	VAT	Net
		£	£	£
1 June	J K Smith	460.00	60.00	400.00
1 June	R F Jones	722.66	94.26	628.40
2 June	B J Watts	113.07	14.75	98.32
4 June	XYZ Ltd	1,067.36	139.22	928.14

The inclusion and operation of VAT will be explained later.

Each of the items in the total column will be posted, ie transferred, to the debit of the customer's account in the ledger.

It might be as well to explain the meanings of the words debtor and creditor at this stage as they cause endless confusion. The Americans express these words graphically by the use of the words 'receivables' and 'payables'. The first item would be posted to the sales or debtors ledger account of J K Smith, namely the total of £460.00 only. Therefore J K Smith is shown in the ledger as a debtor or a 'receivable'. When he settles the account the money will go into cash received and be posted to the credit of his account.

Debit and credit confuse because they are often used in connection with bank accounts. A debit balance or overdraft means the customer owes money to the bank. In the books of the bank the customer is a 'receivable'. Conversely in the books of the customer, if kept correctly, the bank is a creditor or payable. If the customer has a credit balance it means the bank owes the customer money and in the customer's books the bank will be a debtor or receivable.

Many concerns use the sales day book to analyse their sales. The simple method is to have a columnar day book where the sales, net of VAT, are extended into further columns according to the nature of the items sold. Sometimes the analysis is into separate columns according to the salesman whose commission is then calculated. It is, of course, possible with computers to analyse basic sales data in a variety of ways and so produce valuable information simply as a by-product of a suitable software program.

It is usual to keep money received for sales in a separate column in the cash book so that it is possible quickly to reconcile the sales ledger. This is done by taking the total sales for the period from the day book, to which, after the first period, will be added the debtors at the commencement. The sales monies received plus the total of the debit balances in the sales ledger at the end will, if the records have been kept correctly, amount to the same figure as the earlier total. This account, described as a total or control account, is demonstrated as follows:

Year 19XX:

		£	£
1 Jan	Opening Debit Balance per list brought down	19,832.48	
31 Mar	Sales per day book for the period	248,964.82	
31 Mar	Cash received from Sales		239,628.39
Closing Debit Balances per list carried down			29,168.91
		268,797.30	268,797.30
1 April	Opening Debit Balance per list brought down	29,168.91	

The purchase day book and ledger work on exactly the same principle. The purchase day book is a list of goods and services purchased. The total amount of each invoice from each supplier is entered in the purchase day book and posted to the purchase ledger to the credit of the supplier's account. When the account is settled the amount is entered as a payment in the cash book and posted to the debit of the supplier's account.

Practices vary as to what expenditures are passed through the purchase day book. Many concerns put only expenditure on the purchase of raw materials and stocks through their accounting system, other payments being posted direct to the nominal or private ledger as will be explained later.

The control or total account for the purchase ledger might look like this:

Year 19XX

		£	£
1 Jan	Opening Credit Balances per list brought down		11,649.32
31 May	Purchases per day book for the period		112,462.47
31 May	Cash paid for purchases	108,364.20	
Closing Credit Balances per list carried down		15,747.59	
		124,111.79	124,111.79
1 April	Opening Credit Balances per list brought down		15,747.59

THE CASH BOOK

This is the record of the bank transactions. Transactions in actual cash are recorded in the petty cash book although in many instances the amounts involved are anything but petty. It is a ledger account not a journal or day book.

In strict theory there should be a journal — not just the sales and purchase journal but a further book which records all the transactions which have not been passed through the sales or purchase journals. These three journals are called the books of prime entry.

Although not generally used, the journal can demonstrate the effect of the twofold nature of each transaction. If used at all the journal should contain a narration after each entry as shown opposite.

In practice the amount received for share capital would be entered in the cash book on the debit side (left-hand side), and posted directly to the credit of the share capital account in the nominal ledger. The payment of the company formation expenses would be shown on the credit side of the cash book (the right-hand side), and posted to the debit side of the account in the nominal ledger of which more later.

Usually the cash book would have a number of columns; the total would be entered in the total column and the amount would be extended to the appropriate column. Occasionally a payment may be extended to two or more columns. Payment to an employee for travelling expenses of, say, £52.80 and reimbursement of postage he paid of £22.40 might be entered as £75.20 total, and the two amounts put in the appropriate columns.

Year 19XX

		Debit £	Credit £
1 Sep	Bank Account (cash book) Dr Share Capital Account Being the payment for 100,000 ordinary shares of £1 each by the shareholders to the company	100,000.00	100,000.00
6 Sep	Company Formation Expenses Dr Bank Account (cash book) Being the payment of expenses on formation of the company	2,826.42	2,826.42
8 Sep	Wages Account Dr Bank Account (cash book) Being the payment of wages for the week	1,409.43	1,409.43
8 Sep	Wages Account Inland Revenue Being the PAYE and NHI deducted from wages above	242.21	242.21

The determination of the headings on the columns, which might amount to 12 or more, would be governed by the frequency of payments. Weekly wages would probably have a column to themselves. Infrequent payments such as company formation expenses (which are hardly likely to recur at all), would appear in the 'sundries' column. When the accounts are drawn up, or at the end of each month in many cases, the totals of the columns are posted to the appropriate accounts in the nominal ledger and the 'sundries' individually to their accounts. Note that the word 'sundries' in this sense does not necessarily mean petty expenses but infrequent ones.

The last item shown in the journal entries would not appear in the cash book at all since no cash movement was involved at that stage. When the PAYE and National Insurance were eventually paid they would appear as a payment in the cash book and be debited to the Inland Revenue. The PAYE and NI in the wages account would be added to the net wages paid to give the total cost of the wages.

At any time the total payments can be deducted from the receipts, after taking in the opening balance to give the cash at bank or, if it is a minus figure, the bank overdraft.

It is unlikely that the balance shown in the cash book will be the same as in the bank statement at the same time. The reason for this is the time taken for cheques and cash paid in and cheques withdrawn to reach the bank. If all monies received are paid in to the branch where the account is held they will probably get in quickly but often monies are collected in various places and paid in at different branches or even different banks if there is not a branch of the firm's bank nearby.

Therefore it is necessary to reconcile the cash book balance with the bank. It ought to be emphasized that the cash book balance is the true balance. Cheques despatched to suppliers and not presented must be met. The way this is done is to check the items in the cash books with the bank. Those not included in the statement are described as lodgements not credited where credit has not been given for amounts paid in and outstanding cheques where amounts paid to suppliers have not reached the payee's bank. An example follows:

Bank Reconciliation as at 30 September

		£
Balance at bank per statement		3,879.62
Add Lodgements not credited:		
29 September		498.81
30 September		1,726.40
		6,104.83
Less Outstanding Cheques:	£	
23 September	192.48	
23 September	643.90	
23 September	104.22	
24 September	269.30	
25 September	843.97	
30 September	1,426.44	3,480.31
Balance per cash book		2,624.52

Before doing this the accountant or bookkeeper will examine the statement for any items charged but not entered in the cash books such as bank charges, commission interest etc. They should be entered in the cash book thus reducing the cash book balance (or increasing the overdraft if such is the case).

It is the cash book which is the record of the cash flow.

VALUE ADDED TAX

VAT plays a big part in accounting and must be included for that reason, although the tax is described as being 'neutral' in the sense that it is not meant to be suffered by the business. This means that the business is acting as a tax collector (unpaid, of course).

There are two rates of VAT at the time of writing, namely standard (15 per cent) and zero. The essential difference between zero rate and exemption is that input tax can be claimed against zero rated output but not against exempt output.

Exemption can be claimed because the business is too small or because the output is exempt. Zero rating applies to output which is specifically defined by law such as direct exports, books, newspapers and food (basic food for consumption off the premises — not chocolates for instance). Everything else is subject to VAT at standard rate except interest and dividends which are outside the scope of the tax.

The vast majority of businesses account for VAT at standard rate, zero rate or both. The important point is that they are, therefore, entitled to input allowance for the VAT they expend on their purchase of goods or services.

Each quarter the business must make a return to HM Customs & Excise for VAT and account for that collected or claim for that due to be refunded.

The information for the return will usually be the VAT recorded in the sales journal (output tax), and the purchase journal (input tax). The difference if output is greater than input will have to be paid, and if the other way round, recovered. This is simple enough in that the sales journal total will be credited to the VAT account, the purchase journal debited and the difference settled one way or another, thus balancing the account.

The one complication is VAT on expenditure not passed through the purchase journal: stationery for instance, or purchase of fixed assets. Many concerns have a VAT column in the cash book for these items which can be posted to the VAT account. It is important to emphasize that only VAT on those amounts should be entered in the VAT column in the cash book; if the VAT part of the payments made for items passed through the purchase journal and ledger is included the inputs will be inflated and the VAT underpaid or over-recovered. This would not please the VAT inspector.

Stocks are ignored, in that it is the VAT suffered on purchases which gives rise to input allowance. Note also that it is not relevant whether the purchases made have been paid for or the sales money due has actually been received.

THE NOMINAL, PRIVATE OR GENERAL LEDGER

This is the record of the total transactions of the business. The sales, net of VAT, total of the sales day book will, usually at the end of each month, be posted to the credit of the sales account; the purchases, similarly, to the debit of purchases account; other expenditure from the cash book to the debit of the appropriate accounts. Any money received, other than for sales, will be posted to the credit of the appropriate accounts.

It is this ledger that, together with the cash book (which is in theory part of the nominal ledger), provides the items for the trial balance. If all has been done correctly the debit balances will come to the same total as the credit balances. The importance of this operation is that it proves the arithmetical accuracy of the bookkeeping, although it does not show errors of principle, eg if payments for stationery have been incorrectly posted to another account.

The trial balance is the basis for the preparation of the profit and loss account for the period concerned and the balance sheet at the end of it; see the example:

Adjustments to Trial Balance Leading
to Profit & Loss Account and Balance Sheet

	£
Stocks Opening (included in Purchases a/c)	42,987.38
Closing as taken	56,439.28

To adjust for stocks the Purchases Account in the Nominal Ledger would be like this:

		£
Opening Stocks	b/d	42,987.38
Add Purchases		597,808.84
		640,796.22
Less Closing Stocks	c/d	56,439.28
Cost of Goods Consumed		584,356.94
Opening Stocks (next year)	b/d	56,439.28

Audit fees would not normally be payable until after the end of the year and a provision would be made:

Journal		£	
To Audit Fee	Dr	2,000	
Messrs Check and Tick			2,000.00
Being audit fees for the year			

Other expenses might be in arrear

		£
Light and heat	Dr	3,000

Telephone	Dr	600	
General expenses	Dr	100	
Sundry creditors		3,700	
Provisions for Expenses not exactly known but estimated.			

	£	
Depreciation	25,702,98	
Plant and machinery		22,864.94
Motor vehicles		2,838.04
Being Depreciation written off		

Trading and Profit & Loss Accounts for the year ended 30 September 19XX

	£	£
Sales		1,149,384.60
Opening Stock	49,987.38	
Purchases	790,808.84	
	840,796.22	
Less Closing Stock	56,439.28	784,356.94
Gross Profit		365,027.66
Wages and salaries	273,187.46	
Light and heat	15,987.28	
Rent and rates	14,682.94	
Telephone	7,422.76	
Printing and stationery	2,469.38	
General expenses	8,569.22	
Audit Fee	2,000.00	
Depreciation	25,702.98	350,022.02
Net Profit		15,005.64

Balance Sheet at 30 September 19XX

	£	£	£
Share Capital			100,000.00
Profit & Loss Account			15,005.64
			115,005.64
Fixed Assets	Cost	Depreciation	Net
Plant and machinery	228.649.38	22,864.94	205,784.44
Motor vehicles	28,380.46	2,838.04	25,542.42
	257,029.84	25,702.98	231,326.86
Formation Expenses			2,826.42
			234,153.28

Current Assets			
Stocks at Cost		56,439.28	
Debtors		183,926.31	
Cash in hand		78.24	
		240,443.83	
Less Current Liabilities			
Sundry Creditors	138,587.43		
Bank Overdraft	90,994.04	229,591.47	
Net Current Assets			10,852.36
			245,005.64
Less Long-term Liability			
Bank Loan			130,000.00
			115,005.64

FIXED AND CURRENT ASSETS

The expression 'fixed assets' (sometimes referred to as 'capital assets') does not necessarily mean assets which are bolted to the floor. Indeed, one of the most common fixed assets in business are motor vehicles which are clearly mobile! Fixed assets simply means assets purchased for the purpose of use rather than to be processed or resold. Whether an asset is fixed or current is therefore very much determined by the nature of the business rather than the nature of the asset.

A motor vehicle can illustrate this. The manufacturer fabricates the chassis, puts it on the production line and as it passes along, bits are added, until at the end it becomes a finished vehicle. The chassis and the parts are raw material stock. When they are added together but not finished they become work in progress. On completion they are finished goods. All of these are current assets.

The finished vehicle is then sold, usually via distributors and agents, in whose hands it is still stock (a current asset) until it is sold to, say, a company in the food trade which buys it for its business. At that point it becomes a fixed asset. It is to be used to transport people and goods in the food trade.

When it has reached the end of its useful life it may be traded in and for the motor dealer involved it becomes stock or a current asset again.

Put another way, fixed assets are those normally expected to be used and be useful for more than a year. On the other hand, current assets are those which change their nature in weeks or months.

The most common headings for fixed assets are:

- Land and buildings

- Plant and machinery
- Motor vehicles
- Office equipment.

These are all tangible assets in that they can be seen and touched. There is another type of fixed asset which is intangible, such as patents, trade marks, copyrights and goodwill. These will usually only show in the accounts of a company if they have been purchased rather than generated within.

The terminology in this field can be confusing: note that current assets are sometimes also known as liquid assets or working capital and might include:

- Cash at bank
- Cash in hand
- Debtors (receivables)
- Stocks and stores (often shown as one total figure)
- Work in progress.

LONG-TERM AND CURRENT LIABILITIES

Long-term liabilities are those which are not payable for a year or more. They may include debentures, which are really long-term loans at interest, and may or may not be secured mortgages usually on land, buildings and loans.

Current liabilities are those which have to be met within weeks or months; the mirror image of current assets, usually consisting of unpaid accounts for current supplies. Bank overdrafts are usually included under this heading although a long-term bank loan would be treated as a long-term liability.

DEPRECIATION

Fixed assets are normally subject to depreciation. There are many theories about depreciation but the basis is that assets gradually deteriorate due to age and use (as distinct from obsolescence which can happen suddenly or not at all).

Usually, fixed assets are shown in the balance sheet at cost. Depreciation is then calculated, in theory, to reduce the figure in the balance sheet by the amount used up in producing the profit for the period, the profit being reduced by the depreciation written off. In practice, companies usually have standard rules such as 10 per cent per annum on all plant and machinery.

The figure in the balance sheet is usually the cost less the depreciation written off, described as the written down or book value. It may or may not bear any relation to the value of the asset. Though it can be quite meaningless decisions have been made on the basis of the book value of fixed assets.

TYPES OF LIABILITY

There are three types of liability in the sense of how they may be settled:

1. Secured liabilities

Mortgages or charges over the company's assets. These creditors have priority compared with others in that if anything goes wrong they can take the asset(s) on which they are secured, sell them, and recover their money from the proceeds. If there is anything over they must account to the company for the difference. If there is not sufficient they rank as ordinary unsecured creditors for the balance.

Such liabilities must be shown in the balance sheet separately as secured liabilities. The most common are loans for the purchase of freehold or leasehold property which are similar, in effect, to the mortgage an individual may raise to buy a house, and floating charges, favoured by banks, which means they may recover their money from any or all of the assets, other than those already specifically secured.

All secured liabilities must be registered with the Registrar of Companies and open to public inspection.

2. Unsecured liabilities

These will be 'ordinary' usually current liabilities for the supply of goods or services. They have no priority and if things go wrong they get nothing until secured claims have been settled in full.

3. Subordinated creditors

Rare but not unknown these are amounts borrowed which will not be repaid until all the others have been paid in full.

The reason that concerns have different types of liability is the relationship of risk and return. A 'safe' investment tends to generate a low rate of interest. Therefore, if a company has, say, freehold property, and needs money, it will get it at a lower rate of interest by offering this as security, sometimes known as 'putting it in hock' than by simply negotiating a loan.

Conversely, if the company has little or no security which appeals to a potential lender it may have to take a subordinated loan at very high cost.

As a general rule secured liabilities tend to be long term, ie payable a year or more after the balance sheet date, whereas unsecured, which include subordinated for this purpose, tend to be shorter.

CONTINGENT LIABILITIES

These will not show in the accounts as such but by way of an additional note. They are items of expenditure which at the time the accounts are prepared are uncertain.

A typical example might be a claim. The note on the accounts might appear like this:

'There is a claim against the company in respect of alleged faulty works amounting to £15,000. The claim, which is not covered by insurance, is being defended by the company.'

CAPITAL COMMITMENTS

Where there are forward commitments for capital expenditure those are also shown by way of note on the accounts, eg: 'The company has contracted to construct a new warehouse costing £86,000, expected to be completed in the next year.'

BAD DEBTS

There are occasions when customers themselves get into difficulties and there is doubt about their capacity to pay. In such cases it is usual to make a provision for what are known as 'bad and doubtful debts'. The debtors on the balance sheet are reduced by the provision which reduces the profit by the same amount. If the debt(s) turn out to be good in the next year there may be an item in the income side of the profit and loss account 'bad debts recovered'.

PROVISIONS

A provision is an amount set aside for an expense the existence of which is known but the amount is not. A typical example is electricity. In the accounts of a company up to say, 30 September, the last electricity may have been paid up to the end of August. The account in the nominal ledger might look like this:

	£		£
31 Dec Cash	4,286.49	1 Oct Provision B/d	1,200.00
31 Mar Cash	5,928.62	30 Sep Profit and loss	19,453.75
30 Jun Cash	3,876.45		
28 Sep Cash	4,962.19		
30 Sep Provision C/d	1,600.00		
Total	20,653.75		20,653.75
*Account up to 31 August		1 Oct Provision C/d	1,600.00

While the amount is an estimate, it is based on a reasonable guess at the actual amount used in September for which an account has not been rendered.

MANAGEMENT ACCOUNTING

The object of management accounting is to write the profit and loss account in advance, together with the cash flow to indicate the expected future results. It is a very useful form of information for management to make decisions and arrange for finance in advance of need.

Unfortunately there is a tendency to complain if actual results do not match forecasts, but in reality it is rare for the actual outcome of any plans to be completely in line with the financial and accounting records and forecasts. It must also be remembered that the plans as shown in the financial forecasts will only be the translation into money terms of the plans of others, eg marketing, production, personnel and so on.

COST ACCOUNTING

The object of costing is to analyse expenditure to identify the amount spent on a unit of production. A manufacturer of a product will try and identify the resources needed to produce a unit (which may be a single item or a number; for instance a manufacturer of bottles might cost on the basis of 1000 bottles as one unit).

The usual key items will be:

- Material
- Direct labour
- Ancillary items.

These will total the direct or marginal cost of each unit. To this may be added a proportion of the overhead expenses to give the total cost.

Difficulties arise as to how to allocate overheads (which are all the other expenses which cannot be directly allocated to a given product or activity but have to 'spread' across the whole range of business activities). Many concerns stop at direct cost and compare this with sale price, the difference being described as the 'contribution'. In any plans the contribution must at least equal the overheads over any period of time and, hopefully, exceed them, thus producing profit.

If these figures are prepared in advance they are described as standard costs, and actuals are measured against them. Golfers will understand that standard costs are the same as par!

BUDGETS AND BUDGETARY CONTROL

Budgetary control is standard costing applied not to units of production but to items of overhead expenditure.

Before the commencement of a financial year management will estimate the necessary expenses to run the business together with the expected sales and production costs. This is put together to become a budget. Control throughout the year is exercised by comparison of actual expenditures with budget.

If circumstances change during the year (and they are almost bound to do so) a sensible management will alter (or flex) the budget to take account of the new situation.

INFLATION ACCOUNTING

For many years accountants have been experimenting with various methods of accounting properly for inflation. There have been conferences, articles, arguments and high level committees endeavouring to find an acceptable method of accounting for inflation. None has worked. Probably the reason is that there is no clear information as to what the rate of inflation is. There are, of course, various indices but they are too broad to apply to individual concerns. Nearly everyone endeavouring to solve this problem has now given up. One hopes that the single digit inflation at the time of writing (1986) will continue or reduce further and the whole wretched nonsense can be forgotten unless inflation levels again reach alarming proportions.

RATIOS

A business can make a profit without being profitable. An investment of £1 million which produces £10 profit is not much good. Profitability is measured by taking the profit related to the capital needed to produce it and expressing it as a percentage.

Ratios and percentages are used for many purposes, far too many for them all to be included here. See also *Ratios*, page 294.

They can be very useful, particularly for setting standards and targets in advance: some of the more common are outlined below:

1. *Current ratio* measures a company's short-term liquidity. It is a guide to ability to meet liabilities when they are due.

   $$= \frac{\text{Current assets}}{\text{Current liabilities}}$$

2. *Acid test ratio* measures the extent to which assets can be converted into liquid (cash) resources.

   $$= \frac{\text{Quick Assets}}{\text{Current liabilities}}$$ (Cash, marketable securities and debtors due)

3. *Inventory to working capital* gives an indication of the dependence of working capital on inventory and ultimately sales.

   $$= \frac{\text{Inventory (average value)}}{\text{Working capital}}$$

4. *Profit (net) margins* indicates what proportion of sales income is net profit.

   $$= \frac{\text{Net income}}{\text{Sales income}}$$

5. *Assets turnover* measures the extent to which assets produce sales revenue.

   $$\frac{\text{Sales for period}}{\text{Total assets employed}}$$

6. *Return on assets* $= \frac{\text{Net income for period}}{\text{Total assets}}$

CAPITAL INVESTMENT

The purpose of capital investment is to produce profit. Therefore managements want to forecast the expected income (or expenditure saving which is, in effect, the same thing) to be generated by the investment. The usual straightforward way is to calculate the return on the amount to be spent. If £10,000 investment in a new machine produces £2000 per annum, that would be a return of 20 per cent per annum except that the new machine would not last for ever so account must be taken of depreciation. This is known as the accounting rate of return method.

Pay-back method simply looks to the quickest way to get the investment back.

The above methods are the most common; there are others, in particular discounted cash flow and net present value calculations. These take into account the time the investment is made and the time the income arrives. This method is too complicated to describe here but can be very effective. Further information will be found in some of the sources listed in Chapter 16.

AUDIT

There are two types of audit; internal and external.

Internal audit is an on-going review of methods and techniques — not just in finance — carried out by employees of the company (usually) and is part of the management process.

External audit is the checking of the financial activities throughout the company mainly carried out after the end of the financial year to produce the annual accounts duly audited for presentation to the Annual General Meeting of the members (the shareholders). These accounts must comply with the Companies Acts and the auditors must not be directors or employees of the company.

Originally auditors were introduced to protect the shareholders against the directors and they are still appointed by the shareholders. In recent years the auditors have been held to be liable to others than the shareholders, eg potential shareholders, creditors, the Inland Revenue etc.

13

INSURANCE AND RISK MANAGEMENT

C S C Bennett

INTRODUCTION

Some insurances are compulsory but others are effected as a matter of common prudence. The business owner or manager must focus on insurances imposed by statute, which often represent a minimum requirement. The reader should also be aware that the need to insure may be imposed by contract.

The law is reluctant to interfere with freedom of choice in the effecting of optional insurances; consequently, a business must use its own judgement. This chapter will help business owners and managers approach insurance in a more knowledgeable way. An otherwise well run business could be put in jeopardy by ignorance in this matter.

RISK MANAGEMENT

The nature of risk

A distinction is made between 'risk', which is insurable, and 'true uncertainty' which is not. Profit is the reward to businesses for facing true uncertainties such as changes in the level of demand. Risk becomes insurable when past data makes it possible to predict or draw inference of what will happen in the future. The science of inferential statistics is important to insurance. These techniques are based around probability theory and the 'law of large numbers'. While the outcome may be uncertain for an individual, predictions can be made with an acceptable degree of accuracy in regard to sufficiently large groups. Consequently, predictable risks are insurable but true uncertainties, which do not lend themselves to a similar scientific base, are not.

An alternative approach to risk is based on effects. The outcome of a pure risk is from loss to no change, ie premises not damaged by fire gives no change while fire damage gives rise to a loss. Such risks are likely to be predictable and insurable. A speculative risk ranges from loss to gain. The results are not predictable but the prospect of profit induces risk taking. Insurance, rightly, is not available in regard to speculative risks as, in the interests of business efficiency, reliance should be placed on sound business practices, such as market research, cost control, stock control etc.

Responses to risk

Businesses should identify and respond to risks. The most common responses are:

Risk avoidance
The shrewd businessman avoids risk when refusing to purchase stock previous experience says is unsaleable. Here risk avoidance is appropriate but if that is the response to every opportunity, he will cease to be in business. If drug companies, following the thalidomide tragedy, marketed only aspirins and cough mixtures, then the cost in terms of alternatives forgone (ie the benefits obtainable from the many new drugs) would have been considerable.

Risk prevention
This takes many forms, such as improved physical standards, road systems, training and education. It plays its part in preserving life and property and minimizing economic waste. However, it cannot eliminate

accidents, and sometimes its costs outweigh the benefits. In short, risk prevention is highly desirable but has its limitations.

Risk assumption

Unplanned risk assumption commonly occurs where the risk has been given no previous consideration because of its relatively inconsequential nature (eg leaving a blank audiotape on the train).

Planned risk assumption occurs where the risk is identified and carried by the firm without making prior financial provision for it. When, and if, the awaited event occurs, payment is made out of current resources so that the loss is treated like a normal business expense. A nationwide supermarket may choose not to insure its plate glass windows against damage. Given a spread of risks, it is unlikely that more than a small number of breakages will occur in any one year. For such a firm, the amounts involved are relatively insignificant and easily funded out of working capital. There seems little point in hiring the risk spreading services of an insurer, whose expenses and profit would have to be met, when the firm can spread its own risks. The firm's freehold property risk is similarly spread but planned risk assumption would be unsuitable as the larger amounts involved would create cash flow problems and disrupt financial planning even for very large concerns. Smaller firms have less scope for planned risk assumption but should consider it whenever the loss is capable of being met out of working capital. Planned risk assumption works best when:

- a geographical spread of risks exist;
- maximum probable loss in one event (or time period) is relatively small.

Self-insurance, at its simplest, means deducting from the firm's surplus each year to create an insurance reserve. The approach may be used when there is no spread of risk and/or potential losses are of a size to make planned risk assumption unworkable. The ultimate in self-insurance is the creation of a captive insurance company to cover the risks of the parent company. This approach gives the firm, of necessity a large one, the advantage of direct access to the reinsurance market.

Risk distribution

This describes the incorporation of a firm as a limited liability company. It is a common response to speculative risks with ownership and risk distributed among shareholders whose liability is limited to the share capital they have agreed to subscribe.

Risk combination
This is linked to the law of large numbers. Two people agreeing to share each other's risks brings no substantial advantage. Combining large numbers reduces uncertainty in regard to the group as the outcome of most pure risks can be predicted with an acceptable degree of accuracy.

Risk transfer
This occurs when the landlord makes a tenant responsible for damage to the premises. It also occurs when payment of an insurance premium shifts the risk from an insured person to the insurer. Insurance is in fact *risk transfer and risk combination* based on the ability to predict future losses.

The economic value of insurance
Its origins lie in:

- minimizing the cost of public reaction to risk;
- the promotion of loss prevention.

Insurers minimize the cost of risk, it may be contended, by:

Stimulating business enterprise
Without insurance, risk avoidance might be more widely practised. Also, individuals would be less willing to convert their wealth into assets such as cars, houses, factories etc, if required to carry the risk of financial loss resulting from loss or damage to such tangible assets. The absence of car insurance, for example, would seriously limit the demand for new cars and the level of activity in that industry. The absence of fire insurance would discourage investment in premises. Insurance serves as a basis for credit. Banks etc are often only prepared to advance funds if the revenue-generating assets are insured. If firms relied upon their own contingency funds (self-insurance) they would need to be held in short-term financial assets whereas, for the price of a premium, the funds could be employed more productively in profit-earning assets.

Higher prices
These may result from the absence of insurance as the hoarding of contingency funds for self-insurance may lead to lost production and loss of economies of scale. Risk assumption, an alternative to insurance, involves higher risk and may result in creditors seeking higher rates of interest. Also, except for the largest concern, risk assumption leads firms to make crude estimates of their potential losses. Such estimates may well be excessive, leading to higher prices.

Increased imperfections in the market-place
If risk assumption unsupported by contingency funds is practised then more bankruptcies will result, caused not by inefficiency, but by random events such as fires. Thus, efficient firms could be driven out of business. Insurance is especially needed by small firms the absence of which would increase the barriers of entry into business and prevent competition with, or service to, large firms.

Insurance promotes loss prevention in a variety of ways — discriminatory premium rates to penalize or reward particular features of the risk, the employment of surveyors to advise, participation in a variety of research and publicity activities.

The process of risk management

Risk management is not synonymous with insurance management. It is a broader concept which stresses identification, evaluation and control of risks. Risk management is 'the protection of assets, earnings, liabilities, and people of an enterprise with maximum efficiency and at minimum cost'. In running a business it has long been recognized that managers can, and should, control speculative risks. In recent years greater attention has been paid to protection against pure risks — and not only by insurance. Risk management uses insurance as one of many important risk control tools. In large firms a risk manager may head a specialized department but in the small firm, the owner may make the risk management decisions himself. In all cases the following procedure should be adhered to:

1. Identify the risks to which the organization is exposed.
2. Evaluate the risks by establishing the probability of the risk event occurring.
3. Control the risk by physical or financial means.

Risk management checklist

1. *Identify* risks by one, or a combination of, the following methods:

   (a) Review:

   - all relevant data on business assets
   - all activities
   - all personnel.

   (b) Check:

   - all financial statements to identify sources of loss

- each item in the balance sheet and profit and loss account to determine loss exposures.

(c) Prepare:

- a flow chart to show all operations of the business or activity
- a note on all loss possibility situations at various points in the purchase-process-distribution sequence.

(d) Carry out:

- physical inspections of the firm's premises and other places where work and activities take place
- an update of the checklist as the business expands or when processes or conditions change.

2. *Evaluate* and analyse the risks identified by:

(a) measuring or estimating the potential frequency of losses
(b) assessing the potential impact of such losses and the potential variation in losses
(c) ranking potential losses according to importance to the firm.

3. Decide how to handle or *control* these risks by considering which, if any, can be:

(a) avoided
(b) prevented (eg physical improvements, new systems, training etc)
(c) minimized
(d) geographically separated without impairing efficiency (The cost-effectiveness of the above measures should be considered using, where appropriate, capital budgeting techniques.)
(e) related to statutory requirements
(f) transferred to customers, suppliers, tenants or others
(g) retained (ie assumed) having regard to the firm's ability to meet losses out of normal working capital
(h) retained by self-insurance
(i) insured.

4. In regard to risks capable of being retained, has the firm considered:

(a) the ancillary services of insurers
(b) the advantages of certainty as to time of premium payment (aids cash flow management etc), and certainty as to amount which facilitates more accurate costing and pricing?

5. Has the firm prepared an insurance programme by:

(a) assuming that all insurable risks will be insured
(b) classifying the insurances into three categories:

- essential (required by law or necessary to ensure the firm's survival)
- desirable (losses that would disrupt the business but from which recovery could be made)
- available (less severe losses not posing serious financial problems)

(c) comparing each item in the programme with other risk management tools to decide whether or not to insure?

6. Implement risk management techniques by:

(a) informing all affected employees about the risk management objectives and the role they are expected to play
(b) purchasing insurance
(c) administering risk prevention and other measures.

ARRANGING THE INSURANCE

The insurance market

Consists of suppliers, intermediaries, and buyers. A brief outline of this complex market will suffice.

Suppliers (hereafter referred to as insurers)in Britain include:

Authorised insurers (848 in 1985) but the number is not necessarily a good guide to extent of market competition. Some companies write only one class of business (eg life assurance); authorised mutual companies (180 in 1985) mostly write only a single class of business. Besides the companies, Lloyd's is a significant supplier.

Authorised insurers are those that have met Department of Trade requirements. Following the insolvency of an authorised insurer, the insurance industry, under the Policyholders Protection Act 1975, is called upon to deal with outstanding claims up to 90 per cent (100 per cent for compulsory insurances) of their value. In life assurance, another company, subject to possible adjustments in the benefits, takes over the policy. Non-authorised insurers are not covered by the provisions of the Act which applies to insurances taken out by individuals (including sole traders and partnerships) but not companies.

Proprietary companies, those registered with limited liability under the Companies Act, must, inter alia, have a minimum paid-up share capital of £100,000 to secure authorisation. Mutual companies are notionally owned by the policy holders who share in the profits in the form of lower premiums. For a life office, all of the declared profits go to the 'with profits' policyholders. Industrial life assurance companies and friendly societies commonly issue life policies for modest sums assured with the premiums collected frequently from the home.

Lloyd's is a corporation providing facilities for thousands of individuals (known as 'names') to transact insurance by forming themselves into syndicates. Each member has unlimited liability for his own share of any risk. Lloyd's insurances are not covered by the Policyholders Protection Act but Lloyd's has its own scheme to cover the unlikely event of any individual becoming insolvent. Insurance at Lloyd's can only be transacted through a Lloyd's broker.

Insurance intermediaries are known under a variety of nomenclature, but the principal distinction is between insurance brokers and agents.

(a) *Insurance brokers* hold themselves out as full-time specialist consultants. In order that the public should not be deceived by inexperienced people using the style 'broker', brokers are regulated by law (Insurance Brokers (Registration) Act 1977). Consequently, insurance brokers have to be registered and this obliges them to adhere to a code of conduct, be truly independent of insurers, and carry professional indemnity insurance. Brokers, as with other intermediaries, are generally remunerated by way of a commission paid by the insurers.

(b) *Agents* are unregistered and, while many will be part-time non-specialists, some will be full-time. Some of the latter style themselves 'insurance consultants' and may be both experienced and competent. However, the terms 'insurance consultant' and 'adviser' are available to the inexperienced and it would be unwise to rely solely upon such terms when selecting an intermediary.

Part-time agents are appointed because their professions etc may leave them well placed to introduce business, eg garage proprietors or estate agents. Home service representatives employed by industrial life offices normally work for only one company and are not true intermediaries.

Buyers of insurance are many and varied. This section concentrates on business buyers.

The duty of utmost good faith (uberrimae fidei)

This applies to insurance contracts. This is more stringent than caveat emptor (let the buyer beware) which applies, subject to statutes like the Sale of Goods Act, to commercial contracts generally. In the latter, nothing obliges the seller to point out to the buyer any of the defects of the product or service, but in insurance, utmost good faith obliges both parties to the proposed contract to make a full disclosure of all material facts whether or not the specific information is requested. In practical terms, this duty weighs more heavily upon the party seeking insurance. The theory (often true) is that the insurer comes to the bargaining table knowing nothing of the proposed risk and can normally only acquire specific information by way of the proposer's own disclosure. Failure to disclose, or misrepresentation of, a material fact, even if innocent, gives the insurer the option to avoid the contract ab initio (from the beginning). A fact is material if it will influence the judgement of a prudent underwriter in his assessment of the risk. An insured is not penalized for failing to reveal facts he could not reasonably be expected to know. Utmost good faith is pre-contractual and, in the absence of policy conditions, does not oblige the insured to disclose increases in risk during the currency of the policy. However, the renewal of an annual insurance amounts to a new contract and the duty revives at a renewal. Life assurances are permanent (ie for a definite term of years) and the duty applies only at the inception.

Proposal forms

These are used in some classes of insurance (commercial and industrial fire insurance is a notable exception). A proposal form may be seen as a vehicle of information. By raising specific questions the form heightens the insured's awareness as to what is material, but a full and accurate completion of the form does not necessarily guarantee that the proposer has fulfilled his obligations to disclose. Issues peculiar to the insured may not have been covered by the form (Lambert *v* CIS Ltd (1975)), although it is hoped that such instances are rare. At common law it is for the insurer to prove the materiality of the issue. However, it is customary for insurers to extend the inherent duty of utmost good faith to a contractual duty by using a declaration and warranty at the foot of the form. The proposer warrants the truth and accuracy of his statements and agrees that they should become the basis of the contract. As a result, any inaccuracy, regardless of materiality, entitles the insurer to avoid the policy (Dawsons Ltd *v* Bonnin (1922)). In the matter of private insurances, the insurers, by way of a Statement of Practice, have agreed not to rely upon mere technicalities. There is no such agreement for business insurances, and although British insurers have a record of integrity, it is important to complete proposal forms accurately so that policies can be enforced as of right rather than having to rely upon an insurer's goodwill.

A warranty, unlike a term of the same name in commercial law, has to be absolutely true and literally complied with as, subject to the insurer's discretion, breaches will be fatal to the contract. As the duty of utmost good faith revives at renewal, and the practice is not to issue fresh proposal forms, the insured who fails to notify any changes will be taken to have repeated his earlier warranties. Businesses are strongly advised to keep copies of all proposal forms and to check them when renewing.

In commercial and industrial fire insurance, where proposals are not usually used, the insurers rely for their information on their surveyor's plan and report, but this in no way mitigates the duty of disclosure except in regard to such facts that the survey should have established.

Self-regulation

In insurance, self-regulation is partly the result of the exemption of insurance contracts from the Unfair Contract Terms Act 1977. The Association of British Insurers, representing over 420 insurers, has issued Statements of Practice which apply to insurances taken out by UK residents in a private capacity. Businesses are not protected — the plumber who effects insurance on his van gets no protection but he is no more knowledgeable than when buying a household policy, for which protection exists. The answer is for businesses to use a broker as:

- professional expertise becomes available.
- brokers may be liable for, and are insured against, professional negligence leading to loss.

The Law Commission Report 1980

Despite the foregoing, the Report calls for legal reform. The Commission wishes to change the test of materiality from the view of the prudent underwriter to the view of a reasonable insured. Other recommendations include:

1. *Proposal forms*: a proposer should sign only 'to his best knowledge and belief'.
2. *Warranties*: a claim should only be avoided if the breach is directly relevant to the claim.
3. *Basis of contract clauses*: should become ineffective as regards past or present facts and would only apply as continuing warranties in guaranteeing the state of future events, eg the presence of safety precautions.

The government indicated in 1983 an intention to implement these recommendations, but it is vital that businesses should note that they will apply only to private policyholders and not industrial or commercial concerns.

Fixing the amount of insurance

Insurances (other than life and other insurances on the person) are subject to the principle of indemnity. The aim is, within the limits of the insurance, to place the insured in the same financial position after a loss that he occupied before it, ie give an exact financial compensation. In practice it can be very difficult to measure the exact indemnity due. Indemnity links with insurable interest, another fundamental principle, in that indemnity should be measured by the extent of the insured's interest in the event or the property concerned. For example, no loss means no claim. Mr Badcock's lease expired and he vacated the premises. He took no steps to cancel his policy, during the unexpired period of which a fire occurred. He was unable to claim, as, having no interest, he had suffered no loss; neither could he transfer the policy to the property owners upon whom the loss fell. Insurances are personal contracts and not generally freely transferable without the consent of the insurers. If property of any sort is acquired, the new owners should not rely on 'handed over' policies unless the insurers have agreed.

Insurers have responded to some of the practical difficulties of indemnity by the provision of policies on special bases.

1. *Reinstatement policies* are found principally in fire insurance on buildings and machinery. Such policies pay for the cost of reinstating or replacing damaged property without making a deduction for wear and tear or depreciation. An indemnity policy would make a deduction in such circumstances. In reinstatement policies the sum insured must reflect reinstatement/replacement costs as under-insurance is penalized by an 'average' clause.
2. *Valued policies* are issued on works of art, antiques etc which do not have an easily assessable market value. It is easier to fix the indemnity for a total loss at the inception than at the time of claim, when no account of appreciation or depreciation in value is taken. By means of a policy term, partial losses are dealt with on a normal indemnity basis.
3. *Additional cost clauses* allow, up to specified sums, for certain additional costs in the event of loss. Examples: debris removal clause and public authorities clause which both allow for more than an indemnity. In the latter case after fire, additional costs may arise because of public authorities' requirements.
4. *First loss insurances* may be suitable when a total loss is very unlikely. The sum insured represents the maximum likely loss not the maximum value at risk. In theft (or water damage insurance) with extensive and very durable property at risk, this approach may be used. When a loss occurs, the insurer pays up to the agreed

amount with no deduction for under-insurance unless the actual value at risk is higher than the declared value. The rate of premium is higher than with a normal policy, as with all policies, partial losses are more likely than total losses.

5. *Average clauses* seek to penalize under-insurance and account should be taken of it when the insurance is arranged.
   (a) *Pro rata average.* If at the time of loss, the sum insured is less than the value at risk, the insured is deemed his own insurer for the difference and bears a rateable proportion of each loss accordingly.
   (b) *75 per cent condition of average.* The pro rata average clause could produce hardship in agriculture where fluctuating values can create under-insurance. If the sum insured represents 75 per cent of the value at risk at the time of loss, the under-insurance is ignored and the claim settled in full up to the policy limit. Only in the more serious cases of under-insurance (ie when the 75 per cent is exceeded) is pro rata average applied.
   (c) The two conditions of average are applicable when property may be insured under more than one policy — there may be a specific and a general policy covering the same goods. Under-insurance may be penalized and therefore the adequacy of the combined insurances should be checked.
6. *Declaration policies,* a feature of fire insurance, covering stock are designed to allow the insured to maintain full insurance on fluctuating values without over-insuring. The sum insured is the maximum amount at risk at any one time, but the insured pays a provisional premium of three-quarters and submits, usually monthly, declarations of the actual value at risk, permitting an end of year average to be produced. The insured can then receive a refund or pay an additional premium depending on whether the average is more or less than three-quarters of the sum insured.

Liability policies

Sums are not insured as potential liabilities are unlimited — instead limits of indemnity are fixed. In some instances policies (eg employers' liability) give unlimited undemnities, but the tendency is to fix high limits; some insurers regard £500,000 for any one occurrence as a minimum.

Combined or separate policies?

Smaller businesses, especially shops, can purchase much of their insurance in the form of a combined policy. This covers a fixed range of hazards at a standard premium which varies according to the trade and district. The advantages are:

1. The tendency for relatively high minimum premiums for small risks makes the 'packaged' purchase of insurance more economical.
2. Less administration — one renewal date etc.
3. Same insurer ensures dovetailing of insurances to avoid gaps in cover.
4. Optional extras available.

Office and surgery policies are also available on a package deal basis.

Combined policies also arise in the field of liability insurance where their use is not confined to small firms.

Checklist for arranging the insurance

1. *The insurer*

   - Are insurances placed with authorized insurers or Lloyd's?
   - Do the chosen insurers belong to the Association of British Insurers?

2. *The intermediary*

   - For any insurances placed directly with insurers do you gain any advantage?
   - If you have not chosen a registered broker, are you satisfied as to the competence and experience of the intermediary?
   - Is your chosen intermediary insured against professional negligence?
   - Standards vary among registered brokers. Choose a broker whose size, organization and strengths suit your needs. Is he large enough to cope with your needs? If you are a small firm would the broker regard you as a valued customer? Does the broker specialize? What special services does he offer?
   - Has your trade association entered into special negotiations on behalf of all members?
   - Risk management consultants, some of whom are independent of brokers and insurers, may be consulted for a fee.
   - To assist the intermediary, give a full explanation of your business and keep him informed of changes.

3. *Negotiating the contracts*

   - Inform the insurer of all material facts before policy inception.

- Keep an accurate record of your insurance and loss history.
- Be aware of the insurances where changes and increases in risk have to be notified during the policy term.
- Check all proposal forms before signing, even when completed by the insurer's official or your broker.
- Keep copies of all proposals and check them when renewing policies and pointing out any changes in the information previously supplied.
- When insurance surveys are conducted ensure that full and proper access is given to surveyors.
- Have you ascertained if a long-term agreement is available and considered the implications thereof? (These agreements are mainly a feature of fire insurance — in return for a discount, eg 5 per cent for three years, 7½ per cent for five years, the insured agrees to renew with the insurers for a specific number of years.)

4. *The sum insured on property*

- This must, unless agreed, be the full value of the property at risk, as under-insurance is penalized in all claims.
- If you are insured for full replacement/rebuilding costs, ensure that the sum insured is the full value of the latter and not market value.
- Are any 'special arrangements' appropriate?
  (a) First loss policies (ie total loss highly improbable)
  (b) Declaration policies (stocks of fluctuating value)
  (c) Valued policies (works of art etc)
  (d) Removal of debris, public authority clauses and the like should be considered.

5. *Liability insurances*

- Take advice before fixing the limits of indemnity. Normally £500,000 should be a minimum.

6. *Combined or separate policies?*

- Is a combined policy available as an alternative to a number of separate policies?
- Have you considered the adequacy of the combined policy and taken advice on the optional extras?
- Does a combined policy add to your cost by providing more cover than you need or is this an economic way of purchasing insurance?
- When purchasing liability insurance, enquire into the possibility of a combined liability policy.

MAKING A CLAIM

Conditions of the contract

Every policy contains conditions as to what needs to be observed to keep within the contract and how to proceed when a claim arises. The breach of some conditions (eg utmost good faith) may cause the policy to be avoided ab initio, the breach of others gives the insurer the right to avoid from the date of the breach, while breaches of so-called 'conditions precedent to liability' merely entitle the insurer to avoid the claim to which the breach relates. This section is concerned mainly with conditions precedent to liability, the features of which are noted below:

Claims notification
Most policies require the insured to notify the insurer immediately of any event and supply full details within 30 days (or later if agreed). It is for the insured to show that he has suffered a loss from an insured risk and prove the amount of that loss.

Reinstatement
If the insurer decides, or is compelled to reinstate any property instead of paying cash, the insured must produce any plans or documents reasonably required.

Investigation
Policy conditions may permit the insurer access to premises and, in the fire policy, take possession thereof where damage has occurred and deal with any salvage, but this does not entitle any insured to abandon property to the insurer. In practice, where the claim is large insurers often appoint loss adjusters to investigate the claim and negotiate for them. There is nothing to preclude the insured from securing professional representation provided he meets the cost.

Admission of liability
Where the insurance is of liability, the insured should not make any admission of liability. Any letter, writ, claim or process must be sent to the insurer as soon as it is received. Similarly, any notice of intended police prosecution, magistrates court summons, or notice of an inquest, should be passed unanswered to the insurer. Provided there is a claim within the policy, the insurer normally arranges legal representation at these proceedings.

Recoveries

An insured may have a right of recovery of his insured loss against a third party (eg a landlord with a fire claim may also have a claim against his tenant by way of a clause in the lease). At common law, once an indemnity payment has been made, the insurer is subrogated (ie entitled to) the insured's rights against the third party. However, by way of a condition the insurer is entitled to exercise these rights before the indemnity is paid. A delay in pursuing subrogation rights might jeopardize the chance of making a recovery. The insured is expected to help the insurer in these matters.

Establishing the cause of loss

The policy sets out the insured perils and then proceeds to cut down its scope by means of 'expected perils'. The loss may be the outcome of a sequence of events (or concurrent causes) in which there are competing causes. If one is an insured peril and the other excepted then it has to be determined which is the real, ie proximate cause of the loss. The doctrine of proximate cause is well-known in insurance and legal circles. The onus is on the insured to prove that his loss is caused by an insured peril and an insurer, who wishes to rely upon an exception, must prove his point. Proximate cause is sometimes modified by policy conditions and not necessarily to the insured's detriment. A detailed examination of the doctrine is beyond the scope of this book but it is reassuring to note that it follows common sense principles.

Overlapping insurances

A policy of restricted perils (eg fire) is capable of overlapping with a policy of wide perils (eg comprehensive) protecting the same interest. Where such policies are based on indemnity, the insured cannot, despite double insurance in the area of overlap, profit from the loss event. By way of a policy condition he must limit his claim against any single insurer to a rateable proportion of his loss. In order to avoid these 'contribution' situations, insurers sometimes use non-contribution clauses and similar devices such as:

- More specific insurance. If another insurance is more specific the insurer ceases to be liable under his policy.

- Market agreements, eg the Common Law Agreement where an employer, faced with a claim by an employee injured in a vehicle, may have valid claims for indemnity against both his motor and his employers' liability insurers. Employers' liability insurers have agreed to deal with such claims without enforcing contribution rights against motor insurers.

Claims disputes

Arguments may arise as to whether the insurer is liable at all or, if liability is admitted, as to the amount of the claim. Negotiations can often solve the problem without recourse to court proceedings. Arbitration is an alternative to litigation and policies often contain an arbitration clause. The arbitration clause requires that in a dispute about quantum (the amount to be paid under a policy) then the parties must go through the process of arbitration before they can pursue litigation. A dispute about liability may go straight to court. The legislation governing arbitration is the Arbitration Act 1979.

Business policyholders should note that the arbitration mechanisms of the Insurance Ombudsman Bureau and the Personal Insurance Arbitration Service provide them with no help. Both arrangements have as their central idea the provision of an independent body to whom personal insurance policyholders can refer disputes.

Checklist: making a claim

1. *Claims procedure*
   (a) Notification to the insurer
   - Check the relevant conditions of the policy.
   - Give immediate notificàtion in the form required.
   - Comply with any requirements as to submission of a detailed claim (eg fire insurance — 30 days) but seek agreement to extend the period if necessary.

   (b) Complete the claim/accident report form
   - Write 'not applicable' rather than leave blank spaces which will prompt unnecessary enquiries from the insurer.
   - Many questions will be similar to the original proposal. If your claim form shows the proposal as having been incorrect, prepare a careful explanation, as you may have breached the policy. Do not be tempted to make the claim form match the proposal. Departures from the truth could jeopardize an otherwise valid claim. Criminal convictions

now spent, under the Rehabilitation of Offenders Act 1974, need not be repeated in the claim form.

- Attach any estimates for repair or replacement to the claim form but do not delay submission of the form if estimates, which can follow, are awaited.
- Where possible get two (or even three) estimates as this may help the insurer.
- Keep copies of all letters, forms and estimates supplied.
- Be prepared for a reduction in your claim if you are under-insured.

(c) Investigation

- You may have to allow insurers access to premises, paper and property.
- A specialist loss adjuster is likely to represent the insurer for large or complicated losses.
- You may appoint a specialist at your own expense, eg loss assessor, surveyor, to represent you. You may have provision in your fire policy to cover architects' and surveyors' fees in repairing the damaged building.

(d) Subrogation rights

- Do not give away or limit your alternative rights of recovery. Under a contract of indemnity they belong to your insurer.
- You must assist your insurer both before and after payment of the loss in the exercise of these subrogation rights.

(e) Contribution among different insurers

- If you are insured twice for the same loss, inform both insurers.
- Each insurer is entitled to limit his payment to a rateable proportion of the loss.

(f) Arbitration.

- If the insurer disputes liability for your claim, you may, if negotiations fail, proceed to litigation
- If the dispute is over the amount of the claim, liability admitted, the insurer may invoke the arbitration clause.

2. *Some special cases*

(a) Liability claims

- Do not admit liability. Pass all communications received directly to your insurer without delay.
- Obtain and supply names of witnesses.

(b) Vehicle claims

- Make a sketch plan of the accident scene, take measure-

ments and a note of road and weather conditions.
- Obtain details of witnesses and others involved, including their 'insurances'.
- Do not admit liability etc.
- Report personal injury cases to the police (and other cases if names and addresses are not exchanged).
- Keep your insurer informed even if you do not intend to make a claim.
- If you have uninsured losses for which you believe others are liable, discuss the matter with your broker, solicitor or legal expenses insurer, if any.
- Ascertain the extent to which you can authorize repairs.
- After repair, you will be expected by the repairer to sign a satisfaction note. If in doubt take advice from your solicitor or insurer.

(c) Business interruption insurance
- Keep accurate records.
- Engage an accountant to prepare your claim.
- Can you trade from alternative premises or, if the interruption is at your suppliers' premises, find alternative suppliers?
- Keep a record of increased cost of working during the interruption period.

3. *After the claim*

- Consider the cause thereof and decide how to avoid such events.
- Consider the effect of the claim on the sum insured (or limit of indemnity). It may be necessary to reinstate the sum for future protection if reduced by the amount of the claim.
- Record the details for disclosure in future proposals.

INSURANCES BUSINESSES MUST HAVE

Compulsory insurances

These exist but generally common prudence plus an entitlement to insure is all that is required. This entitlement arises whenever the party seeking insurance has a financial involvement with the risk concerned, ie an insurable interest. This interest links with indemnity as the extent of the insured's interest measures the amount of the loss. For example, no financial interest in a property equals no loss and therefore no claim under a contract of indemnity. (See Badcock's case, page 398.)

The reason for compulsory insurance is to ensure that there are funds for the victim of the accident etc. It is not the intention to see that the wrongdoer is indemnified.

Statutes imposing insurance

Road Traffic Act 1972, Section 143 makes it an offence for users of motor vehicles to cause or permit the use of motor vehicles unless insured (or secured) in compliance with the Act.

Section 145 provides that the policy must:

(a) be issued by an authorized insurer
(b) insure liability in respect of the death or bodily injury of any person caused by, or arising out of, the use of a vehicle on a road
(c) cover liability to pay emergency treatment fees.

The policy does not have to cover liability where death or injury arises (i) out of or in the course of employment, or, (ii) out of contract.

The law does not at present insist on insurance against:

- liability for damage to property
- injury caused off a road.

It would, however, be imprudent to limit insurance to Act requirements only. Insurance should be against injury and damage to property wherever it occurs — the law of negligence, unlike S 145, makes no distinction between roads and private property. The standard policy goes well beyond the minimum Act requirements.

NB. By S 146 a security involving the deposit of £15,000 with the Accountant General of the Supreme Court is a rarely used alternative to insurance.

Employers' Liability (Compulsory Insurance) Act 1969 obliges employers to insure their legal liability for death, injury or disease to employees when such death etc arises out of and in the course of employment. The key provisions are:

(a) the insurer must be authorized
(b) the limit of indemnity must be a minimum of £2 million for any one occurrence
(c) certain policy conditions are prohibited in order to protect employees but an insurer may endorse the policy to establish a right of recovery against an insured who has breached one of these conditions. The conditions concerned include conditions precedent to liability, ie they relate to post-loss matters such as omission to notify as required, or admission of liability. Other prohibited conditions include failure of the insured to take

reasonable care, compliance with enactments, keeping of specified records.

The Act does not require an employer to insure in respect of specified relatives although it would be imprudent not to do so. Large local authorities and nationalized industries are not obliged to insure.

Riding Establishments Act 1970, Section 2 (1) obliges licensed establishments to insure against liability for injury to those who hire a horse for riding or use during instruction and also insure such persons for liability they may incur in respect of bodily injury.

Solicitors (Amendment) Act 1974 makes solicitors effect professional indemnity insurance. Solicitors have a duty of care towards clients and others who rely on their advice.

Insurance Brokers (Registration) Act 1977 obliges brokers to register as required by the Insurance Brokers Registration Council which has used its powers to insist that registered brokers insure under professional indemnity policies.

Nuclear Installations Act 1965. The operator of a nuclear installation is strictly liable for damage or injury caused by nuclear risks and must insure this liability up to £5 million. (The government compensates for damage in excess of this sum.)

Merchant Shipping (Oil Pollution) Act 1971. Merchant vessel owners may, in certain circumstances, be strictly liable for spillage of oil into the sea from an oil-carrying vessel and must insure against this risk.

Insurances may be imposed by contract

The requirement to insure may be imposed by contract, eg a landlord may oblige his tenant to insure the property against fire. A finance house is likely to require insurance as a condition of a loan for the purchase of an asset. Standard form contracts frequently include insurance clauses. Under Clauses 20.1 and 20.2 of the JCT Standard Form of Building Contract, the employer (ie the principal) seeks certain indemnities from the contractor in regard to personal injury and damage to property. To ensure that the contractor will be able to meet these obligations, he is obliged (Clause 21.1) to insure his liabilities. Employers' liability and public liability policies provide the relevant protection. Under Clause 21.2 the contractor may be required to effect a 'non-negligent' third party insurance (otherwise known as 'nuisance perils' cover) for the benefit of the employer. Clause 23 of the Institute of Civil Engineers Conditions of Contract calls for insurance to cover liability under Clause 22, ie an employer's and public liability insurance.

Checklist: compulsory insurances

1. Motor vehicles
   - Do you use motor vehicles on a road?
   - Do not be satisfied with an 'Act' only policy.
   - Ensure that for all vehicles you have evidence of your insurance (certificates or cover notes).
   - Insurance must be with an authorized insurer.
2. Employers' liability
   - Effect a policy for any form of employment even though it may be casual or part-time.
   - You do not have to insure if you employ only family labour, but you are strongly advised to do so.
   - Display your insurance certificate at your place of business and keep the policy available for inspection as required by regulations.
3. Quasi-compulsory insurances
   - If you are a tenant, which insurances, if any, must you effect under the terms of the lease?
   - Check other contracts to ascertain if you must act upon any insurance clauses.
   - If a standard form contract is used, have you familiarized yourself with clauses concerned with indemnity?

INSURANCES OF BUSINESS PROPERTY

This section deals with business property excluding motor, marine and aviation risks.

Business property exposed to risk may include premises, fixtures and fittings, plant and machinery, stock-in-trade, goods in trust or on commission, materials, packaging, work-in-progress, patterns, models, moulds, plans and designs. Separate amounts are insured on buildings as distinct from contents and contents are normally further subdivided among different classes of property.

Sums insured according to different classes of property

Buildings. The usual basis of value is the amount it would take to repair or reinstate after damage. Often betterment occurs and/or the insured might take the opportunity of extending or altering the building: in general, improving it over the state it was in before the damage. Negotiation takes place about the degree of betterment and the loss payment adjusted accordingly.

Machinery. When a total loss occurs the measure of value is the replacement by as near as possible the equivalent second-hand machinery, ie same type, same age, same condition etc. With the increasing sophistication of machines and rapid obsolescense this is virtually impossible. Rather than insure machinery on an indemnity basis one approach is to insure on a reinstatement basis (see *Fixing the amount of insurance*, page 398).

Computer systems records, patterns, models, moulds and designs. Often a simple piece of paper or card is worth a tremendous sum if a process is dependent upon it. That worth is not covered by material damage policies. Items such as these are insured only against the cost of labour and materials necessary to reproduce them.

Stock (retail, manufactured, work-in-progress). The insurance value for retail stock is the price that the retailer has paid to acquire the stock. If the selling price were used then the insurer would be paying for a consequential loss, ie the amount of the retailer's mark-up. Some stock may have depreciated to a significant degree (eg fashions or toys no longer 'all the rage'). In these cases market values will be paid if they are less than the cost of acquisition. The insurance value for manufactured goods is the cost of production, ie cost of materials, labour and processes. Again, the selling price is not used. For work-in-progress the materials cost plus processing cost to date of loss gives the relevant figure.

Principal forms of material damage policies available

Fire insurance

Cover is provided under a standard fire policy in respect of three perils: fire; lightning; explosion of domestic boilers or gas used for domestic purposes.

Fire following explosion is considered as loss by fire but there are excepted perils and excepted forms of loss. These are as follows:

(a) Property undergoing its own spontaneous fermentation (an excepted form of loss so damage communicated to other property is covered).
(b) Property undergoing any process involving the application of heat (as in (a) above).
(c) Earthquake.

(d) Subterranean fire.
(e) Riot or civil commotion.
(f) War and kindred risks.

Some important policy conditions:

- Alteration of risk or alienation of interest. If property is removed, or if the insured's interest ceases, the policy is rendered void in respect of the item affected, unless such alteration has been admitted by the insurer.
- Exclusions: (a) radioactive risks; (b) goods held in trust or on commission, money, securities, stamps, documents, manuscripts, business books, computer systems, records, patterns, models, moulds, plans, designs, or explosives (this property must be specifically mentioned in the policy if it is to be insured).
- Other conditions include claims notification, insurer's rights after a fire, arbitration. A further condition, 'property under contract for sale' which gives a purchaser the benefit of the vendor's policy where the latter has contracted to sell his interest in the property, the purchase not having been completed at the time of sale.

Special clauses in fire policies

(a) Architects' and surveyors' fees. Fees incurred in repairing buildings are not automatically covered unless specially included. Fees can be insured by separate item or included in the sum insured on buildings.
(b) Public authorities clause. Following a loss necessitating repair, the local authority may take the opportunity to insist upon certain alterations being incorporated in the reinstatement. This clause enables the insured to meet the costs of such requirements provided adequate provision exists within the sum insured.
(c) Removal of debris. Normally this cost is within a fire policy but sometimes there may be extra costs due to the nature of the risk. A damaged building may block a road or waterway. The clause makes the insurer responsible for the extra costs provided there is a separate item or adequate sum insured.

Additional (or special) perils insurance

These perils can be added to a standard fire policy. They include: aircraft; explosion; riot and civil commotion; malicious damage; storm and tempest; flood; bursting or overflowing of water tanks, apparatus or pipes; impact by vehicles or animals.

Most proposal forms give a useful description of the cover. Policies include an excess (£25–£100) for the water damage claims and it is a condition of this cover that the premises, water tanks etc be maintained in a good and substantial state of repair. For the impact cover there is a £25–£100 excess if the damage is caused by the insured's own vehicle. Subsidence and landslip cover has assumed importance in recent years and can be added to the range of perils in acceptable cases subject to a sizeable excess.

Sprinkler leakage insurance

Sprinklers are undisputed leaders in the field of fire protection equipment. Accordingly, fire insurers offer very significant savings in premiums to those who install them. A problem arises in that having a building covered by a series of pipes and sprinkler heads, creates the risk of water damage if there is an accidental discharge, eg installation damaged by a fork-lift truck. Another danger is the water freezing in the pipes. A sprinkler leakage policy pays for damage from the accidental discharge of water from the system.

Theft insurances

This sub-section extends beyond theft or burglary policies to consider other important forms of insurance wider in scope but having theft as a main element of cover.

Theft insurance

The form of words employed by insurers varies but the general intention is to cover theft involving entry to or exit from the premises by forcible and violent means. In essence there needs to be some form of attack on the premises. Pilfering is not insured as there would be problems in establishing proof and the extent of loss. Moreover, such losses are, for retailers, something like a recurring business expense. Individually, such losses are relatively small and well-spread and in such circumstances there is hardly a need for the risk-spreading facility that insurance provides.

Underwriters are influenced by the degree of attraction of the goods, their portability, security, nature and location of the premises, and previous loss experience. Surveys of premises are the rule rather than the exception and often cover is granted only subject to improvements in the security.

The policy provides insurance against:

(a) loss or damage to the property (ie stock etc) while contained in the premises;
(b) damage, failing to be borne by the insured, to the premises.

The exceptions are:

- fire damage;
- damage to plate or decorated glass;
- loss or damage to money, securities, coins, stamps, business books, computer systems records etc (this is similar to the exclusion in the fire policy and exists for the same reason).
- loss involving a person lawfully on the premises or brought about with the connivance of an employee or family member (this is a fidelity guarantee risk).

One important aspect of the claims condition is that the police must be advised of the occurrence.

Money insurance
For the purpose of the policy 'money' includes: cash, bank and currency notes, cheques, postal orders, money orders, postage stamps, and luncheon vouchers.

Cover is provided on an 'all risks' basis in six categories:

(a) In actual transit.
(b) In a bank night safe.
(c) In a locked safe or strongroom outside business hours subject to an agreed limit.
(d) On the premises outside business hours but not in a safe or strongroom (normally limited to £250).
(e) In the insured's private residence (or that of employees) up to £250.
(f) In the custody of travellers or collectors (normally a 24-hour limit applies here).

The policy insists that all keys to safes and strongrooms be removed from the premises outside business hours. Premium is calculated on the amount of money carried during the year with an adjustable deposit premium charged. Exclusions include: dishonesty by employees not discovered within seven days; shortages due to errors or omissions; losses from unattended vehicles; contents of coin-operated machines.

Goods in transit
This 'all risks' insurance covers goods while in transit anywhere in Great Britain. Cover operates during loading, carriage, unloading or tempor-

ary garaging of all vehicles and trailers. Two main types of policy are issued covering:

(a) an insured's own vehicle with a sum insured per vehicle;
(b) all goods despatched by the insured on his own or road hauliers' vehicles, goods carried by rail or goods sent through the post. Here there is a sum insured per consignment.

Excluded property is similar to that of other policies and embraces goods of a hazardous nature (explosives and acids), attractive and brittle goods (jewellery, clocks, watches and antiques). Cover can be specially considered in the case of some excluded property. Excepted risks include theft or pilferage by employees, moth, vermin, delay, deterioration and inherent vice.

NB. Road hauliers are a special category and can consider effecting an 'all risks' insurance on the property they carry or they can effect a liability policy indemnifying them only when legally liable for loss or damage. The premium is generally adjustable depending on the level of activity which is measured by the level of haulage earnings.

Glass insurance

This may be insured separately but with smaller risks is often a part of a combined policy. Large supermarkets (see page 391) are more likely to practise risk assumption than insure. The policy covers breakage from all causes, including the cost of boarding up, with the exception of the fire risk which is covered under the fire policy. Cover can be extended to include (a) cost of removing and replacing fixtures and fittings involved in the breakage of the insured glass, and (b) damage to goods in the shop window (excluding fire and theft risks).

Engineering insurance

This is based largely on an inspection service provided by the insurers' engineer-surveyors with insurance added as outlined below. Various Factories Acts, and the Health and Safety at Work Act have laid down requirements for inspection. Cranes, boilers and pressure plant must be inspected once every 14 months (other lifting appliances every six months). Inspection services are available for engine and electrical plant but are not compulsory. There are four principal headings under which plant may be grouped:

(a) Boilers and pressure plant are insured against damage to the boiler etc and surrounding property consequent upon explosion or collapse.

(b) Engine plant (eg steam and diesel engines, refrigeration equipment) is insured against mechanical breakdown and damage to surrounding property caused by flying fragments.
(c) Electrical plant (electric motors, generators, etc) is insured against mechanical or electrical breakdown.
(d) Lifting machinery (cranes, hoists, passenger and goods lifts etc) is insured against breakdown.

Checklist: insurance of business property (material damage policies)

1. *Fire insurance*

- Larger risks. As it is unlikely that a proposal form will be completed, refer to your risk management checklist (and your insurance programme; see *Risk Management*, page 389. Ensure that you have identified *all* property in *all* situations.
- Smaller risks. In addition to the above refer to the proposal form which should be sufficiently itemized to help avoid omissions.
- Check the excluded property and negotiate amendments if necessary.
- Sums insured on buildings and machinery should represent current reinstatement costs.
- Always insure for full value.
- Special clauses. Consider making provision for architects' and surveyors' fees and/or removal of debris.

2. *Additional perils insurance*

- Insurance against the full range of perils is advised.
- Excesses are applied in regard to water damage perils and certain aspects of the impact risk.
- Subsidence insurance has to be specially negotiated.

3. *Sprinkler leakage insurance*

If sprinklers have been installed effect this policy. The risk of accidental water damage is not covered by the additional perils insurance.

4. *Theft insurance*

- Cooperate with your insurer if improvements in security are sought.
- Insurance is not available for theft unaccompanied by an

'attack' on the premises (eg sneak thefts, pilfering). Control those risks by other measures.
- Insure for full value at risk on the basis of acquisition costs not selling prices.
- Check the excluded property and negotiate amendments if necessary.

5. *Money insurance*

- Record the amounts in transit for premium adjustment purposes.
- Do not exceed the agreed limit for money in safe or strongroom.
- Do not leave safe or strongroom keys on premises out of business hours.
- Do not exceed the limit applicable to private residences.
- Cover in respect of collectors is limited to 24 hours. Does your system of check take account of this limitation?

6. *Goods in transit*

- Ensure that full values are insured.
- Itemize all forms of transit (own vehicles, rail, road hauliers, post etc).
- Ascertain the restrictions that will apply in regard to overnight parking (especially in London, Liverpool and Glasgow) of unattended vehicles. What forms of property are excluded?
- Do not release road hauliers and other carriers from their responsibilities without informing your insurer (subrogation rights could be affected).

7. *Glass insurance*

- Large companies with a spread of risks should consider risk assumption.
- Ensure that any chosen insurer is capable of carrying out window replacement without delay.

8. *Engineering insurance*

- The risks covered vary according to the plant concerned. Where damage to surrounding property is covered (eg boilers and engine plant) ensure that the sum insured is adequate to pay for such damage.
- Be aware of those items of plant for which inspection is compulsory. Inspection and insurance can be combined.

INSURANCES OF PECUNIARY INTERESTS

Pecuniary risks may arise from bad debts, dishonesty of employees, interruptions to business, loss of book debts due to destruction of records, extra cost of fulfilling uncompleted work by contractor, indemnifying the revenue in respect of non-payment of duties or improper use of dutiable items, and other risks leading to pecuniary loss.

Business interruption insurance

Otherwise known as loss of profits, it complements material damage insurance by providing protection for subsequent loss of earning power. Such consequential losses can often be more serious than the material damage to property. When production is halted or reduced in scope not only will net profit be eroded but there will be standing charges, eg rent and rates, to meet during the interruption. There will, however, be a proportionate reduction in some expenses such as power and raw materials. Cover is available for:

(a) Loss of gross profit. Sales revenue less cost of purchases (or cost of putting the goods into a saleable condition) during the period of interrupted trading following damage insured under a material damage policy.

(b) Increase in cost of working, incurred to avoid a loss of gross profit during the interrupted trading.

(c) Auditors' or professional accountants' charges, for producing and certifying a business interruption claim. The insured must fix the indemnity period, ie the maximum time needed to get the business working and earning again after the most serious damage. It fixes the insurer's maximum liability in time. It is then necessary to forecast the gross profit for the maximum indemnity period.

Some noteworthy aspects:

- An interruption policy operates in conjunction with a fire or additional perils policy. If a claim has not been admitted under the fire or additional perils policy then the business interruption policy will not operate.
- Increase in cost of working. By paying extra costs often a shortfall in production can be reduced, eg rent of alternative temporary premises, payment of overtime. Such costs are paid by the insurer if not exceeding the loss of gross profit thereby avoided.
- The premises need to be fully identified to include all sources

of revenue. Also income could be eroded by damage occurring on sites where work is carried out. Other 'away from premises' extensions available are: suppliers' premises, neighbouring property (denial of access), customers' premises, and failure of public utilities.

- The insured may wish to treat wages as a standing charge and insure 100 per cent of his wages in the gross profit item. This is known as payroll cover. Alternatively, he may treat labour as capable of being hired or fired at short notice and so deduct wages when fixing the gross profit item (when treated in this way wages are, in policy terms, a 'specified working expense'; such expenses are not at risk of loss and therefore deducted from the gross profit item). However, an employer may have union agreements with regard to minimum notice and would not want to lose a skilled labour force following an interruption. Between the two extremes is partial wages cover known as the dual basis. This allows 100 per cent wages cover for a selected number of weeks and then a selected percentage of the wage roll for the rest of the indemnity period, eg 100 per cent for the first ten weeks and 50 per cent thereafter. An option to consolidate exists, ie 100 per cent cover can be increased by abandoning partial cover. In the example, say, the 100 per cent cover can be increased to 30 weeks with no partial loss cover. The option is useful to handle interruptions that exceed the initial period but fall short of the full indemnity period.
- The policy insures future trading expectations. A Special Circumstances Clause allows adjustments to figures from previous trading. Where there is no previous trading, eg construction of a new brewery, an interruption may delay the plant coming on stream causing a future financial loss. Advance profits policies cover the loss between the actual and anticipated dates of production.

Engineering consequential loss

Cover in engineering insurance works in a similar way but there are differences:

(a) Cover is in respect of specific machinery and the perils are sudden and unforeseen damage and failure of the public utilities.

(b) Excesses and franchises are applied to the indemnity period to avoid small losses.

Credit insurance

This aims to indemnify against loss arising as a consequence of a buyer's inability to pay for goods or services supplied on credit. There is no indemnity against the loss of profit on credit transactions. For this reason, and to ensure that the insured is selective in giving credit, the policy never covers 100 per cent of the risk. This produces a co-insurance situation. Policies are available in two main forms:

(a) *Specific account policies* covering known danger spots. These covers are tantamount to selection against the insurer and carry high rates of premium.
(b) *Whole turnover policies* cover the whole credit risk of the firm, subject to the co-insurance aspect referred to above. The spread of risk results in an averaged rate of premium.

Credit insurance is designed to protect a business asset, trade debtors. It does not extend to transactions between businesses and individuals purchasing as private consumers.

The Export Credits Guarantee Department (ECGD) is a government department providing credit insurance. In addition to commercial failure, cover is also provided against loss due to economic or political frustration of payment. Further cover is available against expropriation of overseas assets. ECGD covers encourage exports and overseas investment by removing the consequences of a major possibility of loss.

Fidelity guarantee insurance

Fidelity guarantee insurance is issued to commercial organizations to indemnify an employer against direct pecuniary loss and losses of stock through acts of dishonesty by employees. Several types of policy are available:

(a) *Individual policy* covering a named person for a specific amount.
(b) *Collective policy* covering a number of named employees either for specific individual sums or for an overall amount.
(c) *Blanket policy* covering all staff (unnamed) with a total sum guaranteed.
(d) *Positions policies* cover particular persons in the firm, such as the cashier, without specifying names. Where employees are named, the insurers make detailed enquiries of the employee's background. When unnamed employees are insured, the insurer accepts the information supplied by the employer. In all cases the insurer will enquire into the system of control over stock and money. Some insurers provide cover in respect of an employee for

up to 18 months after he has ceased to be employed to allow sufficient time for discrepancies to be traced.

Court bonds

These are needed to ensure that no loss arises when the courts appoint people responsible for the safekeeping of other individuals' property. The Court of Protection may appoint a receiver to manage the estate of someone who is mentally ill, or senile and not capable of managing their own affairs. To protect against possible loss the receiver must take out a Court of Protection Bond. Also a judge may appoint a receiver for a minor or for property subject to litigation. Again the receiver will administer the estate and must take out a bond, known as a Chancery Guarantee, to guarantee the security of the estate.

Government bonds

They fulfil a similar function to court bonds: the guarantee of payment (in the event of something happening to frustrate payment) of revenue due to HM Customs & Excise. The best example is the removal of goods from a bonded warehouse without the payment of excise duties. A General Warehouse Bond or a Removal Bond would ensure that excise duties were paid.

Bankruptcy and liquidation bonds

They guarantee a trustee in bankruptcy appointed by the creditors. The trustee has control of the bankrupt's assets and should the trustee fail to carry out his duties correctly, the bond will make good the loss suffered by the estate.

Local government bonds

Are used in connection with the accounting and clerical staff of local authorities. These cover parallel commercial fidelity guarantees taken out by the private sector.

Contract guarantee bonds

Are arranged to ensure that work contracted for is actually completed. Before awarding a building contract, a negotiator might require a bond to cover the extra cost of completion in the event of the builder's insolvency. The owners of small firms may be required by the insurers to enter into personal guarantees to secure every effort in the performance of the contract.

Contingency insurances

These are varied and cover special legal risks. For example, the vendor of property may impose restrictions on the use of land. With the passage of time (and death of the vendor), the covenant becomes dated with apparently no one interested in its enforcement. Nonetheless anyone who develops the land contrary to the covenant is taking a risk and should therefore effect a restrictive covenant insurance. Missing documents (share certificates, title deeds etc) may necessitate the issue of duplicates. Indemnity may be required against possible claims if the original document is found. Other insurable contingency risks relate to defective title, film producer's indemnity (abandonment of film due to incapacity or death of star).

Loss of book debts

The loss of records after fire may lead to substantial financial loss. As such debts originate in the period before the peril leading to damage and interruption, they are outside the business interruption policy. The cover is in respect of the loss of outstanding debit balances but a deduction is made in respect of amounts received or traced (failure to collect after tracing is a matter for credit insurance). Additional expense in tracing the debts is covered, if previously consented to by the insurer. A separate item insures auditor's charges payable by the insured in connection with the claim.

Checklist: pecuniary insurances

1. *Business interruption insurance*
   (a) Consider the effect on your earning power of:
   - Fire or other perils at your premises, sites, suppliers' or customers' premises.
   - Denial of access to your premises following damage nearby.
   - Failure of public utilities.
   - Breakdown etc of specific plant and machinery.

   (b) Estimate the maximum length of interruption period and the gross profit therefor.

- Exclude from the gross profit items not at risk of loss through fire etc.
- Wages and salaries need careful consideration as full payroll cover is desirable and some insurance essential.
- An interruption policy operates only if a claim is admitted under a material damage policy.

2. *Loss of book debts*
   (a) Could you trace monies owing to you if your records were destroyed?
   (b) What extra expense would you incur in tracing the amounts due?
   (c) Insurance is available against: fire, special perils and theft; 'all risks'.

3. *Credit insurance*
   (a) Establish a sound credit control system.
   (b) If your trade debtors are significant secure a quotation from a specialist insurer.
   (c) You will have to carry a proportion of any risk insured.
   (d) Compare specific account cover with whole turnover cover.
   (e) If you export or invest abroad, contact the Export Credits Guarantee Department.

4. *Fidelity guarantee insurance*
   (a) Select staff with care and check references.
   (b) Establish sound systems of control over staff with control over stock or money.
   (c) Consider the fidelity insurances available — loss due to dishonesty of staff is *not* covered by a theft policy.
   (d) If a loss occurs, you must assist the insurer in any civil action against the defaulter.
   (e) Policies have a 'discovery' period, which should not disadvantage an employer with an adequate system of control.
   (f) Notify the insurer as soon as you have reasonable grounds for suspicion.
   (g) Do not promise the defaulter that you will not prosecute and inform the insurer if holding money on the defaulter's behalf.

5. *Other pecuniary risks*
   Are any of the following likely to apply to you:

   (a) Court of Protection Bonds or Chancery Guarantees?
   (b) General Warehouse Bonds or Removal Bonds?
   (c) Contingency risks such as:

- Restrictive covenants;
- Defective title;
- Missing documents?

INSURANCES OF LIABILITY

Liability insurance provides an indemnity when there is liability at law for accidents causing bodily injury or damage to property. This section deals with the main liability risks other than motor, marine and aviation. Liability insurance can be purchased in a combined policy or by way of separate policies. For purpose of exposition, separate policies will be outlined.

Before a liability insurer makes a payment to a third party, *two aspects* have to be considered:

(a) was the insured legally liable for the injury/damage?
(b) does the policy apply to the circumstances of the case?

Legal liability arises through tort (eg negligence), under contract, or breach of statutory duty.

The employer's liability policy

This covers legal liability to pay damages to employees for bodily injury/disease arising out of or in the course of employment. The indemnity, which is unlimited in amount, extends to claimants' costs, and insured's own costs if incurred with the insurer's consent. The policy also covers the requirements of any contract for the work of a principal ('employer' in the terms of the JCT Standard Form of Building Contract). The principal, who is often in virtually the same position as the insured in relation to the insured's employees, is indemnified directly or indirectly if he observes the policy terms.

The policy is close to being exclusionless but may be endorsed to exclude certain kinds of work, thus obviating the payment by low risk categories of premiums for risks they do not run. Cover is restricted to employment within Great Britain and, in effect, visits abroad (provided subsequent court actions are in Britain).

Extended definition of employees. The use of labour-only subcontractors in the construction industry gives rise to doubt as to their status, but the employer's liability insurer deems them to be employees for the purpose of the policy. Indemnity to others (at insured's request) is available for any director, or partner, as well as officers, committee members, and canteen members etc. Activities of sports organizations and the like are regarded as part of the 'business'. Most policies cover directors and employees against the cost of defending prosecutions brought against them personally under the Health and Safety at Work Act 1974. (Any fines are not, of course, covered.) The policy similarly covers the solicitor's fee for representation at any coroner's inquest or fatal accident enquiry or criminal proceedings arising out of breaches of the Factories Act and similar legislation.

Public liability

Public liability covers legal liability for accidents causing bodily injury (to persons other than employees) or damage to property arising out of, or connected with the 'business'. Claims by the public can be founded on statute but usually they are based on negligence (eg defects in premises, negligence by outworkers involving the employer in liability to others). Thus, cover is not limited to a premises risk. It extends to work away provided such work is within the description of the 'business'.

The policy applies to accidents occurring during the policy period even though the negligence may have been earlier. There is normally a limit of indemnity for any one occurrence but some policies may add a limit for any one year. The indemnity not only covers the damages payable to third parties but also claimants' costs and expenses and the insured's own costs when consented to by the insurer. Claimants' costs and expenses are not made subject to the limit of indemnity.

Exceptions are necessary as some risks need individual consideration while others are more suitably insured under separate policies. Contractual liability (apart from an indemnity to principals as in the employer's liability policy) and accidents outside Great Britain are (except for business trips), and pollution are all matters needing special consideration. Employer's liability, third party motor risks, liability for boilers, waterborne craft and aircraft, professional negligence, liability for defective products are all more suitable for separate insurances. The policy also excludes liability for property in the insured's custody or control as insurance on a material damage basis is usually more appropriate. As with the employer's liability policy, the premium is adjustable on the basis of annual wages declarations except for smaller risks where flat premiums may be charged. Indemnity to persons other than the insured follows the line of the employer's liability policy as does the extended definition of employees.

Products liability insurance

Injury may result from consuming unfit ginger-beer or from the malfunctioning of a defective component in a jumbo-jet. Such is the range of risks which may be covered under a products liability policy, although in simple cases the exclusion relating to goods sold in the public liability policy may be modified.

The products liability policy provides indemnity arising out of goods sold or supplied or installed, erected, altered or treated by the insured where the accidental injury/damage occurs elsewhere than the insured's premises.

Points to note:

(a) The policy does not cover failure of the product to perform (but consequential injury/damage is covered), neither does it cover the replacement of defective products.
(b) The date of manufacture is not relevant as the policy covers loss/damage occurring during the period of insurance.
(c) The accident etc can occur anywhere in the world but the goods must have been supplied from Great Britain in connection with the 'business'.
(d) The limit of indemnity is normally expressed in relation to any one period of insurance rather than any one occurrence.
(e) The indemnity in terms of damages and costs etc follows the lines of the public liability policy.
(f) Most policies exclude advice and treatment (professional indemnity risks) and some also exclude specifications for the same reason.
(g) Products for use in aircraft, hovercraft or watercraft are excluded as individual consideration is needed.
(h) Premiums are adjustable in accordance with changes in the level of turnover.

Products guarantee insurance

This covers legal liability to replace or repair the defective product and liability for failure of the product to perform its intended function. Plant and machinery may be expensive to repair or replace. Such costs are covered together with losses arising from loss of production. A more restricted insurance is 'financial loss cover' covering financial loss (eg from loss of production) unassociated with injury/damage. Such losses are within the products liability insurance only when flowing from injury/damage which is the basis of a claim against the insured.

Professional indemnity insurance

A professional person (eg solicitor, accountant) may be liable to clients in contract for a breach of the duty of care or they may be liable to third parties who reasonably rely on their advice (Hedley Byrne *v* Heller & Partners (1963)). The outcome may be in the form of financial loss as opposed to bodily injury or damage, although the medical professions are affected by the latter. High standards are required in the exercise of particular skill and judgement, and, consequently there is a considerable demand for insurance from those in the professions. Doctors normally look for indemnity from their own Medical Defence Union and there are others with similar mutual protection arrangements.

Points to note include:

(a) The indemnity is extended to the insured, those who are his partners from time to time, and, sometimes senior members of staff.
(b) Cover is on a 'claims-made basis', ie it is the manifestation of the claim that matters, not the act or omission constituting breach of duty. Consequently, 'occurrences' disclosed at inception are excluded.
(c) As incoming owners normally assume all liabilities on change of ownership, the insured's indemnity extends to include the acts/omissions etc of predecessors.
(d) The policy does not apply to non-professional occurrences (injury due to defective premises) so it is essential for professional persons to maintain other insurances (eg public liability).
(e) The limit of indemnity is expressed in relation to any one year.
(f) To avoid publicity a professional person may prefer to settle rather than contest even an ill-founded claim. The insurer may prefer to resist the claim. The conflict is resolved by the QC Clause whereby the insurer agrees not to defend in the courts unless a mutually agreed Queen's Counsel advises that the claim should be contested.

Checklist liability insurance

1. *General*

   - Give the insurer a full description of your 'business' and ensure that this is accurately shown in the policy.
   - Update the insurer whenever the activities change.
   - Keep a proper record of any variable factor (eg wages, turnover) upon which the premium is adjusted. Supply declarations as required.
   - Fix adequate limits of indemnity.

2. *Employer's liability insurance*
    - This is a compulsory insurance (See Checklist on page 409).
    - Note that the basic policy does not insure overseas risk (other than 'visits').
    - Check 'trade endorsements', if any, and inform the insurer if and when they become inappropriate to your activities.
3. *Public liability*
    - Insurance is not compulsory but is essential.
    - Check the policy exceptions and seek individual consideration or separate policies as appropriate. If different insurers are used for different liability risks, ask your broker or adviser to ensure that no gaps emerge.
    - Some exceptions may be 'excluded forms of loss' rather than 'excepted risks', eg damage to that part of any property being worked upon.
4. *Professional indemnity insurance*
    - Ascertain to whom the indemnity is granted (insured, partners, staff, predecessors) to establish possible gaps.
    - Check the exceptions including those relating to dishonesty and libel and slander (special extensions or separate policies can be considered).
    - Occurrences notified during or within three months of policy expiry will be deemed, if claims materialize, to be claims within the policy provision. This closes the gap that would exist on change of insurer when the new one excludes occurrences notified at the inception.
    - Your professional institute may have negotiated favourable terms for its members.
5. *Products liability insurance*
    - Products liability insurance is needed whenever potential liability arises from sale, supply, installation, erection, alteration or treatment of products.
    - The policy does not cover failure to perform or replacement of defective products. Additional protection may be available through products guarantee or financial loss cover.
    - Products for use in aircraft, hovercraft and watercraft are excluded. Individual consideration is needed.
    - Cover is on a 'claims-made' basis.

MOTOR VEHICLE INSURANCE

Motor vehicle risks include injury/damage to third parties; loss or damage to the vehicle itself; injury to the insured, loss of personal effects and other incidental risks. For insurance purposes, vehicles are considered in three main categories: private cars, commercial vehicles, and motor cycles. Other classes include motor trade vehicles, agricultural vehicles, and special types (eg bulldozers). Vehicles may be insured on the following bases: (a) comprehensive, (b) third party fire and theft, (c) third party only. A more restricted policy, known as 'Act only', covering only the minimum compulsory insurance requirements, is issued to risks unacceptable for wider cover but is rarely used.

Private car insurance

Comprehensive policies have three main sections:

(a) *The 'own damage' section* which is essentially an 'all risks' insurance covering loss or damage to the motor car and its accessories and spare parts on the car or in the garage. Certain forms of loss are excluded: depreciation, wear and tear, mechanical or electrical breakdown, tyre damage from braking or punctures, and loss of use. This section carries an excess (varying from £25 to £100) for accidental damage losses (ie not fire and theft losses) when young or inexperienced drivers have charge of the car. The section covers cost of delivery after repair and indicates the extent to which the insured can authorize his own repairs. There is no 'sum insured' as such, but the insured's own declared value sets the upper limit under this indemnity contract. Some policies provide that if a total loss of a new car occurs in the first year or cost of repairs exceed 50 per cent of car value, the insured will be paid the cost of a new car.

(b) *The liability to third parties section* indemnifies the insured in connection with legal liability for bodily injury or damage to property of others caused by accidents connected with the car. Damages and claimants' costs plus the insured's own costs (if consented to by the insurers) form the basis of the indemnity. The insurer also pays the solicitor's fee for representation in any court of summary jurisdiction, or inquest following an event which may be the subject of a claim. Others indemnified are: (a) any permitted driver; (b) any permitted user (who is not driving); (c) the employer or partner of any person whose business use is permitted by the policy; (d) any passenger. The insured, but not others, is indemnified in the terms of this section in connection with the driving of other cars or motor cycles not belonging to him. This 'driving of other cars' clause is not applicable if the insured is a limited company.

Exceptions include: injury to employees; damage to property in the custody or control of the person seeking indemnity.

(c) *Additional benefits* include limited personal accident insurance for the insured and spouse, medical expenses, emergency treatment (necessary for 'Act' purposes), loss or damage to personal effects. A 'no claim discount' is set out, as well as 'territorial limits' (Great Britain, but with an automatic extension to ensure that the policy meets with the minimum requirements of other EEC countries). A foreign use section makes it possible for the insured to seek full cover when travelling abroad. In addition to the exceptions within each section there are 'general exceptions', one of which relates to 'limitations as to use'. Most insurers recognize three classes of use:

- *Class 1.* Social, domestic and pleasure purposes and business use by the insured. (Note the business use element is for the insured alone and not others who may be indemnified.)
- *Class 2.* Social domestic and pleasure purposes, and for business or trade purposes of the insured, his employer or partner, excluding commercial travelling or the motor trade.
- *Class 3.* As for Class 2 without the exclusions.

All classes exclude, inter alia, use for motor trade hire or reward. Exclusion of motor trade does not affect the cover while the car is with the motor trade for overhaul, upkeep, or repair. Where the cover is to be third party only, then there will be no cover under the 'own damage' section and no additional benefits in terms of personal accident, personal effects or medical expenses. When cover is to be third party fire and theft, the third party policy is extended to add loss or damage to the car if caused by fire or theft.

Commercial vehicle insurance

Many different vehicles are involved (goods carrying, coaches, public authority vehicles, eg ambulances; special types, eg bulldozers) and use the same policy form. Agricultural vehicles and motor trade use special policy forms. The general policy has much in common with the private car form but provides little by way of additional benefits. Special features are:

(a) Loading and unloading risks are included in the third party section subject to exceptions which should be compared with the cover available for such risks under a public liability policy. There should be no gap between the two.

(b) Damage to any bridge, viaduct, weighbridge, or road by vibration or weight of the vehicle is excluded.
(c) Towing of other vehicles (other than for hire or reward) is allowed.
(d) Trailers are commonly covered to the same extent as the insured vehicle to which they are attached except that the operational risk of mobile plant trailers is covered only for 'Act' liability.
(e) The indemnity for third party property damage (unlike private car insurance) is limited to £1 million any one occurrence.

Motor trade cover

This is available in two main forms — road risks and internal risks (accidents on own premises). These policies, treated separately here, may be purchased in a combined form.

(a) *Road risks* protects the trader when using the vehicle on a road and it may be third party or comprehensive protection. The cover operates when any vehicle is on a road or temporarily garaged or parked during a journey on premises other than the trader's own. It extends to garaging at the private home of the trader, partner or employees. The vehicles covered and use thereof are intended to meet the needs of a trader but these matters should be carefully checked when the insurance is arranged.

(b) The *internal risks* policy is the trader's version of a public liability insurance but the exclusion of property in the insured's custody or control may not be acceptable to a trader within customers' vehicles. Thus, the trader may select cover which extends to provide protection for such vehicles and even his own when on the premises. The indemnity for bodily injury is unlimited but property damage is limited normally to £500,000 for any one accident. An important extension of cover is liability arising from defective workmanship and sale of goods on the lines of product liability insurance.

Agricultural and forestry vehicles

Cover includes a special section — indemnity to hirers and drivers. Farmers may find it more economical to hire equipment than to buy. When they hire from other farmers the policies will meet the situation by 'treating as though he were the insured any person who is the hirer, or who is driving on the order or with the permission of the insured or such hirer'. Cover operates while agricultural trailers are attached. Extra premium may be required for third party cover while trailers are detached and out of use.

Motor cycles

Cover follows private cars. Theft of accessories and spare parts (like commercial vehicles) is only covered if the whole of the machine is stolen. Cover is limited to driving by the insured but additional drivers can be added. There is a compulsory accidental damage excess for all machines over 50cc. The policy extends to cover business use, so consequently loading/unloading risks are covered as under the commercial vehicle policy.

Contingent liabilities

When an employee uses his own car on the employer's business, the latter (see *Private car insurance*, page 428) is indemnified under the employee's car policy. If that policy fails (breach of utmost good faith or policy condition), the employer may well find himself with an uninsured liability to a third party. To overcome the problem the employer can effect a contingent liability policy indemnifying him, when liable but unable to claim under the employee's breached policy. A Road Traffic Act certificate is not required for this type of policy. Also in need of such a policy is someone hiring a vehicle with driver and indemnified in the first instance under the existing policy on the vehicle.

Fleet insurances for the larger user

Fleets exceeding 10 vehicles (five for some insurers) can be specially rated and should be considered by the larger user. Insurers ascertain an average gross premium per vehicle (no deduction for no claim discount) and compare this with claims cost during the previous three years. If the loss ratio is materially under, say 60 per cent, the gross average premium is diminished by a discount, but for loss ratios in excess of, say 62½ per cent, a loading is added. Insurers can give more individual attention on fleets, advising upon maintenance, good driving bonuses, and good discipline. The sensible fleet manager should benefit from this approach. Often the larger the size of the fleet, the less insurance protection is needed (large numbers again). A firm can accept a fairly high excess in return for a premium discount. Not only is premium saved but there will be administrative savings by eliminating small claims. The really large fleet owner could meet repairs and third party claims as they occur with insurance to provide protection in the event that claims in the aggregate should exceed a predetermined figure during the year.

Checklist motor vehicle insurance

1. *General*
   - Road Traffic Act 1972 makes insurance compulsory. Do *not* be satisfied with an 'Act' only policy (see *Statutes imposing insurance*, page 407).
   - Choose comprehensive; third party fire and theft; or third party insurance. Be guided by the cost of insurance in relation to the value of the property at risk. Third party insurance amounts to risk assumption as regards loss or damage to the vehicle (see *Risk Management*, page 389).
   - Complete proposals accurately and take copies.
   - When travelling abroad notify your insurer. It may be necessary to extend cover and/or obtain a green card (international certificate of insurance).
   - All policies contain limitations as to use. Ensure that your policy meets your requirements.
   - Instruct employees (and other permitted drivers) what to do and what *not* to do (ie admit liability) after an accident.
   - If you have 10 vehicles (some insurers consider five) you may be eligible for a fleet policy.
   - Some insurers permit payment of premium by instalments.
   - There may be restrictions on theft (or frost damage) cover for vehicles normally parked in the open overnight.
   - Voluntary excesses and driving restrictions (eg insured and spouse) may earn premium discounts.
   - Be familiar with the customary accidental damage excess for both young and inexperienced drivers.

2. *Private cars*
   - Special schemes are available (eg certain occupation groups, total abstainers) as well as premium concessions for some groups (eg young married persons not loaded as much as single young persons of same age).
   - The 'driving other cars' indemnity applies to the insured only in respect of third party cover only.

3. *Commercial vehicles*
   - Check that all drivers hold current licences.
   - Consider whether cover applies on trailers while attached to, and/or detached from the insured vehicle.
   - For special 'plant type' vehicles (eg cranes, mechanical navvies, excavators) consider the insurance of the 'third party working

risk', especially if the plant digs below its own wheel base.

4. *Motor trade*
   - Effect both 'road risks' and 'internal risks' cover preferably in a combined policy.
   - Under both forms of cover, there are optional extras which should be very carefully considered with the guidance of your broker.
5. *Agricultural and forestry vehicles*
   - The 'hirer's indemnity' is an essential part of the cover.
   - The policy should cover hiring or lending to public authorities (eg snow clearance), but haulage of trees on a road entails extra premium and therefore special arrangements.
6. *Motor cycle insurance*
   - Most policies contain compulsory excesses.
   - Driving by persons other than the insured has to be specially arranged.
   - Insured may under some policies 'drive other cycles' for third party risks subject to the cycle not exceeding a prescribed engine size.
   - Policies are available on a 'rider' basis as an alternative to policies on specific machines.
7. *Contingent liabilities*
   - You need this insurance if:
     (a) your employees use their cars on your business.
     (b) you hire a vehicle with driver even if the vehicle owner has indemnified you under his policy.
   - This insurance is sometimes arranged as a part of a combined liability policy or an extension of a public liability.

MISCELLANEOUS INSURANCES

Introduction

The insurance industry reacts swiftly to the risk management needs of business. New types of contracts and special schemes continually come on to the market. In these circumstances it would be unwise to promise more than an overview of a selection of the schemes and new contracts available.

Legal expenses insurance

This is relatively new and has undergone significant growth in recent times. It is available on a personal or corporate basis. Often legal rights are sacrificed when an individual or firm (particularly a small one) is faced with a more financially capable adversary. Equally, there are many contentious areas of which even the normally law-abiding can fall foul. Typically, a policy pays legal fees and associated expenses incurred by the insured in pursuing or defending legal rights in specified circumstances. Some insurers offer a legal counselling service on matters likely to give rise to a claim. The indemnity varies between £5000 any one event to £500,000 any one year depending on the type of cover. In civil cases the insurer pays the third party's costs if they fall upon the insured. In criminal cases, any fines or prosecution costs are not covered. A hidden cost is the payment of wages to directors or employees while attending a hearing or tribunal. The policy compensates the insured for wages payable in respect of resultant absences from work due to attendances as a defendant or witness. The sections under which cover is generally available are as follows:

(a) *Contract of employment disputes* with the optional extra of cover in respect of the compensation or awards made or agreed in respect of unfair or wrongful dismissal.

(b) *Prosecution defence* cover giving an indemnity for costs of defending criminal proceedings arising under such legislation as the Factories Act, Control of Pollution Act, Health and Safety at Work Act, Trade Descriptions Acts, revenue laws etc. Offences deliberately committed are excluded from the insurance. Cover is available for employers and employees according to the insured's requirements.

(c) *Goods or services contract cover.* All goods and services bought and supplied by the firm are subject to contractual obligations and capable of being the origin of many disputes (eg late delivery, inferior quality). The cover is for costs of fighting or defending claims involving suppliers or customers provided the dispute involves an amount over £200.

(d) *Property legal protection cover* embraces expenses arising where loss or damage to property is caused by a negligent third party (eg loss of power due to severing electricity cables). Also covered is the pursuit of nuisance claims against neighbours.

(e) *Data protection cover* includes appeals to the Data Protection Tribunal, defending proceedings under the Act, and an indemnity for liability to pay compensation to data subjects.

(f) *Inland Revenue investigations and VAT.* Tribunals can impose heavy cost by way of professional fees and expenses for representation at a Commissioner's hearing or a VAT tribunal. Optional extras include lease or tenancy disputes.

Builders and contractors

(a) Under Clause 21.2 JCT Standard Form of Building Contract property developers, despite engaging contractors, may incur liability (Gold *v* Patman & Fotherinham (1958)) for damage to adjoining property on the grounds of nuisance. Developers use the clause to oblige the contractor to arrange an appropriate insurance. The clause is more likely to be invoked when the work is in a Georgian terrace than on an isolated site. The policy, which insures the 'nuisance' perils, covers the liability of the developer and damage to his property subject to fairly large excesses. Negligence of the contractor, being covered under the public liability policy, is excepted.

(b) *Contractors' all risks insurance* protects against physical loss or damage to or the destruction of the works. All materials are covered as well as machinery and plant against loss or damage from any cause except for excluded risks, eg war or radiation. The policy contains liability insurance sections. Where major projects are concerned separate policies are arranged but smaller firms taking on numerous minor contracts may find it more convenient to insure on an annual basis for a fixed sum.

Farmers' combined insurance

Groups in one document most of the insurances needed by a farmer. In addition to the insurances described in the preceding sections insurance is available for theft of produce, horses and cattle. Fatal injury to livestock is also insurable under the policy. It is possible to insure pigs against swine fever, and both pigs and sheep can be insured while being transported to or from market. Other risks relevant to farmers include sheep worrying, foot and mouth disease, specified diseases for all forms of livestock, and crop spraying. Fruit growers can obtain special cover for growing apples and pears against weather damage caused by frost, hail and windstorm.

Computers

Insurance is available to cover loss or damage to: (a) equipment; (b) computer systems records and the cost of their reinstatement; and (c) business interruption in consequence of damage to equipment or computer systems records. There is also a limited market to provide a package insuring against computer fraud, whether perpetrated by employees or third parties, and also legal liability arising from fraud, together with the cost of rewriting or amending the software program after the loss.

Exhibitions and conferences

Packages are available to insure losses arising from cancellation/abandonment/postponement of the event; non-arrival of exhibits; liabilities for failure to vacate. Cover can be arranged on an all-risks basis including transit risks. Legal liability insurance can extend to full contractual liability. Loss or damage to the venue is also a common feature of this type of policy.

Kidnap, ransom, hijack

Insurance may be effected by commercial companies to protect key personnel. The market for this cover is very restricted and made subject to very large excesses.

Licence

Some traders, eg licensed victuallers, may insure against loss through forfeiture of their licence, or failure to obtain renewal through circumstances beyond their control. Block policies are available for breweries and the like with numerous licensed premises. Also at risk of loss through loss of licence etc are those who run gaming clubs and betting shops.

Special schemes for retailers

These include: antique dealers whose policy needs to cover a variety of premises (eg repairers', clients', antique fairs) and transits. Jewellers who, in addition to normal risks, can include fidelity, loss of keys, hold-up insurance, defective title, and transit by parcel or letter post. Special personal accident insurance can also be obtained in view of the risk of assault.

Schemes arranged by, or through, trade associations

Many special schemes involve trade associations and can result in favourable cover for members. Often the association works in conjunction with insurance brokers. A good example is the Bookcover Plan set up by the Booksellers' Association and their brokers. The policy covers five main areas — stock and trade contents, loss of income, loss of money, personal accident, and legal liability. A special feature is the insurance of stock on an 'all risks' basis. The policy operates for stock anywhere in the United Kingdom or on the continent including periods of transit or at customers' or hirers' premises. Cover under all sections is more extensive than that normally available. Premiums are competitive.

Checklist miscellaneous insurances

1. *Legal expenses insurance*
   (a) Do you sacrifice legal rights because you feel legal costs:
   - may outweigh the value of any award?
   - are a barrier to action given the uncertainty of the outcome?
   - are excessive in relation to your financial resources?
   - are a barrier when your adversary is more financially capable of sustaining legal action?

   (b) Businesses are exposed to the risks of disputes, prosecutions, and civil actions and costly legal expenses in defending actions, civil or criminal.
   - These risks may arise from a complex variety of legislation (eg race relations, sex discrimination, industrial relations, health and safety, control of pollution, VAT, data protection etc).
   - They may also arise from trading activities or the occupation of premises.

   (c) Study company proposal forms and brochures for use as a checklist as to the headings under which cover is available. However, consult your broker or adviser when effecting cover.

   (d) Some insurers provide a legal counselling service.

2. *Builders and contractors*
   (a) Your employer may use contract documents to oblige you to effect for his benefit a policy in accordance with Clause 21.2 of the JCT Standard Form of Building Contract.

   (b) Contractors' all risk insurance should be arranged for the contract works.

3. *Farmers*
   (a) Use company proposals etc as a checklist, as some combine as many as 16 sections in one document, but choose your cover and insurer with your adviser or broker.
   (b) Special schemes exist for dairymen, fruit growers, estates, bloodstock, and livestock.

4. *Special schemes*
   (a) Check the availability of special schemes with your trade association. Compare cover offered with that otherwise available.
   (b) Check the *Insurance Buyers Guide* (published annually by Kluwer Publishing Ltd) for a summary of schemes, packages, and unusual risks.

LIFE AND DISABLEMENT INSURANCE

Introduction

The life assurance industry has devised many different kinds of contract to meet the varying needs of individuals and businesses. The industry is divided into two branches — ordinary life assurance and industrial life assurance. The latter involves smaller sums assured with premiums being collected frequently from the home (hence the term 'home service') and is not in any way covered here. Instead attention is directed towards the business world.

Business assurance

(a) Most businesses have an urgent need of the benefits life assurance can bring. A sole trader at, or just beyond, the start-up stage, may have committed the family's capital to generate a future income. Premature death means loss of capital and no stream of income. Also, the business may depend on borrowed funds which a surviving family would find difficult to repay. Third, there is retirement which is covered under *Personnel Management*. In a partnership there is the prospect of the withdrawal of capital on the death or retirement of a partner. A business may be heavily dependent on one or more individuals, 'key men', whose premature death could mean of loss of income and/or extra expense. Subject to exemptions, capital transfer tax is payable when an individual transfers assets on death or gifts them during his lifetime. If no funds are available at the time, a forced sale of the business, possibly on disadvantageous terms, may be necessary to raise the amount due.

Suitably arranged life assurance avoids this situation. Also, firms extending credit may wish to insure the lives of their debtors.

(b) Business people, like others, are exposed to the risks of accidental injury leading to death, loss of limb, loss of sight, permanent or temporary disablement. There are also the risks of disablement from working through sickness or disease which may be temporary or permanent. Policies exist to meet these needs.

Types of ordinary branch life policies available

The following is a summary of policies with a note of the purpose for which they are used. Insurers introduce new contracts all the time, but most are combinations of three basic types: term assurance, whole life, and endowment.

Term assurance
A life policy for a fixed sum for a fixed term. If the individual survives the term, nothing is payable by the assurers, who, having been on risk, retain the premiums. The assurance is not expensive as no survival benefit is payable. It gives a high level of protection at low cost (eg young sole trader who has recently invested his own or borrowed funds in business).

Convertible term assurance
The assured person has the opportunity of converting to different types of term assurance policy (ie one containing an investment element) before expiry regardless of changes in health. This type of policy gives high cover at low cost but as income increases, the assured, eg sole trader above, can, as a result of conversion, use the policy for other purposes, such as repayment of mortgage or finance the replacement of fixed assets. Such policies are useful in terms of estate planning and partnerships giving the partners maximum cover per pound of premium when income is low but leaves scope to provide for retirement matters when the firm can afford it.

Decreasing term assurance
Similar to a term assurance except that the sum payable on death decreases as time goes on. Some may be sold under labels such as Mortgage Protection and Family Income Benefits. A 30-year old may effect a £30,000 policy for 30 years. If death occurs at 40 then, for example, £10,000 is payable. In this example, the sum assured has decreased uniformly throughout the term but that is not always the case, especially with mortgages.

Increasing term assurance

Similar to convertible term but generally for shorter periods (eg five years). In addition to the normal conversion option, the assured has the right to effect further cover without evidence of health and increase the sum assured by, say 50 per cent, if desired. Business owners are never sure of the future especially in the early days of their business. Term assurance of this kind provides flexibility.

Whole life assurance

Pays a sum on death whenever it occurs; it thus becomes a permanent assurance from the time effected. The term of premiums is often fixed so that no further premiums are payable after a certain age, eg 60 or 65, but cover continues. Policies are available with or without profits. The same premium outlay, of course, secures more initial cover for a without profits contract but offers a lower return in the longer term. Such policies are often written under the Married Women's Property Act 1882, the aim of which is to improve the position of married women. Proceeds become payable direct to the beneficiary and avoids waiting for grant of probate; it may provide the funds for payment of capital transfer tax; it prevents the proceeds being claimed by creditors if the deceased died bankrupt. Whole life policies may be converted to endowment with the option sometimes being written into the policy.

Endowment assurance

A policy under which the sum assured is payable on death or upon survival of a given term of years, whichever shall occur first. Policies are with or without profit and carry a substantial investment element. Policies can be used to repay a loan or mortgage, provide a pension or 'nest egg'. Endowment policies build up a surrender value and become suitable as security for loans from banks or the assurers themselves.

Group life assurance

Available to persons who are part of some form of group. Often employers will provide automatic life cover for employees, the sum assured usually being a multiple of the salary. Group life cover is a feature of many pension arrangements.

Other life contracts

These include joint life policies when the sum is payable on the first or last death. Another variation is the contingency (survivorship) assurance with the sum payable only if one party, X, dies before another party, Y. The policies are applied in specialist situations, usually protecting a reversionary interest in property subject to a life interest.

Some additional applications of life assurance

Partners

Life assurance is used to: (a) maintain capital following withdrawal of a deceased partner's capital and/or (b) provide a fund to buy out a deceased or retiring partner's share. A number of different methods are used. For example, effecting joint life policies on the partners' lives or taking out individual policies cross-assigned. With partners of different ages, the younger partner(s) in effecting policies on their own lives obviously pay a lower premium than the older for the same cover. As the younger partners are more likely to benefit some adjustment is frequently necessary. Specialist advice is needed to ensure that money is in the right hands at the right time and that the method chosen is tax efficient.

Key man assurance

A business should identify its 'key men' (or women). The sum assured selected should take account of the short run (ie job not being done or done by consultants etc), the cost of finding a replacement, and allow for the time it will take for the replacement to generate profits to the level of the deceased. Key man insurance is often arranged between 3 and 15 times the salary, but individual circumstances may call for other multiples. In choosing a policy some flexibility is advisable. A variety of plans is offered by assurers and specialist advice is needed. The premiums payable may rank as a business expense but this could lead to the proceeds being taxed as a trading receipt. Again, advice is required.

Share purchase assurance schemes

These schemes enable a group of shareholders to purchase the shares of a deceased shareholder at a price fair to the latter's family. The group can thus continue to run the business without the introduction of new influences. The company itself benefits in terms of minimum disruption. The three main methods are: (a) 'Life of another policies' with each insuring the lives of others for their own benefit; (b) 'Own life' trust policies with each insuring his own life for the benefit of other shareholders; (c) Corporate policies which enable the company to acquire the deceased's shares at the time of death. A variety of policies may be used and the actual choice should provide flexibility given the rapid changes that can occur.

Some miscellaneous features of life assurance

(a) Creditors have insurable interest in the lives of debtors. A creditor can effect a policy on the life of a debtor but often the latter is required to effect the policy and assign it to the creditor.

(b) Female proposers, because of greater longevity, benefit from lower premiums than males of comparable age, all other things being equal.

(c) *Surrender.* If the assured wishes to cease paying the premium under an endowment or whole life policy he may cancel and receive a proportion of the amount that he would have received at maturity or death. Surrender values may be greater than the initial sum assured under 'with profits' contracts if sufficient bonuses have accumulated. Alternatively, the assured may cease to pay the premium but keep the policy in force. On its maturity, he will receive a lower amount than otherwise payable.

(d) 'With profits' policies attract bonuses which, when declared, are added to the basis sum and guaranteed to be payable with the sum assured in due course. Periodically offices value their life funds (accumulated premiums and investments) and declare their surpluses from which the bonuses are found. The amount is not dictated by the value of any particular investments but by the actuary's view of the value of the fund. An alternative is unit-linked life assurance under which the bulk of the premium goes to purchase units in a unit trust. The proceeds payable under the policy fluctuate according to the value of the underlying units but can go no lower than the minimum sum assured. Over a period the value of the units would be expected to increase significantly.

Accident and sickness insurance

Personal accident insurance may be sold alone or with sickness cover; sickness cover is not sold alone. In many cases where personal accident cover or personal accident and sickness is sold, permanent health insurance may have been more appropriate. It is important to know the distinction.

Personal accident cover

Normally gives '24 hours' protection covering accidents at work, at home or leisure etc, unless specifically excluded. Capital sum benefits are available for death by accident, or accident causing loss of limb, sight, or permanent disablement. Weekly benefits are payable for up to two years for temporary total disablement from working. The more hazardous the trade or occupation the higher will be the premium. Exclusions often relate to extra-hazardous activities, eg motor-cycling, mountaineering etc, but can be deleted upon payment of an additional premium. A personal accident and sickness cover adds an additional benefit.

Policies are annual contracts and subject to review by the insurers. Thus, if the insured has a disease that is likely to recur, the insurer can refuse to renew, or renew only if diseases attributable to that cause are excluded. From the insured's point of view, this is the main disadvantage of personal accident and personal accident and sickness policies. The cover could be withdrawn at the moment of greatest need, eg a self-employed person suffering from a disease causing permanent incapacity. Group policies are available for employers to cover employees.

Permanent health insurance

Overcomes the problem of withdrawal or restriction of cover at renewal, as, once effected, it cannot be cancelled or restricted by the insurer. The latter is obliged to accept renewal premiums offered by the insured up to a predetermined age, eg 60 or, say, whenever retirement with pension comes on stream. Once the benefit becomes payable it continues for as long as the disablement persists. The potential cost to the insurer is enormous and consequently underwriting follows the more searching approach of the life assurer than that of the personal accident insurer. Premiums too are higher but useful economies can be made if the insured is willing to accept deferred periods.

Employers may do well to improve the employment package by purchasing cover in this form on a group basis. In approved cases employers may be able to secure tax relief on the premiums. Policies, individual or group, do not normally provide capital sum benefits and the weekly benefit (which may be fixed or variable) is designed to make up the insured's lost income (up to 75 per cent of income received while working).

Checklist: life assurance

1. *Sole traders and partners*
   (a) Life assurance can be purchased through a variety of channels. Before entering into discussion ensure that you have thought carefully about your own needs so that you are not vulnerable to biased sales talk.
   (b) Select your intermediary or broker with care. It does not necessarily follow that your motor insurance broker is a good life broker.
   (c) Determine your own priorities — high protection or good investment — but look for flexibility.
   (d) In selecting an investment policy, find out about the

assurers' track record (journals such as *The Economist, Planned Savings, Money Management* and *Which?* should be consulted).

(e) In fixing sums assured, take account of inflation and future changes in responsibilities and/or income levels.

(f) How old will you be when your policies expire? What are your expected life assurance needs at that age?

(g) Consider the uses of life assurance in terms of mortgage repayment (including the low cost method), repayment of loans, as security for loans for those policies having a surrender value, and funding the payment of capital transfer tax.

(h) No tax relief is allowable on premiums for policies effected since 13 March 1984. The policy proceeds should emerge as a tax-free sum, but if cashed in during the first 10 years are likely to be subject to tax.

(i) Special terms are available for non-smokers and members of some professional associations.

(j) After completing a proposal form (single premium policies excepted), you have the right to change your mind (there is a 10-day cooling-off period). The assurer will inform you of the procedure.

(k) People who insure with non-authorized assurers are not protected by the Policyholders Protection Act.

2. *Matters for partners only*

(l) Ensure that your partnership assurance:

- Places money in the right hands at the right time.
- Is tax efficient.
- Is flexible.

3. *All employers*

(m) Key men are business assets. Carefully consider the effect on the business of the premature death of key men.

(n) Consider how life assurance can be used to improve the fringe benefits of the employment package. Group life assurance may be bought separately or as part of a pension plan.

(o) Life assurance may provide funds for the payment of capital transfer tax and for the purchase of shares of a deceased shareholder.

Checklist: personal accident and sickness insurances

1. Three types of insurance are available — personal accident, personal accident and sickness, and permanent health insurance. Ensure that you understand the difference.
2. Personal accident cover carries exclusions. Check them carefully as in many cases they can be deleted if they relate to risks that you run.
3. Permanent health insurance is cheaper the longer the deferred period selected. The risk of short periods of disablement can often be assumed and the policy used to guard against the more serious risk of long-term disablement. This may be more sensible than a personal accident and sickness insurance that pays an immediate benefit. Compare premiums and benefits with your own needs.

14

EXPANSION, MERGERS AND ACQUISITIONS

Annabel C Beerel

INTRODUCTION

Nearly all businesses that survive in the medium to longer term are faced with the stresses and strains of expansion and/or merger and acquisition activities. It is commonly held that big is beautiful, or big is successful. Consequently, most companies, whatever their present size, strive to grow as fast as they can.

The past two to three years have seen the merger and acquisition season in its most frenetic and buoyant mood. The number and value of acquisitions and mergers during the period have surpassed previous records.

The environment has been characterized, among other factors, by:

- the pursuit of growth;
- rationalization of sectors served by corporate entities, ie a move away from conglomeration;
- innovation in bids, counter-bids and bid defensive techniques;
- large premiums being paid over the net value of the target company;
- vast advertising expenditure to entice shareholders either to sell or hold on to their shares.

The motives for acquiring or merging target companies are legion. The primary motivations will be discussed later.

Research into the recent merger and acquisition activity has indicated that the main beneficiaries are the shareholders of the target company and not the acquiring company. This means that the acquirers have been tempted to overpay the offerees for their shares amounts which, in the short to medium term, they have been unable to recoup. Evaluating whether they would have done better or worse without making their move is always a very difficult question on which to obtain an economically objective answer. Suffice it to say that prudent evaluation of the projected returns of mergers and acquisitions, especially to the acquirer company, is essential. Like any marriage, it is relatively easy to enter into but the exit ramifications have an intensified whirlpool effect. One needs to establish, therefore, whether a high probability of success for the future marriage exists.

The number of small, private company mergers far exceed those of the large listed companies. Historically, the vast majority of mergers and acquisitions involve amounts less than £1 million in total settlement costs. The mega-acquisitions and mergers that hit the headlines are the exception rather than the rule. This book is aimed at the small to medium-sized business and the merger and acquisition opportunities open to them. We shall emphasize the implications for these targeted businesses rather than the recent exotic performances of the large corporate conglomerates.

DEFINITIONS

Expansion is the term commonly used to indicate growth which is generated by the income-producing capacity of the company. Growth might mean an increase in product range, markets served or customer base, and is reflected by quantum leaps in the net asset value of the company without its having merged or acquired other businesses.

On the other hand, mergers and acquisitions are a method of *externally* generated expansion.

The terms merger and acquisition are often used interchangeably whereas they are not in fact entirely synonymous.

A merger occurs where two (or more) companies combine their net assets under common management and common ownership in pursuit of their business objectives. Usually a single company is formed to hold the combined interests, the owners of which are the original holders of most of the ownership interests in the constituent companies.

An acquisition (takeover) occurs where one company, or group of companies, takes over the shares or assets of another company or group of companies. A significant part of the ownership interests in the acquired company is eliminated, ie new management exerts control over the newly combined entities.

There are essentially three types of acquisition namely:

- *Horizontal,* the combination of similar businesses with similar products and/or markets and usually motivated by the need to capture market share or to benefit from economies of scale.
- *Vertical,* the combination of businesses which operate at different stages of the production/marketing process. For example, a retail store acquiring one of the factories manufacturing the clothes that it retails, or purchasing fruit and vegetable farms in order to secure sources of supply for its fresh food outlets.
- *Conglomerate.* A conglomerate is a group of companies whose products and/or markets can be considered unrelated. For example, a group of companies which includes tobacco interests, hotels, leisure and spa resorts, as well as retail shops.

The past decade has seen a move away from the formation of large conglomerates with investments in highly diversified interests. There are essentially two reasons for this. First, it is currently held, and some researchers believe adequately proved, that management achieves better results by concentrating on those businesses that it knows and understands.

By endeavouring to manage a variety of businesses, not only are management's efforts dissipated but insufficient time is left to focus on those businesses which they understand best — a state of affairs which leads to poor performance all round.

The second reason often cited against conglomerates is the possible conflict of interest between shareholders and management, especially when these are different parties. It is argued that shareholders can diversify their interests and thus spread their risk by holding shares in different companies with different business interests. They would be better off doing this than holding all their shares in one group of companies made up of multifarious unrelated business. On the other hand, managers might wish to spread their risk by involving themselves in several different types of business. After all, if they manage only one type of business, and the economy does not bolster its performance, management might be out on its ear! Management might thus hedge its chances — a move not necessarily in the best interests of the shareholders.

EXPANSION

Expansion would appear to be regarded as a necessary business virtue. Stagnation or even diminution of a business, on whatever basis it is measured, usually attracts depreciatory comments or reviews. It stands to reason that while most if not all firms strive to expand, some will not achieve it and will either be swallowed or wound up.

Motivation to expand

Expansion is the evidence of increased sales, profits, capital, assets, employees, market share or a combination of these. A psychological factor which, it is postulated, is inherent in the drive for expansion is the desire for power, the need to control one's own environment, and a spirit of independence. These traits are held to be most evident in the small and medium-sized businesses where managers and shareholders are most often one and the same group.

The need for expansion

Why do organizations need to expand? The pursuit for growth could be:

- to achieve a higher market share and possibly more customer loyalty
- to achieve economies of scale and thus reduce unit costs
- to hinder market entry by competitors via control of the market
- to enhance bargaining power with suppliers
- to attain break-even levels as quickly as possible
- to reduce distribution unit costs
- to improve returns on capital/investment.

There are many reasons why organizations might need to grow beyond merely the requirement or satisfaction of being big. Some might argue that large, geographically spread, widely diversified businesses have a better opportunity of minimizing risks than the smaller, more contained organization. Evidence would suggest that this does not always hold true.

Financing expansion

Fast-expanding businesses gobble up cash. Many a profitable business has overtraded resulting in a critical liquidity squeeze which has precipitated corporate failure. Growth plans should naturally form part of business planning and along with it the required finance should be projected. Internally generated finance will usually be profits and possibly the sale of unwanted assets; for example, the sale and leaseback of factory property or premises. External finance could be provided by a range of sources in differing forms. (See Chapter 2.)

Finance for growth is essentially needed for increased working capital, and investment in plant and technology in order to provide increased capacity and efficiency.

Internal or external growth

Whether to pursue growth by developing it within the organization or by following the merger or acquisition route (the external growth path) depends on each firm's circumstances. The external route may prove faster and more efficient; however, combining two or more organizations is sure to create that much more risk. If the returns exceed the related risks, merging or acquiring might be the optimal alternative.

MERGERS AND ACQUISITIONS

The motivation to merge or acquire

The motivation underlying a potential merger or acquisition is one of the critical factors that will precipitate its success or failure. It has equal relevance to the small and medium-sized growing business as to the larger more established one. Some of the most profitable businesses can be traced to small enterprises whose growth was judiciously managed by astute mergers and acquisitions in the early years.

Mergers and/or acquisitions should form part of a company's overall, predetermined business strategy. Naturally, the timing and exact profile of the target company will vary from plan according to the market conditions prevailing at the time of execution. The acquisition policy and criteria should form an inherent part of the strategic (or corporate) plan which each company has, albeit in the managing director's head.

Smaller companies may not have as structured a planning procedure as the larger, more formalized organizations. It is essential, however, that mergers and acquisitions form part of the development of the company and are executed in an ordered, pre-planned fashion rather than in a random, haphazard manner.

Figure 14.1 shows how the mergers and acquisitions process can be viewed.

Business objectives

These are the main objectives on which all the efforts of the business enterprise should be ultimately focused. These objectives should be clarified in the annual financial statements (or in the management accounts for smaller businesses) and should be sanctioned by the shareholders. Management, which has stewardship of the company assets, is obliged to employ those assets in the most effective manner possible so as to achieve the predetermined business objectives. Part of defining the objectives is setting out: products and markets in which the

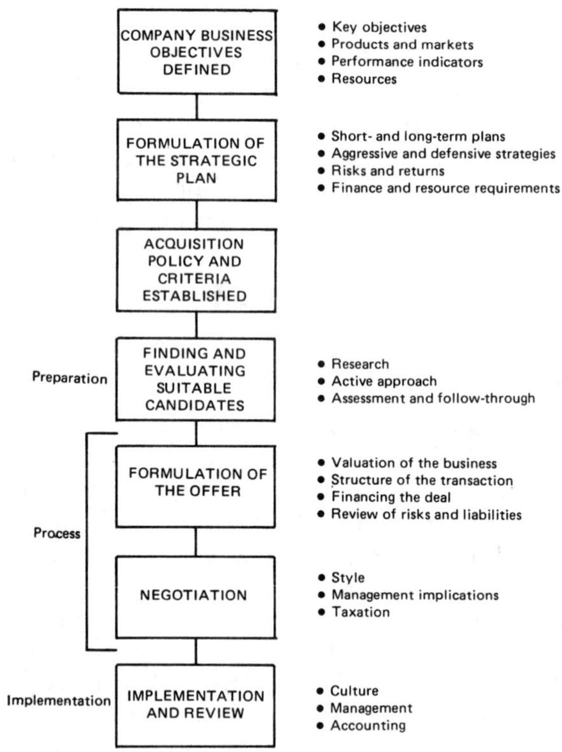

Figure 14.1 *The merger/acquisition process*

company will participate; key performance indicators which will reflect the success or otherwise of achieving objectives; and the resources required, the resources available and the resource gap.

The strategic plan

The strategic plan sets out the various alternatives available to achieve the business objectives. Although the plan might be a formal document it should remain sufficiently flexible to be realistic without continuous alteration. The plan should set out:

1. Short- and long-term potential strategies;
2. Aggressive as opposed to defensive strategies and what the implications could be;
3. The likely *risks* and *returns* associated with the alternatives;
4. How the resource gap will be addressed;
5. The financial requirements in both the short and long term.

A strategic plan might highlight that an acquisition could provide the most cost-effective method of achieving a market share objective, for example. It is important to identify the risks and returns associated with strategic alternatives so as to ensure that all aspects are thought through.

Acquisition policy and criteria

Usually a company establishes some kind of acquisition policy which is formally or informally expressed. For example, acquisitions should only be made of related businesses, or all acquisitions should be for a 100 per cent shareholding.

Acquisition criteria which stem from the basic acquisition policy could include: the type and size of the business; its location, state of technology and management; the size of investment, returns and payback period; and, the risks involved. Acquisition criteria provide a benchmark against which to evaluate and compare potential target companies.

It is unlikely that any company will meet all the criteria but a comparison of risks and possible returns should highlight the more attractive alternatives.

Reasons for mergers or takeovers

Many reasons are cited for following the merger/acquisition trail. In practice the primary motivation is not always a rational, commercial one, but an emotional reason is often rationalized as having a commercial purpose.

Commercial reasons for mergers

- Achieve economies of scale
- Transfer resources to more capable management
- Reduce competition
- Exploit overseas markets from a stronger base
- Optimize distribution channels
- Share research and development expenditure.

Commercial reasons for acquisitions

Production

- Increase capacity
- Achieve economies of scale
- Acquire technical skills
- Achieve stronger purchasing power
- Secure sources of supply.

Marketing

- Expand the product range
- Have access to new customer bases
- Attain patent rights or access to licensing agreements
- Build market share
- Optimize use of distribution networks
- Reach new markets in new locations
- Raise the barriers to new market entrants.

Financial

- Acquire cash-generating businesses
- Acquire undervalued businesses and generate cash by asset-stripping
- Obtain tax advantages
- Reduce the average cost of capital of the combined group.

Other

- Putting off a potential bidder of one's own organization
- Buying management skills
- Diversification
- Exploiting a stock market opportunity, eg reverse takeover.

Implications

The implications or consequences of a merger/acquisition are many. The decision is not a light one and must be taken seriously: in thinking through the detailed implications and preparing for implementation should the bid be successful, use of the appropriate professional advisers is essential.

In broad terms the consequences are likely to impinge on:

People
- Changes in management
- Cultural issues
- Changes in work groups
- Trade union issues
- Changes in reporting structure
- Rewards and performance recognition procedures.

Systems
- New/different systems
- Different reports and controls
- Change in technology.

Finance and accounting
- Different financial structure
- Change in shareholder demands
- Different taxation implications
- Accounting policies
- Pension commitments
- Capital expenditure demands.

Other
- Premises-related issues
- Technology
- Public relations.

The consequences of a merger/acquisition will be unique to each business. Too often these are not considered in detail in advance of the execution of the deal and thus cause unnecessary costs and aggravation at execution.

The regulatory framework

A vast regulatory framework surrounds the area of acquisitions and mergers. This has increased as the tide of merger activity has risen and innovative management keep moving the game to new playing fields.

The management of all organizations that plan to become, or who are already involved in merger activity, are advised to consult appropriate experts on the regulations that might impinge on their activities.

In this chapter the key aspects only will be discussed in general terms. For more detailed discussion you are referred to the further reading in Chapter 16.

The Monopolies and Mergers Commission

Under the Fair Trading Act 1973, mergers may be referred to the Monopolies and Mergers Commission (MMC) for investigation:

- Where the merger creates or adds to a market share of 25 per cent or more; or
- if the value of the assets taken over exceeds £30 million.

The Commission is essentially there to establish whether two or more enterprises cease to be distinct in nature and whether the future operations of the combined entity will be against the public interest.

Usually officials of the Office of Fair Trading will hear about mergers as a result of notification by the parties themselves, the press, or from interested groups who are against the deal being concluded.

If the Commission believes that, as a result of its investigations, the merger is against the public interest, the Secretary of State may:

1. Prevent a merger, or require divestment if it has already occurred;
2. Allow it, possibly subject to certain conditions or undertakings about future behaviour.

In determining whether any merger is likely to operate against the public interest the MMC will enquire into matters on a confidential basis.

The MMC, in reviewing the nature of the transaction, is desirous of maintaining and promoting:

(a) Effective competition between suppliers;

(b) the interests of consumers in respect of:
- prices
- quality
- differentiation
- information
- accessibility.

(c) The reduction of costs, the use of new techniques, product development, and the facilitating of entry of new competitors into markets;

(d) The balanced distribution of industry and employment in the UK;

(e) Competitive activity by UK suppliers in markets outside the UK.

The implications of an MMC referral by public listed companies wishing to merge or take over are complicated by the requirements of the City Code. Both legal and accounting experts can be very helpful in guiding management through this potential minefield.

Merger by scheme of arrangement
Where a significant number of shareholders are involved, a merger is often effected by a 'scheme of arrangement' under Sections 425 to 427 of the Companies Act 1985 with the approval of the court. Refer to the Companies Act 1985 and the Third EEC Company Law Directive.)

Stock Exchange requirements
The Stock Exchange 'Yellow Book' requires those operating under its control to comply with the 'City Code on Takeovers and Mergers' (the Code). This is separately administered by the Panel on Takeovers and Mergers.

The Companies Act 1985
The Companies Act has several sections which will affect merger and acquisition activities of incorporated companies. Aspects to be considered are:

Articles of Association
Meetings and resolutions
Capital and reserves
Accounting policies
Annual financial statement disclosure
Rights of minorities
General disclosure and conduct
Financial assistance to purchase shares
Allotment of shares.

EEC law
The EEC legislation is having increasing impact, bolstered by its programme of harmonization of company law, management structures and employee protection.

Preparation for merger or acquisition

Finding suitable candidates
The successful pursuit of organizations with which to merge or acquire demands:

- Vision
- Commercial judgement (prudence)
- Understanding of human factors
- Tenacity.

Finding a suitable company that meets a substantial part if not all of the acquisition criteria is usually not a simple task. The majority of transactions originate from direct approaches by either a buyer or a seller who has knowledge acquired as a result of detailed research or existing commercial relationships.

We have discussed some of the motives for buying. In seeking a target company it is worth putting the shoe on the other foot and considering why a business might be for sale:

- People who have founded a business may want to capitalize on its success by retiring or diversifying their risk by accepting cash or shares in a larger concern;
- Management problems, eg no suitable successors;
- A need for cash injection;
- In order to put off an unwanted bidder companies sometimes come to an agreement with a third party (white knight);
- Poor management combined with militant trade unions results in uncompetitive organizations. New owners can often impose new management and arrange new agreements with the labour force;
- Existing management and shareholders do not see eye to eye;
- Industry fragmentation where only larger, combined groups with larger market shares can be profitable in the longer term;
- Taxation implications.

Identifying acquisition candidates

The method of identifying potential candidates can be viewed as a 'passive' or 'active' approach.

Passive approach includes:

- Alerting advisers (eg lawyers, accountants, bankers) to the acquisition strategy and criteria in the hope that they might have suitable clients or contacts;
- Carrying out industry and market desk research;
- Approaching merger and acquisition brokers who specialize in finding and matching buyers and sellers. They also assist in financial analysis, pricing and negotiation. Although they may speed up the process they are not cheap.

The passive approach is usually the cheaper method and can produce equally good results.

Active approach. This involves a fair amount of extra work on the part of the acquirer but is likely to achieve an optimum result in a shorter time. Dedicated resources are required to carry out the merger or acquisition search in an optional amount of time and to give it the necessary focus. This method includes:

- Primary research, ie interviewing people in relevant trades or industries;
- Desk or secondary research;
- Discussions with advisers;
- Trade and/or credit agencies might be approached, eg Dun & Bradstreet;
- Company searches can be carried out at Companies House;
- Merger and acquisition brokers might be approached;
- Review of the press, magazines and other media will highlight general and specific achievements of both public and private businesses.

A range of potential candidates having been identified and general information obtained, a dossier might be opened on those companies on which further research and follow-up would seem appropriate.

Details of:

- Products and services
- Markets and customers' assets
- Assets
- Geographical areas of operation and distribution
- Organizational strengths and weaknesses

are likely to be collected.

Information relating to the predefined acquisition criteria should also be collected so that comparisons between companies can be made based on accurate data.

Assessment and follow-through

The amount of information that the acquirer will have been able to gain about his potential candidates will vary greatly. This will depend on whether they

- are public or private companies;
- are regularly in the media for any one or a host of reasons;
- operate in obscure markets or locations;
- are part of a larger group;
- have a wide as opposed to a narrow shareholders' base;
- are themselves assertive or defensive in the market-place.

The assessment procedure should cover questions such as:

- The target company's strengths and weaknesses

- Details of the existing management
- Who should manage the new business; whether existing management should be retained;
- Which business objective and corporate strategy acquiring this business will satisfy;
- What actually is being purchased, eg:
  - assets
  - growing profits
  - market share
  - customer base
  - patents;
- How much cash the target company will generate or absorb, in the short and long term;
- Could there be unrecorded liabilities and if so what, eg warranty agreements or product liability claims?
- What could or should be the feature of the negotiations?
- How much you should pay;
- How you should pay, bearing in mind the future involvement of present management and their motivation for selling;
- What increased cost could the acquirer company incur over and above the purchase price?
  - implementation costs
  - the purchase price, eg:
  - costs of redundancy
  - dislocation costs
  - costs of standardization
  - retraining expenditure;
- A list of further information required.

The working checklist on pages 461–464 should be helpful in developing a detailed merger and acquisition proposal.

At the end of the day no matter how much objective information and how many statistics have been called in support of the proposal, qualitative factors and subjective judgement will always play a major part. In order to minimize the effect of this one might rank the acquisition criteria and the respective information of each company against them. A weighted score of each alternative should automatically reveal the best fit. Although this can be helpful, few businessmen will allow statistical ranking scores to take precedence over experience and intuition.

Based on a combination of subjective and objective information a short list of prime targets can be developed. One of the candidates is likely to be considered the best alternative. At this point a direct approach is likely to be appropriate. The method of contact is important as this will set the tone for the rest of the process and the deal-clinching or deal-aborting negotiations. It is advisable to approach the right person, possibly by telephone and to get some feel for his response. Follow-up discussions and exchange of letters can then proceed without prejudice to either side.

Should the management and/or shareholders reject any approach outright, the acquirer needs to consider very carefully whether his own organization and its management team can sustain and win a hostile takeover situation. The amount of time, effort and cost will be greatly increased. If the target company is privately held a non-breakthrough situation could exist.

Shares are likely to be fairly tightly held and often managers are the major shareholders. Also, it will be more difficult, if not impossible, to get more information about the company, as private companies have only to file limited information for public consumption. On the other hand, if management of a public company rejects the approach both companies could be drawn into a highly expensive slanging match from which, it can be argued, only the advisers and advertising agencies really benefit. The path followed will ultimately depend on the importance of merging with or taking over the identified target.

Once a suitable candidate, who is prepared to consider a sale, has been found there is usually an exchange of information and assurances. There will be the completion of the list of outstanding information as well as the verification of the important items necessary to provide sufficient comfort so that negotiation proceedings can begin. It is accepted practice that an offer is conditional upon an investigation of crucial areas to be carried out by relevant independent experts or teams set up by the purchaser. Areas on which comfort might be sought could be:

1. Production capacity and efficiency of manpower utilization.
2. Quality of products or services
3. Various financial aspects, eg: projections; reliability of information; value of stock; and, cash forecasts
4. Market analysis
5. Competence and quality of management.

The preliminary assessment of the acquisition candidate should have highlighted some of the areas which warranted detailed independent investigation.

Checklist for developing a merger/acquisition proposal

1. How does the merger/acquisition add to the overall business objectives?

2. Describe how the merger/acquisition fits into the overall strategic plan.
3. Describe the alternatives available with respect to a merger or acquisition in both quantitative and qualitative terms, eg own expansion.
4. Set out briefly the profile of the potential candidates which could fit into the organization's acquisition policy:
   — type of business
   — size of business
   — special features of the business, eg markets, customers, suppliers
   — management staff and strength of the business
   — history of the business (quantitative and qualitative terms)
   — details of asset backing
   — description of the cash generating ability.
5. Set out a summary of the weighting of the alternatives and the conclusion which has been reached. Highlight the best fit candidate.
6. Set out the strengths, weaknesses, opportunities and threats of that candidate.
7. Profile of candidate:
   — group/company legal structure
   — description of main types of business
   — management and organizational structure
   — profit summary — last five years
   — identify major sources of profit/loss
   — balance sheets
   — details of latest audited group/company balance sheet
   — cash flows
   — details of latest source and application of funds and/or management accounts cash flows
   — group/company prospects
   — three years' projections of profits, cash flows and balance sheets.
8. History and business of candidate:
   — brief history
   — details of net assets and profits
   — description of business including location of premises and the operations conducted therefrom
   — employee details
   — details of any associated companies
   — share capital — details
   — description of borrowing powers

- — details of legislation peculiar to the particular industry, if any
- — product range
- — sources of supply and purchasing procedures
- — production processes and methods
- — warehousing methods
- — marketing policy
- — distribution policy
- — royalty agreements and licences
- — research and development plans in both quantitative and qualitative terms.

9. Management:
   - — directors' and senior executives' qualifications, experience, salaries and benefits
   - — Memorandum and Articles in relation to directors' powers and interests
   - — management structure and reporting procedures
   - — assessment of key individuals
   - — succession plans
   - — deployment of employees
   - — details of training programmes
   - — details of pension arrangements.
10. Financial systems and control:
    - — details of accounting systems
    - — details of management reporting procedures.
11. Accounting policies:
    - — list of key accounting policies which affect major items of income determination and asset valuation.
12. Comment on past trading results and future projections:
    - — unusual exceptional items
    - — trends in turnover
    - — trends in gross profit
    - — trends in selling and administration
    - — taxation
    - — earnings per share trends
    - — dividends policy
    - — gearing effects
    - — comparisons with other businesses in the same industry
    - — key ratios.
13. Prospects:
    - — consider the objectives of management
    - — detailed profit forecasts
    - — detailed cash forecasts

- detailed balance sheet forecasts, with particular reference to the asset quality and mix
- review with great care the assumptions upon which all forecasts are based.

14. Miscellaneous issues:
    - insurance
    - legislation and government codes
    - memorandum and articles
    - patent and trade marks
    - royalties
    - capital commitments
    - contingent liabilities
15. Ensure the listing of all assumptions and aspects of the business that you consider to be outstanding, unanswered or ambiguous.
16. Summary, conclusions and recommendations.

Regulatory framework

Fair Trading Act 1973 — Monopolies and Mergers Commission
Industry Act 1975 — Relates to important manufacturing undertakings
EEC Law
Competition Act 1980
US and UK anti-trust laws
The Stock Exchange Rules and Regulations
Companies Act 1985

The process

The process of formulating the offer and then negotiating can be the most time-consuming part of the deal. Thorough preparation as well as careful consideration of the alternatives and the role played by the human element should minimize undue inefficiencies or complications at this stage. In order for the deal to be a success *both* parties must believe that they have gained and not that one party is better off at the expense of the other.

The price, the manner in which it is settled, and the style of negotiation, will be influenced by the seller's motivation for agreeing to the merger or takeover. Failure to recognize the underlying dynamics could jeopardize successful negotiation.

The price
Arriving at a value for a going concern is a very arbitrary process. A roomful of advisers is likely to arrive at a range of different values based

on different assumptions and different perceptions of what is basically being valued; not to mention how the seller's and buyer's views might differ. Value is thus a highly subjective concept and can best be expressed as a range within which *one price* must be struck, which will satisfy both the buyer's and the seller's expectations. It is important that the buyer establishes an upper and a lower price limit based on his valuation of the business.

Lower limit. This is the investment or market value of the business as it currently stands.
Upper limit. This is the market value of the business less costs plus synergistic benefits of being combined with the acquirer.

It is between these two limits that the buyer will endeavour to negotiate his price. Once he starts negotiating beyond his upper limit emotions would seem to have taken over as he is prepared to pay more than the investment's apparent worth.

Methods of valuation

The methods used for valuation will largely depend on whether the target company is:

1. A public company which is listed on a stock exchange
2. A private company
3. A sole trader or partnership.

Listed company. If a company is quoted on a stock exchange it is obvious that the consideration offered by the purchaser must exceed the current quoted price to induce shareholders to part with their shares. Once the market gets a whiff of an acquisitive company seeking to take over quoted shares the share price inevitably rises. The purchaser can thus find himself chasing an upward spiral of share prices until sufficient shares are secured to render the offer unconditional. Research has revealed that, typically, the share price of an undefended bid can go up by 30 per cent and a defended bid as high as 60 to 90 per cent.

Listed companies are thus usually valued based on:

- Current market price
- Net present value of projected further earnings (NPV method)
- Basis of asset backing, ie value of net assets less goodwill, intangibles, borrowings, tax liabilities and minority interests.

Unlisted company. These are usually valued on either an earnings basis or a net asset value basis. *Earnings basis* includes:

- *Price earnings multiple.* Applying a P/E ratio of a comparable quoted company to the projected average future earnings of the company (a weighted average over, say, five years).

- *Net present value.* This is calculating the net present value of future cash earnings over a period (usually 10 years with a terminal value) by applying a discount rate which management believe includes the time value of money and a perceived risk factor. This is also known as the *discounted cash flow* method and is considered to be the most sound.
- *Dividend yield.* This method is rarely used and then only if it applies to the purchase of a minority holding. The method is used to calculate the net present value of future dividends which might be earned by a minority shareholder based on future earnings, market value and dividend payout assumptions.

Net asset value basis includes any one or a combination of the following:

- Book value of net assets
- Replacement value
- Realisable value
- Economic value, ie the cash generating ability of the net assets.

The method used will depend very much on the state of the company, its asset rise and its future prospects. A review of asset backing might reveal surplus assets which can be sold off without impairing the operating performance of the business. The market value of such surplus assets should be added to the earnings based evaluation.

Sole traders and partnerships. As for unquoted companies, there is no yardstick for arriving at a market value. The same valuation methods are typically used as for unquoted companies. In establishing the true earnings potential care must be taken to adjust for any allowances in the accounts so that figures reflect the true economic value. For example:

- The proprietor might not take a market-related salary;
- The proprietor might own the business property and charge an uneconomical rent;
- Accounting policies might not be sufficiently prudent, eg depreciation.

Whatever method the acquirer applies it is essential that he has some bench-mark return that he requires the potential acquisition to satisfy. This will be influenced by the returns achieved on current operations as well as what could be received on comparable investments. Added to this an evaluation of the asset backing will influence the returns required and the risk. If the assets have quality this will reduce the risk and hence the required rate of return (discount rate or IRR, depending on how the present value cash flows are approached).

Factors influencing valuation

The following factors affect the valuation of a business:

- The marketability of its shares
- The size of the valuation, ie majority versus minority
- The industry sector
- The quality of the assets (asset backing)
- The target company's market share in its major product markets customer/client goodwill.

Figure 14.2 gives an example of financial analysis for the purchase of 100 per cent of the interests in a takeover target.

Figure 14.2. *Financial analysis of 100 per cent acquisition*

A. *Investment*
Purchase price (cash + market value of shares issued)
+ Capital required for immediate investment
– Expected net proceeds of selling surplus assets

B. *Estimated annual cash inflows*
(Year by year for n years)
Present profit before tax on operations retained
+ Synergistic benefits (less costs)
+ Profits (less losses) from new investments
– Profit before tax
– Tax = Profit after tax
+ Depreciation
= Internal cash flow
– Investments in fixed assets and working capital (a) to maintain earnings, and (b) for growth
= Net cash to be generated from acquired company

C. *Terminal value*
Profit after tax (in year n) × the selected discount rate.

D. *Internal rate of return*
Equates (B) annual cash inflows + (C) terminal value to (A) investment.

E. *Maximum purchase price*
Estimated net cash generated + terminal value, both discounted at the *required* rate of return – adjusted for immediate (i) new capital required, less (ii) proceeds from sale of surplus assets.

Structure of the offer
Most small business acquisitions involve a direct contract between the purchaser and the selling shareholders.

Assets or shares? The question of whether shares or assets should be acquired will largely depend on whether the purchaser is negotiating with one (or a few) or with numerous, widespread shareholders.

Factors to be considered are:

Purchase of shares

1. Where the purchaser intends purchasing the entire business and he is satisfied that no large uncertain liabilities exist a share transfer would seem appropriate.
2. The purchaser of shares will not obtain any tax relief on the consideration paid. Asset purchases will, however, qualify for tax relief on those assets purchased which are subject to capital allowances.

   The vendor of shares will suffer tax at capital gains tax rates on any capital gain realized. If the vendor sells assets he may pay:
   - initial tax on the sales of his trading stock
   - possible capital gains on the sale of other assets
   - a further tax charge on the distribution of the company's profits to him by way of dividend.
3. A purchaser buying shares automatically inherits the employees of the vendor company. This will apply if he purchases the business as a going concern but not if he purchases specific assets.
4. If the business to be acquired has major long-term contracts or licences which are critical to the future of the business, by purchasing the shares the purchaser can ensure continuation. By purchasing certain assets only contracts will normally have to be renewed with the supplier or licensor.
5. Stamp duty implications are complex and need to be considered.

Purchase of assets

1. The purchaser can purchase those distinct assets which he requires and leave the liabilities to the vendor.
2. Often the most significant asset of the business is goodwill. There is no precise definition of goodwill but it is evidenced in loyalty by customers, good credit standing, outstanding order books and the like. Non-completion clauses in the sale agreement can prevent the vendor from setting up a similar business around the corner and thus eroding any goodwill transferred to the purchaser.
3. The assets to be purchased must be carefully identified, legal

ownership established and valued. These aspects may form part of the accountants pre-acquisition investigation.

The pros and cons of the purchase or sale of shares versus assets depends on the unique circumstance of each business. Again, you are advised to seek expert help in working through all the issues.

Paying for the acquisition. Consideration for an acquisition or merger can be in the form of cash, shares, loan stock (which can be convertible) or a combination of these.

The method adopted is usually affected by:

- Market conditions
- Current trends
- The apparent cost to the acquirer
- The purchaser's own financial gearing
- His cash resources
- The tax position of both parties.

Cash. This is the simplest and usually the most acceptable form of purchase consideration. This will affect the vendor's tax liability.

Loan stock. From the purchaser's point of view the advantage of loan stock (typically debentures) financing is that his earnings per share are likely to be improved (as long as the profits from the acquisition more than cover the interest payments on the debt). Vendor shareholders often view loan stocks as an attractive alternative especially if conversion rights are attached. There is also an opportunity to defer capital gains tax under certain circumstances. Loan stocks are either secured on specific assets or unsecured.

Shares. This is a popular form of payment, especially for a listed company when the market is booming. Shareholders in the acquiring company might not be happy with this arrangement as their shareholdings could be diluted by an issue of new shares. The Companies Act 1985 as well as the City Code imposes several constraints with respect to a share offer.

In offering his own shares the purchaser is also required to substantiate the value of his shares. This particularly affects private companies and could further complicate the negotiation procedure with the vendor.

Timing of the payment. This will vary depending on whether public or private companies are involved. For public companies there is usually little scope for deferral of the consideration to be paid. In the case of private companies all kinds of arrangements can be entered into subject to the receipt of sufficient comfort by the acquirer, arranging of warranties and indemnities, as well as the delivery of assets where appropriate. If existing management in the vendor company stays on, put-options are sometimes granted in order to encourage performance and effectively defer part of the payment for future earnings.

Financial implications

The proposed structure of the deal and the method of payment obviously have a direct impact on the financing capability of the acquirer and on the group structure once the deal is executed.

The acquirer needs to consider:

- His organization's resources and accessibility to acceptable sources of funding
- The impact on the debt: equity structure (gearing) of the present group and on the combined group
- Whether a vendor placing can be organized.

The acquirer needs to ensure that the financing of the purchase will not put such strains on the business that implementation of the deal will be constrained by insufficient resources. Having carried out his homework, the acquirer should also be reasonably certain that the after-tax returns of the combined group exceed the after-tax cost of funding. Detailed cash flow analysis is a prerequisite for carefully reviewing the financial implications and for showing lenders and investors that financing will be under control.

Accounting and tax aspects

Accounting

The nature of the consideration paid and the size of the equity investment will affect how the new group will account for the acquisition.

An investment can be categorized as:

1. An *investment* — this is typically a shareholding of less than 20 per cent.
2. An *associated company* — this is a company in which there is an investment of at least 20 per cent and up to 50 per cent, where the company does not qualify as a subsidiary.
3. A *subsidiary* is a company that is controlled by another, either by virtue of a holding greater than 50 per cent or where the holding company controls the board of directors.

The Companies Act 1985 and the published statements on generally accepted accounting practice prescribe the accepted alternatives for both merger and acquisition accounting. Merger accounting in particular has been the subject of a great deal of debate and the accounting experts can probably best advise on this.

The two key areas that require attention in accounting treatment are:

- Goodwill arising on the acquisition;
- Pre-acquisition profits earned by a subsidiary.

The implications of these should be thought through when the offer is being structured.

Taxation

The sphere of tax implications with respect to acquisitions and mergers is large and beyond the scope of this book. The purchaser and vendor are likely to have different tax profiles which will often materially influence their perception of the benefit of the deal.

As highlighted under the *Structure of the offer* (page 468), whether shares or business assets are sold will have a material affect on tax planning.

Your accountant should be continually on the alert for tax opportunities and pitfalls throughout the process and you are advised to rely on his expert advice.

Negotiation

By the time formal negotiation is entered into each party will have a reasonably good idea of the other's stance. Both buyer and seller will usually have in mind a range of acceptable prices around which they will bargain.

During the negotiation stages, the ranges often change. However, in principle, if they overlap or are close to overlapping then a deal should be possible. Every negotiation is different but there are a few general rules:

1. The fewer people involved in negotiating the better.
2. Advisers can be used with great effect to explore the other side's position.
3. Be well prepared.
4. Have a strategy.
5. Find out areas of agreement and use them to build up trust.
6. Isolate main points of difference.
7. Find out what the other side wants.
8. Be prepared to listen.

The future of the management in the selling organization will influence the style and the sensitivity related to the negotiating procedure.

The taxation profile of both purchaser and vendor will also influence the negotiations, especially with respect to the manner of and timing of payment.

Implementation

If you have ploughed your way through the details of mergers and acquisitions this far you are sure to believe that by now the worst must surely be over. Sadly, not so. That is why tenacity was prescribed as one of the characteristics required of an acquirer or vendor.

Everything, with the exception of negotiation, has been on paper until this stage. Now is the time to implement possibly months of planning. Good planning always incorporates the implementation steps, as this exercise compels one to think through the practical implications of objectives and policies.

Typically there are three broad categories which are most likely to cause implementation complications, should there be any:

1. Overcoming cultural differences and varying management styles;
2. The implementation of new management and/or changed reporting lines for existing management;
3. Management information system alteration and implementation.

These three areas in particular can cause untold agonies to management of the new group and, in effect, this is part of the high risk element attached to the merger and acquisition route.

POTENTIAL RISKS AND LIABILITIES ASSOCIATED WITH MERGERS AND ACQUISITIONS

1. *Property*
   - leasehold versus freehold
   - unknown rental commitments
   - repairs and maintenance warranties
2. *Plant and machinery*
   - state of repair
   - fairness of book valuation
   - state of obsolescence
3. *Stock*
   - amount of slow moving/obsolete stock
   - valuation
   - vulnerability to commodity prices

- contract price agreements

4. *Debtors*
   - accuracy of outstanding amounts
   - collectibility
5. *Intergroup services and charges*
   - It is often difficult to establish the benefit and cost savings of intergroup charges arising possibly out of group purchasing power and often allocated on an arbitrary basis to group companies.
6. *Potential redundancy and closure costs*
7. *Overdependence on any suppliers or customers*
8. *Unrecognized tax liabilities*
9. *Pension liabilities and/or under-funded pension funds*
10. *Pending litigation and disputes*
11. *Outstanding contractual commitments*
12. *Potential compensation payments to retiring directors or officers*

    The usual methods for guarding against the above include:
    - accountants' investigations
    - use of advisers and consultants
    - discussions with lawyers and solicitors
    - warranties and indemnities.

MANAGEMENT BUY-OUTS

The growth of management buy-outs in the UK has accelerated at a fantastic rate over the past two years. The trend has emerged as part of world recession and the changing attitude of conglomerates that managing related businesses is far easier than handling a diversified group.

A management buy-out is an acquisition which results in the former management or employees acquiring a substantial equity stake in that business. The participants in a management buy-out may consist of a team of the most senior management, or it may include an employees' cooperative. The best example of the latter was the buy-out of the National Freight Corporation by 26,000 of its managers and employees during 1981.

Opportunities for management and staff

Management buy-outs in the present receptive climate provide some very positive aspects to the purchasing team, namely:

1. An opportunity to purchase the business at a substantial discount on net assets
2. The support of City institutions is often more forthcoming than with the conventional acquisition
3. Financiers are usually prepared to accept a higher level of financial gearing in the financing of a management buy-out
4. In many cases deferred payment terms can be negotiated with a willing seller in the holding company
5. The current tax environment is extremely favourable for the employee. Tax relief is available for interest paid on loans to enable him or her to finance equity investments in certain trading companies which are also close companies.

Reasons for disposals

Below are set out some reasons for a disposal to be made by the holding company:

1. The parent company could be in financial difficulties;
2. The company to be disposed of may not be meeting group objectives;
3. There could be a general lack of fit;
4. Other external or market factors.

Businesses suitable for management buy-outs should have a reasonable history of profits (often they are turnaround situations), acceptable cash flows and good prospects. Most of all, they should have proven management, especially if that management is undertaking the buy-out.

Financing the buy-out

Financing a buy-out is obviously simplified if it has the blessing of the vendor. Care must be taken, however, that this is not achieved at an overrated buy-out price. If the prospects for the company are good and management is able to put up a portion of the funds institutional money is usually not difficult to come by. A common feature of management buy-outs is that the managers contribute a relatively small part of the total financing requirement and acquire a relatively large part of the equity. The percentage holding that the institution will obtain in return for its investment and whether it is an active or a passive investor are issues that the buy-out team need to think through clearly prior to clinching the deal. A high proportion of the equity plus an active style might inhibit management and affect the culture of the entity.

In raising finance the assets of the business are most often used as security. Care must be taken not to run foul of Section 151 of the Companies Act 1985 with respect to financial assistance directly or indirectly for the purpose of acquiring shares in that company. This applies both to limited and unlimited companies. There are exceptions to the rule and the Companies Act should be carefully studied in order to ensure that the regulations are adhered to.

In choosing the institution that is likely to be the most sympathetic partner it is important to consider:

1. The period it is likely to allow before it wishes to exit and realize its investment;
2. Whether it will be prepared to provide further financing for growth;
3. What other services the institution is able to provide.

Another source of finance could be through a Business Expansion Scheme (BES) investment. The BES provides an incentive to outside investors to put money into unquoted trading companies. This scheme enables UK investors to claim tax relief at their top rate on investments of up to £40,000 per annum. Individuals connected with the company are precluded from this opportunity.

Other sources of funds for buy-outs include pension funds, a range of government grants and the personal wealth of the new management/shareholders.

In order to raise the finance and convince investors that the position is backable, a *business plan* is required setting out the objectives of the business, how it intends to achieve them and the anticipated risks and returns.

It would seem that the trend in management buy-out activity will continue. It is argued that it is an all-win situation in that everyone comes out better off:

1. The parent company is rid of an unwanted subsidiary;
2. Employees/managers enjoy a new sense of purpose in taking charge of their own destiny;
3. The country's employment situation is said to be improved if the smaller business sector is bolstered;
4. Investors are more ready to part with their funds as they view the venture as having less risk due to growth opportunities and proven management.

SELLING YOUR BUSINESS

Much of what has already been said applies to the vendor of a business as much as to the purchaser. The vendor naturally approaches the process from his standpoint with his perceptions of how to make an optimal exit: optimal from both a psychological and a monetary viewpoint. A small to medium-sized business vendor has usually to consider, among other points, the following factors when negotiating a sale:

1. Are shares or business assets to be sold?
2. Will any liabilities remain?
3. What is a fair valuation of the assets?
4. What can be deemed goodwill and will he (the owner) be restricted by restraint of trade agreements?
5. Can any valuable contracts be taken over?
6. What indemnities and warranties is he likely to have to supply?
7. If the property on which the business is run is leasehold will the landlord give consent to assignment?
8. What are the implications with respect to patents?
9. What basis of valuation should be applied to stocks?
10. Normally the vendor retains the book debts — can he rely on the purchaser who usually acts as collecting agent?
11. What are his family circumstances, does he need to consider estate planning not to mention detailed tax planning?

CONCLUSION

The subject of acquisition and mergers is wide and complicated. Only general guidelines can be given as, not only is each transaction unique, but market conditions change and new approaches are continuously being developed.

The merger/acquisition decision is an important one. Not only will it test the vision, commercial judgement and tenacity of management, it can probably be deemed the highest risk project to be taken on by any organization.

Prudent use of professional advisers should enhance objectivity and reduce or eliminate the unnecessary risks.

15

LEGAL ASPECTS OF BUSINESS

Helen Johannsen

Tortious liability
The law of contract
Sale of goods
Consumer credit and hire purchase
The law of property
The Rent Acts
Intellectual property

INTRODUCTION

Every aspect of business activity involves some form of risk. The prudent entrepreneur should therefore consider his legal liability as well as his financial and contractual responsibilities. Businessmen have contracts to comply with, orders to meet, customers to satisfy and properties to maintain. Naturally, every responsible role attracts liability. Common law and statute clearly define these limits of liability and the procedures to follow to avoid liability. It is essential to understand the elements of every legal relationship, in particular the Law of Contract. It is also important to appreciate that the interest of the inventor, the employee and the consumer are fully recognised by the law. This chapter briefly discusses the basic aspects of business and is not intended to provide exhaustive coverage of legal liability. In legal matters, a 'little learning' can so easily be dangerous and sometimes lead to disastrous consequences. Independent legal advice should therefore be sought at all stages of business.

TORTIOUS LIABILITY

A tort constitutes a wrongful act which is neither a crime nor a breach of contract. If someone has suffered injury as a result of another's wrongful act, then he may be able to claim compensation in the form of damages. The basis for any successful claim rests on whether or not the injured party can establish that he has suffered harm and that the wrong-doer has violated a legal right of his. Claims in tort, as with all other civil actions, aim to compensate the injured party and not to punish the wrong-doer.

The law of torts is not a clearly defined area of law, as new torts continue to be created and others are redefined by the courts. However, the following are well recognized specific torts.

Trespass

There are three forms of trespass:

Trespass to the person may take the form of an *assault,* an attempt or threat to apply force to someone else; *battery,* the application of force however slight; and *false imprisonment,* the deprivation of someone's liberty.

Trespass to goods involves direct wrongful interference with someone else's goods, that is either taking goods from someone or interfering with them while he is in possession of them.

Trespass to land occurs when one person enters upon the land in possession of another without lawful justification. Trespass to land is also committed when objects are thrown or placed on land.

Nuisance

Acts of nuisance are either private or public.

A public nuisance is usually defined as 'some unlawful act or omission to discharge some legal duty, which act or omission endangers the lives, safety, health or comfort of the public or by which the public are obstructed in the exercise of some common right'. It must be noted that a public nuisance is a crime.

A private nuisance is a tort only and amounts to an unlawful annoyance which interferes with a person's use and enjoyment or with the use of certain rights which accompany the use of the land, such as the right of way or the right to light.

Negligence

Negligence is a tort in its own right which is committed when a person has breached a legal duty to take care not to damage the person or property of another. It is essential in any claim of negligence to establish that a duty of care exists between the two persons involved and that the duty has been broken, resulting in actual damage or loss. Broadly speaking, a duty of care is said to exist when one person can foresee that his acts or omissions are likely to injure another. Further, the damage or loss must be reasonably foreseeable.

Once the duty of care has been established, further efforts must be made to show that the duty has been broken. The standard applied to this test is a standard which could be expected of an ordinary reasonable man. Naturally, certain activities require a higher standard of care than others and the reasonable man is expected to adapt his standards accordingly. Finally, the loss or damage suffered must be directly attributed to the negligent act.

Situations may arise when the act speaks for itself and the doctrine of 'res sipa loquitor' can be applied. The maxim means that the wrongful act raises a strong presumption of negligence and no evidence is required to prove how the accident occurred.

The Law Reform (Contributory) Negligence Act 1945 introduced the concept of contributory negligence. Accordingly, where any person suffers damage as a result partly of his own fault and partly of another person's, the damages recoverable shall be reduced to such an extent as the court thinks just and equitable.

Defamation

Defamation is commonly defined as 'publication of a statement which tends to lower the person in the estimation of the right thinking members of society generally'. There are two forms of defamation.

Libel is a defamatory statement in permanent form, such as writing or printed matter. Broadcasting on television and radio, if defamatory, is now categorized as libel. Libel is actionable without proof of special damage.

Slander is a defamatory statement which is not permanent, namely an oral statement or a gesture. Slander is only actionable if the plaintiff can show that he has actually suffered damage.

No action for libel or slander will succeed without proving that the statement was published to a third party.

Further, whereas libel is a crime as well as a tort, slander is only a tort, unless the words were spoken to create a breach of the peace.

Where a defamatory statement has been made innocently, an 'Offer of Amends' can be given.

Defences to defamation include *justification,* that the words spoken or written are true; *absolute privilege,* that the statements were made in parliament or court proceedings; *qualified privilege,* that a statement was made by a person under a duty to make it to a person under a duty to receive it; and *fair comment,* ie an honest statement of opinion made in a matter of public interest.

Passing off

This tort is essentially concerned with damage to business interests. The tort is committed when a person pretends that his business or goods are those of another, so as to attract business away from the other. Imitating or adopting another's trade mark, design, label or shop front and style all constitute the tort of passing off. All that needs to be proved in a passing off action is that the goods are so marked, described or identified as to be calculated to mislead ordinary purchasers and to lead them to mistake the imitation goods for the real thing. Passing off is actionable without proof of damage.

Strict liability

In general, tortious liability requires that someone must be proved blameworthy. However, there are certain areas of tortious liability which are strict, in the sense that no proof of fault or blame is required. The law has imposed strict limits on a person's freedom in particular areas, so that a person becomes absolutely liable for his acts or omissions which cause damage or loss to another irrespective of any fault or negligence on his part. Examples of strict liability are:

Rule in Rylands v *Fletcher*

This famous case has created an onerous duty on occupiers of land. Any occupier of land who, for his own purposes, brings and keeps on his land anything not naturally there and which is likely to cause damage if it escapes, must keep it at his peril. If he fails to do so he is fully liable for the direct consequences of its escape, even if he has not been guilty of negligence. The rule has been applied to water, acid, fires, gas fumes and people.

Liability for fires

There can be no responsibility attached to the owner of land for fires created or spread by strangers. However, a landowner will be strictly liable for the fires of his incompetent employees. Further, he will be strictly liable for fires created by negligent even disobedient independent contractors during the course of their contractual obligation. If a fire has spread to another's premises, the person who created the fire will have no excuse. Accordingly, anyone who starts or uses fires or fire-making equipment or even just allows them on his premises must control them.

Breaches of statutory duty
Many Acts of parliament such as the Factories Act impose strict duties on the persons to whom they apply. Breach of such duty generally renders the offender liable for damages irrespective of any fault or negligence.

Liability for premises

Not only does the duty doctrine apply to individuals but it has also been extended to cover land and premises, so that an occupier of land owes a duty of care to those who enter his premises and he is liable for any damage or loss caused as a result of the defective land, premises or structures erected thereon.

Occupier's liability
The Occupier's Liability Act 1957 clearly classifies the extent of an occupier's responsibility towards his visitors. An occupier, for the purposes of the Act, is the person who has the effective control of the premises, be he the owner, the landlord or the manager. A person is in control of premises if he is in a position to know the state of repair of those premises and has a control over who he allows on to them. The Act further states that the occupier only owes a duty of care to people who have been given express or implied permission to enter. Such people are 'visitors' and have lawfully entered the premises. Visitors include guests, visiting maintenance engineers and those who come in the exercisable right conferred by law.

The occupier must take all reasonable steps to see that the visitor will be reasonably safe using the premises for the purposes for which he is permitted by the occupier to be there. The occupier's duty increases if his visitor is a child. An occupier must be prepared for the fact that children are less careful than adults, hence a warning of danger on the premises will be sufficient for an adult, but not for a child. However, if the visitor has special knowledge and has called for a specific purpose, he is expected to guard against any risks ordinarily incidental to that calling.

An occupier of premises will not be liable for work done on his premises by an independent contractor, provided he can show that he has taken reasonable steps to satisfy himself that the contractor is competent and has carried out the work properly.

The occupier's obligation to people entering his premises under the terms of a contract, such as hotel guests and theatre goers, will be governed by the terms of the contract. However, in the absence of express terms a common duty of care will always be implied.

Someone who enters land without an invitation is a trespasser and by virtue of the Act is afforded no protection. However, if the occupier is aware of a regular trespasser, for example someone who uses a regular right of way across his land, the standard obligation may arise and the occupier must then treat the trespasser with 'ordinary humanity'. Recent case law has increased the occupier's obligation. The occupier must now take heed of the potential trespasser and if he creates a danger on his land and he knows there is a chance that someone may trespass, he must take reasonable precautions to prevent accidents.

Contractors' liability

The Occupier's Liability Act does not apply to building contractors or other workers in connection with installations or maintenance of equipment on premises, unless they are in actual occupation of the property. However, the general duty of care or neighbourhood principle is applicable, in that the contractors will be responsible to people they can reasonably foresee are likely to be affected by their work or installations.

The Defective Premises Act 1972 deals specifically with contractors' and builders' obligations. A duty is owed to every person who acquires an interest in the building to see that the work is done in a workmanlike manner with proper materials, so that the building will be fit for human habitation.

Landlord's duty to tenant

The Defective Premises Act 1972 states that where a landlord, under the terms of a tenancy, has an obligation to maintain and repair those premises, the landlord owes a duty to all persons who might reasonably be expected to be affected by the defective state of the premises. The landlord must therefore take such care as is reasonable to see that they are reasonably safe from personal injury or damage to property.

Employer's obligations to his employees

The employer's obligations to his employees are, to a large extent, governed by numerous Acts of parliament, such as the Factories Acts, Health and Safety at Work Act and the Employer's Liability (Defective

Equipment) Act 1969. The employer's liability is usually 'strict', that is he will be liable whether or not he has been negligent. The general rule is that the employer always owes a duty to his employee to ensure that the working environment is reasonably safe and that the employee is not exposed to unnecessary risks. The employer's obligation is wide and encompasses all aspects of the conduct of his business. Not only must the employer ensure that his staff are competent, that the equipment, machinery and materials are safe, but also that the system of work which has been devised is reasonably safe. Naturally, the obligations required depend in each case upon the particular circumstances of the employment. Whatever conditions prevail, the employer's obligations are always personal to him; he cannot evade liability by stating that a particular duty has been delegated to another. Furthermore, it has been established that the obligation exists even if the employee was not acting in the course of his employment and even if the employee was not authorized to be on the premises or any part of them.

Finally, the employer cannot allege that the employee was well aware of the hazardous working conditions because, in such circumstances, the duty to provide a safe system of work prevails.

The obligations during employment are not all one sided, in fact the employee owes an obligation to the employer to use reasonable care and skill in the performance of his duties. If the employee fails he will be required to indemnify his employer if he causes him injury.

Liability for employees

Not only are employers under numerous obligations to their employees, they must also accept responsibility for torts committed by their employees during the course of employment. In such circumstances, the employers are 'vicariously' liable. The liability is far-reaching and extends to torts committed by the employee, which are not authorized or ordered or prohibited by the employer. The liability also extends to torts which arise out of the improper or negligent execution of the employee's duties. The general rule is that an employer is only vicariously responsible for employees who are under a contract of service. In determining whether a person is an employee, regard must be had to the extent of supervision and control, the employer's rights of dismissal, the manner of payment, the skill of the employee and the responsibility and integration involved.

Clearly an employer cannot be made liable for every wrongful act of his employees, hence the limitation that the act must have been committed during the course of employment. Whether a particular act falls within the scope of employment must largely depend upon the special circumstances and facts involved. If an employee has acted for his own benefit, or has acted outside the class of acts which he is employed to do, or has gone off on a 'frolic of his own', the employer will not be held liable. In any event, the onus will be on the plaintiff to establish that an employee was acting during the course of his employment.

Liability for independent contractors

As a general rule employers are not liable for torts committed by independent contractors, namely those persons employed to do a particular job under a contract for services. This rule extends to the employers or agents of the independent contractors.

As with all general rules there are a number of exceptions. The employer will be liable where the nature of the contractor's work is particularly hazardous and is likely to cause danger to the public. The employer cannot evade liability for the dangerous operation even though the liability is not strict. Further, the delegation of works to an independent contractor does not prevent the employer being liable for strict liability torts or offences. If the employer expressly or impliedly authorizes the independent contractor to commit a tort he will be liable.

An employer must furthermore be careful to select competent independent contractors and give adequate instructions, otherwise he will be responsible for his own negligence if the tort is committed by a contractor he knew to be incompetent or a contractor who was not sufficiently directed or advised.

If an employer hires out his employee to another employer the liability rests on the employer who exercises the control both as to what the employee is to do and how he shall perform his work. An employee cannot have two employers. The original or general employer will not be liable if he can establish that the vicarious responsibility has been transferred to the new or special employer. As in all cases, the individual facts of each case will highlight the particular relationship.

Liability for agents

An agent derives his authority from his principal and if that principal has authorized him to commit a tort or assists in the commission of it or in fact ratifies the commission of it, he will be liable.

An agent is a person who acts on behalf of another and may have been appointed expressly or impliedly. A relationship arises between a principal and agent similar to that of the employer and employee. A principal will only be vicariously liable for acts committed by his agent during the course of employment. What distinguishes an agent from an employee or independent contractor, is that the agent conducts business or performs various acts on behalf of and not for another. In reality, the distinction between an employee and an agent may become extremely blurred and particular attention should be paid to the facts and circumstances of each individual case.

Liability for partners

The law relating to partnerships is governed by the Partnership Act 1890. A partnership is defined as the relationship which subsists between persons carrying on a business in common with a view to a profit. Although a partnership is not a legal person, because it is a joint enterprise, all partners are taken to be each other's agents in respect of all acts done in or about partnership business. An act committed by one partner in furtherance of partnership business will bind the other partners even if he has done so without authority.

If a partner causes loss or injury to a member of the public by an act or omission in the course of partnership business, the firm as a whole will be vicariously liable, not just the partner involved. The limitation on this provision is that the act must have been committed during the course of business, which is a fact to be determined by the circumstances of the incident.

THE LAW OF CONTRACT

A contract can simply be defined as a legally binding agreement, that is an agreement which can be enforced by the courts. At the root of every contract there must be an agreement between two or more people. There must be 'consensus ad idem', ie a meeting of minds. If the parties to an agreement are mistaken as to each other's intention, there cannot possibly be 'consensus'.

Further, a binding contract will not exist purely because there is consensus between the parties. There must be a definite intention to create legal relations. Mere domestic or social agreements are not usually intended to be legally binding and are therefore not contracts. A thorough examination of the facts surrounding the formation of the contract must be made in order to establish the necessary intention. A term of the agreement may especially state that legal relations were not intended, which the courts, more often than not, uphold. The courts will, when deciding whether the intention exists, presume that a commercial agreement is always a legally binding contract and that a social family agreement is not.

A contract will not necessarily exist because there is a consensus and intention. There must also be a definite offer by one party to another which is accepted. There must be consideration and certainty of terms. The contract must not be illegal or impossible to perform and the parties to a contract must have the requisite capacity to contract.

The offer

Contrary to popular belief, an offer does not have to be in writing; indeed, it can be oral or even implied from a person's conduct. An offer can be made to a particular person or group of persons. The offer, however made, must be communicated to the other party, he must be aware of its existence and its terms, which must be unequivocal and certain. Naturally, problems may arise as to what constitutes an offer. If a party makes an announcement as to his intention or communicates information during negotiations, is he making an offer? Is, for example, an offer made by a shop keeper who displays his goods in a shop window or catalogue? The answer is no. He is merely tempting or inviting you to make offers. These invitations are commonly classed as 'invitations to treat'. So anyone who selects an item from a self-service store is making an offer to purchase. The offer is accepted by the cashier when the goods are rung up on the till. An offer cannot exist indefinitely and usually the offeror will set a time limit within which it must be accepted. If the offer is not accepted within the stated time, it will lapse after a reasonable time.

Every offer subsists until it is accepted or revoked. The offeror can revoke the offer at any time before it is accepted but his revocation must actually be communicated to the offeree, before the offer has been accepted. The revocation can be communicated directly or indirectly through a third party.

Acceptance

As with an offer, an acceptance can be oral, written or implied from conduct. Acceptance must be a positive act and must comply with the terms of the offer, especially if the offer specifies the manner of acceptance. An offer is not accepted if the acceptance has been made subject to a particular condition. Further, if a counter offer is made there is no acceptance and it causes the original offer to lapse. The positive act of acceptance requires that the offeree communicates his acceptance to the offeror.

Problems arise where the offeree communicates his acceptance by post. The offer is accepted as soon as the letter is posted, provided it is properly stamped and addressed, even though the letter of acceptance may never reach the offeror. The offeror is nevertheless deemed to have received the acceptance; this is known as the 'post rule exception'.

Consideration

All simple contracts must be supported by valuable consideration, otherwise they are void. Consideration does not only mean money but something that is measurable in money's-worth, ie goods and services. The term 'valuable consideration' simply means that the consideration must be capable of being valued. Consideration involves an element of exchange. One party must benefit while the other suffers a detriment. Consideration must, like all the essential ingredients of a contract, be certain, not vague or indefinite. However, the consideration need not be adequate. The contracting parties are at liberty to decide what price to set. The payment of a smaller sum than originally provided for in a contract will not discharge liability to pay the whole sum.

Certainty

Even if there has been a firm offer which has been accepted and supported by valuable consideration, there will be no contract if the terms are uncertain. If the contractual terms are too vague the contract will fail for uncertainty, unless there is a provision in the contract to resolve the ambiguity. Alternatively, the courts may decide that a term should be implied from the course of dealing between the parties or certain trade customs or statutes.

The terms of a contract should determine the obligations and duties of each party and should, for the avoidance of ambiguity, be expressly stated. There are two kinds of terms, namely conditions and warranties.

Conditions and warranties

A condition is a term which goes to the root of the contract and is fundamental to its existence. A breach of condition entitles the injured party to treat the contract as discharged or sue for damages.

A warranty is a non-fundamental term and subsidiary to the contract's main purpose. Breach of warranty entitles the injured party to sue for damages only. Should problems arise as to the meaning or certainty of terms, then the language used must be construed to give effect to the intention of the parties. The contract should be construed strongly against the party who drafted the contract.

Capacity

The general rule is that all persons have full capacity to make contracts. However, contracts made by minors, ie those under the age of 18 years, are subject to certain rules.

A company can make any contract as long as it is within the powers granted to it in the Memorandum of Association. If the company acts outside its powers, ie 'ultra vires', the contract will be void. The members cannot ratify the contract if it is ultra vires, although they could of course vote to alter the objects clause of the Memorandum of Association to ensure that future contracts of a similar nature are not void. If, on the other hand, the directors act beyond their powers but within the company's powers, ratification is possible.

Remember that contracts with foreign sovereigns and diplomats cannot be enforced in the courts because one of the parties would have diplomatic immunity!

Void, voidable and illegal contracts

Void contracts

Void contracts are those where either one or both of the parties to a contract has made a mistake as to a basic fact of the contract which is fundamental to their agreement. It is essential that the mistake shall have been as to a fact and not to a point of law. The old latin maxim of 'ignorantia legis non excusat' (ignorance of the law is no excuse) applies.

A 'common' mistake occurs when the same mistake is made by both parties. Such a common mistake could relate to the existence of the subject matter of the contract, for example, both parties were unaware that the contractual goods had been destroyed in a fire. A mere mistake as to the value or quality of the subject matter will not suffice.

A 'mutual' mistake means that both parties have made different mistakes. There must have been a misunderstanding and hence no consensus.

A 'unilateral' mistake is a mistake made by one party only. A mistake in such a case is only operative if the other party knew or ought to have known of it.

Misrepresentation

A contract will be voidable where one party has been induced to enter into the contract by another who has made a false statement of a material fact. In contractual terms this is called a misrepresentation. The party who has been induced or misled has the option whether or not to treat the contract as voidable. It is important to note that neither party is under a duty to disclose all the facts to the other. The maxim which is traditionally applied in such cases is 'caveat emptor' — let the buyer beware. The injured party will not be able to treat the contract as voidable unless he can establish that he relied upon the statement and that it was the statement alone which induced him to enter into the contract.

An innocent misrepresentation is made by someone who honestly believes that his statement is true. On the other hand, a person who knows that his statement is false or does not care whether or not it is, makes a fraudulent misrepresentation. The remedy for the injured party in this case is to rescind the contract and to take an action for damages. The victim of an innocent misrepresentation also has the right to damages as well as rescission, subject to certain conditions.

Duress and undue influence

A party may enter into a contract because he has suffered or has been threatened with violence against himself or his family. If such is the case, then he is said to have been induced by 'duress', and the contract will be voidable.

If a party to a contract has been pressurised or coerced into that contract without the elements of duress, to such an extent that he does not enter into the contract by exercising his free judgement, then the contract has been induced by 'undue influence' and is voidable only at the court's discretion. Where one person is in a position to influence the other unfairly, undue influence is presumed. Such is the case of parent and child, teacher and pupil, doctor and patient etc. In all other cases, unless undue influence is alleged, it must be proved by the party alleging it.

Illegal contracts

A contract is void if it is for an illegal purpose or its purpose is contrary to public policy. No recourse to the courts is possible by either party even if hardship results. Further, no money is recoverable. If a contract is not wholly illegal the courts may intervene and sever the illegal terms and enforce the legal terms. However, severance is only possible where the terms are wholly independent. Some contracts are made specifically illegal by statute, such as gaming and wagering contracts.

Contracts in restraint of trade

Contracts which restrict a person from freely exercising his trade or profession are contracts in restraint of trade. They may be general, namely preventing trading in a particular country; or specific, that is preventing trade within a particular area. The general rule is that such contracts are void, but they may be enforced if it can be established that there is a legitimate proprietary interest to protect and it is reasonable between the parties and the public interest.

The question whether it is reasonable to restrain a person will be for a judge to decide, and usually will depend upon the particular circumstances of each case. In any event, such contracts will not be enforced if no vaulable consideration has been given.

A typical restraint of trade contract is a 'solus' agreement between a garage proprietor and an oil company. The garage proprietor contracts to sell only the oil company's petrol and goods etc.

An employer can restrain his employee from working in a particular area or field of work. However, the courts will only enforce such agreement if the employee is in a position to prejudice his employer's business, for example by disclosing confidential information or trade secrets. Further, the restraint must be reasonable having regard to the area of restraint and type of employment and the length of restraint.

Restraints on sale of a business

On the sale of a business, clauses are commonly present in the sale agreement restraining the seller of that business from setting up in competition with the purchaser. The purchaser naturally intends to protect the goodwill of the business he is buying and the courts appreciate this fact and tend to enforce such covenants. The clause must be reasonable having regard to the nature and extent of the business and the area and the time of restraint.

Discharge of contracts

Contracts once made can be discharged by performance, agreement, frustration or breach of contract.

Performance

Performing the exact terms of the contract will discharge the contract once the performance is complete. Substantial part performance of a contract will not discharge the contract unless the part performance is voluntarily accepted by the promisee.

Agreement

Contracts can simply be discharged by either party whether or not they have been performed in whole or in part by either or both of the parties. The contract can also be discharged by both parties by substituting a new agreement for the old. The variation of the contract by agreement is possible at any time. However, if one party unilaterally makes a material variation without the consent of the other, the contract is discharged.

Frustration
A contract is frustrated when there is a supervening event which makes the contract impossible to perform. That is, when the basis of that contract is destroyed, or a certain event upon which the contract is dependent fails to occur. A contract for personal services will naturally be frustrated if the person dies or is ill for a long time. A change in the law of governmental interference may further operate to frustrate the contract. The frustrating event must not be self-induced. Often, express contractual terms make provision for possible frustration and provide that if such an event occurs the contract will subsist. The courts generally will respect the express terms and not interfere.

Breach of contract
A breach of contract at its simplest means that one party to the contract fails to perform his part of the bargain, as to the manner and/or time of performance. A breach of contract may be a breach of warranty or condition. If there is a breach of a non-essential term, ie a warranty, the injured party can only sue for damages. The contract must continue as the breach does not operate to discharge the contract.

On the other hand, a breach of condition will enable the injured party to elect to treat the breach as a breach of warranty and sue for damages. Alternatively, he can treat the breach of condition as automatically discharging the contract. Damages for breach of contract constitute compensation to the injured party for his actual loss, which must not be too remote from the breach. The loss must be a natural consequence of the breach or if not, at least the damage should have been foreseen. The damages awarded are purely compensatory and not punitive, although there is a duty on the injured party to minimize the damage as far as possible.

The situation may arise where a party has the option either to sue for damages for breach, or sue for the work he has partially completed. In such cases a claim can be made for work actually done.

The concept of privity of contract

A party to a contract only owes a duty to the other party to that contract. The contract is a personal relationship and no other party can acquire rights or incur liabilities under it. A person who is not a party to a contract cannot sue on it or be forced to perform certain duties.

The rule of privity of contract does not apply, however, if the contract was made by an agent or trustee. Rights and liabilities can, however, be transferred or assigned to another, and if done with the agreement of the other or the authority in the contract, a new relationship will arise between the assignee and the original contracting party. The assignor will be free from the bonds of privity of contract.

SALE OF GOODS

The law relating specifically to the sale of goods is substantially contained in the Sale of Goods Act 1979. The Act strictly governs sale of goods operations by implying terms into every contract. The Act only applies to goods and chattels but can include crops and minerals. The sale of goods contract is described by the Act as 'a contract whereby the seller transfers or agrees to transfer the property in goods to the buyer for money consideration or the price'.

The following conditions and warranties are implied into every contract for the sale of goods, unless expressly excluded by the parties.

Title

A condition that the seller has or will have the legal right to sell the goods and a warranty that the goods are free from encumbrances are implied into every sale. The Unfair Contracts Terms Act 1977 forbids the exclusion of the condition as to title in a domestic contract, although the seller can contract to give limited title only. A business contract can exclude the term completely.

Description

In a sale by description there is an implied condition that the goods shall correspond to their description. The condition applies only if the buyer describes the type of goods he wants to purchase and the supplier merely supplies the goods as requested.

Merchantable quality

Where a seller sells in the course of business, there is an implied condition that the goods supplied under the contract are of merchantable quality. The condition does not apply to defects specifically drawn to the buyer's attention before the contract, or defects which his pre-contract examination, (if any), ought to have revealed. The Act implies another condition that the goods should be reasonably fit for the buyer's purpose, where this is made known, unless the buyer does not rely or it is unreasonable for him to rely, on the seller's skill or judgement.

Sample

Conditions are implied that the bulk of the goods shall correspond with the sample in quality. Further, the buyer should have a reasonable opportunity of comparing the bulk with the sample and ensuring that the goods shall be free from defects rendering them unmerchantable.

The Unfair Contract Terms Act 1977

This Act provides that where the buyer 'deals as a consumer', the seller cannot exclude any of the implied conditions. However, if the buyer does *not* deal as a consumer, ie he purchases the goods during the course of business, then the conditions may be excluded so long as the exclusion clause is reasonable. The seller must therefore prove that the exclusion clause is a fair and reasonable one to be included in the contract, having regard to the circumstances which were or ought reasonably to have been known to or in the contemplation of the parties when the contract was made.

The passing of title of goods and risk of loss

Problems have arisen in the past as to when the title of goods passes from the seller to the buyer. The Sale of Goods Act specifically states the point of time at which the seller ceases to be the owner of the goods.

The Act makes a distinction between specific or ascertained goods and unascertained and future goods. The distinction is important because the Act states that no property passes until the goods are ascertained.

Specific goods are goods which are clearly identified and agreed upon at the time of contract. The transfer of ownership of such goods will depend on the intention of the parties. However, if no intention can be ascertained, the ownership will only pass if the goods are in a deliverable state. If the goods are in a deliverable state then the ownership passes when the contract is made, irrespective of the time of delivery or payment. Further, where goods are not in a deliverable state, the passing of ownership is delayed until they are made deliverable and the buyer is aware that they are. If the seller has to weigh or measure the goods in order to ascertain the price then property does not pass until he has taken these steps.

Unascertained goods are goods to be manufactured or acquired by the seller after making a contract for sale. The Act provides that, where under a sale of unascertained goods the goods are later ascertained and in a deliverable state, the ownership passes upon appropriation by one party with the other's assent. The other party's assent can be inferred from the contract itself or implied by the actions of the parties.

The passing of ownership and goods as specifically described by the Act determines also when the risk of accidental loss occurs. The Act provides that the risk of accidental loss passes with the ownership of goods. This provision confirms that the seller is released from all responsibility for the goods once the ownership passes. However, where specific goods perish before contracting, without the seller's knowledge, the contract is void simply because the subject matter does not exist. Also, where specific goods perish without fault after the contract but before the risk passes the contract is avoided.

Title to goods

A buyer who discovers that the seller was not the owner is entitled by the Act to remedy in damages against the seller. The general rule is that 'the buyer acquires no better title to the goods than the seller had'.

The bona fide buyer may, in some circumstances, obtain title to the goods even though the seller did not have the title to pass on. The first exception to the general rule is where a person sells goods under the authority or with the consent of the owner. The exception applies to those who sell goods with actual authority or ostensible authority. The essential point in both cases is that the seller or agent acts within that authority. Even if the goods are sold without authority the true owner may adopt the transaction if he was represented to be the owner, by the agent.

The second exception states that the title will only pass where the true owner is precluded from denying the seller's authority, such as allowing possession of the goods *and* also some indication that the seller had title. Mere possession of the goods by the seller is insufficient. The effect is that the owner is holding the seller out as being the owner to anyone who has dealings with him.

The third exception encompasses sales by commercial dealers or mercantile agents as they are called in the Act. A mercantile agent is someone who must normally be in the business as a buyer or seller of goods. The mercantile agent must also be in possession of the goods which have been entrusted to him in his capacity as agent.

The fourth exception is where a seller, having sold the goods, continues or is in possession of the goods or documents of title. The transfer or delivery of the same goods to any person receiving the same in good faith without notice of the previous sale shall have the same effect as if the person making the delivery or transfer was expressly authorized by the owner of the goods to make the sale. Accordingly, title will pass to the second buyer irrespective of the first contract.

The fifth exception is where a person having bought or agreed to buy goods obtains, with the seller's consent, possession of the goods or documents of title. The delivery or transfer by that person of the goods or documents to a bona fide purchaser with knowledge shall pass good title. This exception applies to the situation where a buyer has 'bought' the goods even though he may not have actually paid for them but nevertheless has obtained possession of the goods with the seller's consent.

Sales to private purchasers of motor vehicles which are delivered on hire purchase or conditional sale agreements, are the sixth exception. Where there is a disposition of a car to a private purchaser in good faith without notice that the car was subject to a hire purchase or conditional sale agreement, the disposition shall have the same effect as if the owner's title had been vested in the hirer or buyer immediately before disposition. Accordingly, good title is passed even though the buyer has not yet acquired it. The essential element in all such transactions is that the purchaser was acting in good faith.

Performance

The Act not only governs the terms of the contract but also performance of the contract. The performance of the contract involves the delivery of the goods by the seller and their acceptance, plus payment of the price by the buyer. The Act specifically states that it is the seller's duty to deliver the goods and the buyer's duty to accept them and pay for them in accordance with the terms of the contract.

Delivery can mean simply making the goods available for collection by the buyer. The Act does, however, describe delivery as being the voluntary transfer of possession of goods to another. Delivering goods to a carrier is deemed to be delivery to the buyer, unless the contract specifically requires the goods to be delivered to the buyer's premises. If goods are subject to a shipping CIF contract then the seller's obligation to deliver is not performed until he tenders the shipping documents to the buyer, who then is obliged to pay.

The carrier is presumed by the Act to be the buyer's agent, even though chosen by the seller. The seller, however, may be responsible in damages if the goods are lost or damaged in transit, because he placed them with an unsuitable carrier. The prudent seller should therefore select a suitable carrier having regard to the nature of the goods and the circumstances.

If the goods are to be carried by sea, then the seller must inform the buyer so that the buyer can make provision to insure the goods. If the seller fails to notify the buyer, then the goods will be at the seller's risk. The provision does not apply to CIF contracts where it is the seller's duty to insure. There is no express provision relating to carriage by land, and much will therefore depend upon commercial practice in a particular trade and the terms upon which the carriers are likely to handle the goods. The principle that the seller must inform the buyer, although not directly applicable to land transport, would usually be extended to afford the buyer the same degree of protection.

If the seller delivers the wrong quantity or delivers a consignment of goods mixed with goods of a different description, the buyer is entitled to reject the whole consignment if he wishes, or accept the contractual goods and reject the rest. However, if goods of the wrong description are delivered, then there has been a breach of condition and the contract is void. The buyer may therefore reject the goods and claim damages for breach of contract.

Delivery of the wrong quantity of goods may entitle the buyer to reject the goods only if there has been an excess or deficiency in quantity. If there has been a minor error in the quantity delivered, the buyer may not be entitled to reject. What constitutes the minor deviation would depend much on the circumstances. Further, unless otherwise agreed, the buyer is not bound to accept delivery of goods by instalments.

The counterpart of the seller's duty to deliver the goods is the buyer's duty to accept and pay for them in accordance with the terms of the contract. The delivery of goods and the payment of the price are concurrent conditions unless otherwise agreed between the parties. The seller must be ready and willing to give possession of the goods in exchange for the price, and the buyer must be ready and willing to pay the price in exchange for possession of the goods.

The acceptance and delivery of the goods do not necessarily go hand in hand. The Act provides that where goods are delivered to the buyer, who has not previously examined them, he is not deemed to have accepted them until he has had a reasonable opportunity of examining them for purposes of ascertaining whether they are in conformity with the contract. In fact, the seller is under a duty to allow such examination. The right to reject the goods as not being in conformity with the contract only extends to the buyer so long as he has not 'accepted' the goods within the terms of the Act.

Acceptance occurs by virtue of the Act when the buyer intimates to the seller that he has accepted them. Alternatively, when the goods have been delivered to the buyer he carries out any act in relation to them which is inconsistent with the ownership of the seller, or when, after a lapse of reasonable time, he retains the goods without intimating to the seller that he has rejected them. Acceptance may therefore prevent the buyer from rejecting the goods.

CONSUMER CREDIT AND HIRE PURCHASE

Consumer credit law is essentially governed by the Consumer Credit Act 1974, which has been enacted to govern the operation of the numerous forms of credit available to the consumer. Quite simply, credit is buying something and being given time to pay for it, or alternatively borrowing money and paying it back at a later date. Credit is available in many forms, some of which are briefly discussed below.

Hire purchase

A hire purchase agreement is an agreement for the hire of goods under which the consumer or hirer may buy the goods at a later date. Usually the vendor will sell the goods to a finance company. The finance company will then hire out the goods to the consumer in return for regular hire purchase instalments. A deposit may also be required. The consumer is not, however, the owner of the goods until all the instalments have been paid and he has exercised his option to purchase them. If the consumer falls behind in his payments, the owner is entitled to take the goods back. Also, the hirer cannot sell the goods while he is still paying for them. The Act provides protection only for a consumer where the amount of credit does not exceed £5000.

Credit sale

A credit sale agreement will have the same characteristics as the hire purchase agreement; however, the consumer becomes the owner of the goods as soon as he buys them. Generally, a shopkeeper will sell the goods to a finance company which will sell them to the consumer who agrees to pay by instalments. As the consumer owns the goods immediately, he can sell them before the final instalment has been met. The instalments will, of course, still be outstanding and the consumer may be required to pay off the outstanding balance upon sale. The Act only applies to consumer sale agreements where the credit is greater than £30 and less than £5000.

General provisions relating to hire purchase and credit sale agreements

The Act provides that certain described information must be set out in the agreements, such as the price, the rate of interest and the credit given, in order to be enforceable. Generally, once an agreement is entered into, the consumer cannot cancel it. He will be in breach of contract if he defaults. There are, however, two occasions when the consumer can withdraw from the agreement.

A consumer can withdraw from a credit agreement before the finance company accepts and approves the consumer's application for credit. Further, a consumer who has signed a credit agreement with a seller who has made representations to him at his home, ie off trade premises, is given special protection by the Act. A copy of the agreement must be left with the consumer when the sale is made and another copy of the signed agreement must be sent within seven days. The consumer then has a five-day cooling-off period during which he can back out of the agreement. The consumer can cancel the agreement in writing within five days of receiving a second copy agreement. The consumer's right to cancel must be mentioned in the agreement. The effect of cancellation is to treat the agreement as if it never existed. Therefore, goods and money must be returned by both parties. It is the seller's duty to collect the goods and the consumer's duty to take reasonable care of them.

Goods purchased under credit sale agreements belong to the consumer; he cannot therefore cancel and return the goods to the finance company, unless they are faulty. Goods subject to a hire purchase agreement do not belong to the consumer until all the instalments have been paid. They can be returned to the owner if the consumer is up to date with instalments and has paid half the credit price for the goods.

Credit cards

The consumer can purchase goods by producing a bank credit card, store credit card or budget account card. The vendor then invoices the credit card company or store. An account settled by a given date entitles the consumer to interest-free credit. Interest will be charged after a given date on a sum outstanding. On signing a card a cardholder becomes bound by the conditions of use sent to him with his card. Conditions of use must be sent to the cardholder on issuing every new card. If a card is lost after signature, the cardholder will only be liable for the first £30 of losses if it is misused, even if he does not inform the card company of loss. However, if a card is misused by someone with the cardholder's consent, the cardholder is liable for all losses. A cardholder will not be liable for losses after notification to the card company of its loss. The advantage of buying goods with a credit card is that if the goods are faulty or defective in any way, then the cardholder has equal rights against the card company and the shopkeeper, because this makes the card company jointly liable for the shopkeeper's breach of contract.

Credit reference agencies

Whenever a consumer borrows money, hires or purchases goods on credit, the creditor may consult a credit reference agency in order to ascertain whether the prospective borrower, buyer or hirer pays promptly, has been taken to court regarding his debts or is generally suitable to contract with. The Act provides that the consumer is entitled to know what information the agency holds on him. Further, if the information is wrong and the consumer is likely to suffer as a result, it can be corrected. A consumer who has been refused credit and wishes to find out why can ask the creditor in writing within 21 days from the last dealing with him for the name and address of the agency consulted. The creditor must reply within seven working days. The creditor is, however, under no duty to disclose the contents of the agency's report or give reasons for his refusal to grant credit. A written request can be made by the consumer to the agency, who must send a copy of the file and a statement of the consumer's rights within seven days of receipt of the request. A further written request can be made to the agency to correct any false information or incorrect facts. If the agency does not do so, the consumer can compose a 'Notice of Correction', up to 200 words. If no action is then taken by the agency, the consumer should report the matter to the Director General of Fair Trading.

Licensing under the Consumer Credit Act 1974

Under the Consumer Credit Act 1974 licences are required for the various business activities of the consumer credit and hire industry. If a person wishes to engage in a business covered by the Act he must first obtain a licence from the Director General of Fair Trading. The licences are not given automatically. A licence is not required, however, if the credit business is related to lending money, giving credit or hiring goods to limited companies. Further, a licence is not required merely to accept someone's else credit cards or simply to allow customers to pay bills at the end of a given period. Generally, a licence must be obtained for the consumer credit and consumer hire business, credit brokerage, debt adjusting, counselling and collecting and the credit reference agency business.

The Act also places restrictions on canvassing off trade premises. Broadly speaking, this term means calling uninvited on individuals to try and persuade them to enter into credit or hire agreements. Dealings with limited companies and corporate bodies are outside the Act. The term does not cover any other form of canvassing, such as using the telephone or sending letters or circulars. Briefly, you cannot call upon people uninvited to sell credit linked to the supply of goods or services, unless you have a licence issued under the Act with the endorsement authorizing 'canvassing off trade premises'.

Data Protection Act 1984

New rules have been introduced by the Data Protection Act 1984 restricting access to computerized data and allowing individuals to check on information stored about themselves. The legislation is intended to deal specifically with the problems arising from new technology. The information need not be purely related to a consumer's credit rating. Details of employment history, political activities and welfare records are covered by the Act. The Act, however, specifically relates to 'personal' information, that is it must relate to a living individual. The Act offers protection to the individual against expressions of opinion only. The Act requires that the organization, ie a building society, employer or agency, holding personal information on a computer, must be registered. The organizations must observe the procedures set down by the Act for the collection and storage of data. The personal information must be accurate and up to date, collected legally, held no longer than necessary and stored securely.

The individual's right of access to data becomes enforceable in November 1987, after which the individual will be entitled to ask the organization if any personal information is held by them. If so, copies of the information must be provided within 40 days, in a non-technical manner, upon the individual's written request, failing which the individual can initiate proceedings under the Act for compensation for damages due to unauthorized disclosure of data and the holding of inaccurate data. The courts will have the power to order the information to be corrected or deleted. The Act, however, specifically excludes government computers, and data contained in manual files.

See also Chapter 4, pages 118–121.

THE LAW OF PROPERTY

This section offers a brief summary of the complex Law of Property Act 1925 which deals with essential aspects of land ownership. For the Act's purposes the term 'land' encompasses the house or flat or other building which is erected on it and also gardens, allotments or estates. The landowner can either have a freehold or a leasehold interest in the land. The freeholder owns the actual land forever and is entitled to do with the land as he wishes subject, of course, to planning permission and restricted covenants.

Leasehold

The leaseholder owns the land only for a fixed period of time. The leaseholder will have been granted a lease by the owner of the land, entitling the leaseholder to occupy the land for a specified period only, upon payment of ground rent and subject to certain terms. The land will revert to the landlord when the term of the lease expires. The leaseholder will usually be subject to covenants in the lease requiring him to keep the property in good repair and to maintain it properly. In addition, the leaseholder may be required to contribute towards the cost of maintaining the common parts.

Freehold

On the other hand, a freeholder is under no obligation to repair the property, unless a mortgage deed requires him to do so. Furthermore, a freeholder can effect alterations or extensions to his property in whatever manner he wishes, subject to planning permission and restrictive covenants. A leaseholder would generally have to obtain the landlord's prior consent to any alterations or additions. The leaseholder will usually be able to enforce covenants against other leaseholders, such as the covenant of support and maintenance. Mutual repairing covenants should be evident in every lease of a flat in a building, so as to maintain the structure of the building as a whole. A freeholder will have great difficulty in restricting other freeholders' use of their land.

Restrictions on freeholders and leaseholders

The rights of freeholders and leaseholders are further restricted by the rights given to government bodies, institutions and officers and members of the public. A building society will, for example, have certain rights of re-entry and sale. A local authority has rights of compulsory purchase and can control hygienic living conditions. The local authority can also carry out various building works and repairs on properties. The police and other officials also have rights of entry. The planning legislation can control the use and size and alterations carried out to the property.

The freeholder and the leaseholder may also be subject to their tenants' rights of occupation, their neighbours' rights of light, air and way. Rights can be acquired over land by deed or long usage. A right will only be acquired by long usage if it has been exercised without permission, force or security and, generally, it must have been in continuous use for a period of 20 years.

Land registration

A system of registration of land was introduced in the 1960s and it is hoped that in time all property in England and Wales will be registered at its local district land registry. Certain areas of the country have been designated for compulsory registration and a transaction involving land in those areas will require to be registered for the first time. If the land has already been registered the purchaser knows that the seller's title has been checked by the government, that is the seller's title has been guaranteed. The purchaser can simply request a copy of the registered title and check the entries. Unfortunately, if the seller's title is not registered the purchaser must examine the chain of transactions for the previous 15 years to ensure that legal title is valid and that it will be passed on to him.

As discussed previously the essential difference between the freeholder's and the leaseholder's interest is that the leaseholder's comes to an end when his lease expires. The leaseholder will then lose his home. However, the provisions of the Leasehold Reform Act have to a large extent mitigated the harshness of this rule. The Act allows the leaseholder of a house to buy a freehold of the house or alternatively to obtain a 50-year extension to the lease. Flats are specifically excluded from the provisions of the Act. The lease must also be for more than 21 years and the leaseholder or his family must have lived there for the last three years. The Act is, unfortunately, very complicated and the various conditions must be satisfied before the option to purchase the freehold or extend the lease can be exercised. The freeholder may, in certain circumstances, be able to prevent the enforcement of the provisions of the Act taking place, but will have to pay compensation to the leaseholder in these circumstances.

The leaseholder of the flat will, on expiry of the lease, and subject to certain conditions, become a protected Rent Act tenant. The landlord will therefore have to commence possession proceedings in order to regain possession of the flat. The landlord will only be successful if he can prove one of the statutory grounds for repossession, such as rent arrears and/or breach of the tenancy agreement.

THE RENT ACTS

The law governing the relationship between a landlord and a tenant is extremely complex and detailed, and it is possible to give only a brief summary here. To avoid having to study the numerous statutory provisions relating to tenancies, the simplest approach is to ask whether a tenancy is within the Rent Acts or not. The tenancy must, to be within the Rent Acts, be of a residential dwelling. The tenant must have exclusive possession of at least part of the property and the rateable value and rent must be within certain limits. Most lettings by private landlords are regulated tenancies, ie regulated by the Acts.

If the landlord is a resident landlord, that is he and the tenant live in the same house or flat, the Act does not apply. The landlord cannot evict a regulated tenant unless he obtains a possession order from the court and this can only be granted in certain limited circumstances, such as misconduct by the tenant or because the landlord requires the accommodation for himself or his family. Further, either the landlord or the tenant can apply to the rent officer for a fair rent to be registered; this will then be the most that the landlord can charge.

A regulated tenancy can either be 'protected' or 'statutory'. The difference is that a protected tenant has security by virtue of his contract with the landlord. A statutory tenant has security by virtue of the protection given by the Rent Acts. There are also some special types of regulated tenancy where the landlord has a guaranteed right to repossession at the end of the tenancy, eg where a landlord lets his home which he intends to retire to.

A shorthold tenancy is a new type of regulated tenancy introduced by the Housing Act 1980. The main feature of a shorthold tenancy is that the tenancy must be granted for a fixed period between one and five years. At the end of the fixed period the landlord has the mandatory right to repossession, subject to certain conditions.

Restricted contract lettings are where the landlord and the tenant live in the same house or flat. Tenants of resident landlords do not normally have long-term security of tenure. The landlord can apply to court for a Repossession Order once he has brought the letting to an end and the court must grant the order, but may suspend its operation for up to three months.

General points

It is a criminal offence for anyone unlawfully to turn a residential occupier out of his home or to drive him out by threats, violence or withholding services.

Before a landlord can try to get a possession order against the tenant, he must serve a Notice to Quit the premises. The notice must be in writing and served upon the tenant at least four weeks before it is due to expire.

If a tenancy is granted after 24 October 1961 and is for less than seven years, the landlord is responsible for the repair of the structure and exterior of the dwelling. The landlord must also repair the basins, sinks, baths and gas and water installations. Otherwise, the responsibility of the landlord and tenant will largely depend upon the agreement between them.

The landlord must provide a rent book containing certain prescribed information to all weekly tenants.

A landlord cannot charge a premium, that is a lump sum, to a prospective tenant for the right to occupy premises. Merely asking for a premium is a criminal offence. The landlord may require the tenant to purchase the fixtures and fittings at an inflated price. The tenant will then be able to recover a sum of money over and above the actual value of fixtures and fittings.

The payment of a deposit greater than two months' rent will usually be regarded as an illegal premium.

It is an offence not to provide in writing the details of the landlord's name and address within 21 days of a request.

The landlord cannot levy excessive service charges, ie a charge for the cost of maintenance, redecoration, insurance and administration of the property. The landlord must obtain estimates and consult the tenants before incurring expenditure over a certain value. The landlord must also supply a copy of estimates and a notice of works to be carried out and allow the tenants to make representations.

A criminal offence may be committed if the premises are overcrowded. Premises are overcrowded if the square footage of the property and the number of bedrooms and living rooms are under a recognized minimum for a given number of people. The landlord is entitled to evict a tenant who has been found guilty of an overcrowding offence at the premises. A tenant who is on the council's waiting list cannot, however, be evicted from overcrowded premises.

Licensees

A licensee is a person who is allowed on to someone else's property with permission, but without legal rights. Licensees are not tenants. A hotel guest has a permission to occupy a room for a certain number of nights; he is not a tenant and is not entitled to Rent Act protection.

It is important to distinguish between a tenancy and a licence because if there is a tenancy the tenant will be entitled to full protection or at least restricted protection depending on the circumstances. If there is a licence, the occupier can never have full protection. Naturally, some landlords have tried to draft tenancy agreements so that they look as though they give the occupier a licence and not a tenancy. In practice, the courts examine these documents very closely and are reluctant to enforce them as they are usually shams and a device for trying to avoid the Rent Acts. Recently, authorities have stated that a test whether an occupancy of residential accommodation is a tenancy or a licence rests on the true construction of the agreement and whether the occupier had been granted exclusive possession of the accommodation for a fixed or periodic term at a stated rent. The intention of the parties, as manifested in the agreement, is generally irrelevant.

A person who occupies premises without permission is a trespasser and has no rights over the land. Such a person is commonly called 'a squatter', a word which is not known to the law. Squatting itself is not illegal; however, it can lead to the commission of other criminal offences, such as causing criminal damage. The Criminal Law Act 1977 created three separate offences purely to deal with the position of squatter. Entering the property with an offensive weapon, which may simply mean a torch or a spanner, is an offence. Refusing to leave when asked by someone who was previously living there or intends to live there, is an offence. Also, a squatter who resists or intentionally obstructs a bailiff, who is enforcing a possession order, commits an offence.

Since 1977 a squatter cannot be physically ejected without a court order. It is an offence to threaten or use violence to obtain entry. However, a displaced residential occupier can use threats of violence but not actual acts of violence to secure entry. Such course of action is not recommended, especially as expeditious methods are available to the landlord to obtain a possession order at the high or county court.

INTELLECTUAL PROPERTY

Statutes have been enacted over the years to protect the interests of artists, authors, inventors and designers, so that they may be entitled to derive benefit from the products of their labour. The Copyright and Patents Acts grant exclusive rights of reproduction and use, subject to certain conditions, to anyone who has created a work of art, a design or devised an invention. The rights extend for specified limited periods only. If the rights are infringed the injured party is entitled to seek financial redress. Therefore, full investigation of existing copyrights and designs must be made by anyone who wishes to reproduce or use a product. A thorough examination of the Patents Register must be made by anyone who proposes to launch a new invention. Further, the inventor, in order to obtain statutory protection must first obtain a patent and then register it. Unnecessary research and production expenditure and legal fees can therefore be avoided if full searches are made at the outset.

Copyright

Copyright can briefly be described as the exclusive right of printing or otherwise reproducing an original work. That is, an author, artist or composer has the right to prevent all others from copying his work. The infringement of this right is called piracy. Copyright extends to original artistic, dramatic and musical works and to recordings, films and broadcasts.

The law on copyright is mainly contained in the Copyright Act 1956. The Act defines separately the various matters in which copyright can exist, how that copyright is infringed and the period for which it extends. Where an original literary, dramatic or musical work has been published, copyright subsists for 50 years from the end of the calendar year in which the author died. If the work has not been published or any of the other acts specified in the Act have been satisfied, the copyright subsists from 50 years from the end of the calendar year in which the publication takes place or such other specified act is done.

Copyright in a literary, dramatic or musical work is infringed by reproducing the work, performing it in public, broadcasting the work or causing it to be transmitted. The Act does, however, make provision for the reproduction of literary, dramatic or musical work for the purposes of judicial proceedings and reports or for the use of schools etc. Reproduction of this kind is termed 'fair dealing' and does not infringe the copyright law, so long as sufficient acknowledgement identifying the author is made.

Copyright in artistic work subsists in paintings, sculptures, drawings and photographs and in general subsists for 50 years from the end of the calendar year in which the artist died. In the case of a photograph, the copyright exists for 50 years from the date of publication of the photo. An artistic copyright is infringed by reproducing it in any material form, including broadcasting.

The copyright in any literary, dramatic, musical or artistic work usually vests in its author. However, where the author has created the work during the course of his employment, with a newspaper or other publication, the proprietor is entitled to the copyright in respect of the publication in its newspaper or other periodicals only. In any other case, subject to an agreement to the contrary, the copyright in work made during the course of the author's normal employment is the property of the employer. Where a person commissions a photograph or painting, the person commissioning the work is entitled to the copyright.

A copyright can be assigned, but the assignment must be in writing. An agreement in writing to assign future copyright automatically vests the copyright in the assignee when the copyright comes into an existence.

Where a manuscript of a literary, dramatic or other such artistic work is bequeathed to another, the copyright will pass to the beneficiary in the absence of contrary intention.

Copyright law is governed by a number of Acts and further amendments and new Acts are being introduced to protect the interests of the artists and authors. The law is making an attempt to keep in line with the various new forms of reproduction of works and new bills are regularly being submitted for approval.

Patents

The law relating to patents is now largely contained in the Patents Act 1977. Broadly speaking, a patent confers on the applicant the right of exclusive use and benefit of a new invention. An application to the Patent Office for a patent may be made by any person who must identify the actual deviser of the invention. In order for the application to be successful the invention must be novel, new and it must involve an inventive step, ie not obvious to the skilled inventor, and it must be capable of industrial application. The Act does not make provision for scientific theories, literary, dramatic, musical and artistic works, mathematical methods or computer programs. Furthermore, a patent will not be granted if the invention is offensive, immoral or anti-social behaviour is likely to result. Also, a patent will not be granted for biological processes involved in breeding animals or plants, medical or surgical methods of treatment.

An application for a patent can be made in the prescribed form on payment of a fee to the Patent Office. Within 12 months of filing the application further specifications and details must be lodged, giving a clear description and technical information regarding the invention. The examiners at the Patent Office will make a thorough search of their records to ensure that the invention is in fact new and inventive. Applications for patents are published by the office and publication then confers certain rights on the applicant to take action for damages for infringement. The purpose of publication is to invite public response and criticism. A further examination is then carried out on payment of a further fee by the examiners. The examiners will make their final decision whether they are satisfied that the invention is novel and inventive. If a case is proved for a patent, the Grant of Letters of Patent will be published. The patent will then continue for 20 years from the date of filing the application only upon payment of the annual renewal fee. Non-payment of the renewal fee will cause the patent to lapse.

As with a copyright, a patent can be assigned or mortgaged. However, to be valid, the assignment or mortgage must be in writing. The patent can be registered thereby giving notice of its existence. The register of patents also establishes the priority of applications. A later registered patent will have priority over an earlier unregistered one. Also, no claim for infringement of a patent can be made for unregistered patents.

Inventions devised during the course of employment are governed by the rules embodied in the Patent Act 1977. The employee-inventor will be able to patent an invention only if it was not invented during the course of his normal duties. Naturally, each case will turn on its own particular facts and the particular duties of the employee in question. If the invention does *not* belong to the employer, the employee is entitled to cash compensation from the employer if the employer has derived outstanding benefit from the patent. The employee can make a claim for compensation at any time during the duration of the patent. However, no compensation will be forthcoming if the employee works under a collective agreement and is entitled to compensation for inventions made at work. The collective agreement, which usually makes generous provision for the employee's inventions, will prevail over the Act's provisions. Naturally, the employee will only reap the benefits of a collective agreement if he is a member of that particular trade union.

A patent is infringed if, while it is in force and without the patent owner's consent, where the invention is a product, a person makes, disposes of, uses or imports the product. Where the invention is a process, the person simply needs to use or offer the process for use or import or dispose of the same. The proprietor will be able to seek an injunction preventing further use of the patent and/or an order requiring the infringer to destroy or deliver up the products made in infringement and/or damages on account of loss of profits.

Separate legislation governs the use and restriction of designs and is constantly being updated by various rules, to protect the interests of the designer. For legislative purposes a design has been defined as 'the features of shape, configuration, pattern or ornament applied to any article by an industrial process or means, being features which the finished article appeal to and are judged solely by the eye'. A design does not include a method or principle of the construction. Registration provides the designer with copyright protection for five years from the date of application and can be extended for two further periods of five years. The effect of registering the design is that the designer is bestowed with the exclusive right to use the design for business and trade purposes. The designer's remedies for infringement are an injunction, or an order for delivery up of the infringing copy and/or damages. However, no damages will be awarded where there has been an innocent infringement.

Although designs are not published in the same way as patents, the Register of Designs is still available for public inspection. As with copyrights and patents, a design can be assigned or licensed and any such transaction should be registered, although non-registration of the transaction will not affect the damages awarded for infringement.

16

BUSINESS INFORMATION SOURCES

Hano Johannsen

INTRODUCTION

This chapter highlights the key sources of business information and is divided into two parts. Part 1 covers general sources; Part 2 provides detailed sources of further information chapter by chapter (organizations, books and journals).

PART 1: GENERAL SOURCES OF FURTHER INFORMATION

Today the range of sources of business information is vast and changing rapidly. While personal and business contacts, Chambers of Commerce and trade and professional associations often provide the answers to a wide range of problems, keeping up to date with current developments and finding information on specialist topics calls for an understanding and knowledge of the many centres which collect, organize and make business information available and how they do it.

The aim here is to suggest a broad spectrum of potential sources. Some of the long-established national organizations will be familiar but many of the more specialized sources may be unknown.

It is important to recognize that while some business information is very visible in the sense that access is available from libraries, local and national information and advice centres, it is by no means all about the published word (directories, books, journals, newsletters). There are also vast 'hidden' sources. These provide information in the form of specialist audio or video cassette updating 'magazines'. Examples include the Management Tape (produced by Audio Magazine Co, Didasko House, Warboys, Huntingdon, Cambs) and the Financial Training Video (a VHS tape available on subscription from Financial Video Training, 60 Kennington Oval, London SE11 5SW).

A growing number of computer online information services (on company information, for example, provide individual user access to major databases) plus a host of unpublished and semi-published reports and statistics. The latter are often unique sources and can be extremely useful but they tend to be little known outside a narrow circle. It is this category of information which includes specialist working party reports, survey reports, statistical data collected by trade associations, as well as numerous limited circulation reports and newsletters. Also in this category is other material such as the helpful series of checklists and reading lists produced by the British Institute of Management. For example, BIM produce reading lists covering books and journal articles on over 200 business and management subjects.

Additionally there is a vast range of visual and audio-visual material. Though primarily aimed at the training and education markets, much of this material can also be regarded as a valuable information source (see *Know Your Training Films*, a two-volume directory including index, 2nd edition, Management Update, 1987).

It is the ongoing nature of information - it is always out of date immediately it is produced - plus the range and variety of potential sources and the varied stocking and indexing habits of numerous libraries etc which make it very difficult to point to any one key source of information on any given subject.

There is also the question of definition. While business and commercial information may at first sight appear to be an easily defined area, in reality it is not. There are numerous topics which are regarded as peripheral or borderline in the sense that they are seen by some as being technical or scientific. British Standards, patents and product information are examples which can easily be classified as 'non-business' but are nevertheless of key concern to many sectors of the business community.

The result is that although one should find the bulk of relevant material in commercial or business libraries and information centres, one should remember that what material is collected in any given library or information centre is mainly a result of its purchasing and staff resources and the subjective judgement of what users are likely to require.

ONLINE BUSINESS INFORMATION SERVICES

So called 'online' information services are developing rapidly. In the main they provide the user with access to highly specialized and large databases of information which are regularly updated. By means of a terminal, a visual display unit, a telephone link (and a subscription fee), they enable a user in any location to gain access to vast central collections of data. The number of subscribers to some new services has not always met market forecasts, suggesting that some potential users may not yet be ready to take the plunge.

The range of services covers a large field including, for example, JORDANWATCH, McCARTHY ONLINE (for company information), British Telecom's business HOTLINE, HARVEST (covering market research reports), KOMPASS (a service replacing EKOL and specializing in company information), DATASTAR (covering *Harvard Business Review* articles), the recently relaunched MANAGEMENT and MARKETING ABSTRACTS (produced by Pergamon in association with the British Institute of Management and PIRA) and MARISNET (for open learning training materials).

So many new services are being developed and marketed that it is best to keep up to date by referring to *Online Business Information*, a monthly magazine or the *Online Business Sourcebook*: both are published by Headland Press and details are available from Freepost 22, London EC1A 7QT (telephone enquiries 0429 31902).

BUSINESS LIBRARIES AND INFORMATION CENTRES

The first port of call when seeking business information externally should be the leading local public library. Many hold a range of valuable collections of reference material of interest to the businessman. Although the scope of the collections vary, they all have experienced staff who can not only provide access to their own collection of reference material but can be particularly helpful when it comes to tapping into other library and information resources. The layman is often unaware of the vast 'hidden' resources available via the British Library Lending Division at Boston Spa and the day-to-day contacts with many other libraries which can be accessed through the local library system.

The major cities and many county library services operate comprehensive specialized business or commercial libraries making available a wide range of journals and specialized information sources. Some have comprehensive information retrieval systems, and the more specialized centres have experienced staff who usually have detailed knowledge of business topics and sources.

Specialized libraries

British Library Business Information Service
Southampton Buildings
25 Chancery Lane
London WC2A 1AW
01-405 8721

City Business Library
55 Basinghall Street
London EC2V 5BX
01-638 8215

Statistics and Market Intelligence Library
1 Victoria Street
London SW1H OET
01-215 5444

In major cities and towns check with the Central or County Library services for further details

Professional bodies etc

Most professional associations provide a library and information service: some are restricted to members' use. The following lists some of the key organizations. ASLIB (listed below) is a useful 'signposting' organization if you are unsure where to go for specific types of information.

ASLIB (Association of Information Management)
26–27 Boswell Street
London WC1N 3JE
01–430 2671

BACIE (British Association for Commercial & Industrial Education)
16 Park Crescent
London W1N 4AP
01-636 5351

British Institute of Management
Management House
Cottingham Road
Corby
Northants NN17 ITT
0536 204222

The Chartered Institute of Management Accountants
63 Portland Place
London W1NN 4AB
01-580 6542

Design Council
28 Haymarket
London SW1Y 4SU
01-839 8000

Industrial Society
Peter Runge House
3 Carlton House Terrace
London SW1Y 5DG
01-839 4300

Institute of Chartered Accountants in England and Wales
PO Box 433
Chartered Accountants Hall
Moorgate Place
London EC2P 2BJ
01-628 7060

Institute of Data Processing Management
50 Goschen Buildings
12–13 Henrietta Street
London WC2E 8NU
01-240 3304

Institute of Directors
116 Pall Mall
London SW1Y 5ED
01-839 1233

Institute of Management Services
1 Cecil Court
London Road
Enfield
Middx EN2 6DD

PART 2: DETAILED SOURCES OF INFORMATION FOR EACH CHAPTER

The following list highlights useful sources of additional information for each chapter: in most instances sources are listed under three headings:

Sources of further information,
Further reading and
Key journals.

For general sources of business information see also Part 1.

1. BUSINESS ORGANIZATION

Sources of further information

Alliance of Small Firms and Self-employed People Ltd
42 Vine Street
East Molesey
Surrey KT8 9LF
01-979 2293

Association of Independent Businesses
Trowbray House
108 Weston Street
London SE1 3QB
01-403 4066

Business Management Association
St Mark's Hall
Balderton Street
London W1Y 1TG
01-493 1001

Companies Registrar (England and Wales)
Companies House
55 City Road
London EC1Y 1BB
01-253 9393

Companies Registrar (Scotland)
102 George Street
Edinburgh EH2 3JD
031-225 5774

Companies Registrar (Northern Ireland)
Department of Commerce
43–47 Chichester Court
Belfast BT1 4PJ
0232 234121

Confederation of British Industry (CBI)
Centre Point
New Oxford Street
London WC1A 4DD
01-379 7400

Co-operative Development Agency (CDA)
Broadmead House
21 Panton Street
London SW1Y 4DR
01-832 4300

Council for Small Industries in Rural Areas (CoSIRA)
141 Castle Street
Salisbury
Wilts SP1 3TP
0722 336255

Greater London Enterprise Board (GLEB)
63–67 Newington Causeway
London SE1 6BD
01-403 0300

Industrial Common Ownership Movement (ICOM)
7 Corn Exchange
Leeds LS1 7BP
0532 961737

Institute of Directors
116 Pall Mall
London SW1Y 5ED
01-839 1233

Management Consultancies Association
11 West Halkin Street
London SW1X 8JL
01-235 3897

Wales Co-operative and Training Centre
55 Charles Street
Cardiff CF1 4ED
0222 372237

Further reading

Brech, E F L, *Principles & Practice of Management*, Longman, Harlow, 1975
Brooks, M J, *Sources of Free Business Information*, Kogan Page, London, 1986
Chaplin, P, (ed) *Choosing and Using Professional Advisers*, Kogan Page, London 1986
Child, J, *Organisation: A Guide to Problems and Practice*, Harper and Row, London, 1977
Her Majesty's Stationery Office (HMSO), official source for all Acts of Parliament, Command Papers, Statutory Instruments etc, and a vast range of business publications produced by government departments and agencies. (HMSO bookshops in major cities or order titles from local bookseller agents.)
Johannsen, H (ed), *Company Organisation Structure*, British Institute of Management, London, 1970
Johannsen, H, and Page, G T, *International Dictionary of Management*, 3rd edn, Kogan Page, London, 1986
Knight, K (ed), *Matrix Management*, Gower, Farnborough, 1977
Mahler, W B, *Structure, Power and Results: How to Organise Your Company for Optimum Performance*, Dow Jones-Irwin, Homewood, 1975
Pugh, D S and Hickson, D, *Organisation Structure in Its Context*, Saxon House, Farnborough, 1976
Scrine, A J, *Be Your Own Company Secretary*, Kogan Page, London, 1987
Winckles, K, *The Practice of Successful Business Management*, Kogan Page, London, 1986

2. FINANCE

Further reading

Beerel, A C, *The Realities of Raising Business Finance*, Management Update, London, 1986
Dewhurst, J and Burns, P, *Small Businesss – Finance and Control*, Macmillan, London 1983
Midgley, K and Burns, P, *Business Finance and the Capital Market*, 3rd edn, Macmillan, London, 1979
Ray, G H and Hutchinson, P J, *The Financing and Financial Control of Small Enterprise Development*, Gower, Aldershot, 1983

Samuels, J M and Wilkes, F M, *Management of Company Finance*, 3rd edn, Van Nostrand Reinhold, 1982
Woodcock, C, *Raising Finance: The Guardian Guide for the Small Business*, 2nd edn, Kogan Page, London, 1985

3. PROPERTY AND PREMISES

Sources of further information

British Coal Enterprise
NLA Tower
12 Addiscombe Road
Croydon CR9 3JH
01-686 0366

British Technology Group
101 Newington Causeway
London SE1 6BU
01-403 6666

Commission for the New Towns
Glen House
Stag Place
London SW1E 9BJ
01-828 7722

Council for Small Industries in Rural Areas (CoSIRA)
141 Castle Street
Salisbury
Wilts SP1 3TP
0722 336255

Department of Employment
Small Firms Service
Ring the operator on 100 and ask for Freefone Enterprise. You will be put in touch with your nearest branch.

Sixth Floor
Ladywood House
Stephenson Street
Birmingham B2 4DT
021-643 3344

Fifth Floor
The Pithay
Bristol BS1 2NB
0272 294546

Carlyle House
Carlyle Road
Cambridge CB4 3DN
0223 63312

16 St David's House
Wood Street
Cardiff CF1 1ER
0222 396116

120 Bothwell Street
Glasgow
G2 6TU
041-248 6014

1 Park Row
City Square
Leeds LS1 5NR
0532 445151

Graeme House
Derby Square
Liverpool L3 9HJ
051-236 5756

Ebury Bridge House
2–18 Ebury Bridge Road
London SW1W 8QD
01-730 8451

Third Floor
320–325 Royal Exchange Buildings
St Ann's Square
Manchester M2 7AH
061-832 5282

Centro House
3 Cloth Street
Newcastle upon Tyne NE1 3EE
0632 325353

Severns House
20 Middle Pavement
Nottingham NG1 7DW
0602 581205

Abbey Hall
Abbey Square
Reading RG1 3BE
0734 591733

The Welsh Development Agency
(Small Business Section)
Treforest Industrial Estate
Pontypridd
Mid Glamorgan CF37 5UT
0443 852666

The Scottish Development Agency
(Small Business Division)
102 Telford Road
Edinburgh EH4 2NP
031-343 1911

The Local Enterprise
Development Unit
Lamont House
Purdys Lane
Newtownbreda
Belfast BT8 4AR
0232 691031

Design Council
28 Haymarket
London SW1Y 4SU
01-839 8000

English Estates
St George's House
Kingsway
Team Valley
Gateshead
Tyne and Wear NE11 0NA
0632 878941

53 Fore Street
Bodmin
Cornwall PL31 2JB
0208 3631

Hallgate House
19 Hallgate
Doncaster DN1 3NN
0302 66865

Sandon House
157 Regent Road
Liverpool L5 9TF
051-933 2020

Forster House
Allensway
Thornaby
Cleveland TS17 9HA
0642 765911

Salterbeck Industrial Estate
Workington
Cumbria CA14 5DX
0946 830469

Fire Protection Association
140 Aldersgate Street
London EC1A 4HY
01-606 3757

Health Education Council
78 New Oxford Street
London WC1A 2AW
01-631 0930

London Docklands Development
Corporation
West India House
Millwall Dock
London E14 9TJ
01-515 3000

Merseyside Development
Corporation
Royal Liver Buildings
Pierhead
Liverpool L3 1JH

Royal Institute of British Architects
(Clients Advisory Service)
66 Portland Place
London W1N 4AD
01-580 5533

Royal Town Planning Institute
26 Portland Place
London W1N 4BE
01-636 9107

Further reading

Biekowski, M and Allen, K, *Industrial Aids in the UK: A Businessman's Guide,* Centre for the Study of Public Policy, University of Strathclyde, annual

Business Location Handbook, Beacon, Northampton, 1986

Dewis, M (ed), *Health and Safety at Work Handbook,* Tolley, London

Duffy, F, *Planning Office Space,* Architectural Press, London, 1976

Farrell, P, *How to Buy a Business,* Kogan Page, London, 1983

Green, H, Chalkley, B and Foley, P, *How to Choose Business Premises,* Kogan Page, London, 1986

Harkness, S and Groom, J N, *Building Without Barriers,* Watson-Guptill, New York

Johannsen, H (ed), *Business Relocation,* Management Update, London, 1983

Man, D, *Shops: A Manual of Planning and Design,* Architectural Press, London, 1981

Saphier, M, *Planning the New Office,* McGraw-Hill, New York, 1978

Key journals

Commercial Property Register
(10 × pa)
Tophill Press
Unit 4 Sevenoaks Station
Kent TN13 1DP

Industrial Property Register
(10 × pa)
as above

Premises Management
(Quarterly)
J Allen Publishing
Unit 2 Haslemere Estate
Armadale Road
Feltham
Middx TW14 0WL

4. PERSONNEL MANAGEMENT

Sources of further information

Advisory, Conciliation and
Arbitration Service (ACAS)
Head Office
11–12 St James's Square
London SW1Y 4LA
01-214 6000
and regional offices

Department of Employment
Head Office
Caxton House
Tothill Street
London SW1H 9NF
01-213 3000

Data Protection Registrar
Springfield House
Water Lane
Wilmslow
Cheshire SK9 5AX
0625 535777

Health and Safety Executive
Regina House
259–269 Old Marylebone Road
London NW1 5RR
01-229 3456

Industrial Participation Association
78 Buckingham Gate
London SW1E 6PQ
01-222 0351

Industrial Society
Peter Runge House
3 Carlton House Terrace
London SW1Y 5DG
01-839 4300

Institute of Personnel Management
IPM House
Camp Road
London SW19 4UW
01-946 9100

Irish Management Institute
Sandyford Road
Dublin 14

Pre-Retirement Association of Great
Britain and Northern Ireland
19 Undine Street
London SW12 8PP
01-767 3225

Royal Society for the Prevention of
Accidents (ROSPA)
Occupational Safety Division
Cannon House
Priory Queensway
Birmingham B4 6BS
021-233 2461

Wages Councils
Steel House
11 Tothill Street
London SW1H 9NF
01-213 3881

Further reading

Armstrong, M, *A Handbook of Personnel Management Practice*, 2nd edn, Kogan Page, London, 1984

Armstrong, M, *Personnel Management: A Handbook for Employers and Line Managers,* Kogan Page, London, 1982
Armstrong, M and Murlis, H, *A Handbook of Salary Administration,* Kogan Page, London, 1980
Biddle, D, and Everden, R, *Human Aspects of Management,* Institute of Personnel Management, London, 1980
Cuming, M C, *Theory & Practice of Personnel Management,* Heinemann, London, 1980
Dickinson, A W, *The Industrial Manager's Guide to Personnel Practice,* Gower, Epping, 1974
Fisher, M, *Controlling Labour Costs,* Kogan Page, London, 1981
Hawkins, K, *A Handbook of Industrial Relations Practice,* Kogan Page, London, 1979
Honey, P, *Solving People Problems,* McGraw-Hill, London, 1980
Thomason, G F, *Textbook of Personnel Management,* Institute of Personnel Management, London, 1978

Key journals

Anbar Personnel & Training Abstracts (8 × pa)
PO Box 23
Wembley
Middx HA9 8DJ

Employee Relations (Quarterly)
MCB University Press Ltd
62 Toller Lane
Bradford BD9 9BY

Employment Gazette (Monthly)
Department of Employment
HMSO

Industrial Relations News (Fortnightly)
MCB University Press Ltd
62 Toller Lane
Bradford BD9 9BY

IPM Digest (Monthly)
IPM House
Camp Road
London SW19 4UW
01-946 9100

Personnel Management (IPM) (Monthly)
1 Hills Place
London W1R 1AG

Personnel Review (Quarterly)
MSC University Press Ltd
62 Toller Lane
Bradford BD9 9BY

Chapter 5. Training

Further sources of information

Industrial Council for Education and Training Technology (ICETT)
Leicester House
8 Leicester Street
London WC2H 7BN

Institute of Training & Development (ITD)
5 Baring Road
Beaconsfield
Bucks HP9 2NX
04946 3994

Further reading

Belbin, R M, *Management Teams,* Heinemann, London, 1981
Dean, C and Whitlock, Q, *A Handbook of Computer-Based Training,* Kogan Page, London, 1984
Directory of Trainer Support Services 1987, Kogan Page, London, 1987
Hague, H, *Executive Self-Development,* Macmillan, London, 1974
Pepper, A D, *Managing the Training and Development Function,* Gower, Aldershot, 1984

Key journals

Health & Safety at Work (Monthly)
PO Box 109
Maclaren House
Scarbrook Road
Croydon CR9 1QH

Industrial & Commercial Training
(6 × pa)
MCB University Press Ltd
62 Toller Lane
Bradford BD9 9BY

Personnel and Training Abstracts
(8 × pa)
Anbar Publications Ltd
PO Box 23
Wembley
Middx HA9 8DJ

Personnel Management (Monthly)
Institute of Personnel Management
IPM House
Camp Road
London SW19 4UW
01-946 9100

Training & Development (Monthly)
100 Great Portland Street
London W1N 5PD

Training Officer (Monthly)
25–27 Cross Street
Manchester M2 1WL

Transitions (Monthly)
1 Hills Place
London W1R 1AG

6. ADMINISTRATION AND OFFICE SERVICES

Sources of further information

Institute of Administrative
Management
205 High Street
Beckenham
Kent BR3 1BA
01-658 1071

Institute of Data Processing
Management
50 Goschen Buildings
12–13 Henrietta Street
London WC2E 8NU
01-240 3304

Institute of Management Services
1 Cecil Court
London Road
Enfield
Middx EN2 6DD
01-363 7452 & 7457

National Computing Centre
11 New Fetter Lane
London EC4 1PU
01-353 4875

National Reprographic Centre for Documentation
Hatfield Polytechnic
Bayfordbury
Hertford SG13 8LD
0992 552341

Further reading

Cemach, H P, *Work Study in the Office* (6th edn, revised by R Revell), Anbar, Wembley, 1986

Checkland, P B, *Systems Thinking, Systems Practice,* Wiley, Chichester, 1981

Comer, M K, *Corporate Fraud,* McGraw-Hill, London, 1977

Currier-Briggs, N (ed) *Handbook of Security,* Kluwer-Harrap, London, 1975

Denyer, J C, *O & M and Management Services,* Macdonald & Evans, Plymouth, 1976

Fletcher, J and Gowing, D, *The Business Guide to Effective Writing,* Kogan Page, London, 1987

Knight, P A, *Installing a Small Business Computer,* National Computing Centre, Manchester, 1982

Knox, F M, *Managing Paperwork: A Key to Productivity,* Gower, Farnborough, 1980

Mills, G and Standingford, O, *Office Organisation and Method: A Manual of Administration Management* (6th edn), Pitman, London, 1978

Oppenheim, P and Derrick, J, *A Handbook of New Office Technology,* (2nd edn), Kogan Page, London, 1986

Seymour-Smith, L, *Making Your Meetings More Effective,* Management Update, London, 1985

Shaw, J, *Office Organisation for Managers,* Macdonald & Evans, Plymouth, 1978

Wainwright, G, *Report Writing,* Management Update, London, 1984

Key journals

Anbar Work Study & O & M Abstracts (8 × pa)
PO Box 23
Wembley
Middx HA9 8DJ

Business Systems & Equipment (Monthly)
Maclean House
76 Oxford Street
London W1N 9FD

Computer Weekly
Quadrant House
The Quadrant
Sutton
Surrey SM2 5AS

Micro Decision
Evelyn House
62 Oxford Street
London W1A 2HG

7. MARKETING AND SELLING

Sources of further information

AGB Research plc
London International Press Centre
76 Shoe Lane
London EC4A 3JB
01-583 8888

British Direct Marketing Association
1 New Oxford Street
London WC1A 1NQ
01-242 2254

CBD Research
154 High Street
Beckenham
Kent BR3 1EA
01-650 7745

British Overseas Trade Board
1–19 Victoria Street
London SW1H 0ET
01–215 7877

Bill of Entry Service
Statistical Office
HM Customs & Excise
Portcullis House
27 Victoria Avenue
Southend SS2 6AL
0702 49421

Building Research Establishment
Department of the Environment
Bucknalls Lane
Garston
Watford WD2 7JR
0923 674040

Business Statistics Office
Government Buildings
Cardiff Road
Newport
Gwent NPT 1XG
0633 56111

The Central Statistical Office
Press and Information Service
Great George Street
London SW1P 3AQ
01-233 3000

Dun and Bradstreet
26-32 Clifton Street
London EC2P 2LY
01-588 3881

Economist Publications
40 Duke Street
London W1M 5DG
01-493 6711

Euromonitor Publications
87 Turnmill Street
London EC1M 5QU
01-251 8024

Extel Statistical Services
Extel House
37 St Paul Street
London EC2A 4PB
01-251 0344

Financial Times Business
Information
102 Clerkenwell Road
London EC1M 5SA
01-251 9321

Industrial Market Research Association
11 Bird Street
Lichfield
Staffs WS13 6PW
0543 263448

Institute of Marketing
Moor Hall
Cookham
Maidenhead
Berks SL6 9HQ
06285 24922

Institute of Public Relations
1 Great James Street
London WC1N 3DA
01-405 5505

Inter Company Comparisons
81 City Road
London EC1Y 1BD
01-251 2828

Kompass Sales Information Services
Windsor Court
East Grinstead
West Sussex RH19 1XD
0342 26972

Marketing Surveys Index
22 Wates Way
Mitcham
Surrey CR4 4HR
01-640 6621

Market Location
17 Waterloo Place
Warwick Street
Leamington Spa
Warwickshire CV32 5LA
0926 34235

Mintel Information Services
7 Arundel Street
London WC2R 3DR
01-836 1814

NEDO
Millbank Tower
Millbank
London SW1P 4QX
01-211 5989

A C Nielsen
Nielsen House
London Road
Headington
Oxford OX3 9RX
0865 64851

Science Reference Library
25 Southampton Buildings
Chancery Lane
London WC2A 1AY
01-404 0406

Statistics and Market Intelligence Library
1 Victoria Street
London SW1H 0ET
01-215 5444

Further reading

Abell, D F and Hammond, J, *Strategic Market Planning*, Prentice Hall, Englewood Cliffs, 1979

Andrews, B, *Creative Product Development*, Longman, London, 1975

The AZ of UK Marketing Information Services, Euromonitor, London

Baker, M J, *Marketing Strategy and Management*, Macmillan, London, 1985

Bolt, G J, *Market and Sales Forecasting*, Kogan Page, London, 1983

Bonama, T V, *The Marketing Edge: Making Strategies Work*, Macmillan, London, 1985
Brann, C, *Cost Effective Direct Marketing*, Collectors' Books, Kemble, 1984
British Overseas Trade Board, *Industrial Marketing Researcher Check List*, HMSO, London, 1979
Carter, H C, *Effective Advertising*, Kogan Page, London, 1985
Chisnall, P M, *Marketing Research - Analysis and Measurement*, McGraw-Hill, Maidenhead, 1975
Christopher, M, *Effective Marketing Management*, Gower, Farnborough, 1980
Current British Directories, CBD Research, Beckenham
Gabor, A, *Pricing: Principles and Practice*, Heinemann, London, 1977
Hague, P N, *The Industrial Market Research Handbook*, Kogan Page, London 1985
Heller, R, *The Naked Market: Marketing Methods for the 80's*, Sidgwick & Jackson, London, 1984
Kotler, P, *Marketing Essentials*, Prentice Hall, Englewood Cliffs, 1984
Lace, G, *Marketing and Public Relations Handbook*, Kogan Page, London, 1986
Levitt, T, *Marketing for Business Growth*, McGraw-Hill, Maidenhead, 1974
Linton, I, *Promotion for the Professions*, Kogan Page, London, 1985
McDonald, MHB, *Marketing Plans: How to Prepare Them, How to Use Them*, Heinemann, London, 1984
The Marketing Research Sourcebook, Headland Printers, Hartlepool
Morse, S P, *Management Skills in Marketing*, McGraw-Hill, London, 1982
Patten, D, *Successful Marketing for the Small Business*, Kogan Page, London, 1985
Piper, J (ed) *Managing Sales Promotion*, Gower, Farnborough, 1980
Rines, M (ed) *Marketing Handbook* (2nd edn), Gower, Aldershot, 1981
Rogers, Len, *Selling by Telephone*, Kogan Page, London, 1986
Smith, R D and Dick, G, *Getting Sales*, Kogan Page, London, 1984
Sweeney, W R, *Managing a Sales Team*, Kogan Page, London, 1982
Thorelli, H B and Becker, H, *International Marketing Strategy*, Pergamon, Oxford, 1980
White, R, *Advertising: What it is and how to do it*, McGraw-Hill, London, 1980
Wilson, A, *The Assessment of Industrial Markets*, Hutchinson, London, 1986

Key journals

European Journal of Marketing (3 × pa)
MCB University Press Ltd
62 Toller Lane
Bradford BD9 9BY

Industrial Marketing Digest (Quarterly)
Old Rectory
Ranmore Common
Dorking
Surrey RH5 6SP

Marketing Week (Weekly)
60 Kingly Street
London W1R 5LH

Quarterly Review of Marketing
Institute of Marketing
Moor Hall
Cookham
Maidenhead
Berks SL6 9QH

Sales & Marketing Management (11 × pa)
13 Vaughan Road
Harpenden
Herts AL5 4HU

8. PHYSICAL DISTRIBUTION MANAGEMENT

Sources of further information

Centre for Physical Distribution Management
Management House
Cottingham Road
Corby
Northants NN17 1TT
0536 204222

Further reading

ABC Freight Guide, Kogan Page, London, annual
Burton, J A, *Effective Warehousing* (3rd edn), Macdonald & Evans, Plymouth, 1981
Gattorna, J (ed), *Handbook of Physical Distribution Management*, (3rd edn), Gower, 1983
Lowe, D, *The Transport Manager's Handbook 1987*, Kogan Page, London, 1986
Mann, C, *Commercial Vehicle Buyer's Guide*, (10th edn), Kogan Page, London, 1986
Murphy, G J, *Transport and Distribution* (2ncd edn), Business Books, Southport, 1978

Key journals

Focus (6 × pa)
Centre for Physical Distribution Management
Management House
Cottingham Road
Corby
Northants NN17 1TT

Freight (Monthly)
Hermes House
St John's Road
Tunbridge Wells
Kent TN4 9UZ

Transport Management (Quarterly)
32 Palmerston Road
Southampton SO11 1LL

9. PURCHASING AND SUPPLY

Sources of further information

British Standards Institution (BSI)
2 Park Street
London W1A 2BS
01-629 9000

Design Council
28 Haymarket
London SW1Y 4SU
01-839 8000

Institute of Purchasing and Supply
Easton House
Easton on the Hill
Stamford
Lincs PE9 3NZ
0780 3994

Institute of Quality Assurance
54 Princes Gate
London SW7 2PG
01-584 9026

Further reading

Aljian, G W, *Purchasing Handbook,* McGraw-Hill, London, 1981
Attwood, P A, *Planning a Distribution System,* Gower, 1978
Bailey, P J H, *Purchasing and Supply Managment* (4th edn), Chapman & Hall, London, 1978
Bailey, P J H and Farmer, D J, *Purchasing Principles & Management,* Pitman/Institute of Purchasing and Supply, London, 1981
Buckley, J (ed), *Guide to World Commodity Markets* (5th edn) Kogan Page, London, 1986
Burton, J H, *Stores Accounts & Stock Control,* Pitman, London
Compton, H K, *Storehouse & Stockyard Management,* Pitman/Institute of Purchasing and Supply, London
Compton, H K, *Supplies and Materials Management* (2nd edn), Macdonald & Evans/Institute of Purchasing and Supply, Plymouth, 1979
Farrington, B, *Industrial Purchase Price Management,* Gower/Institute of Purchasing and Supply, 1980
Lee, L and Dobler, D W, *Purchasing & Materials Management,* McGraw-Hill, London, 1984
Lysons, C K, *Purchasing,* Macdonald & Evans, Plymouth, 1981

Marsh, P D V, *Contracting for Engineering and Construction Projects* (2nd edn), Gower/Institute of Purchasing and Supply, 1981
Parsons, W J, *Improving Purchasing Performance*, Gower, 1982
Redmond, P W D *Mercantile Law* (5th edn), Macdonald & Evans, Plymouth, 1979
Thomas, A B, *Stock Control in Manufacturing Industries* (2nd edn), Gower, 1980
Warman, J, *Warehouse Management*, Heinemann, London, 1971
Watling, T F and Morley, J, *Successful Commodities Futures Trading* (2nd edn) Business Books, 1978
Woodroffe, G, *A Buyer's Guide to the Supply of Goods & Services Act 1982*, Institute of Purchasing and Supply, 1982

Key journals

Purchasing (Monthly)
Morgan Grampian House
30 Calderwood Street
London SE18 6QH

Purchasing & Supply Management (Monthly)
Institute of Purchasing and Supply
Easton House
Easton on the Hill
Stamford
Lincs PE9 3NZ

10. MANAGEMENT TECHNIQUES

Sources of further information

British Institute of Management
Management House
Corby
Northants NN17 1TT
0536 204222

Institute of Management Services
1 Cecil Court
London Road
Enfield
Middx EN2 6DD
01-363 7452 and 7457

Operational Research Society
6th Floor Neville House
Waterloo Street
Birmingham B2 5TX
021-643 0236

Society for Strategic and Long Range Planning
15 Belgrave Square
London SW1X 8PU
01-235 0246

Further reading

Argenti, J, *Practical Corporate Planning*, Allen & Unwin, London, 1980
Armstrong, M, *A Handbook of Management Techniques*, Kogan Page, London, 1986

Barnes, R M, *Motion and Time Study: Design and Management of Work,* Wiley, Chichester, 1980
Battersby, A, *Network Analysis for Planning and Scheduling* (3rd edn), Macmillan, London, 1978
Carson, G B, *Production Handbook,* Ronald Press, USA, 1972
De Bono, E, *Lateral Thinking; A Textbook of Creativity,* Penguin, Harmondsworth, 1977
Finch, F, *Concise Encyclopedia of Management Techniques,* Heinemann, London, 1976
Greenwood, W T, *Decision Theory and Information Systems,* South Western Publishing, USA, 1969
Hammond, J, *Understanding Human Engineering,* David & Charles, Newton Abbot, 1978
Helfert, E A, *Techniques of Financial Analysis,* Dow Jones-Irwin, USA, 1977
Juran, J M, *Quality Control Handbook* (3rd edn), McGraw-Hill, London, 1974
Miles, L D, *Techniques of Value Analysis and Engineering,* McGraw-Hill, London, 1972
Murrell, K F H, *Ergonomics,* Chapman & Hall, London, 1985
Rawlinson, J G, *Creative Thinking and Brainstorming,* Gower, 1981
Rickards, T, *Problem Solving Through Creative Analysis,* Gower, 1974
Westwick, C A, *How to Use Management Ratios* (2nd edn), Gower, 1987

Key journals

Journal of General Management (Quarterly)
108 Cowley Road
Oxford OX4 1FJ

Long Range Planning (6 × pa)
Pergamon Press Ltd
Headington Hill Hall
Oxford OX3 0BW

Management Decision (6 × pa)
MCB University Press Ltd
62 Toller Lane
Bradford BD8 9BY

Management Services (Monthly)
1 Cecil Court
London Road
Enfield
Middx EN2 6DD

Management Today (Monthly)
30 Lancaster Gate
London W2 3LP

11. TAXATION

Further reading

Hambro Tax Guide, Macdonald, London, annual
Horner, J, *Tax Facts,* Mistsave, Stockport

Moullin, M and Sergent, J, *Guide to the Taxation of Companies*, McGraw-Hill, London, 1982

12. ACCOUNTING

Sources of further information

Chartered Assocation of Certified Accountants
29 Lincoln's Inn Fields
London WC2A 3EE
01-242 6855

The Chartered Institute of Management Accountants
63 Portland Place
London W1N 4AB
01-637 2311

Chartered Institute Public Finance and Accounting
3 Robert Street
London WC2V 6BH
01-930 3456

Institute of Chartered Accountants in England and Wales
PO Box 433
Chartered Accountants Hall
Moorgate
London EC2P 2BJ
01-628 7060

Institute of Chartered Accountants in Ireland
87–89 Pembroke Road
Dublin 4
0001 680400
and
11 Donegall Square South
Belfast
0232 221600

Institute of Chartered Accounts of Scotland
27 Queen Street
Edinburgh EH2 1LA
031-225 5673

Institute of Internal Auditors
82 Portland Place
London W1N 3DH
01-580 0101

Further reading

Batty, J, *Accountancy for Managers* (3rd edn), Heinemann, London, 1982
Edey, H C, *Introduction to Accounting* (4th edn), Hutchinson, London, 1978
Goch, D, *Finance and Accounts for Managers*, Kogan Page, London, 1986
International Labour Office, *How to Read a Balance Sheet*, Geneva
Jones, D M C, *Management Accounting for Non-financial Managers*, British Institute of Management, London, 1978
Kellock, J, *Elements of Accounting*, Heinemann, London, 1978
Reid, W and Myddelton, D R, *The Meaning of Company Accounts* (3rd edn), Gower, 1982

Sayle, A J, *Management Audits*, McGraw-Hill, Maidenhead, 1981
Whitehead, G, *Success in Principles of Accounting*, J Murray, London, 1977

Key journals

Accountancy (Monthly)
40 Bernard Street
London WC1N 1LD

Accountant's Magazine (Monthly)
27 Queen Street
Edinburgh EH2 1LA

Management Accounting (Monthly)
63 Portland Place
London W1N 4AB

13. INSURANCE AND RISK MANAGEMENT

Sources of further information

British Insurance Association
Aldermary House
Queen Street
London EC4 4JD
01-248 4477

British Insurance Brokers Association
10 Bevis Marks
London EC3A 7NT
01-623 9043

Further reading

Anderson, R, *The Insurance Buyer's Guide*, Kluwer, London, annual
Bennett, C S C, *Economics for Insurance*, Lesley & Page, Bracknell, 1984
Bennett, C S C, *Insurances of Liability*, Lesley & Page, Bracknell, 1986
Catchpole, W L, *Business Guide to Insurance*, Heinemann, London, 1974
Collins, M G, *Insurances of the Person*, Lesley & Page, Bracknell, 1986
Collins, M G, *Introduction to Insurance*, Lesley & Page, Bracknell, 1984
Dacey, M S, *Principles and Practice of Insurance*, Lesley & Page, Bracknell, 1986
Dacey, M S, *Property and Pecuniary Insurance*, Lesley & Page, Bracknell, 1985
Eaglestone, F N, *Insurance for the Construction Industry*, George Godwin, London
Muckleston, R, *Risk Management for the Smaller Company*, Association of Insurance and Risk Managers in Industry and Commerce, 1979
Society of Company and Commercial Accountants, *Fleet Motor Insurance*, 1983

14. EXPANSION, MERGERS AND ACQUISITIONS

Further reading

Bean, D G, *Financial Strategy in the Acquisition Decision,* Gower, Epping, 1975
Begg, P F C, *Corporate Acquisitions and Mergers,* Graham & Trotman, London, 1986
Goldberg, W H, *Mergers, Motives, Modes, Methods,* Gower, Farnborough, 1983
Lawson, M K, *Going for Growth,* Kogan Page, London, 1987
Morris, M J, *Successful Expansion for the Small Business,* Kogan Page, London, 1984
Reid, S R, *Mergers, Managers and the Economy,* McGraw-Hill, London, 1968

Key journals

Investors Chronicle
40 Greystoke Place
Fetter Lane
London EC4A 1ND

15. LEGAL ASPECTS OF BUSINESS

Further sources of information

Advisory, Conciliation and
Arbitration Service (ACAS)
Head Office
11–12 St James's Square
London SW1Y 4LA
01-214 6000
and regional offices

Chartered Institute of Patent Agents
Staple Inn Buildings
355 High Holborn
London WC1V 7PX
01-405 9450

Law Society
113 Chancery Lane
London WC2A 1PL
01-242 1222

Further reading

Clayton, P, *Law for the Small Business* (5th edn), Kogan Page, London, 1987

Cornish, W R, *Intellectual Property: Patents, Copyright, Trade Marks and Allied Rights,* Sweet & Maxwell, London, 1981
Goode, R M, *Commercial Law,* Penguin, London, 1981
Mitchell, E, *The Business and Professional Man's Lawyer,* Business Books, London, 1981

Williams, J F, *A Manager's Guide to Patents, Trade Marks and Copyright*, Kogan Page, London, 1986

Key journals

Professional journals covering the law are aimed at the legal profession rather than the layman. Most business journals include articles on legal aspects of business.

Index

add = address